MIRACLE

ALSO BY PETER GOLENBOCK

Wrigleyville
Amazin'
American Zoom
The Last Lap
NASCAR Confidential
No Fear (with Ernie Irvan)

MIRACLE

Bobby Allison and the Saga of the Alabama Gang

Peter Golenbock

ST. MARTIN'S PRESS ≋ NEW YORK

www.stmartins.com

Design by Phil Mazzone

Library of Congress Cataloging-in-Publication Data

Golenbock, Peter, 1946–
    Miracle : Bobby Allison and the saga of the Alabama gang / Peter Golenbock.—1st ed.
      p. cm.
    ISBN 0-312-34001-X
    EAN 978-0-312-34001-8
    1. Allison, Bobby.   2. Automobile racing drivers—United States—Biography.   I. Title.

  GV1032.A3 G65 2006
  796.72092—dc22
  [B]   2005044609

First Edition: February 2006

10 9 8 7 6 5 4 3 2 1

To Cliff and Adrienne Powers, courageous people themselves, whose friendship and support have been constant lo these many years.

CONTENTS

Contents

Contents

I first became involved with NASCAR and the Allisons in 1991 when I researched and wrote *American Zoom,* my oral history of the Daytona 500 and of NASCAR as well. The track's Donna Friesmuth was kind enough to provide me, my wife, Rhonda, and our then five-year-old son Charlie with tickets to the 1992 Daytona 500, and before the race she arranged to introduce him to Davey Allison, who tousled Charlie's hair and signed a postcard to him. I was struck by Davey's gentleness, and when he was killed the next summer in a helicopter accident, the tragedy really hit home.

I thought then about how devastating the loss of a child must be. For Bobby and Judy Allison, this was doubly hard, because, the year before, their younger son, Clifford, had been killed when he crashed during practice at Michigan. Clifford's death hadn't gotten much notice, but Davey's became national news, and it was then that the public became aware that Bobby and Judy had lost both their sons. I thought then, *How can Bobby and Judy Allison survive this?* Adding to his misery, in 1994 Bobby's protégé, Neil Bonnett, died in a racing accident. *When will it stop?* I wondered. And then later I read that Bobby and Judy had gone their separate ways. Job, the biblical character who epitomizes suffering, immediately came to mind.

Then, a couple of years ago, at the dinner at the International Motorsports Hall of Fame in Talladega, Alabama, librarian and factotum Betty Carlan, who has more friends in racing than Carter has Little Liver Pills, casually mentioned to me that Bobby and Judy had remarried.

"I am thrilled for them," she said. "They deserve a little happiness."

That's when the lightbulb went on. If I could provide the details of Bobby and Judy's ordeal, along with stories of their sons Davey and Clifford, brother Donnie, and friends Neil Bonnett and Red Farmer, I would have one hell of a dramatic book. And it would have a happy ending.

I mentioned the idea to Betty.

"If you do it," she said, "you ought to start with Eddie Allison. You'll love Eddie. You'll see."

"Eddie Allison?" I said. "Who's Eddie Allison?"

It turned out that Eddie Allison is Bobby and Donnie's older brother, a man who helped both to become great racers, only to leave the sport and return to civilian life way before his time. As Betty suggested, I called Eddie first, and the eloquence and wonderful storytelling of Eddie Allison became my first great surprise.

During our conversation, Eddie spun stories of brother Donnie, telling tales of his toughness and skill, and he also spoke of other brother Bobby's brilliance, both as a racer, an expert on making a car run fast, and an airplane engineer. I had read several books and many articles about Bobby, and my sense was that after Bobby had suffered terrible brain injuries after a crash at Pocono in 1988, he probably wouldn't be much help. My second great surprise came after I called him.

During thirty years of interviewing athletes, I have rarely met a person so smart, so analytical, and so precise in his memories. With the exception of events from a year or so on either side of the crash in 1988, Bobby Allison was able to recall *everything* about his life in spectacular detail. His recovery, as it turned out, took him a full fifteen years. He experienced enough pain and hardship during those fifteen years for two lifetimes.

My third big surprise was learning of the tenacity of Judy Allison in the recovery of husband Bobby. She was the Florence Nightingale of Alabama, driving the doctors and nurses crazy, but all the time focusing on whatever she could do to aid in his return from the dead. To me, Judy is as big a hero as anyone in this book. She needs to be noticed and honored. Her gift of shooing away all negativity in the face of tragedy should not be overlooked.

I owe a tremendous debt of gratitude to a lot of wonderful people in the writing of this special book. In addition to Bobby, Judy, and Eddie Allison, I wish to thank Pat Allison, Donnie's wife; Susan Bonnett, Neil's wife; Liz Allison, Davey's wife; Red Farmer; Hut Stricklin; my friend, the late Ralph Moody; another friend, the late Bob Latford; Fred Lorenzen; the always fascinating Humpy Wheeler; one of my favorite people in all of racing, crew chief Larry McReynolds; Paul Goldsmith; the bubbly Wanda Lund; Waddell Wilson; Junior Johnson; Bud Moore; Buddy Baker; Bob Tomlinson; Jimmy Makar; Robin Pemberton; Bill Ingle; Ed Carroll; Benny Parsons; Jake Elder; and fellow St. Petersburgian, racer John Bailey. You all have a spot in my Hall of Fame.

I want to mention Greg Fielden, my partner in the NASCAR Racing Encyclopedia, whose series of books, *The Forty Years of Stock Car Racing*, are the foundation of any NASCAR library. His scholarship made my research so much easier. I also want to thank Ben White for his friendship.

I would also like to recognize the exceptional reporting over the years of Ed Hinton, Shav Glick, Beth Tuschak, Liz Clarke, Raad Cawthon, Sandra McKee, Mike Downey, Robert Markus, Michael Vega, Steve Hummersports, Larry Woody, plus some of the best sports journalists in the country from my hometown *St. Petersburg Times*, Bruce Lowitt, John Romano, Cary Estes, and Darrell Fry. I appreciate all your great work.

Writing a book is always a team effort, and no one has ever had a better team than I. Managers Neil and Dawn Reshen and their efficient, helpful staff have made it possible for me to work with a minimum of distraction; the wonderful Rhonda Sonnenberg, princess of the universe, blesses me with her aura every day; our talented, personable son, Charlie, sometimes says he feels he can never measure up to our standards, but he should know he sits tall on a pedestal, no matter what.

I want to thank my agent, Frank Weimann, for his hard work and also praise Marc Resnick, my editor, who is always a joy to work with. Marc trusts me implicitly, and I him, and you can't do any better than that. Thanks, too, to Donald J. Davidson who copyedited the manuscript with great care and skill.

Lastly, I want to thank Davey Allison, who treated my son so kindly on that February day in Daytona. You left us too soon, and we'll never forget you.

MIRACLE

Clifford and Davey.

CHAPTER 1

The Photograph

Bobby Allison, who kept his memories locked inside him, carried one photograph in his wallet. "This tells the whole story," Bobby says. The picture was taken in the spring of 1992 while his sons were sitting together at dinner. Clifford is holding up two fingers to make a "devil sign" in back of Davey's head.

"There's Davey, doing what he's supposed to do, smiling for the camera," Bobby says. "And there's his little brother, giving him a set of horns and loving it, and Davey doesn't know."

It wasn't supposed to end like this. At one time, Bobby Allison, racing champion of 1983 and winner of eighty-five Winston Cup stock car races, was the toast of all of stock car racing. Then he almost died in a horrific crash. After that, the tragedy that followed him and his wife, Judy, is almost unimaginable. And yet, despite all the heartbreak, Bobby's deep faith and his inner strength have made him an inspiration for all Americans.

People have compared Bobby Allison to the biblical figure Job, who is the poster boy for suffering and trouble.

Bobby himself says he is no Job.

"Job was an entirely different kind of man," he says. Only because, unlike Job, Bobby refuses to forgive those who he feels have wronged him.

Bobby's priest, Father Dale Grubba, suggests Bobby had it tougher. "Job never had a head injury, with all the frustration, the confusion, the self-doubt to come with it. God left Job his clarity, so that he could reason through his trials."

Bobby's story and that of his brothers, Eddie and Donnie, his sons, Clifford and

Davey, and his friends, Neil Bonnett and Dale Earnhardt, may be less catastrophic than that of Job, who was tested time and time again by God, only to keep the faith. Like Job, Bobby and Judy had to suffer indescribable loss and pain. *Miracle* is a tribute to their faith and courage.

CHAPTER 2

Pop and Kitty

"Daddy could fix anything, and he passed that on to us."

—**Eddie Allison**

You'll be surprised to learn Bobby Allison's dad was not a Southerner. Rather, he was a Yankee from Pearl River, New York, a town a stone's throw from the northern border of New Jersey. Bobby's mom came from Park Ridge, New Jersey, on the other side of that border. They were both devout Catholics, and they met and fell in love.

Edmund J. "Pop" Allison rode motorcycles as a teen, but his love affair with his Harley ended after he ran into the back of a car, flew over the top of it, and was injured badly.

He then turned his attention to cars. A master mechanic who could fix anything, Pop Allison opened a car repair shop in Pearl River.

In 1935 he went to help a friend who had a garage on Staten Island fix a car. While working on it, he was almost killed by carbon monoxide poisoning. His doctor told him he needed to live where he could get fresh air. His parents and brother had moved to Miami and highly recommended it, and so shortly thereafter Pop Allison and his wife, Kitty, moved to South Florida.

Pop and Kitty Allison faced tragedy early when their first baby died in childbirth. After a daughter, Claire, was born, Patsy came next, and then came a son, Eddie, born on September 19, 1936. He was soon followed by Bobby, born December 3, 1937, and Donnie, born September 7, 1939. More children would follow: After Tommy, Mrs. Allison suffered the loss of three children in a row. Stanley lived four days. The cause of death was a mystery. Then came Mary Catherine, who was diagnosed with cystic fibrosis and only lived nine months. The next sister, Margaret Mary, lived to be sixteen She, too, had cystic fibrosis.

"We thought she would make it," said Eddie. "There's no telling how much money Daddy spent on medicines to keep her alive. Even when she died, you never heard him complain. He was a fantastic man. I didn't have any trouble burying him, but I sure do have trouble talking about him, because he was so great. And he doesn't hold a candle to the woman he married."

Jeannie, Aggie, and Cindy followed, and adding to the din of the Allison home were foster children.

"My mom and dad took in children from Catholic Charities, a boy here, a girl there," said Bobby. "They would try to give them a little bit of a home life. Those children had to do their chores like we did. They had to go to church and say grace before meals. I would say over the years there were ten or twelve. I haven't seen any of them in a long, long time."

Every Sunday afternoon two large tables were set for dinner. For many years the two-story house would be filled with the laughter and horseplay of children.

"The family always ate meals together, and every meal started with grace," said Bobby. "Dad worked a lot at night. He built and repaired gas stations, and in his business he would do the repairs at night so the place could be open during the day. If my dad worked all night Saturday night, he'd come home Sunday morning and bathe and put his suit and tie on—he always wore a tie to church—load us up in the car, and we would all go to Mass. Then he would come home and go to bed."

When Pop Allison moved to Florida, he started a company that supplied service station and garage equipment. As part of the construction he installed gas pumps and tanks.

"My dad was a healthy, six-foot, 190-pound, very strong man physically," said Bobby. "He worked very hard."

The work included the laying of concrete floors.

"He was a master at concrete finishing," Bobby said. "He could lay a large slab of concrete and finish it without a flaw on the top surface. His concrete jobs were supersmooth and superstraight, and he was always very proud of that."

When the Japanese attacked Pearl Harbor on December 7, 1941, and war was declared, Pop Allison wasn't drafted because he had so many dependents. But he did not shirk his duty. He went to work for the navy at its base at Opa-Locka, a town near Miami. To take advantage of his expertise, the navy placed him in charge of the fuel systems of the Black Widow fighter planes. Before he arrived, the planes would regularly crash after takeoff. When he got there, he determined there was a problem with the purity of the fuel, so his first order was for his men to go down into the gas tanks and thoroughly flush them out. Problem solved.

He also devised a new fueling system. It took three sailors on the wing to hold the nozzle, because the hose acted like a whip when the fuel was shut off. It took the strength of those three men to keep it from knocking them off the wing. He solved that problem, too.

When the war ended, Pop Allison resumed his civilian work installing gas pumps and tanks. One of his jobs was to install the first service station lift to pick up a car on the island of Key West, Florida. The Boca Chica Bridge had yet to be built, and he had to ferry the equipment there.

In 1948 he helped build and equip a local Firestone store, and as part payment, he received one of those newfangled television sets.

"We were the only family on the street with a TV," said Eddie Allison, "and when the TV broke, Daddy didn't call a repairman. He fixed it himself. Daddy could fix anything, and he passed that on to us. I, myself—there is nothing I can't do. I could have been a rocket scientist if I had wanted to. A rocket scientist is just a man. You do what you want to do."

After the war ended Pop Allison took his young boys to work with him. Though Bobby was a small child—he didn't grow tall until he was nineteen—early on, when he worked for his dad, he became proficient at digging holes.

"One of the really special people my dad had working for him a long time was an old colored fellow by the name of Sam Hepburn," said Bobby. "Sam was nearly as tall as my dad, and he really knew how to dig. He made sure every shovelful he picked up had a good amount of dirt. And he never had to go far with it. He figured out how to move the most dirt with the least amount of work and effort. He showed me how to do that, so I became really good at digging small holes for my dad, even though I was small myself."

Above all, Pop Allison set an example for his children. He believed in spare the rod, spoil the child. Eddie and Bobby at times feared him but always respected and even revered him.

"My dad always set a very good example," said Bobby. "I never heard my dad say a cussword—never. As I was getting older, I was still a little bitty guy, but I would work with the colored laborers who he hired from a street corner in downtown Miami. Sam Hepburn would govern their work production. They would jump on the truck and work hard, digging a ditch or a lift hole, and the colored laborers used a lot of bad language. Those guys didn't have any language rules.

"One day I was digging a ditch, and I was practicing some bad words, damn and hell, not really bad stuff. I was digging this damn ditch and throwing a damn shovel of dirt over. My dad walked up behind me, and I thought, *Oh no, I'm going to get murdered*. Because I was a little bitty guy, and my dad was a big and strong man, and when he'd lose his temper, he would swing. Instead of a spanking, it would be a beating. If you did something wrong, you would get hurt.

"I'm not sure I had ever done anything as wrong as this up to this point. And I had already gotten hurt. He put his hand on my shoulder, and he said, 'Come here with me.'

"We went behind a big pile of dirt where a dump truck had left it. I was really concerned.

"He said, 'Let me tell you something: There's a proper word for what you're trying to say. Why let the whole world know how stupid you are by using that kind of language?'

"And it impressed me to such a degree. I thought, *Here's the biggest, strongest, and best man I've ever known, and he's telling me why should I let the world know how stupid I am?* It really helped me. I've always appreciated that, and I've told that story to youngsters along the way."

If Bobby worked hard for his dad, his brother Eddie worked harder. Eddie began going to his dad's jobs when he was as young as five years old.

"Eddie was very, very industrious and very dedicated to our dad," said Bobby. "He worked a lot of nights with Dad even when he was still in high school. He would work late into the night and occasionally all night long. Eddie picked up on mechanical things quickly and got interested in the mechanics of automobiles even before I did.

"Eddie was always wanting to take the lawn mower apart. My interest was the outboard motor. Dad had an outboard motor and a little boat, and I would drag that motor down to the canal, which was a block and a half to the Miami River from our house. It was a 3.3 Evinrude, little, but really heavy, and it was a lot of work to drag it to the river, but I would do it. I made a deal with a guy in the neighborhood for a dump of a little boat, a real piece of junk, but it floated, and I would put that motor on that boat, and I would go up or down the river to fish or to look around, while Eddie was over helping dad."

"Daddy didn't believe in doing anything but right," said Eddie. "It's our forte. Why did we work the way we did? Because of our daddy. And then my mother made sure we stayed straight. She beat our butts if we didn't.

"We were taught how to live the way people are supposed to live. That's what made us what we are. We could whup the world because we knew how to live in the world. As we were doing it, we didn't think we were doing such a great thing, but when you get to be our age and you look back . . .

"They raised us as perfect as a man and a woman could raise a family," he said.

After the war, Pop Allison rented property where he kept his service station and garage equipment. He decided that as long as he had the space, he should start a business in which he bought junked cars and sold car parts.

"He built it into a major operation," said Eddie.

"My dad always wanted a junkyard," said Bobby. "It should be called a used auto parts facility, not a junkyard. He really felt that was a great business. He had a great interest in cars and the mechanics of cars. That facility was something he always had as a special dream. It was a way to allow him to get away from the hard labor."

The city of Miami was a terrific place for the Allison kids to grow up. Miami was a tropical playland. The weather was ideal, and in the mid-1950s it was safe from crime.

When the boys were growing up, no one locked his doors. The Allison kids didn't even have a key to the house. Eddie would walk down the streets of Miami with a cigar box under his arm, selling chances to raise money for his school. "I never worried that somebody was going to touch it," he says.

When the temperature and humidity rose, the boys were never far from the water. There was a canal a couple of blocks from their house, and the boys had the little dingy "to mess with." Eddie, Bobby, Donnie, Tommy, and their friends would head out onto Biscayne Bay to fish or just enjoy themselves.

The brothers Allison were tough kids who were always up for a challenge, no matter how daunting.

One time Eddie, Bobby, Donnie, and Tommy decided they would ride their bikes to a spot where they were sure to catch the largest bass: the forty-Mile bend on the Tamiami trail. All four brothers got on their bikes, and they tied a rope to six-year-old Tommy to make sure he kept up. It wasn't long before their dad got wind of what they were doing. Dad went out and retrieved Eddie and Bobby. A friend in another truck went and got Donnie and Tommy.

"Not a lot of words were spoken," said Eddie, who added, "You have no idea how much fun our life was. And we did it all with nothing."

Their home was located at the corner of Northwest Fifteenth Street and Thirtieth Avenue in the northwestern section of the city of Miami, a stone's throw from the Miami airport. The Pan American Airlines office was three blocks away. The property had a large field with palmetto trees scattered every ten yards. The boys used it as a football field.

Across from the Pan Am offices was an electricity plant that supplied the power to the neighborhood. It was privately owned by a man named Ware, the inventor of aluminum storm windows. Ware put the wires underground, so when hurricanes hit, no one lost power. The plant had three cooling pools for the generators, and the boys would fish there for bass.

"It had fish you couldn't believe," said Eddie.

The boys lived within a couple miles of the West Flagler Kennel Club, a dog track. They loved to go watch the greyhounds when they ran schooling races, practice races during which there was no betting.

When Eddie was ten, eleven, and twelve, he was a batboy for the Miami Sun Sox, a minor league affiliate of the Brooklyn Dodgers. After Brooklyn completed its training at Vero Beach, the Dodgers would travel south to Bobby Maduro Stadium in Miami to play their spring training games. They brought their own batboys, but they hired the visiting batboys from among the locals. Eddie retrieved bats for the visiting players from 1949 through 1951. On April 12, 1951, *Life* magazine published a picture with a caption that read, "Leo Durocher and his son." But it wasn't Durocher's son. It was Eddie Allison.

"I knew it was me," said Eddie. "It was a black-and-white picture, and I didn't have a uniform on, but I was wearing cleats, and my cleats had yellow shoelaces, so in the black-and-white picture they really stood out." Eddie's mom had the picture on her walls for years.

The visiting player Eddie remembers most fondly was Stan "the Man" Musial, the star first baseman for the St. Louis Cardinals.

"It was 1950, and I had worked all summer for my dad, and I made two dollars," said Eddie. "The Cardinals played three games, and before they left, Stan gave me five dollars.

"The next year, when the Cardinals came back, I was in the tunnel going from the home clubhouse with a double armload of towels and wash rags to put in the locker of the visiting team. Stan came bopping down that tunnel from the other direction, and he grabbed me and said, 'Hi, kid.' We shook hands, and he had one of those wind-up hand buzzers, and he shocked me, and he laughed, and then he gave me another five dollars. Stan Musial was a fantastic human being.

"I had a fantastic life growing up," said Eddie.

Pop Allison made a decent living, but there were so many kids to feed and clothe there wasn't much money for frills.

"There were eight or nine kids to raise," said Eddie. "It was such a neat life for people who didn't have any money. We had *no* money. Absolutely no money. We had enough clothes to wear, enough food to eat. Back then you wore shorts and no shirt and you didn't have shoes. Your feet were tougher than shoe leather. You could walk on the asphalt without wincing when it was ninety-five degrees out.

"Right above the Hialeah racetrack was a dairy farm, where Mom and Dad drove to get the fresh milk. My mother was a real shopper. She knew how to grocery shop. We ate everything on our plate. Even today, I love leftovers. Bobby can't stand them. But that's different personalities. I could eat food until it's gone."

Pop Allison and his wife, moreover, were determined that no matter what the cost, their children would all receive a Catholic school education. The boys went to elementary school at the First Avenue and Second Street Primer. By the time Eddie reached the eleventh grade, the archdiocese had closed all the existing Catholic schools in Miami and opened two brand-new ones, Notre Dame for girls, and Archbishop Curley for boys.

When Eddie graduated from Archbishop Curley High School in June 1954, he became the first person in the history of the school to get a diploma. He was in the first graduating class, and he was the first student whose last name began with the letter A.

"I was the very first Curley graduate, alphabetically and sizewise," he said. "I was the shortest."

Around this time Pop Allison became very sick, and he had to stop working. "He had worked so hard that he was knocked for a loop," said Eddie.

"He had begun developing stomach and digestive problems," said Bobby. "He continued to work until he wore himself down physically to the point that he just nearly collapsed one day. A doctor friend operated on him and took his gall bladder out and repaired a hernia in the stomach. It took him quite a while to recover from that.

"When Dad got sick, Eddie really got after his basic business, which was the service station work. Eddie and I both did the junkyard stuff. Early on, Eddie did quite a bit more than I did. He was really into the service station end, did the repair work, went out and fixed pumps and lifts that needed it.

"For quite a while Eddie was my dad's right-hand man. Then both of us did the junkyard part."

Said Eddie, "I begged my daddy. I said, 'You get the work, and I'll do it.' He was too sick. He just couldn't do it anymore."

One reason Eddie and Bobby were determined to keep the junkyard going, even though their daddy was sick, was because of their passion, stock car racing. The parts business was the best way they could get what they needed to build their race cars.

"'Cause we didn't have any money," said Eddie.

CHAPTER 3

Bobby: Exiled to Wisconsin

"At one point he told himself, I'm done. This is it. I'm going under right here."

—**Bobby Allison**

Bobby was only one year behind Eddie at Archbishop Curley High School. Though he weighed only 103 pounds, Bobby drove either an old Chevy or rode on a Harley-Davidson 74 to school. He was so light he needed to have someone ride on the back of the Harley with him so that when he stopped at a red light he could hold up the bike. Bobby, like Eddie and Donnie, had jobs after school. "We figured out at an early age how to buy things," said Eddie.

In addition to riding a motorcycle, at age fifteen Bobby also learned how to fly an airplane. Bobby had a friend, Tommy Chalk, whose uncle owned an airline.

"When I was twelve, I took my first plane ride," said Bobby. "Walter Lang, who my father built a gas station for, had a friend, Zack Mosley, who wrote the Smilin' Jack comic strip, and Mosley took me for a ride in his Piper Cub. I thought it was the neatest thing I ever did. He let me hold the stick while we were en route. I think about it now and really smile.

"Tommy Chalk was a year older than I, a buddy of mine from the neighborhood. He went to public school. His mother and dad were divorced, and he lived with his mother. His father owned an airport in Adel, Georgia, which was a *long* way from Miami. His uncle owned Chalk Airlines, which flew flying boats to the Bahamas from the Miami Causeway. Tommy had a pilot's license, so Tommy and I would earn a few bucks on the weekend and go and rent a single-engine Piper Cub, and we'd leave from Tamiami Airport or South Dixie Airport down U.S. 1, and we'd go flying.

"I was going to take flying lessons under Tommy's observation, but when I went for my physical, I found out I was color-blind. It didn't bother my racing, but I stepped away from flying."

But not forever.

When Bobby Allison was 17 years old, he began racing in the hobby class at Hialeah, a third-of-a-mile track with long straightaways and narrow corners.

Bobby was racing the old Chevy he drove to school. Brother Eddie also was involved in racing, working for an engine builder by the name of Harold Wilcox. Eddie watched Bobby twice turn over his Chevy.

"The car had no roll bars in it. It scared me to death," he says. But the car had such a strong door post that it didn't cave in, and Bobby wasn't hurt.

It didn't take but a couple weeks for Bobby to eliminate his mistakes and pace the field. Eddie saw that Bobby had rare control when it came to driving, whether it was a motorcycle or a race car.

"Instantly, we saw he was going to win races," said Eddie.

"In my senior year of high school, they started an amateur division at Hialeah Raceway," said Bobby. "By then I had become a big racing fan. At first I hitched rides to get to the racetrack. At age fourteen in Florida you could get a restricted driver's license. You could drive a motorcycle, but you couldn't drive a car at night. So I bought a little motorcycle, and I would take it to the races at Hialeah or to the Medley Speedway, which was a little harder to get to. Medley was in the middle of nowhere, but it was a neat racetrack. It was a third of a mile, semibanked. It had a railroad metal guardrail around it, which was really hard on race cars."

The track was owned by John Fitzgibbons, and in the meantime he built a quarter-mile track in Hollywood, Florida, on the site of an old drive-in theater.

"When I was seventeen," said Bobby, "I sold my motorcycle, and I bought a '38 Chevy coupe from a friend, Fran Curci, who was a year behind me at Archbishop Curley High School. Fran was the star of the football team, and I was a football equipment manager, so I was around him some. The car was a '38 standard, which had a solid front axle instead of the knee action that General Motors came out with at the time.

"The only requirements to race were that I had to put a seat belt in it, wear a helmet, and strap the driver's door shut. I had to roll the window and the quarter window in the back down so I could put a belt around three or four times and fasten it.

"I'd take the car out to the track, and I'd take off the muffler and put it in a little cardboard box and take the headlights out. And I'd race.

"I had to promise my mom I'd improve my grades in school for her to sign the sheet to go out and compete. Mom signed the form, thinking it was for one week. Of course, I was thinking it was for a hundred years.

"She signed the form, and I went out there."

Bobby won the third race he entered.

Said Bobby, "I didn't do anything to the engine, but to make the car go around the corner better, I jacked the car up and put a coil spring between the frame on the right front and the U-bolts on the right front spring. It was something I was sure the car needed to turn the way I wanted it to.

"I randomly picked one that looked like it would be the right strength, length, and diameter. The thing actually held itself in place. And it worked.

"In my mind it was like I had just won the Daytona 500," said Bobby.

Bobby also began racing at a track at West Palm Beach. The half-miler was laid out in a real crazy way. When you came off turn two, you had to press your foot to the floor as you headed straight for the fence in order to get the car off the corner. Very few drivers had the nerve to do that, but Bobby did, as did Donnie and an older racer by the name of Red Farmer. All three would go on to win a lot of races there as a result.

Bobby was winning races, and his mom was becoming concerned. No, she was petrified that her dream of his going to college and getting an education was being detoured by racing.

One evening she said to him, "I didn't give you permission to run all these races. I want you to go to college. I want you to get a better education, and I don't want you messing with these greasy old cars and these greasy old people."

To stop him, she realized, she had to send him somewhere where he would get away from the influence of racing. Bobby had graduated from high school in June 1955, and she called her sister Patty and her sister's husband, Jimmy Hallett, who lived in Wisconsin.

She said, "Can Bobby come stay with you?"

"Of course," they said.

Hallett called Bobby and asked him to come stay with them.

Bobby said to Hallett, "I don't want to come for a vacation. I want to go to work."

He said, "You come to Wisconsin and I'll get you a job."

If Kitty Allison had thought things through, she never would have sent Bobby to Uncle Jimmy's. Jimmy Hallett was the national sales manager for the Mercury Outboard Motor Company, which was owned and run by an intense, profane man by the name of Carl Kiekhaefer. In 1955 Kiekhaefer was the owner of the race car that Tim Flock drove to the Grand National stock car championship. You wouldn't think a seventeen-year-old kid who went to work testing outboard engines would end up as a crew member of one of Kiekhaefer's race cars, but that's exactly what happened. It would take the better part of the year for Bobby to do it, but do it he did. With a will as strong as Bobby Allison's, there was always a way.

The Kiekhaefer Mercury Outboard Engine organization had delivery trucks that carted engines all over the South, and three weeks after graduation Bobby was picked up at his house and driven to Fond du Lac, Wisconsin, in a panel truck.

———

The Halletts—Aunt Patty and Uncle Jimmy and their three daughters, Carol, Laurie, and Barbie—lived two blocks from Lake Winnebago, one of Wisconsin's small lakes. His first weekend there Bobby went to the beach, swam, boated, picnicked, and fished.

Jimmy, meanwhile, got Bobby a no-brains job testing outboard engines. The mechanics would build the engines, check them out, and put them on small runabouts, and it was the job of Bobby and three other teens to drive them around the rivers and lakes of Wisconsin for six hours a day. At the end of the day they were to fill out a report on the performance of the engine. For a summer of fresh air and easy money, Bobby was paid $39 a week.

"To drive a boat around the lakes of Wisconsin and get a paycheck every Friday, that was the first home run I hit along the way," said Bobby. "And it was decent money. I knew adults who weren't making $39 a week. This was a great deal."

Bobby paid his aunt and uncle $5 a week room and board, so he had money in his pocket and weekends to do whatever he wanted. It didn't take him long to discover that every town in Wisconsin had a stock car racetrack. If he wanted to, he could go see races seven nights a week, and sometimes on Saturday they raced in the afternoon *and* at night, and sometimes on Sunday they raced in the afternoon *and* at night.

Though Bobby didn't do any racing himself in Wisconsin, there were weeks he went to nine races as a spectator.

The Wisconsin racer Bobby liked the most was Miles "Mouse" Milius. His nickname arose because he was so good at getting through traffic without damaging his car. Most of the tracks were quarter-mile dirt, except the Milwaukee Mile, which was paved. Despite the beating and banging on the dirt, Milius would finish intact, and often won. Bobby took note that Milius kept his car clean. The lettering was neat, and he was amused by the mouse decal on its side.

"I became a fan of his immediately," said Bobby. "He raced at Slinger, a dirt track, and Hale's Corners and Cederberg, and at the fairgrounds track at Oshkosh. He won a lot, and I watched him, and I got to start forming an opinion about how to make it to the checkered flag."

Summer was over. Cold weather arrived in Wisconsin, and Bobby saw something he had never seen in his life: snow. He was still running the outboard engines six hours a day, but now he would put on long underwear and a ski jacket to wear under the life jackets. On his feet he wore tie-up ankle boots. The air temperature dropped to around twenty, and on days like this Bobby and the other boat testers would freeze as they drove to the north end of Lake Buttes des Mortes and headed for the local coffee shop.

"In fact," said Bobby, "we spent a lot of time in the coffee shop. We would leave our engines running at the dock of the coffee shop, and we'd go inside, where it was warm. Carl Kiekhaefer never caught on. Good thing. He'd have beheaded us right there."

On one particularly cold, windy day, Bobby and the other three boat testers put their boats on the cranes that moved them from the boathouse into the water. The other three took off together, heading upriver, when Bobby remembered he had to go back to the boathouse to get something he had forgotten.

When Bobby returned, he saw his boat was leaking, but that often happened before starting a trip. The wooden boat would swell after it sat in the water a while, and the leaking would stop. Bobby paid no mind to the water sloshing around the bottom of the boat, and after he pulled out the bailer plug, the boat emptied of water. He reinserted the plug, revved up the engine, and headed for open water in an attempt to catch up to the others.

Bobby was driving a boat with a Mercury thirty-horsepower engine, capable of going forty miles an hour. Back then it was one of the more powerful engines. He was considerably behind the others, and he pushed the throttle open in an attempt to catch up.

As he rode onto Lake Buttes des Mortes, the waves grew higher than he had anticipated. He hit a wave that bounced the boat out of the water into the air. He shrugged it off and continued. The next wave took the boat way up, and then the tail of the boat hit another wave, which tipped the boat nose down to a third wave, which, as Bobby described it, "made it into a submarine."

The boat flipped up, and the motor headed downward. The nose of the boat was lifted out of the water, and Bobby figured he would hold on to it until help arrived, but the water on the nose of the boat froze, and like Rose's ill-fated lover in the movie *Titanic,* Bobby's hands slipped on the icy surface. He knew he had to swim to shore or die.

The swim was perhaps an eighth of a mile, but the air was freezing, and Bobby was weighted down by his laced-up boots and the heavy jacket. His life jacket allowed him to float with his nose at water level. But with the temperature plunging, staying in the water very long meant certain death.

"Any way you look at it," said Bobby, "I was in trouble."

Bobby began swimming, but the weight of the clothes made the task too difficult. At one point he told himself, *I'm done. This is it. I'm going under right here.* He accepted the inevitable and let himself sink to a watery grave.

Then his feet touched bottom. His head was above water.

I can make it, he told himself, and he exerted more effort until he was able to swim, wade, and walk to shore. He headed for the nearest house, and as he climbed up out of the lake onto a lawn, a dog began barking at him.

A woman emerged from the house, and when she saw Bobby, she told him, "Go to that door right there." Bobby went to her laundry room, where she poured a large tub of hot water. Bobby took off his wet, freezing clothes and got into the tub. He was suffering from hypothermia and had turned blue. After he got into the tub, at first he couldn't feel the heat. Then it began to burn, and she told him, "That's good."

After he had sat in the tub awhile, the woman gave him dry clothes, and he got into bed. When she called an ambulance, she was informed that the roads were too slick for service.

Bobby gave her the telephone number of the boathouse, and two employees of the Mercury Outboard Engines company drove out and got him. They then drove him to Oshkosh Hospital.

Bobby recovered fully, except at times he would feel cold, and his body would spasm for several seconds. The vicious chills went away after about six months.

Carl Kiekhaefer, the company owner, gave Bobby two days off. He spent the two days recuperating at his aunt and uncle's house. In the meantime, the boat testers were gearing up to move their operation to their winter proving grounds in Siesta Key, Florida, at the southern edge of Sarasota. The four adults in charge of the testing operation lived in one cottage. The four teens, including Bobby, lived in another. At the tip of the peninsula was a boathouse. The operation was identical to the one in Wisconsin.

Bobby by then had turned eighteen, and one weekend he returned home to Miami to buy a new car with his earnings. He and his father went to the Chevy dealership, and he bought a '56 Chevy Bel Air hardtop.

"This was a hot deal for me," said Bobby. He drove the car back to Sarasota and parked it by the cottage he was staying in.

Carl Kiekhaefer, who was in the habit of roaming around his various facilities unannounced, came walking into the boathouse where Bobby was getting ready to run an engine for the day.

"Who owns that Chevrolet up there in the complex?" asked Kiekhaefer.

Bobby said, "I do." He was proud of his car, and he had a big smile on his face when he said it.

"I hate Chevrolets," said the dictatorial, unpredictable Kiekhaefer, whose race teams drove Chryslers. "Get it off my property."

Said Bobby years later, "He made me park the car outside the gate of the facility and walk in. A couple hundred feet, no big deal, but here was this great big open area where you could have parked a hundred semis, and he wouldn't let me park my Chevy in there because he hated Chevrolets."

Bobby stayed in Florida all winter running the engines. In April, as winter was leaving Wisconsin, it was time to pack up and move the operation north again.

About then Kiekhaefer returned to Sarasota.

"You," he said to Bobby, "drive my Mercedes to my race car shop in Charlotte, and the truck will come by and pick you up there."

Bobby had wanted to drive his Chevy back to Wisconsin, and this was Kiekhaefer's twisted way of denying him that pleasure. Kiekhaefer thought by doing this Bobby would have to leave the Chevy in Sarasota, but Bobby got one of the other teens, a friend of his by the name of Marlon Felker, to drive it up to Wisconsin for him. Kiekhaefer's vindictiveness would later propel Bobby into Grand National racing.

Bobby drove Kiekhaefer's 190 SL Mercedes from Sarasota to Charlotte. When he arrived, he was introduced to Ray Fox, who was the crew chief for Kiekhaefer's Grand National cars. In 1955 Kiekhaefer had run a car driven by Tim Flock, and

Flock had easily won the Grand National driving championship. Kiekhaefer, who might have served as a prototype for New York Yankees owner George Steinbrenner, was a tyrant who had a lot of money and wasn't afraid to spend it in pursuit of victory, and after Flock was so successful in 1955, he decided that if one top driver was good, five top drivers would be better, so he hired five of the best drivers NASCAR had to offer to race his fleet of Chryslers in 1956.

When Bobby walked into the large car-building facility and met Fox, he was probably five foot four, weighed perhaps 120 pounds. Bobby could see several Chrysler 300s and several Dodge D500s. He noticed several mechanics were inside, but also saw that little work was getting done. Most of them were sitting on the workbenches in small groups talking to each other. Bobby was surprised that no one seemed to be working.

Bobby said to Fox, "I brought Carl Kiekhaefer's Mercedes from Sarasota, and the truck is going to pick me up tomorrow to take me to Wisconsin."

Fox looked at him wearily and said, "Boy, I am really in trouble. Are you a mechanic?"

Bobby said, "Yeah, I'm a good mechanic. Why?"

"Kiekhaefer drafted all of these guys out of different parts of his companies," Fox told him, "and none of them want to be here, and I can't get any work done. Will you work until your guys get here to pick you up?"

Bobby, who was no stranger to work, immediately agreed. Fox said, "We made up a work sheet how to prepare the car for the race. I've selected which bits and pieces to put where to prepare it for the next event. Here is the sheet for the car over there. As you work on it, this sheet will tell you what to do."

None of the steps on the list was unfamiliar to Bobby, but he was surprised at the added details he hadn't considered before. He said to himself, *I can do this,* and as he went from job to job, he worked on the Chrysler 300 with efficiency and skill. A couple of hours later he walked over to Ray Fox and said to him, "I'm done. What else do you want me to do?"

When Fox quizzed him to make sure he had done things right, Bobby assured him he didn't make any mistakes.

"The sheet tells you what to do," said Bobby.

Fox said, "Oh man, what a help you are. Here, do another one." He gave Bobby a sheet for another car. This time Fox offered Bobby the use of his personal toolbox as a token of his appreciation.

Bobby worked, all alone, until ten that night. Before he headed to the hotel, Fox said, "I really appreciate what you're doing. I'll see you in the morning."

When he returned the next morning, Carl Kiekhaefer was waiting for him. The trucks had arrived, and Bobby was expecting to ride to Wisconsin when Ray Fox came over and said, "I told Carl Kiekhaefer I need to keep you here."

It was Bobby's mother's worst nightmare, and a dream come true for Bobby, who told Fox, "That would be great."

Bobby stayed another two months. One of his assignments was working on the car of driver Herb Thomas, who in a Chevrolet had been one of Tim Flock's closest rivals in 1955. The next year Thomas was driving a Chrysler for Kiekhaefer, who gave his drivers the best deal in the history of NASCAR. Not only did they get to keep the entire purse, but they got a salary as well. When Kiekhaefer made Thomas an offer, the gentlemanly tobacco farmer couldn't refuse.

Working on Thomas's race car also meant Bobby got to go to the races. In those days the schedule consisted of more than fifty races, many of them held during the week. Over the next two months, Bobby went to a dozen races.

Humpy Wheeler, who would go on to become the president of the Charlotte Motor Speedway, knew Bobby when he was working at the Kiekhaefer shop sweeping floors and working on the cars.

Wheeler, who was still in high school, worked for Bob Osiecki, a drag racer.

"We all came up together, Cale [Yarborough] and Richard Petty and Bobby Allison," said Wheeler. "We were all the same age, and we were doing various things in racing. I saw Bobby around the track, because I was going to races, too, and working. We all would do anything in those days to get to the track."

In 1956 the Kiekhaefer race team was the class of Grand National circuit, winning sixteen races in a row between mid-March and early June. If Herb Thomas didn't win, then Buck Baker or Speedy Thompson won. Baker would go on to win the racing title in 1956.

Allison also went to a few United States Auto Club races. Norm Nelson and Tony Bettenhausen Sr. drove for Kiekhaefer on that midwestern circuit, with equal success.

"For two months I never saw any but a Kiekahefer car win a race," said Bobby.

Another of Bobby's duties was to drive the truck carrying one of the Kiekhaefer race cars to the next race. The Syracuse race was held on May 30, 1956, Memorial Day, and the order Kiekhaefer gave Bobby and his partner and the drivers of the other truck was to act independently. If the other truck had a flat or engine trouble, keep going.

Bobby and his driving partner, Willard Stubby, left Charlotte for Syracuse with Buck Baker's race car inside the Ford van he was driving. These vans, the first ever to haul race cars, had major brake problems. When the power brakes malfunctioned and the driver was going downhill, suddenly the driver would be without brakes. The driver had to push the brake pedal, let it up a little, push it in, let it up, until finally the power brakes would kick in.

Bobby, who had a great feel for any vehicle he was driving, figured out how to massage the brakes well enough to solve the problem. The driver of the other truck, carrying Speedy Thompson's race car, was not as adept, and he took a detour to a Ford dealership to get the brakes adjusted. As a result Bobby and Willard Stubby arrived in Syracuse around nine on Wednesday the morning of the race, while the Thompson truck was nowhere to be seen.

Kiekhaefer asked him, "Where is the other truck?"

"Sir," said Bobby, "our instructions were to not stick together. They were having brake trouble, and they stopped."

Kiekhaefer, who hated inefficiency and had a short fuse, was mad at Bobby and his partner anyway.

They unloaded the race car and prepared it. When Buck showed up, he was happy to see his car, and he went out and ran some practice laps, and he was fast.

It was almost race time when the other truck arrived. Speedy Thompson missed qualifying, but in those days they didn't have full fields, and he started at the back of the pack. Speedy raced all the way to the front, but then his car broke. Baker went on to win the race.

After the race Kiekhaefer went up to Bobby and Stubby and said, "Okay, you guys have been up all night. We won the race, and I'm happy. You guys go to the motel and get a good night's sleep, and get the trucks back to Charlotte, and everybody will have the weekend off."

It was one of the rare open weekends, and Bobby was excited. He and Stubby were going to jump in Bobby's '56 Chevy and drive down to Myrtle Beach for some R&R. The plan was to return in time for work Monday morning.

The next morning, Bobby headed back to Charlotte, and despite the brake problem, Bobby drove the route quickly, while the other truck again stopped with brake trouble.

When Bobby pulled in, Kiekhaefer was standing there.

"Where is the other truck?" he wanted to know.

"Sir, our instructions were to not stick together. They had brake trouble again."

"Okay," Kiekhaefer said, "you guys have to wait for the other truck to arrive. While you're waiting, go ahead and go to work on the race car for next week."

Bobby, who himself had a temper and who reacted to injustice when he felt victimized, said, "Wait a minute. We've been up all night, and we were promised the weekend off."

"Shut up," said Kiekhaefer, who was not used to being argued with. "I told you to go to work. You're going to wait for the other guys to get here."

So Bobby and Stubby went to work on the race car for the next week. Around noon, Bobby said to Kiekhaefer, "We're going to lunch."

"Make sure you guys are back here," he said. "Don't go sneaking off."

They went to lunch and came back, and around three in the afternoon the other truck pulled in. Kiekhaefer was in a rage, screaming and yelling.

Said Kiekhaefer to the four drivers, "Punch out. Get out of here. All of you."

The four went up front to the little foyer in the front of the shop where the time clock sat, and they stood in line to punch out.

After they punched out, they stood there, discussing whether all four of them should go to Myrtle Beach together, which meant the other two would have to get their clothes. Another consideration was that because there would be four people in the car, some of the suitcases already in the car should be left behind.

While this discussion went on, Kiekhaefer came walking from his office into the foyer area. He walked up to Stubby and said, "What's the matter, Stubby? Are you waiting on the clock?" In effect, Kiekhaefer was accusing him of standing around before punching out so he could make some unearned money at Kiekhaefer's expense. It was a nasty crack, and Stubby, taken aback, said one word: "What?"

"Are you waiting on the clock, you SOB," Kiekhaefer repeated.

Stubby remained confused, and so Bobby said, "No, we're already punched out."

"Shut up," said Kiekhaefer. "I wasn't talking to you." He turned back to Stubby, and he said, "You're fired. Get off my property."

When the other two guys in the other truck tried to object, Kiekhaefer fired them as well.

Bobby said, "Well, I'm gone, too."

"No," said Kiekhaefer, "you can't leave. You got to stay here."

But Bobby made it clear to Kiekhaefer he was leaving.

"You have to leave your tools here," Kiekhaefer said. "Ray Fox has got to okay your getting your tools."

The four of them lived in a large house with twenty-one bunk beds owned by Kiekhaefer. Bobby, a quick read, knew that if he didn't beat Kiekhaefer back to the house, Kiekhaefer would lock them out of the house to prevent them from getting their belongings.

The boys jumped in Bobby's car. Kiekhaefer got into his Chrysler.

Bobby knew a shortcut to the house, and he got there first. They were coming out of the house with their suitcases when Kiekhaefer pulled up. They got in Bobby's car and left.

Bobby drove them to Wisconsin, and while they were there, Bobby went to his aunt and uncle's house. Kiekhaefer knew the connection, and when he arrived, his uncle told him Kiekhaefer wanted to talk to him.

"I need you to come back to work for me," said Kiekhaefer. "When you get back to the shop, talk to Ray Fox. I need you back."

Bobby, massaged, his anger cooled, agreed.

When Bobby returned to Charlotte, his first job was to drive a truck carrying engines to be rebuilt in Wisconsin. He left his '56 Chevy in Charlotte and drove a Dodge van loaded with engines. When he arrived in Wisconsin, Kiekhaefer called him into his office.

Bobby had been getting $1.19 an hour, and he was getting time and a half overtime and double pay Sundays and holidays. He was making as much as $200 a week.

Kiekhaefer said to him, "I'm putting you on salary. I'm going to give you a hundred dollars a week."

Bobby said, "No, I ain't doing that."

Kiekhaefer said, "You're fired." And he added, "And you're not driving my truck back to Charlotte."

Bobby was left stranded in Oshkosh, Wisconsin, with just an overnight bag. He also had a pile of money.

He was given a ride to Milwaukee, where he caught a plane to Charlotte. The flight cost him about fifty dollars.

"He was really something," Bobby said of Kiekhaefer. "He built his race team into an amazing powerhouse. But he drove people to the point of wanting to jump off a cliff."

Bobby learned a great deal from his experience with Carl Kiekhaefer. One lesson he learned firsthand was how destructive having more than one race car on a team could be.

"If I have a teammate who I have to help," said Bobby, "how am I going to get an advantage on him? The only way I'm going to do that is to have an advantage over everybody."

Bobby also learned how difficult a race team owner could be. Bobby wanted to race more than ever. He didn't know what step to take next, but he knew that once he started racing for real, the lessons he learned about the importance of preparation and preventive maintenance would stand him in good stead.

Bobby left Charlotte and headed south to Miami in his Chevy.

The 1956 season would prove to be Carl Kiekhaefer's last. At the end of the season, Kiekhaefer, hounded by Bill France, who fought him hard in order to bring better competition to the NASCAR circuit, and convinced there were no more worlds to conquer in racing, folded his Grand National race team.

CHAPTER 4

Bobby: Bob Sunderman

"I can't let them know I'm racing."

—Bobby Allison

"Look, if you're going to do this, do it under your own name. Just do it with honor."

—Pop Allison

When Bobby returned from working for Carl Kiekhaefer, he had the racing bug bad. He began hanging around the race shop of Bobby Johns, one of the more successful Miami racers. He worked on his car, but didn't get any pay. He watched how they prepared to go race. He rolled tires and loaded equipment into the tow truck.

"I wasn't doing anything important, but I enjoyed being part of this ultracompetitive effort with Bobby Johns and his father, Shorty," said Bobby. "His car wasn't as fancy as Red Farmer's, or Alan Clark's or Rags Carter's, but he beat them more than occasionally. I was so enthused with racing, all I wanted to do was hang out there."

Bobby wanted to race the '38 Chevy he had left behind when he went to Wisconsin, but by the time he got back home, rule changes had made the car obsolete. To race, Bobby needed to find a ride.

After he returned home, his mother quickly saw that his desire to race was even greater than it had been when he left.

"She wanted me to go to college and get some kind of degree and wear a suit and tie," said Bobby.

Bobby's mom was so freaked out and upset, she told him, "You can't race and live here."

Bobby wasn't ready to move out quite yet, so he tried a subterfuge: racing under an alias.

Bobby's oldest sister Clarie was dating a boy by the name of Bob Sundman. He was a little bit older than Bobby, a neighborhood kid he had hung around with for several years. His father, Carl Sundman, owned a race car with a machine shop and welding equipment.

Bobby talked to Bob Sundman about the problem his mother had with his racing. Sundman said to him, "I'll lend you my license, and you can go to Hollywood and race my car there under my name."

"That's a great idea," said Bobby. "My folks will never know that I'm racing as long as I use your name."

Bobby went to Hollywood Speedway, where the pit steward knew both Bobby and Sundman. When the pit steward asked him what he was doing, Bobby told him the truth.

"I can't let them know I'm racing," he said.

Because the pit steward knew Sundman, he told Bobby he was changing the name on Bobby's entry from Sundman to "Sunderman." It fooled exactly nobody.

"It took my dad about one day to figure all this out," said Bobby. "Way down in a little bitty column in the *Miami Herald* it said, 'Sixth place, Bob Sunderman.' I do think somebody probably tipped him off. I don't think he figured it all out by himself. Though he could have."

Bobby's dad came up to him and said, "Look, if you're going to do this, do it under your own name. Just do it with honor." Which was Pop Allison's attitude about everything.

A mythology grew up around Bobby's driving under the Bob Sunderman name. The fact was he drove under that name for two weeks at the most, racing a couple of times a week.

"The Bob Sunderman thing turned into a good story more than anything factual," said Bobby. "A lot of people got a kick out of my driving under an assumed name."

It wasn't long after Bobby returned from Charlotte that he needed to get himself a job. He had put several of his Mercury Outboard Engine paychecks in his glove compartment so, when he got home, he would have money to live on.

"I thought I was rich," said Bobby. "I lived off that for a while, and then one day I realized I didn't have another paycheck to make a car payment." Bobby knew that for him to be able to race, he would have to make some money first, so he got a job as a general mechanic working for Aerodex, a Miami company that rebuilt airplane engines owned by a man named John Fitzgibbons.

What Bobby learned at Aerodex was that he was not afraid to work hard.

"A lot of guys showed up for work and waited for lunchtime, and then they waited for the time to go home," said Bobby. "I looked at a job as *How can I do this job the best? And how can I do it the quickest?* They found out early I was a good worker, an enthusiastic worker, and I moved around in the engine department quite a bit."

Bobby realized that to race it would take more than the $39 a week he was making at Aerodex, so Allison, industrious like his father, took a second job working the night shift at the Streamland Service Station on River Drive near his dad's junkyard.

Bobby would leave Aerodex at five, go home, change out of his greasy clothes into clean ones, and go pump gas at the gas station. He did everything he was asked to do willingly, sweeping the driveway, cleaning the Coke box, wiping the customers' windows, and pumping gas.

Bobby drove his '56 Chevy Bel Air hardtop, and for the fun of it he took part in drag races along the lonely, rural Miami streets. Bobby's Bel Air was painted black and light chartreuse, and it had a little V-8 engine with a little carburetor and a three-speed transmission. Bobby discovered his car was quicker than the three or four cars he raced, and in that short period of time Bobby got a reputation for his drag racing skills.

One afternoon Bobby got off work at Aerodex and headed home. As he neared his house, a car approached. Bobby slowed, and he saw that the driver of the other car, racer Red Farmer, was signaling him to stop.

"We're getting a Chevy ready to race," said Red, "and Homer wants you to help him with the engines." Homer was Homer Warren, Red's engine builder.

"I'm working until nine at Streamland," Bobby said.

"We'll be there after nine," Farmer replied. "We usually work until ten thirty, eleven at night at our race car shop, and you know where that is. It's between your dad's place and Aerodex. When you get off tonight, come on over."

After working his second job, Bobby went to Farmer's shop. He was ushered into a little office where Red and Homer Warren were waiting.

"We want you to help Homer with these engines," Red said, "and we'll pay you, but we don't want the other boys out in the shop to know, because we don't pay them anything."

"You'll pay me?" said Bobby in surprise.

"We'll give you fifteen dollars a week, but you'll have to help Homer with this engine." Bobby was flattered to be asked, and he agreed.

Homer said, "You've been up with Kiekhaefer with the Chrysler 300s that run the dual carburetors, and you have your own car that beats everybody, so we know you know. Here are two brand-new carburetors in boxes. You get these ready to put on this engine that we're putting together."

Said Bobby years later, "I wasn't about to tell them I had never even had as much as a screw out of my carburetor. Or from Kiekhaefer's, either."

Said Farmer, who found out years later, "We didn't know that Bobby really didn't know a hell of a lot more than we did. He was so impressed with being asked to work on our car that he was going to bluff it."

Bobby told them, "I have to take these home." And he told himself, *I have to stop at the parts store and buy an overhaul manual for this carburetor to tell me what the dimensions and settings are supposed to be. Then I'll guess how to go from there.*

Bobby went and bought a manual. He went home, and he took the first carburetor out of the box, took it apart, and started measuring, and the measurements didn't add up to what the manual said the proper measurements were supposed to be.

Said Bobby, "At the time, they had carburetors with metering rods and jets, and the metering rods were set wrong and the floats were set wrong, and what would happen, a racer would put a four-barrel carburetor in his car, and you could rev it, and it would sound real good, but you'd go out on the racetrack and it would stumble and miss and backfire."

When Bobby looked in the manual, he discovered that the floats had not been set properly and needed to be adjusted. He opened the second carburetor and looked at it, and he saw that not only were the metering rods and floats set wrong, but they were set differently from the first carburetor, and they, too, needed adjustment.

It's no wonder everyone is having trouble with these carburetors, Bobby told himself.

Bobby worked until the carburetors were set as instructed in the manual, and he put them in Red Farmer's race car, and then on his own he devised "a beautiful set of throttle linkages." His had both sets of front barrels opening together, and then the rear barrels kicked in, and then he made a little fuel log for the carburetor and after he was done, he took the carburetors and manifold back to Homer Warren, who bolted them onto the engine.

Homer Warren and Red Farmer were about to discover that the kid they hired would turn out to be one of the innovative automotive geniuses of their day. Homer Warren cranked up the engine and it turned over. It purred.

They went to the racetrack, and Red Farmer dominated. He won the first feature he entered with that car at Hollywood Speedway, and then he took it to Medley Speedway and won, and then he won at the half-mile track at West Palm Beach.

Said Farmer, "He showed us what he knew about that Chevrolet motor. We put it together, and Bobby went with us, and we won eight of the next nine feature races with that Chevrolet motor."

Red, a skilled driver and a colorful character, was not satisfied just to win. He wanted to dominate. His goal was to lap the field in a heat race, and he was able to do this in this car with the Bobby Allison–improved engine.

"It was the first V-8 Chevy engine to come into racing down there," said Bobby, "and the V-8 engine was better than anything else at the time. And the dual four-barrel carburetors really, really worked good. So he had a good-driving car, a good-handling car, a good-running car, and he himself really pushed that car to the limit. Red Farmer was the best I've ever seen in my whole driving career driving with the car in a slide. Most racers had to go fast with a car in a slide, but they used the tires up pretty quick. Red could do it right to the point where he didn't kill the tires, but the car would go that little bit faster."

Later on down the road Bobby figured out Red's secret, and the pupil would beat the master.

"He would use his tires up, and then I could pass him and win the race," said Bobby.

While Bobby was going to the local tracks with Red Farmer, one of the friendships he made was with R. H. Ellis, who drove for a car owner by the name of John Russo. Word of mouth in racing is the lifeblood of the sport. Russo had heard about the carburetors Bobby had built for Red, and toward the end of 1957 season Russo asked Bobby to do the same thing for him.

Russo said to Bobby, "If you come fix my Modified car so the carburetor runs right, I'll let you drive my Sportsman car."

After Bobby did the work for Russo, he finally had a car to drive. He headed for the Hollywood Speedway and got behind the wheel of a flathead '37 Ford, which under the rules could run multiple carburetors. The car wasn't working right, he saw, and he took it back to the pits, and he fixed the "tiny" problem in two minutes.

At the Hollywood Speedway, the Modified cars had their own heat race, and then the Sportsman cars had a separate heat race. For the feature, the Sportsman cars started in front of the more powerful Modifieds. Bobby was entered in his car, and R. H. Ellis was driving Russo's Modified car.

It was late in the year and Bobby didn't have any points because he hadn't raced, so he had the worst record. With the field inverted, he started in front.

The first two weeks Bobby finished in front of Ellis. By the third week Bobby won the heat race. It only paid $15, but as far as Bobby was concerned, a win was a win.

He would lead the feature, but then one of the speedway's stars, Red Farmer, Bobby Johns, or Roddy Perry, would pass him with only a few laps to go. Bobby would finish in the top five of the feature even though he was driving the less powerful Sportsman car. He'd earn another $20 for finishing first in his class.

"Boy, all of a sudden I was really in high cotton," said Bobby.

Bobby soon learned about the negative effects of ego and envy. John Russo, angry that Bobby was finishing ahead of R. H. Ellis, told him he no longer could drive his Sportsman car.

But if Russo wanted to keep Bobby from beating Ellis, he was too late. The cat was out of the proverbial bag. Bobby's reputation was made, and quickly he was approached by another car owner, Marty Handshaw. Bobby had been neighborhood friends with a number of Handshaw's crew members, so when Handshaw offered him the same deal Russo had offered him—"Work on my car, and you can drive my Sportsman car"—Bobby accepted.

Handshaw was a better driver than Ellis, so it was harder for Bobby to beat him, but beat him he did. Handshaw became a close friend of Bobby's, and he admired rather than was jealous of Bobby, and for several months Bobby drove Handshaw's car.

Then one day Bobby was accosted by Handshaw's father, who reminded him of Carl Kiekhaefer.

"He was a very mean-acting character with a lot of bad language," said Bobby.

The father didn't like Bobby finishing ahead of his son, didn't even like him running competitively with him.

"You're out of here," the father told Bobby.

"I decided to build my own car," said Bobby. "I built my first '34 Chevy coupe, modified at my daddy's shop on Northwest South River Drive."

Spectators couldn't help notice Bobby Allison out on the racetrack. He was young, and he was faster than most of the older, more experienced drivers.

One afternoon a man by the name of Roy Armstrong came into Bobby's dad's shop, where Bobby was working on his car. Bobby was friends with Armstrong's two sons. Armstrong had been attracted by Bobby's enthusiasm and drive.

Armstrong said, "Okay, kid, I'm here to help you. Shut up, and here's what we're going to do." With Armstrong, it was "I'm going to teach you" or "I'm going to show you."

Bobby was eager to learn, and Armstrong would show up at the shop almost every day. One of the first lessons—and one of the most important—impressed on Bobby was this: "Listen here, kid, every racetrack has two straightaways and *four* corners. We have to handle twice as good as we run."

Armstrong, a skilled mechanic, knew how to make a car handle, and he showed Bobby all the tricks. He also showed Bobby how to work on various aspects of the car and engine and how the various parts related to each other. He also showed him the ins and outs of adjusting a car to race conditions.

His mother had wanted Bobby to go to college. She didn't know it, but Bobby was attending the Roy Armstrong College of Racing.

For no pay, Roy Armstrong became Bobby's first crew chief. Armstrong taught Bobby the fine points of racing, but he taught him other important lessons as well.

"We were at the racetrack one night," said Bobby, "and a little kid asked me for an autograph. I kind of frowned and said, 'What?' And Roy grabbed me by the arm and said, 'Listen here, kid. Every request for an autograph is a compliment.' And that is still true today.

"So at Hialeah and Hollywood and West Palm Beach, and Key West, Florida, and anywhere else where someone would take an autograph, I'd give one. And if they looked like they weren't ready to leave real quick, I'd give them two.

"Roy Armstrong really helped me."

CHAPTER 5

Bobby: Judy

One of the men who supplied Bobby with parts and tires was a racer by the name of Ralph Stark. Ralph carried these items to the track in his race truck, and to make extra money, if a competitor needed a part or a tire, he'd sell it to him.

Bobby occasionally bought something from Stark, an older man who treated Bobby with respect.

"He took a liking to me early on," said Bobby. "He always treated me real good."

After Bobby left the Hanshaw car, Ralph Stark asked Bobby to drive his car.

Stark's wife was named Carolyn, and her sister Arlene was married to a man named Hank who also worked on Stark's race car. Carolyn and Arlene had a younger sister, Judy, aged fifteen, who was living with Carolyn after the death of their father the year before. Though Carolyn and Arlene often asked Judy to go with them to the races, she would beg off.

One night she finally relented and went. Before the feature, Carolyn told Judy that a young man by the name of Bobby Allison would be driving Ralph's car. It was all she knew about him: his name.

That night Bobby crashed, and the car began to flame. In the grandstands a horrified Judy Bjorkman stood up and screamed out Bobby's name, afraid he was badly injured.

Unknown to Judy, sitting four or five rows behind her was Bobby Jannelle, one of Bobby Allison's friends, who took notice when the pretty young girl reacted with horror when Bobby crashed.

After the races Bobby, his crew, and Bobby Janelle went to Nevelle's Barbecue to get a bite to eat. Coincidentally, Ralph Stark, Carolyn, and Judy were already seated at a table when Bobby's group arrived. Jannelle whispered to Bobby, "That's the good-looking girl who was worried when you crashed over there. You ought to go say something to her."

Bobby was with his date, so he wasn't about to go over to introduce himself right then, but he did make his date sit on the other side of the table so he could have a good view of Judy and make eye contact.

That was a Saturday night, and nothing came of it, but on Monday night Bobby drove over to Carolyn's house, where Judy was living. He told Carolyn he needed to talk to Ralph because he needed a flywheel for his race car. What he really wanted was to meet Judy. It was a weeknight, and before he arrived, he went to the trouble of showering, putting on fresh, clean clothes, and combing his hair.

"He's probably over at the race shop," Carolyn said to him, "but why don't you come in?"

So Bobby came inside, and Carolyn introduced Bobby to Judy.

Bobby didn't know it, but at the time Judy was dating a fellow by the name of Russ, who also worked on Ralph Stark's car. Judy and Russ weren't engaged, weren't even going steady, but they had agreed not to see anyone else. Judy was hearing talk that he wasn't keeping his part of the bargain, two-timing her with a girl named Peggy.

Judy was pretty "put out" about the whole situation. After she and Bobby talked for a few minutes, he asked if she would take a ride with him to her brother-in-law's shop. She was pretty shy, but she agreed, figuring that Russ was sure to find out and become insanely jealous.

They drove over to the shop, which was locked up tighter than a drum. Bobby asked her if she wanted to ride around and talk, and she agreed.

"What about we go get a banana split?" he asked.

"That would be fine."

They went to the local malt shop, and according to Judy, Bobby spent the entire evening bragging about his girlfriends and his active social life. In self-defense, she countered with the names of the boys who liked her. When Bobby dropped her off at the end of the evening, Carolyn asked her how it had gone.

"I don't *ever* want to see that guy again," she said. "He is *so* stuck on himself."

A few weeks later Judy went to the races at West Palm Beach, and that evening Bobby crashed, which allowed him to sit up in the stands with her. He asked her if she wanted to ride back to Fort Lauderdale with him.

"I have to check with Hank," her brother-in-law, she said. "He's my guardian. He's in the pits."

Bobby had a blue Chevy pickup with a cartoon of him in a race car on the side. Judy went to talk to Hank, who knew too well what Russ was up to. When Judy asked Hank if she could ride with Bobby, Hank told her cryptically, "If it was me, I'd be sitting in the front seat of that truck when it pulled out of here."

"Hank was telling me to go with Bobby," Judy said years later.

As busy as Bobby was, he found time to visit Judy Bjorkman evenings during the week. One evening Judy informed him that she was moving to Orlando because her mother had found a job there as a beautician. The middle Bjorkman daughter, Connie, had agreed to take them both in until they could find an apartment.

The night before she and her mother were to leave, Bobby and Judy ate at a catfish restaurant, returning to Carolyn's about nine. The two sat in Bobby's truck and talked until five-thirty in the morning. She and her mom were supposed to leave for Orlando at six, and she wasn't even packed. When her mother came outside, she saw them in the truck together and wanted to know what they had been up to.

"Mother," Judy said, "we were just talking. Honest."

Bobby said to Judy, "Give me your sister's address, and if I get a chance, I'll come see you." She wrote the address down and left it in the truck, thinking the while, *Yeah, sure. This is the last time I'm going to see this guy.*

Two weeks later, on a sunny Sunday morning, Bobby drove to Orlando to surprise her. When his blue truck pulled in front of sister Connie's home, Judy was in bed, her hair in curlers. Judy had told Connie about Bobby, but still wasn't sure that he'd show. When Connie saw the truck, she came to Judy's door all excited.

"Get up," she said. "Get up. He's out there. He's out there."

"No way," Judy said.

"He is."

Judy went to the window, and when she saw him, she began pulling all the curlers from her hair. Bobby asked if she would go to Mass with him.

It wasn't long before Judy's mother lost her job in Orlando, and she and Judy returned to Fort Lauderdale. One day when they were visiting Carolyn, her mom was cooking with butter, when there was a fire on the stove and her mother's hands and arms were burned. With her mom disabled, Judy decided she needed to find a way to make a living.

She was fifteen, in the ninth grade, enrolled in the Diversified Education program at Central High School in Fort Lauderdale. Half the day she went to school. The rest of the day she pounded the pavement looking for work. After three months of frustration, Judy asked older sister Carolyn if she could move in with her and borrow the money to go to the beautician school two blocks from Carolyn's home in West Hollywood. Carolyn agreed. Her mom moved in with sister Arlene and her husband Hank in Fort Lauderdale.

The day Judy graduated from the beauty school, she and the other graduates were thrown a party at the school. After she returned home, Bobby pulled up in front of Carolyn's house. He seemed nervous.

"I need you to come out to the truck for a minute," he told Judy.

"What for?"

"I just need you to come out here."

Said Judy years later, "There was no telling what he was going to do. I went out there, and he reached onto the seat and got this little box and handed it to me. I looked at him and he said, 'Open it.' So I opened it, and he said, 'What do you think? Will you marry me?'

"And that was it," said Judy. "I said yes."

It was a total surprise.

They were married on February 20, 1960. He was twenty-two. She was eighteen.

Judy, who had been born Lutheran, went to church but once a year, on Easter Sunday. She had been to services at the Catholic church several times with girl-friends and found herself drawn to it. Soon she was enrolled in catechism class, and it wasn't too long before she decided to convert.

When she told her mother, her mother said, "My gosh, your dad is going to roll over in his grave."

"No, Mother," Judy said. "Everything is going to be okay."

Judy had been born in Sisters of Mercy Hospital in San Jose, a Catholic hospital, and she wondered aloud whether the nuns had put a hex on her daughter.

"Mother," argued Judy, "it's called a blessing."

Judy embraced Catholicism, and from then on you could count on seeing Bobby and Judy in church together Sunday mornings.

In 1958 Bobby was building his own race car, and also fixing up customer's street cars to earn money to keep him racing. He was working on a car when he accidentally dropped a cast iron hydromatic transmission on his left hand, breaking bones and requiring dozens of stitches.

Bobby's dad took him to a doctor friend who spent two hours on a Saturday morning sewing up his hand.

That night Bobby went to the races, but he needed a substitute driver. He got Ernie Reeves, who by day worked as a plasterer and at night had worked for him at his dad's little garage. The car was so good Reeves almost won the feature event, just losing out to Red Farmer right at the end.

Bobby was out of action for nine long weeks. His return came on Memorial Day 1958, a special Wednesday night race at West Palm Beach.

Farmer won the race, and Bobby finished second. Second-place money, $95, was a big night for Bobby.

Among the friends Bobby had made in racing were Gil Hearn, an excellent racer his age, and Kenny Andrews, another guy his age who owned Hearn's car. Andrews's dad was an important part of the local Miami racing scene, supplying the circuit with custom racing wheels.

Hearn and Andrews loved racing in Miami, but they were resentful of the low purses the tracks paid, and so decided to drive up through Georgia and Tennessee to find paved tracks to race. South Florida racers preferred pavement to dirt. All they found, however, were dirt tracks.

The two returned to Miami for the Memorial Day weekend at West Palm. They finished back in the pack, and Bobby had finished second. Young and enthusiastic, they didn't hold it against him. Rather, they suspected the youngster might want to travel north with them in search of bigger purses.

Kenny Andrews said to Bobby, "We were up in Georgia and Tennessee, and the racers there said the tracks in Alabama are really good tracks, and they are paved. So we're going to Alabama. Why don't you come with us?"

Bobby had just won $95 for his second-place finish, and he said, "I got all this money. Yep, I'll go with you."

Bobby went home and told his mother he was going to Alabama, and by now she had resigned herself to the fact that her son was going to be a racer, not a college boy. She even suggested Bobby take younger brother Donnie with him.

Bobby said to Donnie, "Grab your suitcase and your helmet." At the time Donnie had only been running novice class for a neighborhood friend. Donnie jumped in the truck, and the two brothers headed for Alabama.

They started up the highway on a Thursday night. The race at the Dixie Speedway just outside Birmingham was scheduled for Friday night. Around lunchtime Thursday, they were in central Florida, and Bobby said to Donnie, "Instead of wasting our money on food, let's stop and buy a basket of peaches for fifty cents. They really look good."

They bought peaches and ate them for lunch and supper Thursday, midnight snack Thursday, breakfast and lunch on Friday.

The first night in Alabama was spent at the Dixie Speedway at Midfield, a quarter-mile paved track in the Birmingham outskirts. Bobby finished fifth in the heat race, fifth in the semi, and fifth in the feature.

Bobby went to the pay window figuring he'd get a few bucks, buy a hamburger, and sleep in the truck on the way to Montgomery and the next race.

Bobby stood at the pay window, and he was handed $135. Bobby walked away from the window, and he said to Donnie, "We have died and gone to heaven. Look at all this money. We're going to have one of those two-dollar steaks we saw at Miss Mary's Drive-in back over there, and we're going to sleep in a bed tonight."

And that's just what they did.

They went to Montgomery. Bobby went to Bo Freeman's gas station, where racer Sonny Black kept his '34 Cadillac. It was a show car, but it also won frequently. Sonny Black was a bootlegger who raced at night and did well. Sonny hadn't run at the Dixie Speedway because it was a quarter-mile track, and his Cadillac didn't run well there because it was so heavy. When Bobby and Donnie pulled up to Bo Freeman's gas station, they were taunted by Sonny's fans not to bother to go to the Montgomery race because "these Cadillacs are going to blow you out of the woods."

Said Bobby, "My attitude was, I've been in the woods before. I'm going anyway."

They went to Montgomery and qualified on the pole. In those days Alabama tracks paid money to the top qualifiers. Bobby won the heat race, won the semifinal race, and he won an Australia pursuit race, in which the car with the fastest time starts last, and every car he catches has to pull out of the race. Bobby won that race, too.

Bobby sat on the pole in the feature, and the driver on the outside was Sonny Black. The race began, and Black taught Bobby a lesson in staying ahead he never forgot.

When the flag dropped, Black accelerated past Bobby in his powerful Cadillac. He then pulled in front of Bobby and hugged the bottom of the track. Bobby was unable to get under him in the straightaways, and when they got to the corners, Black held him off until they reached the next straightaway.

Black won the race, and Bobby finished second. When Bobby went to the pay window, he was handed $400.

"The stack of money looked like it was a foot tall," said Bobby.

It was Bobby and Donnie's introduction to racing in Alabama.

Their next stop was the Peach Bowl for a Sunday night race. The track was located in the Atlanta stockyard area, near today's downtown. Bobby, this young, new kid, finished fourth, which thrilled him.

"There were a lot of guys behind me," he says.

Bobby and Donnie spent the night there. The next morning Gil Heard told Bobby he was heading to Jasper, Tennessee, to see his girlfriend, whose family had moved there from the Miami area. Bobby knew that Jasper was near Chattanooga, the home of Honest Charlie's Speed Shop, where Bobby could buy the latest in racing parts and pieces. Bobby had money in his pocket, and as well as he was doing, he was dying to make his car go faster.

Bobby and Donnie, along with their two friends Gil Hearn and Kenny Andrews, drove to Jasper, Tennessee, and at night slept in a peach grove outside Gil's girlfriend's family home. The next morning Bobby drove to Honest Charlie's and bought aluminum hubs and an aluminum flywheel. He put them on the car and returned to Alabama to the Dixie Speedway for a Friday night race.

He unloaded the car, ran a couple practice laps, and his engine blew up. Bobby hadn't been prepared for that. Out of the race and feeling dejected, Bobby tried to leave, but couldn't because the races had started. He was trapped inside until the evening was over.

With no place to go, Bobby decided to examine the engine. To his delight, he saw that he had broken an intake valve, but little else. The valve was down in the valve guide, and the piston was hitting it. He pulled the cylinder head off, and he saw the piston wasn't damaged. Neither was the cylinder head.

By the time the races were over, he knew he needed only an intake valve. He would have to take out the engine, but "it was no big deal to fix."

After the final race, Kenny Andrews said to Bobby, "Gil's mad, and he's going home? What should I do?"

Instantly Bobby knew the answer.

"Put Donnie in the car," he said.

The next night in Montgomery Donnie drove his first race in a professional division Modified car.

That night after the races were over, a man walked up to Bobby and offered him help. Bobby was shocked. No one had ever helped him when he was racing in South Florida. The man was Harry Mewbourne, whose driver, Earl Abts, had won the feature that night.

Mewbourne said, "I own the car that just won the race, and I have Chevy parts, and if you want, you can come to my shop, and I'll try to help you."

"What a neat deal," Bobby said. "Thanks. I'll see you in the morning."

Bobby was all alone now. Donnie had gone to drive with Kenny Andrews. Bobby rented a motel room close by the track. Saturday morning he drove to Mewbourne's place, sure all he needed was a head gasket and an intake valve.

Mewbourne sold him the parts he needed for about seventy-five cents, and Bobby drove to Bo Freeman's gas station in Montgomery. He put in the new parts and cleaned everything up. He was late to the track, and he had to start last in the feature event, but he sped from last to first to win the very first race of his long, illustrious career.

Donnie was in the race, and he finished up front.

Bobby headed for Atlanta and the Peach Bowl for the Sunday night race. Donnie and Ken Andrews moved into Sonny Black's house. After a decent finish in Atlanta, Bobby headed back to Miami.

In 1960 Bobby did so well that he would finish second in the nation to a racer by the name of Johnny Roberts for the Modified racing championship. Bobby's success in 1960 would move Ralph Stark to run Bobby in the 1961 Daytona 500.

Stark built a '60 Chevy with a 348 Chevy engine. It was a motor Chevy was very proud of, except it had one major problem: Racers hated it. It's nickname was "the boat anchor."

Bobby, at age twenty-two, was thrilled at the opportunity. He had met several of the Grand National drivers while racing on the short tracks, and he was excited and awed the first time he drove through the Daytona International Raceway tunnel into the infield.

Bobby's car was "terribly slow" compared to the Pontiacs and Fords, and the Chevrolet engine was outclassed.

"We were really, really behind," said Bobby. He ran twentieth in one of the twin 100-mile qualifiers. He won $50. After the race, Carolyn, Judy's older sister, called Bobby to say that Judy was in labor in the hospital. He charged home to their house in West Hollywood and spent the night with Judy. She gave birth to a son, Davey, named after a close friend, Dave Julian. After his son was born, he raced back to Daytona to run the race. Bobby's endurance was amazing.

"In those days," he said, "I had incredible endurance. I could stay up all night, easy. One night. I had to sleep the next night. I functioned really well the following day. And that's what I did. I probably got a nap along the way. I went to Daytona and raced the car."

He started thirty-ninth, and he finished thirty-ninth, still running at the end of the race.

"I went, and I gave it a try, and it was a first step," said Bobby. "It was always something I wanted to do. I didn't do totally bad, because there was somebody behind me, and that's how I gauged my early racing career. I may not have done as well as I wanted to, but I did better than some."

In 1961, between the summer season in Alabama and the winter season in Miami, Bobby won thirty-three feature races. Once in Alabama Bobby wanted Judy to go with him to all the races. A different sort of girl might have balked, but Judy had had some years as a child on the road. Her father, an electrician who lived in Oakland Park, near Fort Lauderdale, at times took jobs in such places as San Jose, where he worked at the shipyards; Kansas City, Missouri; Woodbury, New Jersey; and Augusta, Georgia. When Bobby began his career as a racing vagabond, it was no big deal for Judy.

In Alabama, Judy was fortunate to have friends and neighbors who were able and willing to watch her kids. She would stay home during the week and travel all weekend. But there were times even after Clifford and Carrie were born that Judy would round up her four kids and take them all to the races.

"Everyone helped everyone else," said Judy. "It was pretty neat. As the kids got older, I had to stay home a little bit more because of their activities, but I really did go to an awful lot with him, and not just to the big races on Sunday, but to the little races during the week as well. I went more than any of the other wives who ever went with their husbands. We were a hundred percent dedicated to each other."

Bobby's brother Eddie confirms their mutual devotion.

"We were at Columbia, South Carolina," said Eddie, "and Bobby finished the race second, and a friend of ours from Alabama was there with us, and he had a couple of friends with him, and one of them was the most beautiful woman you ever saw in your life.

"We were standing there, and Bobby was between me and her, and she turned to him and said, 'I want your autograph—in me.'

"My brother turned to me and said, 'Let's go.'

"I was single. I said, 'Wait a minute. Leave me here.'

"'No, you're coming with me,' he said, and we jumped in his Mooney at the airstrip and hauled ass to Hueytown. Now you talk about tough. He's the only man I know who would have done that. That's how tough Bobby Allison is, and how much he loved his wife."

One place Bobby ran after moving north was a little track on the south side of Richmond. Wife Judy was the pit crew. Bobby took his car off the trailer, put it on the track, mashed the gas, and blew everyone away, including veteran driver Emmanuel Zervakis.

What was amazing was that Bobby Allison won all those races with no money behind him and a skeleton crew. Bobby would just bust his butt, working, working, working until he figured out how to make his car last and win.

In 1962 Bobby returned to Alabama, and this time he wanted Judy and the kids with him.

She had gotten a job as a hair stylist at a high-end beauty salon, Richard and David, on Flagler Street in Fort Lauderdale, where she was earning $300 a week doing hair. She had worked there three or four months when Bobby asked her to go to Alabama with him. She gave up her lucrative job to be with him full-time.

When Bonnie was five months old, the family moved to Hueytown, Alabama, along with Donnie and his wife, Pat, and Eddie and his wife, Alberta. For Judy, the change from the informal Miami area lifestyle to the formal Southern belle Alabama society took some getting used to.

"We would go shopping in Birmingham," said Judy, "and you had to dress up with gloves and hats." It would stay like that for another six or seven years until the appearance of shopping malls, when the culture began to change.

The way Judy was raised, when you visited someone's home, you never asked for anything but waited until you were offered. "In Alabama, people wanted you to make yourself at home," she said. "I wasn't used to that. It was really, really different."

In 1960, Bobby, who had supreme confidence in his ability to build and drive a car, took his car up north to New Jersey to race at Wall Stadium. Winning was difficult, because the locals kept trying to wreck him. If they couldn't get into him, he won. But if they did get him, he not only lost, but he had to pay to fix the car.

It wasn't personal. The local track veterans didn't think a newcomer, especially from a place like Alabama, should be able to waltz in and steal their purse money.

Since fixing his car race after race wasn't his idea of what he wanted to do, he returned to the southern tracks, and in 1962 he won forty-one feature races, winning the national Modified-special driving championship. The team of brothers Eddie and Donnie Allison wasn't far behind.

CHAPTER 6

Donnie and Eddie:
Built From the Chassis Up

"Donnie had the feel of the car to the track as good as Bobby did."

—**Eddie Allison**

After Eddie Allison graduated from high school, he went to work for an engine rebuilding company owned by H. C. Wilcox, an automotive whiz who started the firm when he was twelve years old. It was from Harold Wilcox that Eddie learned how to build race cars.

One of the racers who had tutored Wilcox was Ralph Moody, who in the early 1950s came down to Florida from New England when he was young and raced against the best South Florida had to offer. Moody very often left the Miami boys in the dust.

Wilcox knew everything there was to know about motors, so what Wilcox wanted Eddie to concentrate on was how to make the car turn when it got to the corner. Wilcox also knew how to do that, and he gave Eddie a Ph.D. education.

"I am never afraid to ask a question," says Eddie. "And the man who taught me, Wilcox, never balked at a question I asked him. Plus he gave me all the input he could give me. He showed me by example so much, I rarely had to ask him any questions. And he wasn't scared to tell you *why* something was."

By 1957 Eddie and his brothers Bobby and Donnie were getting parts from their junkyard and building and driving race cars. While Bobby and Donnie showed driving talent from the beginning, Eddie spun more often than not.

"My foot was *way* too big" is how Eddie put it. "I couldn't get my foot up off the floor." Eddie would make it through turn two and go into three, but too often he didn't escape turn four. He told his brothers, "I don't need to drive. You guys drive. I'll fix them." Eddie might well have been a star on the superspeedways, where the winners *never* lifted, but this was 1957, and by the time the sport changed from its short-track roots to the era of superspeedways, Eddie's desire to drive was long gone.

Besides, Eddie was his father's boy, and there wasn't anything he couldn't fix. When he was nine years old, he went around the neighborhood offering to fix his friends' bicycles. His mom often didn't have the extra dime for ice cream, but when the Good Humor truck came by, somehow Eddie had the cash in hand.

Though Eddie was becoming expert at making a race car turn, Bobby didn't feel he needed Eddie. Bobby didn't feel he needed anybody. Bobby was a racing genius when it came to cars, airplanes, or anything mechanical. Bobby himself had an instinct for knowing how to make a car turn and knowing how to build an engine. And as a racer, only two others in the Miami area could keep up with him, Red Farmer and his brother Donnie.

Farmer recalled that when Donnie was twelve or thirteen years old he used to come with them to the races.

"Donnie used to come with us to Hollywood Speedway," said Farmer. "After the heat race, I'd get out of the car, and he'd climb in the window and get in the seat and play like he was driving my car. He asked me when he could run. I said, 'When you can reach the pedals.'

"He was small then," said Red. "Donnie always liked to do anything different or wild. He was different from Bobby. Bobby was more conservative, more level-headed. Donnie was like me, crazy. He wanted to do anything that was different."

Acknowledged as the black sheep of the family, Donnie as a youngster was wild.

"He was four times wilder than Bobby and me put together," said Eddie.

Donnie Allison was the best natural athlete in the family. He was the best football, baseball, and basketball player of the brothers. "He was the Natural," says Eddie. But when Donnie was ten or eleven, his dreams were not of major league baseball or even of race cars, but rather thoroughbreds. Not even five feet tall and unable to reach the pedals of a race car, Donnie talked of becoming a jockey.

"Man, Donnie could ride a horse," said Eddie. "Donnie loved horses." Eddie and Donnie used to walk the eight or nine miles to Hialeah racetrack. The trainers at Hialeah didn't mind when the kids came around.

"Donnie was quite small, so the idea of being a professional jockey was attractive to him."

But his dreams of becoming a jockey ended when, as a freshman in high school, he was riding his motorcycle and rammed into the back of a truck and "like to tore his left leg off." He needed 188 stitches and three weeks in the hospital to recover.

"Donnie was dodging a car, and he caught his left leg on the rear bumper of a truck coming in the other direction," said Bobby. "It dug into the flesh and broke it and tore it. The doctor wanted to take the leg off, but Dad said no.

"'You put that thing back together, and we'll take whatever you give us,' he said. 'But you're not going to take it off.' Dad stepped right in."

There were two Seminole villages not far from the Allison home, and Donnie made friends among the young Indians his age. The Indian villages had alligator pens, where the Indians would wrestle the alligators for tourists. According to Bobby, "his adventurous spirit led him to try alligator wrestling."

Donnie "was crazy and liked to have fun," said brother Eddie. Donnie wrestled alligators.

"He could do that, yeah," said Eddie.

Donnie also thought that because he had befriended the Indians, he had license to hunt and kill alligators. He was wrong, and he was once arrested and thrown in jail. Eddie came and bailed him out.

Donnie also was the fighter in the family. Neither Eddie nor Bobby ever looked for a fight, though if cornered, they could respond with fury. Donnie, however, actually enjoyed fighting.

"You didn't want to fight Donnie Allison, because he'd whip your butt," said Eddie. "He was lightning fast and so strong that if he hit you . . ."

Later on, after Eddie and Donnie moved to Bessemer, Alabama, one of the good ol' boys from Fort Payne announced to everyone in the bar that he was going to "whup Donnie Allison." He had heard of Donnie's reputation, and he was trying to make a name for himself. One night, both were there, and Donnie wiped the floor with him.

Donnie didn't go to Archbishop Curley High School like Eddie and Bobby. He first went to Jackson High School, and then he was sent to St. Leo's in northern Florida. Donnie was not an avid student, and as soon as he could, he dropped out of school in order to work and race full-time.

Donnie, Eddie knew, could drive the wheels off a race car.

"Donnie had the feel of the car to the track as good as Bobby did," said Eddie. "But Donnie needed the car to turn. When Donnie drove with me, we made the car turn. Too often when he was driving for other car owners, it didn't."

In 1957 Eddie and Donnie built a race car. They had a '46 Ford and they put a Crosley body on it and installed a 401 Buick engine. They took the car to the Medley Speedway, across the river from the Hialeah Speedway. They were scheduled for a night race. The track was closed for practice when they arrived. The pit steward told Donnie, "You can go out and run three laps."

Donnie cruised around to shake down the car. He mashed it to hold it even for one lap and then he stood on it. When he came in, he said, "Eddie, it won't run."

Eddie replied, "Donnie, that's thirty-hundredths faster than any race car has ever been around this racetrack!"

In the Friday night feature Donnie was trying to pass the leader, Rags Carter. Carter stuck him in the wall. The fence was made of railroad ties, and when Donnie's car hit, the wood grabbed it and tore it up.

Eddie had to work at Wilcox's engine company Saturday morning. Another driver, whose name Eddie remembers as Payne, was kind enough to let him and Donnie take the wrecked car to his body shop. When Eddie arrived at the shop a little after noon, Payne helped Eddie fix the car so it would be ready to run that evening.

That first night Donnie won the heat and the semi. Donnie told Eddie, "If I don't keep my foot on the gas pedal, the thing runs over the ripples." (The ripples were bumps placed along the bottom of the track to warn the drivers not to run too low.) Eddie wasn't surprised. That's how he had built it. In other words, for the car to work at its best, Donnie had to floor it going *into* the corners. It was Eddie's little secret passed on to him by Harold Wilcox.

"That's how you build a car—from the chassis up," said Eddie. "When the car runs in the dirt, you can mash your foot on the gas when everybody has their foot off. So you just go right by them. The gas pedal is what makes the race car handle. The front wheels steer way better with pressure against them than they do coasting. When the back wheels are pushing the front wheels, they stick in the racetrack way tighter than when you have your foot up off the gas.

"No one else did this. You'd think everyone would, but no. But that was what always made my cars win."

Donnie and Eddie ran that car twelve times and won seven features. Of the other five races, it wrecked once, that first night, blew up twice, and finished second twice.

"Donnie started out with the reputation as a hard charger," said Eddie, "but that was because the car would turn. It would go where he put it, so he could hold the gas pedal down, where other people had theirs off."

CHAPTER 7

Pat: Alabamy Bound

"Miami was a wonderful place to grow up."

—Pat Allison

When Donnie met his future wife, Pat, Bobby and Judy were already married and living in Hollywood, Florida. "I would go up there with Donnie when we were dating, and I'd sit with Judy at the race shop," said Pat. "Davey was a baby, maybe three or four months old. Judy and I got to be good friends."

Donnie first met Pat when she was fifteen. Their houses weren't far apart. She lived on one side of Grapeland Heights Park, and he on the other. One day a group of kids came down to the park to play touch football.

"He ended up throwing me in the canal that ran right alongside where we were playing," said Pat. "Of course, I didn't like him."

Donnie asked Pat for a date, and even though she didn't like him, she agreed. Pat and two of her girlfriends went out on a triple date with Donnie and his two best friends. One of them, Kenny Economi, made good money working for a battery company, and so he was able to buy a brand-new 1961 Chevrolet painted red and white. The car was immaculate. Pat was very happy to be traveling in style.

Donnie owned what Pat calls "an old bomb." Once in a while Donnie would pick her up and take her to school, but she would insist he drop her off blocks from the school because she didn't want to be seen in his jalopy. Later Donnie got a job as a service writer at Deal Ford, and he bought a 1961 Chevrolet Impala. After that, Pat was happy to have Donnie drop her off right in front of the Campus Corner drugstore near the school. Inside they drank Cokes and danced to "At the Hop" by Danny and the Juniors on the jukebox. Pat loved to dance, and Donnie was a great dancer.

Pat attended Miami High School. She was a good student and made a lot of friends. When they met, Donnie was out of school.

Pat recalled that "Donnie's dad had a pretty big junkyard in Miami on Northwest South River Drive. It was filled with cars and car parts. It's where Bobby got the parts for his first cars."

According to Pat, Donnie began racing because of brotherly competition. "Bobby told Donnie he couldn't race, and that got the hair on the back of Donnie's neck up, for sure," said Pat. "Donnie is a very competitive person, and he went for it, and he enjoyed it. Throughout his career, he just loved driving. He just loved it."

When they met, Donnie and Bobby had been racing for a couple of years at the Medley Speedway in Miami Springs on Friday nights and at Hialeah Speedway, across the canal, on Saturday nights.

Pat recalls that when the brothers raced, they were fiercely competitive with each other and with Red Farmer and another driver by the name of Herbie Tillman.

"One time after a race Pop Allison had to remind them they were still brothers," said Pat.

"To win, you had to have people to compete against," said Bobby. "I wanted him and everyone else to show up so I could beat them all. Early on, Donnie was just somebody in another car, and later he became a tough competitor, and finally, he became *the* toughest competitor.

"We were very competitive with each other. In one race one or the other of us was going to win, and I guess I began to crowd him, and he began to crowd me, and finally we got to bumping each other.

"I think he spun me out. I'm not sure, but after the race we had words, which delighted some of the fans and pleased the promoter, and then we almost came to blows, and my dad stepped in, and he said, 'I didn't raise you boys this way. You're going to apologize to each other, and you're going to support each other.'

"Our competitiveness didn't lessen, but we gave each other better consideration."

Racing was an important part of Donnie's life when Pat met him, but Pat actually thought it might be a passing fancy, like his jockey obsession years earlier. She was thinking Donnie would settle down with a steady nine-to-five job like most of their friends. Pat figured that there was a raft of solid opportunities in Miami for Donnie to work around cars, parts, or tools, but once Donnie, Eddie, and Bobby headed north, any possibility of Donnie's taking a regular job disappeared completely.

When Donnie went with Bobby and Eddie to Alabama for the 1961 racing season, Pat had no idea what she was getting into.

Said Pat Allison, "The first year Eddie, his first wife, Alberta, his two young boys, Donnie, me, and our daughter Pam, who was six weeks old, moved into a little three-story house in Bessemer." The two families lived in an apartment on the third floor split in two by a wall.

"When I got in there I thought I was going to cry," said Pat. "I wanted to go back to Miami, where everything was nice and new." Bessemer, a steel town, was always gray.

Bobby, Judy, and their two kids lived in Hueytown, the next town over, in a little apartment out in the country. In 1965 Donnie and Pat also moved to Hueytown. They lived there until 1982, when they moved to their farm *way out* in the country. Pat's consolation was that they would be going home to Miami once the racing season ended in the fall.

For years, the local Alabama racers had had the tracks all to themselves, but beginning in 1961, they were overwhelmed by the stiffer competition from what was really the Miami gang: Bobby and Donnie Allison and Red Farmer.

"They came in there like a storm," said Pat Allison. "There were a lot of cars, but only a few good drivers, and they won a lot." Usually the purse for winning was closer to $150, which is why they sometimes raced five nights a week.

"I remember waiting in long lines to get the prize money—in cash," said Pat. "Today it's computerized, and nobody waits anyplace. I can remember a race Donnie won in Memphis. He got paid with a thousand-dollar bill. That was *real* big money back then. It's like a million today."

After the race Donnie and Pat stopped at an all-night restaurant at around two in the morning. They ate. All Donnie had was the thousand-dollar bill. The waitress had to wake up the owner at home.

"He said we could mail him the money when we got home," said Pat.

Most of the local Alabama racers had jobs, and racing was a hobby. The Allisons were different; racing was their livelihood. And where Bobby could keep all his winnings, Donnie and Eddie had to split theirs fifty-fifty.

And so Bobby had more money to race with, while Donnie and Eddie had to scrape along as best they could. While Bobby was buying a new part, Eddie and Bobby would go to a junkyard and get a used part. That Eddie had the ability to squeeze a nickel until the buffalo on the back cried uncle contributed to their success.

"Eddie was in charge of the purse money," said Pat. "I got ten dollars a week for groceries, and he took twenty, because he had two kids and I had one. The rest went back into the car. Bobby had his own team, and he handled his own money. They kept their cars in different places in other people's shops in the beginning, but they helped each other when they needed it."

Donnie and Pat were able to make ends meet because Pat herself was expert at stretching a dollar. And when times got tough, Donnie was resourceful. He could play a mean game of pool.

"The money part of it was like a roller coaster," said Pat. "Now it isn't. Now if you start a Winston Cup race, you can live for half a year on that money. Back then, sometimes it was good, and sometimes it wasn't, and when it wasn't, we made do. I can do anything with money. I learned it over the years. If you have a little bit of money, you just spread it around. Donnie always made enough money to live on, and sometimes it was better than others.

"In the early years, Donnie would go to Pharoah's pool hall in Bessemer. Donnie is competitive, and he's good in every sport he plays. He would go up there when the guys from the car dealerships would go to lunch, and they'd all shoot pool, and he made a lot of money doing that, and I would buy groceries and some other things, too. So Donnie was always creative about money."

Making it easier on the newcomers was the wonderful treatment bestowed on them by the local Alabamans.

"A lot of good people in Alabama helped Donnie, Eddie, and Bobby," said Pat. "We couldn't believe it. People would say, 'Come eat dinner with us.' 'Here are a bushel of peaches.' 'We'd be glad to keep the kids.' 'Come home with us.' It was amazing: we weren't used to Southern hospitality. They were very good, good folks, and we still have good friends from there today."

Judy went with Bobby to the races more often than Pat went with Donnie. Part of it was that Donnie had Eddie's company. The other part was that Pat was more reluctant to leave her youngsters in the care of others.

"At first I would go with him," said Pat, "but when the children came along, I just felt I needed to be with the children more than I needed to be at the track."

They ran on Thursday nights at the Dixie Speedway in Midfield, Alabama. The race was on the radio, so Pat could stay home and listen. Sometimes, if the boys had to travel overnight, she and Judy would leave the little kids behind in the care of Mrs. Jones, an elderly babysitter.

In 1964 the three Miami race teams, Bobby, Eddie and Donnie, and Red Farmer, dominated the competition so completely that they won 96 percent of the races run in the Birmingham-Montgomery area. They made enough money for all of them to continue to fix up their cars and to live. Bobby even made enough money to buy a little Skeeter race car, a midget body converted into a Modified car.

The team of Donnie and Eddie actually won more races than Bobby that year.

"Eddie was the key," said Pat Allison. "Eddie was a one-man Wood Brothers. [Glen and Leonard Wood are renowned for their car-building ability.] He was as good as the Wood Brothers. If he had stayed in racing, Eddie would be a car owner today. He was an excellent mechanic. He and Donnie always worked together. Bobby and Donnie were pretty good mechanics, but Eddie was brilliant when it came to the motor and to handling."

The day after Eddie and Donnie won the 1962 middle-season championship at the Birmingham track with a Buick motor, it blew up. Eddie and Donnie could not afford to put the engine back together again, so Eddie retrieved an old Chevrolet motor that Bobby had taken out of his car and abandoned. It was sitting under a bench, unwanted and unloved, and Eddie borrowed injectors, patched it up, and put it in Donnie's car. And for the rest of the '62 season, Donnie never lost another quarter-mile race.

After winning eight in a row, Donnie entered the final race of the season at

Birmingham. It was 500-mile race. When Donnie crossed the finish line, he was twelve laps ahead of the second-place car.

After the summer season up north, Eddie, Donnie, Bobby, and Red returned to Miami to race in the wintertime.

"It was so much fun you can't imagine," says Eddie Allison.

CHAPTER 8

Red Farmer:
Short-Track Racer

"Dirt is for racing. Asphalt is for getting there. If it ain't in a slide, it ain't worth the ride."

—Red Farmer

"Winning was the only thing. Second place wasn't worth a damn."

—Red Farmer

Charles "Red" Farmer was born on October 15, 1928, in Nashville, Tennessee. His dad was a furniture salesman for Sears and Roebuck. His mom and dad separated, and in 1945 he and his mom moved to Miami, where his grandparents lived. The redhead attended Edison High School.

Farmer had a good friend, Earl Davis, whose dad raced a '34 flathead Ford at the Opa-Locka racetrack.

One day, out of the blue, Earl said to Red, "My dad and his driver had a falling out, and he's looking for someone to drive the car next week." Earl had been impressed with the wild way Farmer drove his street car and told his father.

He asked Red, "Would you like to drive it?"

"I don't know anything about a race car" was Red's first reaction, but then he reconsidered.

"Heck, yes, might as well try it," he said.

Earl Davis, his dad, and Red went to the Opa-Locka race track, the site of an abandoned air force base. The cars ran down the straightaways on asphalt, and then turned through dirt to go to the other runway coming back the other way. There was also a smaller dirt track there, and Farmer began his career running on it.

Farmer had no one to teach him. A driver learned through experience.

"Back in those days there were no Go Karts or anything like that. There were no classes, where you could start off in a lower class and move up. You just went out there, and you got run over until you learned to get out of the way."

Farmer thought he was pretty good, until a racer by the name of Ralph Moody came down from the north and blew all the Miami hotshots away.

"I remember we thought we were pretty good," said Farmer. "Then in 1950 Ralph came down in a red car with a white X on the door, and he won about ten races in a row. He was such a chassis expert, and he had a lot more experience than the guys in the area. Ralph concentrated on handling, while we concentrated on running sideways and spinning the wheels and going out of shape. He kicked our butts."

In 1953 a man by the name of Shorty Sykes offered Farmer the chance to drive in the Daytona beach race in February.

"It was a hell of an experience," said Farmer. "In those days they started everybody who showed up. There were eighty or ninety cars in the race.

"I didn't have a trailer or a truck. Shorty Sykes's car lot offered me a Hudson if I'd take it to Daytona. I built a race car, put a roll cage in it. In those days they were stock cars. Me and my mechanic, Wayne Kackley, put a toolbox in the backseat and the luggage in the trunk. We cranked it up with the lettering on the side, and we drove that Hudson from Miami to Daytona Beach and listened to the radio all the way up driving that race car.

"When we got up there, we jacked it up and took the mufflers off so it would sound like a race car."

Farmer and Kackley were rookies. The car ran fast, and Farmer reached the top twenty before he broke a right rear wheel coming off the dirt bank onto the asphalt on lap 12.

"I didn't know it," said Farmer, "but the hot dogs at the time like Ralph Moody and Tim Flock, they double-plated all their wheels. I had just a regular stock wheel. When I came off the back straightaway in the dirt and hit the asphalt, the wheel broke off and jammed up in the quarter panel."

Back home in Miami, Farmer was hired by John Fitzgibbons, the owner of Aerodex, a company that rebuilt airplane engines. In addition to his interest in planes, Fitzgibbons also loved to race. Fitzgibbons hired Farmer to be his driver.

In 1953 Farmer was leading the points standings for the national Modifieds championship when he was drafted into the army.

When he got out of the service in 1955, Farmer returned home only to learn that Fitzgibbons had another driver, Dur Howe. Rather than fire Howe, Fitzgibbons decided to run two cars, and so he and Farmer traveled to West Palm Beach where they bought a white '37 Ford with the number C-97 on the side. The C stood for Choquette. Jack Choquette had driven C-97 to the Modifieds national championship in 1955.

Farmer was a rugged guy who looked like a gunfighter, but everybody loved him because he was a very nice person. He raced at the Hollywood Speedway, a quarter-mile asphalt track, on Saturday nights, and at West Palm Beach, a half-mile dirt track, on Sundays. Midyear, Farmer had a wreck, and when he repainted the car, he changed the number from C-97 to F-97—"C was for Choquette. F was for Farmer and Fitzgibbons."

Farmer has run car number F-97 for almost fifty years. At the end of the 1956 season Farmer replaced Choquette as the Modifieds driving champion.

The race that gave him the championship was held in Concord, North Carolina. One of the racers he beat was Ralph Earnhardt, a tough customer who also loved to race on dirt. At the awards dinner at Daytona Beach that year, Farmer and Earnhardt, the Sportsman champion, were seated at the same table.

It was the next year when Farmer asked Bobby Allison to help him with his Chevy engine. Allison made a name for himself as a mechanic, and his mechanical ability helped Farmer to greater heights.

"He saw where I was having so much fun winning races," said Farmer, "and boy, I guess he decided he wanted to try it, and he went from drag racing to oval track racing."

Farmer, who preferred to race on dirt, raced against Bobby and the team of Donnie and Eddie on asphalt at Opa-Locka, Hialeah, and the Medley Speedway, which was right across the river from Hialeah.

"Bobby and Donnie didn't like the dirt tracks that much," said Farmer. "I used to kid them. I'd say, 'Dirt is for racing. Asphalt is for getting there.' Or I'd say, 'Asphalt is for sissies.'

"They would say, 'Asphalt is for racing. Dirt is for taters.'

"I would tell them, 'If it ain't in a slide, it ain't worth the ride.'"

Red Farmer and the Allison brothers all became close.

Farmer recalled going to Bobby and Judy's wedding at Miami Springs in 1960.

"It was a Catholic wedding, and me being a Baptist, I went in the church, and though it was the same religion, everything was in Latin, and I didn't understand what they were saying," said Farmer. "All these words were being said and bells were jingling, and it must have lasted an hour and a half, the longest, most drawn-out wedding I ever did see, and of course half the time I didn't know what was going on. It was kind of funny."

Farmer and the Allisons raced against each other in the Miami area until the latter part of 1959, when Bobby and Donnie and Eddie left the city to race on the Alabama circuit. When they returned, they told Farmer about the fantastic tracks there and the money the tracks were paying.

But Farmer, who was an electrician with the International Brotherhood of Electrical Workers Local 349, had a wife and family, and he couldn't just pick up and go off to Alabama. It took the work of Fidel Castro and Nikita Khrushchev to give Farmer the break he needed to put his racing career on a firm footing.

"During the Cuban Crisis in 1962, they had a blockade, and the electrical work came to a screeching halt," said Farmer. "I had a wife, three kids, a mother-in-law, and a grandmother-in-law who lived with me, and the unemployment checks didn't go very far, and that's when I loaded up my coupe behind my station wagon on an open-wheel trailer and towed it to Birmingham to run at the old Dixie Speedway."

The first night Red Farmer raced, he had to start dead last because he hadn't accumulated any points.

The Alabama racers had straight drives with fuel injectors. They pushed the cars to get them started. Red had a '36 coupe with a four-barrel carburetor, a clutch, and a transmission, and the Alabamans laughed when he cranked it up on the trailer and backed it down the ramp.

The laughter didn't last long, as Farmer, starting at the back of the pack, roared past everyone to win. The next night he went to the Montgomery Speedway, a half-mile track, and he repeated his success.

Farmer's two wins were worth $300.

"I had been living on $35 unemployment checks," said Farmer. "That was big money for me."

After running the two races, Farmer loaded his race car on the trailer and drove the twenty-plus hours back to Miami. Before the end of 1962 Farmer decided to move to Alabama permanently.

Bobby had moved to Hueytown, and after a time Farmer moved in next door.

"Bobby's shop is right next to mine right now," said Farmer. "Bobby and I have been next-door neighbors for thirty years. Our property adjoins each other. They live at 140 Church, and I live at 143 Faust, which is the next street over, but the other side of the fence of my property is the Allisons."

In 1966 Bobby went to run the NASCAR Grand National circuit, and Donnie followed a year later. For most of his career, Red Farmer avoided the Grand National/Winston Cup circuit. Over thirteen seasons he ran in thirty-six Grand National races, finishing fourth twice.

"[In 1972,] I finished fourth in the Talladega 500 in a car that I built in my backyard," said Farmer. "That car is in the International Motorsports Museum in Talladega right now."

The reason Farmer didn't move up to Grand National/Winston Cup racing was simple: He hated the politics and the games played on the factory race teams at that level, and he was aware enough to know that if he ran as an independent, he wouldn't be able to compete with the factory teams.

"There was a time when Eddie Allison was working on a Chrysler team with Donnie, and Bobby was with Mario Rossi and the Ford people, and the thing of it was, there was so much politics with the factory teams that Bobby and Donnie were told they were not supposed to talk with each other even though they were brothers," said Farmer.

"That kind of stuff went on, and if you didn't have the factory backing—if you were an independent like Dave Marcis—you were history. I did most of my racing and winning on the short tracks. I did a little Grand National, but I didn't have the backing, and, to put it bluntly, I would rather win on the short tracks than be an also-ran in Grand National and Winston Cup.

"Winning was the only thing. Second place wasn't worth a damn. I wasn't going to sit and run twentieth or twenty-fifth in a Winston Cup race just to say I was a Winston Cup driver. I'd rather go to Birmingham and win a half-mile race out there and be in the winner's circle than be an also-ran in Winston Cup.

"And I could make a living on the Busch circuit, because I ran fifty to sixty races a year, and I could win twenty to thirty features a year, and once in a while I could get a little deal money under the table from the promoters to pay my expenses, entry fees, and pit passes."

Helping Farmer meet his expenses was his sponsor, Long Lewis Ford. In 1962 thirty-five Chevrolets were running at the Dixie Speedway, and a man by the name of Vaughn Burrell came to Farmer and asked if he got him a Ford motor whether he'd build a car to run at the Dixie Speedway. Farmer was spending a lot of his earnings on motors, and here was a chance to get a free motor. Farmer agreed.

Long Lewis Ford supplied Farmer with a 427-cubic-inch engine from Holman and Moody, the Ford parts giant.

"Those were big old fat motors," said Farmer, "weighed about two hundred pounds more than the little motors did. I moved the motor back about six inches from the front wheels to give it more rear-wheel weight, built that car, got it ready to go out to the Dixie Speedway.

"Roy Buckner was Mr. Burrell's partner, and he said, 'I don't know what this car is going to do. Let's not embarrass ourselves and put our name on the car until we can see what it's going to do.'

"I went out there the first night and won the feature. They said, 'Man, I wish we had put the name on that car!'

"I put LONG LEWIS FORD on that quarter panel, and it's been there forty-two years. That's fifteen years longer than Petty had STP. It's the longest sponsorship in racing that I know of.

"It was on a handshake. We made a gentleman's agreement forty-two years ago, and that's the way it's been. We never put a word on paper, no lawyers. Just a gentleman's agreement."

Red added three more championships to his credits, winning the Sportsman national championship—today it's called the Busch series—three straight years, in 1969, 1970, and 1971.

It is October of 2004, and Red Farmer at age seventy-six is still racing. He has 745 wins to his credit. In 2003 he won a 50-lapper at the Dothan Speedway and another 50-lapper at Greenville Speedway.

Because Red Farmer didn't race on the Winston Cup circuit, he never achieved the fame of the other members of the Alabama Gang. But Red Farmer, a pure racer, never cared about the fame or even about the fortune. What he cared about was the joy of racing, something he has never lost, he says, because he has never been involved in the politics of the sport.

"If you drive on a race team," he said, "and if you go to the track and don't win the race, the first thing the owner says is 'How come we ain't winning races?' The crew chief says, 'The driver isn't driving the car.' The driver says, 'The crew chief isn't setting up the car right.' And he says, 'I can't set it up right because the owner won't spend the money to buy me what I want.'

"They're pointing fingers in a circle, and it comes right back to nothing. To me, being an owner, driver, and mechanic, I can't blame anybody but me. And I didn't have to answer to anybody. So I never would go Cup racing.

"I can't have anybody pulling my strings and telling me who I'm supposed to talk to, like Bobby and Donnie did, what I'm supposed to say and give me a script.

"That's the trouble nowadays. We have too many robots out there driving. You come up and stick a mike in their mouth, and they tell you what the sponsor wants them to say, not what they think. You have a few drivers like Tony Stewart, who is a breath of fresh air. If you don't want an honest answer, don't ask the question.

"Too many of them are scared of their sponsors or the owner and walk around like a monkey with someone pulling their strings so they can open their mouths. That's what we had when I was in it, and I said, 'Uh-uh, I ain't doing that. I'm going to go back where I can enjoy racing and have fun.'

"When I ran last Saturday night, I finished my fifty-sixth year driving. Next year will be my fifty-seventh year, but I still enjoy it, still have a good time doing it. If I was in the damn Cup racing, I'd have probably quit twenty years ago."

CHAPTER 9

Bobby:
Nose to the Grindstone

"Here comes the Alabama gang."

—**Local Competitors**

The commute from Miami to the racetracks throughout the South was getting to be too much for the brothers, and the time away from their families too much for their wives, so in 1963 Bobby, Eddie, and Donnie, along with fellow racer Red Farmer, decided to relocate permanently to the Birmingham area.

Bobby and Judy moved to the small town of Reevestown, Alabama, a blue-collar suburb of Birmingham. Tommy Walker, a friend of Bobby's who worked at the local Chevy dealership, rented out a garage apartment. Red Farmer, Eddie, and Donnie moved to Bessemer, another Birmingham suburb a few miles farther north.

While Donnie and Eddie were racing together, Bobby was driving his own car with the help of a friend, Chuck Looney. Bobby and Donnie had met Looney in a local Miami bowling alley owned by former Boston Red Sox first baseman Norm Zauchin, who belonged to the same church as the Allisons. Looney, a top bowler, wore a diamond ring signifying he had bowled a 300 game in a tournament. He worked for Zauchin maintaining the lanes and handing out bowling shoes and score sheets.

Looney and the Allison brothers became close friends, and Looney almost became part of the family. After Bobby began racing, Looney worked for him for years fixing his cars and driving the tow truck.

Bobby won the Modified championship in 1964 and 1965. He ran on tracks all over the South, including the Dixie Speedway, a quarter-mile track at Birmingham; a quarter-miler in Huntsville; a half-mile track at Montgomery, a five-eighths-of-a-mile track in Birmingham, plus tracks like Oak Grove in Tennessee, the Asheville-Weaverville Speedway, and the Nashville Speedway.

"Anywhere there was a race, he ran," said Eddie Allison.

In 1964 Bobby was second in points at the Birmingham Speedway. Donnie was first. Red Farmer was third.

At the Dixie Speedway, Farmer was first, Bobby second, and Donnie third. At Huntsville, the order was Donnie, Bobby, and Red, and at Montgomery it was Red, Donnie, and Bobby. Bobby was second in the points nationally, and Red was third.

That was the year when people saw them coming to the track towing their cars in a convoy, they would cry, "Here comes the Alabama Gang."

In 1964 Bobby bought what the press called a "mystery" 427 Chevrolet engine from Roger Penske. It was an engine that racer Junior Johnson had used in his cars in 1963 and then discarded at the end of the season when Chevrolet did away with it; even the molds for the engine parts were destroyed. The mystery was why it ran so fast. But Penske had a store of them, and he had no use for them. Bobby wanted one because they were still legal on the Modified circuit.

"It was basically a 427," said Eddie Allison, "but the engine was unbelievable. It was made just right. The thing made an ungodly amount of horsepower, and you can do a whole lot with a race car if you've got horsepower."

By 1964 Bobby Allison's name had spread around the racing world, which was always looking for new talent. Ray Fox, a successful car builder and engine man who had been impressed by Bobby when he was a kid working for Carl Kiekhaefer, invited him to come to Darlington to see if he could drive his car in the Rebel 300. Eddie Allison didn't go with him.

"I wish I would have," he said.

Bobby ran a few laps, but the car didn't handle very well, and it didn't go very fast. Bobby was used to setting up the car the way he wanted it. This time he had to do it Fox's way.

LeeRoy Yarbrough, a tough-talking racer who had driven for Fox, came over and said to him, "Looks like you need a driver for that car. I can win with it."

Fox agreed and gave the ride to Yarborough. He flew Bobby home to Hueytown in his private plane.

When Eddie was asked why Fox gave the ride to LeeRoy Yarbrough instead of Bobby, he said, "I can't even imagine. I really can't. And Ray Fox is a smart man. I think LeeRoy made the car go a little bit faster. And LeeRoy was a pretty good race car driver. But nothing in the class of Bobby Allison. After a year or two Ray knew he had made a mistake."

On October 20, 1964, Judy gave birth to her third child, a boy they named Clifford, after Cliff Julian, brother of Dave Julian.

That fall Judy got a phone call from a man named Ed Grady. "He wants to start a Grand National team next year," she said to Bobby, "and he wants you to drive for him." Grady told Bobby he was pointing toward the race at Riverside on January 17,

1965. Bobby knew who he was. He had met a couple of his mechanics on the short tracks along the way at Pensacola.

"Yeah, boy, let's do it," Bobby told him.

What Bobby didn't know was that the man who had given his name as Ed Grady was really Ed Grady Parton. Parton had been part of the Teamsters, a union business agent in Baton Rouge, Louisiana, and he had turned state's evidence against Jimmy Hoffa during the Senate committee hearings in the late Fifties. That Parton wasn't buried under the start-finish line of a racetrack seemed to be a miracle, but he was very much alive. E. G. Parton had read of Bobby's successes in the Baton Rouge newspaper, and he wanted him to be his driver.

John Holman of Holman and Moody, the huge Ford car and parts distributor in Charlotte, had sold Parton a mess of a car. Nelson Stacy once drove it on dirt tracks.

Bobby and Chuck Looney worked on the car in Hueytown, rented a flatbed truck, and headed to California with Parton and an employee of Parton's by the name of David Ashley.

When the car arrived, Norris Friel, the head NASCAR official, shook his head at how many improvements they would need to make to qualify the car. Friel wrote down a long list of things.

"We worked and worked and struggled to get the thing through inspection," said Bobby. "It took us three days to get a Holman and Moody car through inspection."

Bobby was new, and the NASCAR inspectors were being super careful about letting a novice into their race.

Bobby and Ashley worked on it right up to race time, but they still could not complete the list. Bobby was allowed to enter the car only because the field wasn't full. A NASCAR official drove Bobby around the track in the pace car so he could see how it was shaped. He started forty-first and his time on the track was short-circuited when the car overheated. He finished twenty-ninth.

Bobby took the car back to Hueytown and worked on it for two straight weeks. He built his own parts when he had to. No one could have worked harder.

Said Eddie Allison, "Bobby and I had enough brains to understand when a race car told us 'I want this,' we gave it to it. And we knew how to make what we needed. We didn't have to go and buy it. We couldn't have if we had wanted to, because we didn't have any money. Even as much money as we made winning, we had to buy tires, and we had to buy food to eat. So we had to make the parts.

"Years and years later I was talking with a friend. I said, 'The kids today don't know how to do anything, because they don't have to.' I wasn't bragging. I was just stating the facts.

"And you don't get gaga about God over it, but our talent came from somewhere. We believe he gave it to us, and we put it to use. He's not going to put it to use. We have to put it to use. And so Bobby and I had the talent to figure out what was going wrong and fix it. Cause he had given us that talent.

"And we worked hard, but that wasn't unique. I've seen plenty of people in the sport work as hard as we did. But hard work gets you wherever you want to go. You might get kicked in the teeth. You might get your teeth knocked out. But if you get back up and go, you get there. And then you can fix your teeth. But the reason Bobby Allison won races was because Bobby Allison worked his ass off."

When Bobby brought the Parton car to enter the Daytona 500, Friel stopped him after he drove through the tunnel but before he could enter the garage area.

"Is that the same car you had at Riverside?" Friel asked. Allison said it was.

"Then just turn that damn thing around and go back where you came from cause you're not running that car here," Friel said.

Allison told Friel they had done a lot of work on the car. He pleaded with him to at least take a look at it.

Friel couldn't believe it was the same car. Allison assured him it was.

Friel was impressed. He said, "This is the way you bring a car to the racetrack."

For the race Parton bought a new engine from John Holman, the business brains behind Holman and Moody and a man known occasionally to be a hard-ass when it came to accepting the return of parts that didn't meet expectations. In other words, if John Holman sold you a part, you were stuck with it—even if it was defective. You had no choice. He was the only Ford parts dealer around.

When Bobby started the engine, he found water in one of the cylinders and water in the oil, suggesting a cracked cylinder head. Parton, with Bobby in tow, went back to see John Holman.

"Your head is no good," said Holman. "A new head is $300, and if you want one, put your money right here on the counter."

Parton, who was six foot three and very strong, reached across the counter and grabbed Holman, a large, rotund man, by the front of his shirt and dragged him over the countertop.

He said, "Listen here, Porky Pig. You're going to give me a new head for this one right now. I'm going to be back in ten minutes, and if there isn't a new head on this workbench, they are going to find you floating somewhere." And he shoved him backward.

Parton turned and walked away, with Bobby trailing behind him. Holman started yelling to his employees, "Give me a head quick. Get a head. Get a head. That guy is going to kill me."

When Parton returned, he had a new cylinder head waiting for him.

But the incident would hurt Bobby Allison's career badly. Parton—and by association Bobby—had made a powerful enemy. John Holman disliked Bobby until the day he died. Bobby didn't realize it then, and today isn't convinced it was the sole reason because he says, "A lot of people wanted to kill John Holman."

"Might it be one reason?" I asked Bobby.

"That was the start," he said. "Yeah, it certainly was the start of it."

Bobby impressed everyone during Speed Weeks Daytona. He finished seventh in the 40-lap qualifying race behind Darel Dieringer, and when the 1965 Daytona 500 was halted after 332.5 miles because of rain, he was in eleventh place.

When he ran at Atlanta on April 11, he finished seventh, a good effort, but not enough to keep Parton in business.

Like novice car owners before and after him, Parton's experience disillusioned him, and he returned to Baton Rouge. He sold all his equipment to Robert Harper. In his final three races driving for Robert Harper, Bobby finished far back in the pack.

Allison returned to Alabama to drive on the short tracks. In 1965 he won 14 races in 66 starts. That year Bobby won his fourth Modified racing championship.

CHAPTER 10

Donnie and Eddie: Busting Their Humps

"Donnie and I could fix a race car sitting on a nurfing bar talking about it."

—**Eddie Allison**

Like Bobby, the team of Donnie and Eddie had also garnered some attention, but when they were given what they thought was their first opportunity in Grand National racing, something went awry.

In the spring of 1963, shortly after the Daytona 500, Grand National racer Jack Smith said to Donnie and Eddie, "Come and build a car so we can run Atlanta."

Donnie and Eddie arrived at Smith's shop in Spartanburg, South Carolina, to build a race car. Both thought they were building the race car for Donnie to drive.

Donnie and Eddie realized immediately that Smith's crew "didn't know how to make a race car go."

After they arrived, the Allisons became frustrated at the snail's pace of the race team. Smith's mechanics were perfectionists. Said Eddie, "The thing had to be as minutely perfect as they could make it. It would take them three days to make a piece for a car that we could make in an hour."

According to Eddie, it took two of Smith's men three days to build a spindle.

"We could have done it in three hours," he said.

As for the motor, Eddie took one look at it and told them, "All the horsepower is in the tailpipe." When he confronted the engine builder, he was told he was wrong.

"You couldn't tell him anything," said Eddie.

But Jack Smith had a deal with Chrysler, and he had money, and Bobby and Eddie had nothing, so Smith had the power to call the shots. Eddie wasn't given any input.

In the end it didn't matter. It turned out there had been a misunderstanding:

Smith intended to drive the car himself. The Allisons didn't care. Smith had hired them to work on a car, and he had paid them, and they went home a little perplexed but not unhappy.

Said Eddie, "A lot of crazy things like that happen. You just let it go on. It's no hard feelings or animosity. It's just what happened."

Donnie and Eddie returned to Hueytown to build Donnie's Modified car. Donnie had to borrow some money from his father-in-law, Joe Laserra, to build the car for them to run in Alabama.

Said Eddie, "We knew we could win the races at Alabama. We had to make the money to support our families. I had two boys, and Donnie had a boy and a girl. We had to bust our humps."

With Eddie making sure the car turned, Donnie won the last nine races in a row at the quarter-mile Dixie Speedway in 1963.

"Our little coupe with a supercharger on it just annihilated the circuit around there," said Eddie. "The car was so dominant that they changed the rules so it no longer was legal."

A large part of Donnie's success came from Eddie's ability to set up the car and from the close relationship the two brothers had.

"Donnie and I could fix a race car sitting on a nurfing bar talking about it," said Eddie. "And our Modified Special car was a better turner than what anyone else had. 'Cause Donnie and I could talk about that."

Then before the 1964 season the track banned the supercharger under their hood.

Donnie and Eddie asked if they could put a supercharger on a Late Model car, but the track wouldn't allow that either, so in 1964 Donnie decided to leave the Alabama tracks and drive for Bob White, a Chattanoogan who owned Weldon Gas Products, an acetylene oxygen gas company.

Eddie didn't go with him at first. Eddie stayed in Birmingham and worked for a company that repaired machinery equipment. Eddie thought about going home to Miami, but he had leased his house in Hialeah to a woman whose husband was fighting in Vietnam. His house payments were being taken care of, so he figured he might as well stay in Birmingham and work at his job, and on the weekends he would go to Chattanooga, stay at Donnie's house, and watch Donnie run.

The mechanic on Donnie's car was Bob Wright, who had a reputation for wanting to do things his way. Wright at first insisted on working alone on the car, but as the season went on, he and Eddie Allison would talk cars, and Wright saw how much Eddie knew and let him work alongside him before a race. Though Eddie wasn't officially on the race team, Eddie would periodically take off from his job at the machine company and work full-time on Donnie's car.

———

In 1964 Donnie Allison won the first nine races at the Montgomery Speedway. He was racing against Bobby, Red Farmer, Friday Hassler, and all the top drivers he had been running against the past few years.

Donnie had a reputation for being a hard charger, because he could put his car in places other drivers couldn't, but Donnie could do that because his car handled so much better than the other cars.

"I learned the basics at the right place, and our car would turn, so Donnie would put it in places it looked like he shouldn't go," said Eddie Allison. "It wasn't hard charging. We knew we had to get to the front before Bobby and Red, because we didn't have any money. We had to win races to be able to go to the next race. And we were supporting two families when everyone else was supporting one. In the summertime Donnie and I had our families living with us, so we had the expense of paying for houses in both Florida and Alabama. But we did well. We had no complaints."

In 1964 Donnie Allison, driving a '34 Ford, was the track champion at Birmingham and at Huntsville.

At the end of the '64 season Eddie Allison returned home to Miami to work at the junkyard.

"There is no place in the world to live like Miami, Florida. And when I went home, I don't remember fooling with anybody's race car. I was basically done with racing in 1964."

Said Pat Allison, Donnie's wife, "Eddie couldn't take the pressure of what went on in the racing circuits. He had ulcers real bad, and he couldn't handle that, so he went on to a nine-to-five job."

CHAPTER 11

Bobby:
Eddie Makes a Sacrifice

"All racing is is work. You got to work. You can't be scared to work."

—Eddie Allison

When 1966 began, Bobby was driving for Betty Lilly, the wife of a Valdosta, Georgia, industrialist. Lilly assured Bobby she had plenty of money to race competitively on the Grand National circuit. After all, the year before she had backed driver Sam McQuagg, and he had been named Grand National Rookie of the Year. When McQuagg left Lilly to take a ride with Ray Nichels, Lilly chose Bobby to replace him.

Lilly's resources, however, turned out to be less than advertised.

"She talked to Bobby like she was going to be able to afford whatever he wanted to do," said Eddie Allison, "but every time he wanted to do something, she didn't have the money to do it."

Bobby's greatest success driving for Lilly came in the Peach Blossom 500 at Rockingham on March 13, 1966. Bobby finished third in Lilly's car, laps behind Paul Goldsmith and Cale Yarborough. Bobby's purse was $4,500. He also managed a third at the Middle Georgia Raceway on May 10 behind Richard Petty and Tom Pistone. But there were too many blown engines in between. Lilly finally had to admit that racing was too rich even for her blood, and after the Middle Georgia Raceway race, she dropped out of racing.

"It didn't pan out," said Eddie, "so Bobby said, 'I'm building my own car.' "

Bobby knew what he wanted. He had raced on the short tracks with a '64 Chevelle, and that's the kind of car he would build.

Bobby asked Tom Gloor, who owned the local Chevrolet store in Hueytown, to sponsor him. Gloor, a combat pilot in World War II, had sponsored him on the

Modified circuit, but Gloor was not comfortable sending Bobby into battle at the speeds run on the Grand National circuit, and so he lovingly declined.

"Tom just got worried that the money he was giving Bobby would end up getting him hurt," said Eddie Allison, "and he couldn't stand that, so we had to go somewhere else for a sponsor."

Bobby built his little Chevelle with very little help and painted it maroon and white. The car would cost Bobby a total of $7,000.

Bobby and Chuck Looney built the car in a two-car cement-block shed behind Bobby's house at 3352 Crescent Drive in Hueytown, Alabama. That garage, if it is still there, ought to be a shrine for race fans to visit. When racers saw the movie *Days of Thunder,* one of the details they scoffed at was the tiny shed in which the hero of the movie built his race car. But the fact is at least one racer—Bobby Allison—began in just such a tiny shed.

In 1966, when Bobby built his car in his backyard, he was barely scratching out a living. His competitors, the top race teams in Grand National racing, were sponsored and supported by the major car companies. The slogan was "Win on Sunday, sell on Monday." Chrysler and Ford, especially, had deep pockets from which to buy the best parts and hire the best drivers.

Richard Petty was funded by Chrysler, as was Cotton Owens and driver David Pearson. Ford financed car owner Junior Johnson and driver Fred Lorenzen. Bobby Allison, who had no money to speak of, had the confidence, will, and work ethic to enable him to build a car to compete with—and beat—the big boys.

One of the burning questions has always been, What is the hardest single feat in sports? Ted Williams always said that hitting a baseball was the toughest. But if hitting a baseball is the hardest, the next hardest has to be winning a Grand National–Winston Cup–Nextel Cup race. Thousands have tried. Most have failed. Only a handful have won even one race. Bobby Allison, starting from nothing, would win 85.

Eddie had a week's vacation coming in April of 1966, and he decided he would spend it with Bobby. Eddie, his wife, Alberta, and his two little boys, Eddie and Mike, drove to Hueytown for what was supposed to be some rest and relaxation. But Bobby needed all the help he could get on his race car, and Eddie never said no when his help was needed, so Eddie spent the week in the garage working on Bobby's car. That was all right with Alberta. She was used to it. After all, building and fixing race cars was what Eddie had always done.

Bobby had another flirtation with Grand National racing when, on May 22, 1966, legendary car builder Smokey Yunick asked Bobby to drive his Chevrolet in the World 600.

"I think Smokey admired my competitiveness and the success I had up to that point," said Bobby.

———

Chevrolet was out of racing, and Smokey was trying to bring it back in. Bobby went out and tested the car, and it was very fast on the straightaways, but it didn't turn at all when it got to the corner.

"What a handful," said Bobby. "Whoever drove Smokey's car really had his hands full!"

Bobby drove three laps in the race, and he pulled into the pits. He told Smokey, "I don't even know where to start."

"At the time I didn't fit into Smokey's picture, and he didn't fit into mine. So we went our separate ways," said Bobby.

"Smokey and Bobby were super friends after the fact," said Eddie Allison. "If they could have been friends then like they ended up being, Bobby could have driven for Smokey, and Smokey never would have quit racing. Because with Bobby, Smokey wouldn't have had to cheat to win."

At this point Bobby became impatient. He had been shot down by Ray Fox, Ed Parton went bust, and his joining with Betty Lilly hadn't worked very well. When he drove for the best, Smokey Yunick, he ended up going three crummy laps. Bobby decided he would have a greater chance of success in Grand National racing if he built his own cars.

After Eddie and his family drove back home to Miami, Bobby called him to say he needed him. Would Eddie please come back to Hueytown?

There wasn't anything Eddie wouldn't do for Bobby. Eddie had an old car, and he grabbed his tools and drove from Miami back up to Bobby's home in Alabama. He left his wife and two boys back in Miami so the boys could finish school. Every week Eddie sent money home to pay the bills.

The plan was for Alberta to come up at the end of the school year. In the meantime, she fell in love with a male neighbor, and by the time school ended, so had Eddie's marriage. His wife and two sons moved to Fort Valley, Georgia. Luckily for Eddie, the new husband loved the boys, and so Eddie feels no bitterness toward either his ex-wife or her new husband.

"That's life," said Eddie. "It happens. My boys have a fantastic mother. I told her many times, 'You did a fantastic job raising these boys.' I had them in the summertime, and I took care of everything, and I gave her the house we had bought together, so things were cool, and the guy she married really loved my boys, so it made the thing work."

Though Bobby requested Eddie's help, he didn't need Eddie's expertise on making the car turn as much as Donnie did. Bobby had his own ideas on the subject. Bobby, in addition to being perhaps the greatest driver of them all, was also a crackerjack mechanic. He knew how every piece of the car worked and how to fix it. And Bobby was the sort of driver who demanded that things be done his way. And so Eddie knew going in that he wasn't coming to Bobby's race team as a partner, the way he had been with Donnie, but rather as a worker, an employee.

"Bobby would not relate to me the way Donnie would. And I couldn't rebut it, because I was the mechanic, and he was the driver-owner-crew-chief-everything. We would talk about how to make the car go better, but not the way I would do it. Bobby knew how he wanted the car, and we didn't have time to discuss it. We worked twenty-four hours a day, seven days a week to get to the racetrack. If we had stopped to discuss it, we wouldn't have gotten to the racetrack."

Which was fine with Eddie.

"Obviously, what Bobby wanted to do was good enough to win races. Like I say, I'm the most spoiled mechanic that's ever been, because I didn't have to worry about it.

"The biggest problem with NASCAR Cup racing today is the mechanics think they are smarter than the drivers, and you can't be," said Eddie Allison. "The race car has to fit the driver. If you're not sitting in the seat you cannot say, 'We need this to make the race car go faster.'

"My philosophy is this: If the driver comes in and says, 'We need a roller skate up on the roof,' I say, 'Okay, here, I will put it up there.'

"And if the stopwatch moves, I say, 'Do you want another one?' The stopwatch controls the thing."

But in hindsight it's clear that when Eddie Allison went to work for Bobby, he was sacrificing his own career in racing. Had he stayed with Donnie, or had he gone to work for another driver in Grand National racing, Eddie might have been recognized as the outstanding car builder he was. But because he worked for Bobby, the rest of Eddie's career was conducted mostly in the shadows of his famous younger brother. Not that Eddie ever was bitter about the sacrifices he made working for Bobby.

Says Eddie, "It just doesn't bother me, because we did so well. To see Bobby perform, that was the greatest. It flabbergasted people when he mashed the gas pedal of that car."

Bobby Allison had a novel idea—front-end steering—and it was up to Eddie and Chuck Looney to implement it. At the time most cars had the steering mechanism in the back. Bobby believed that a front-steer suspension would absorb the racetrack better than rear suspension.

"This was the first front-steer car," said Eddie Allison. "We took the Ford spindle, and we turned it around, and then we figured out how to hook the General Motors steering linkage to make the car work right. We got the parts from a junkyard. That's all we could do. We didn't have money to go to a car store. We had so many friends in the junk business we could just go get parts and carry them home and see which one we wanted to fit. Bobby was such a likable person, all he had to do was to meet somebody, and they became his friend. And people found out he was as good as he spoke. He never took advantage of the people who helped us.

"We figured out what it took to make the car turn. The beauty part of putting it in the front was that when the car went down the straightaway, it was *pulling* against the linkage instead of pushing against it. We hooked the thing up without a spring and worked it up and down and got the wheel to do what we wanted it to do, and we finally figured it out. And it worked the day we finished it. All we then had to do was make it strong. We could run five hundred miles if we didn't wreck or if the engine didn't blow."

And so Bobby Allison, who had a brilliant mind for automotive engineering, created a new, revolutionary design, one that would have made him a rich man had he had the business sense to patent it. But Bobby Allison was a racer, not a businessman. Bobby never cared much about the money. His idea helped him win races, and that was all he really cared about. Other people would copy his idea and become rich.

"The race cars today are his race cars," said Eddie Allison. "You won't get anybody to admit it. He gave it all away. He carried all the stuff to Mike Laughlin's shop in Greenville, and he gave it to him. The Ford guys were so die-hard on their rear suspension, and it ain't there no more. His is. Every car. It worked then, and it still works. Other guys take credit for it, but it came right off what we built right here in this backyard at Crescent Drive in Hueytown. And again, this is not to brag, but merely to state a fact. It's his brain. He also invented a deicer using the oil out of the engine to deice an airplane.

"Bobby could do anything. It was a thing our daddy taught us, that you can't be scared to try to do something, or you won't do it. Bobby could run a milling machine. A lathe. We learned how to do by doing, and we had enough brains in our heads that we could follow up on that."

In 1966 Bobby left Alabama to compete on the Grand National circuit. Bobby's first attempt in his own car came on June 15 at Beltsville, Maryland, a half-mile track with a mild bank. To go fast you had to turn the corner when you got there.

At the time the rest of the cars were monsters, giant bodies weighing 4,000 pounds, powered by giant 450-horsepower engines. Bobby arrived at Beltsville in his little 3,000-pound Chevelle with a 327 Chevy engine. Few paid him any heed. He was unknown, and his car was underpowered. According to Eddie Allison, he and Bobby knew the car was fast the minute the little maroon and white Chevelle drove onto the track.

After Bobby qualified fourth, his opponents weren't so blasé, but three-quarters of the way through the 200-lap, hundred-mile race his differential broke, and he finished only fifteenth.

One spectator impressed with Bobby's performance was NASCAR founder and czar Bill France, who was always on the lookout to promote and help fresh blood coming into the sport. France knew an up-and-coming driver when he saw one. Bobby was handsome like Gregory Peck. ("Every time I saw him I thought of *To Kill a Mockingbird*," said Humpy Wheeler, president of the Charlotte Motor Speedway.) But France thought Bobby needed a bigger engine than his 327 to run at Daytona in the Firecracker 400, and he told him to go to Junior Johnson's and get one.

Bobby didn't necessarily agree, but when Big Bill France, the founder of the sport, tells you to go to Junior Johnson's place and get a motor, you don't slap him in the face by declining such a generous offer. And when you don't have any money, you don't turn down a free engine.

France called Johnson and told him to help Bobby install one of the big Chevy motors in his Chevelle.

Bobby, Eddie Allison, and Chuck Looney drove up to Wilkes County to Junior's shop in Ronda, North Carolina, to install the engine.

"Chevrolet had given him engines that were sitting idle," said Eddie Allison. "So it was no big deal for him to give us one."

"I remember how race-smart Junior was," said Eddie Allison. "The man was a better mechanic than he was a driver, and he won fifty races. Junior was sharp. Junior knew what it took to make a motor run, which a lot of people don't know. Most engine builders throw parts at it, and it runs faster. Everybody has their quirks, but Junior was an all-right person. We had a good time getting that done."

Bobby's first attempt to race with the big Chevy engine came on July 4 in the Firecracker 400. But the car could only qualify twenty-seventh, and in the race he finished fourteenth.

"We found out at Daytona we didn't want that 427 motor, that our 327 would have done better, but we couldn't get the 350 till the end of the year because Chevrolet wasn't making them," said Eddie Allison. "We had to run a 327, which was the biggest they made at the time."

Three days later, at the Old Dominion Speedway in Manassas, Virginia, Bobby sat on the pole. But in the race the transmission went out, and he finished fifteenth.

"We knew the 427 motor wasn't what we wanted," said Eddie Allison. "The reason we built the car the way we did it was to outrun them in the corners, and the 427 motor took a whole lot of that away, because it was so much heavier."

Three days later, on July 10, Bobby raced at Bridgehampton, Long Island, and in this race he qualified poorly and went out of the race early when the engine blew up and leaked oil all over the track. The 427 was dead. Long live the 427.

The next race was at Oxford Plains, Maine, scheduled in two days. Bobby Allison didn't have a motor. And he didn't have much money. Bobby went to a Chevrolet dealership in Boston and bought a "warranty engine." It had been in a brand-new car bought on the showroom floor, but when the customer found out the hard way its engine didn't work right, he returned the car to the dealer under the warranty and received a new engine. When Bobby asked the dealer if he had any cheap 327 Chevy engines in stock, the dealer showed him the warranty engine. It didn't work right, Bobby was told, but it was cheap. Bobby figured he could fix it, and he bought it along with some racing parts.

Bobby needed a garage to work in, and he contacted Bob Latford, who worked for the PR department of NASCAR and who drove the pace car. Latford then called the Chevy dealer in Oxford Plains, Maine, who said Bobby could use one of his bays until the shop opened in the morning.

Bobby headed for the shop as soon as he arrived. Darkness had fallen. That night Bobby, Chuck Looney, and Bob Latford stayed up all night putting in the engine. Latford, a delightful man who loved the sport and later became known for his racing knowledge as the Shell Answer Man, was part of the caravan of seven or eight independent race teams and NASCAR officials going from track to track. When he learned Bobby needed help, Latford pitched in. Latford wasn't much of a mechanic, but when Bobby told him what bolt to tighten, turn it he did, and if Chuck or Bobby needed another hand, Latford was there to give it to him.

Oxford was a third-of-a-mile track, a beautiful facility seating 13,000 in the middle of scrub oak. The race was held at night, giving the makeshift Allison crew a few more precious hours to prepare the car. To everyone's amazement—everyone except Bobby Allison—he won the pole, and he won the race a lap ahead of the field, the first victory in his illustrious Grand National/Winston Cup career.

"It was the first of Bobby's eighty-five Winston Cup victories," said Latford. "Bobby claims I was his crew chief for that one. It was a thrill."

After the race Bobby was not modest about his accomplishment. He accurately told the writers, "I blew by all the hot dogs."

Fonda, New York, was next, fifty miles northwest of Albany, and with the little engine Bobby started the race eighth, but a wreck caused by J. T. Putney took him out of the race early and shortened the car by two and a half feet on the right side. Tiny Lund was also caught up in the wreck, and after the race was over, Lund walked over to Putney, hit him, and knocked him over.

The next event on the northern tour was at Islip, Long Island, and on the way Bobby stopped at the Dumont, New Jersey, body shop owned by his cousin, Dave Demerest, whose specialty was body work and frame straightening. (Demerest's mom was the sister of Bobby's mom.)

"Dave Demerest was very good at his job," said Bobby. "He knew exactly which piece of metal to touch first to get what we needed. He had a frame-straightening rig. I had never seen one before, but that thing saved us. It pulled the wheels back into position where they needed to be, which gave us the basic four spots on the ground from where to try to throw the sheet metal."

Bobby and Chuck Looney again stayed up all night shaping the sheet metal back into what a Chevelle was supposed to look like. James Hylton, another rookie racer, and his mechanic, J. D. Roberts, also pitched in to help Bobby. Hylton and Bobby would become close friends, with Bobby often staying at Hylton's home in Inman, South Carolina, when he was racing in the Carolinas.

"Boy, both of them were a big help," said Bobby. "James himself was a really good mechanic. They jumped in. If they needed something, I would help him."

The camaraderie of the independents was touching. These racers with little resources had one advantage: They had each other.

"We had a good camaraderie," said Eddie Allison. "No one had any money. We were on the road. If we needed to, we borrowed trailers, borrowed trucks. We did everything to get to the race. People don't understand what it took to get there. Roy Tyner, John Sears, J. D. McDuffie, all them guys, Richard Childress, James Hylton. We all traveled together. We gypsied up and down the road. And if we didn't have time to go back to the shop and work on the car, we'd go to somebody's shop and work on it there. It was a neat camaraderie of people, a lot of fun. Which made it worthwhile, because all it was was work. We got to breathe two or three hours a week. The rest of the time we worked."

Not only did they help repair each other's cars or provide assistance or parts when needed, they also got together and formed a unique pit crew.

"We didn't have the pit crew the Pettys had," said Eddie. "We needed to have a jack man, a gas man, a tire man, and none of the independents had much help, so a group of the independent owners—James Hylton, Richard Childress, John Sears, Roy Tyner—pooled their help to form one pit crew. Childress gave us Tim Brewer. James Hylton had a guy named J. D. Roberts from down in Tampa. Chuck Looney was the gas man from our team. The one crew pitted all our cars. The way we did it, the driver who was highest in the standings in the race got to pit first. Very rarely was someone in our group ahead of us. And even with that makeshift crew, we still beat that [Petty] Plymouth."

When Bobby arrived for the Islip race after a night of working around the clock, the car wasn't painted.

"When I went to the race at Islip, the car had a primered front fender and a wrinkled-up hood," he said.

It sounded like Bobby worked twenty hours and slept four.

"No," he said, "twenty-one and three, and some days, twenty-two and two."

The Islip track officials let Bobby enter, again because they didn't have a full field.

James Hylton, who had made it possible for Bobby to get to the race, led the 300-lap Islip race from lap 147 to lap 282. Hylton's lead was a commanding one—until his car began to sputter at the end. He was out of gas, and Bobby passed him and went on to win his second Grand National race.

He won a third short-track race at Beltsville, Maryland, on August 24, 1966. Richard Petty, the favorite, had a rare engine failure on lap 30, and Allison led the race the rest of the way. No other racer was on the lead lap.

Three days later, on August 27, at Bowman Gray Stadium in Winston-Salem, Bobby crossed swords with another of NASCAR's royalty, Curtis Turner, acknowledged by many as the greatest of the early stock car racers. Turner, like Petty, was used to getting his way, and he didn't like it one bit when newcomers tried to match wits or trade paint with him.

"Curtis showed up that night in a pale-yellow, light-colored suit, with a shirt and tie—fancy dress, and smelling of strong drink," said Bobby.

The confrontation began on the eighth lap when Allison refused to be a gentleman and let Turner pass. Turner, who had more of a temper than Petty, whacked Allison from behind and spun him out.

"There he was in the factory Ford," said Bobby. "The track was close to his hometown. I was in his way. And the only way he could remove me from his way was wreck me while he had a shot at me. Which he did."

Bobby softened, giving Turner the benefit of the doubt.

"I'm not sure whether it was a deliberate act or if he was feeling good enough [from the liquor] that he didn't judge properly."

Bobby was able to resume the race with only a few little dents. He was, however, a lap down.

"I spent all the time catching up, and when I caught him, he was leading, and I attempted to pass him, and he wrecked me again," said Bobby. "He deliberately ran me into the wall, and this time it did damage my car."

After the second incident, Bobby retaliated.

The yellow flag waved, and the pace car came out. Turner, leading the race, was on the other side of the oval creeping along right behind the pace car when Allison decided that the quickest way to his intended target was a straight line.

"I just went across the infield and crashed right into his left front. Wanted to take him out. I was trying to even the score a little bit."

The cagey Turner, keeping an eye out for this newcomer, saw him coming and just managed to avoid terminal damage as Bobby tried to bury the front of his car in Turner's. For the next ten laps the two drivers raced side by side, beating and banging the sides of their cars, trying to get the other driver to say uncle or crash.

Cotton Owens, who owned David Pearson's car and whose pit was next to Bobby's, was standing there holding his hands about two feet apart. Eddie Allison asked him what he was doing.

"I'm hunting a rock," Owens said. Owens wanted to throw it at Turner, who was also banging on his car.

"There was a lot more banging back in those days than we have today," said Humpy Wheeler. "A lot more, particularly hitting the guy on the left rear quarter panel and spinning him out. Or slamming on the brakes and letting him eat his radiator up on your bumper. They didn't know Bobby and Eddie, and they just put them through the paces.

"Bobby was just so mad at Curtis," said Wheeler. "You couldn't stay mad at Curtis, because he was one of those Peter Pan people. But that got everybody's attention. They knew: Don't mess with Bobby Allison anymore."

That day at Bowman Gray, Bobby finished eighteenth, Turner seventeenth, after NASCAR officials tossed them both out of the race. It was just as well, because their cars looked like they had just come back from a demolition derby.

Police had to keep the two drivers—and the riled-up race fans—apart. Turner got in his street car and left. A few days later, at Darlington, Turner and Bobby ran into each other.

Turner said to the youngster, "You and I need to be friends."

"And from then on, we were," said Bobby. "And it made me feel good, because Curtis was the first one who recognized that I was committed to what I wanted to do, that I was talented enough to do well. And he wanted to be my friend. That was pretty neat."

Turner and Allison both were fined $100 for the rough driving. After the race

Junior Johnson, the owner of Turner's car, told his driver. "If you do that again, I'll pay the $100 fine and you can pay to fix the car." Johnson was so disgusted with having to spend all that money fixing a car Turner had turned into a scrap heap that he fired him.

The race proved two things: Bobby Allison wasn't going to back away from anyone, and if you did him wrong, you weren't going to get away with it.

Bobby's immediate problem was that his car was wrecked, the next race was at Darlington, and the drivers had to be there for qualifying at noon on Thursday, September 2. He had exactly seven days to make it.

"We brought the car home to Hueytown from Bowman Gray in a bushel basket," said Eddie Allison. "It was the only car we had. If we don't get to Darlington on time, we don't get to race."

Bobby, Eddie, and Chuck Looney didn't go to bed until they got the car through inspection. It was an impossible task under difficult conditions, but the three men accomplished their goal in the little garage in Bobby Allison's backyard.

"NASCAR would not allow us to bring a raggedy, bent-up, not-painted car to race there," said Eddie. "So we had to do all the things it took to make the car presentable *plus* put it back together again.

"All a race car is is work. You just work. Back then you worked twenty-four hours a day, seven days a week, and when we did it, it was 365 days a year. We'd get up Christmas morning, open the packages, and then go to work on the race car.

"You worked all the time," said Eddie Allison. "All you did was work and get a hamburger and eat your hamburger while you were working on your car. The whole proof of the pudding is work. But it was so much fun . . . and work. That's all it is is work. You got to work. You can't be scared to work. And you better figure out how to prop your eyelids open if the car isn't done and you have to have it there tomorrow. You have to work on it. People don't understand that the world that works, works, and the world that don't, don't."

The race at Darlington on September 5, 1966, was a precursor to the events of the rest of Bobby's season when engine after engine blew up or a part broke during a race. It's what happens when you don't have enough money. It's what happens when you're a rookie on the circuit. It's what happens when you have to trust people you don't know for advice.

At Darlington Bobby bought an engine from someone who said he knew something about engines, but a lap after Bobby passed Buddy Baker to take the lead in the race, it blew up.

"It was a sad deal because we didn't have any money," said Eddie Allison. "Money would have let us hire more help. We worked constantly, so we didn't have time to concentrate on going faster, as much as getting the car back on the racetrack, because Bobby's goal was to make all the races. We couldn't miss a race. So we worked, constantly worked.

"What happened, Bobby listened to a lot of people telling him a lot of junk that cost us motors. One guy in California sent Bobby pieces to put in the motor, and we put them in, and the motor ran three laps. As smart as we were in that department, we didn't have time to double-check. We took people at their word, and we bolted stuff together, and it blew up."

Race fans had no idea how tiny a budget Bobby had to race with. Tom Gloor, who had sponsored Bobby's Modified car and who owned the local Chevrolet dealership in Hueytown, called General Motors headquarters in Detroit and asked them to send him two Chevy 350-cubic-inch motors so Bobby could race at Martinsville on September 25. When the Chevy brass said no, Gloor said, "If you don't send us two motors, there is going to be a Camaro on the showroom floor without an engine in it."

GM sent the motors, and with little time to spare, Bobby and Eddie put the stock, out-of-the-crate 350-cubic-inch motor into the Chevelle and installed the racing camshaft, an oil pan, the four-barrel intake, and the rest of the parts needed to make the car go.

The car ran well, and then the tire changer on the makeshift pit crew cross-threaded one of the five lug nuts, and the NASCAR official in the pits refused to let the car run with only four. By the time they fixed it, the car was down a lap, forcing Allison to run the engine harder than he wanted.

If the engine had lasted, he would have won. The old scoreboard at Martinsville listed the race leaders. As Bobby gained on the field, he was fifth, and the next time around he was fourth, and then third, and then second, and then he took the lead and was the race leader from lap 210 to lap 354.

Bobby was sitting behind Fred Lorenzen, confident he would be able to pass him before they reached the checkered flag, but with six laps to go, Bobby's engine blew. Lorenzen won the race.

Afterward Lorenzen's famed 28 car was sitting on the truck, when Eddie walked by and noticed that one lug nut was missing from the right front wheel.

"He got to run with four," said Eddie, "but they wouldn't let us run with four."

That week *National Speed Sport News* featured a photo of the old Martinsville scoreboard and the car numbers on it, with Bobby's Chevelle on the bottom of the turn passing Lorenzen's Fairlane. It would not be long before Bobby began winning at the superspeedways as well as the smaller venues.

"At the time there were more racetracks in the South than anywhere else in the country per state," said Humpy Wheeler. "Most of the tracks were dirt. We had a lot of race drivers who were coming into the so-called big time who had won hundreds of races. It wasn't like it is now. These were people who had been lower-middle income, so they were hungry, and the talent was much more plentiful than it is today.

"When Bobby first came in, we thought, *He's won a lot of short-track races. Let's see how brave he is when he gets out there at Daytona, Charlotte, et cetera.* And Bobby caught on about as fast as anybody I had seen. Bobby was very competitive and very smooth. He knew when to go and when to slow. Back in those days it was more survival than anything. You go to Martinsville for five hundred laps on asbestos brakes, and it wasn't a question of who had the fastest car but who had brakes with a hundred laps to go. Charlotte was tough. So was Darlington. And Bobby started winning at the big tracks."

In 1966 Bobby Allison won three races in a car he built in his garage, and might have won ten if the engines and parts hadn't broken.

"What Bobby did was unique," said Eddie Allison. It shows you how dedicated and talented he was. He had a talent that so far surpassed everyone else's that it was unreal. Otherwise he couldn't have done it. Because nobody else has done it. Look at how many have tried. Rob Moroso, Tighe Scott. Bobby Hillin. You can go on and on.

"The sad part is that if a person with Bobby's desire, will, and ability came along today, it would be impossible for him to do what Bobby and I did, which is build a Cup car in your backyard and race. Today it takes way too much money to be competitive. It would be impossible. People just don't understand how we did what we did just from nothing.

"To take a car out of the backyard in Hueytown, Alabama, and go beat that [Richard Petty] Plymouth was unreal. It was so neat, because Bobby scared them hot-dog racers to death. This hick from Alabama—he really wasn't a hick from Alabama; he was a well-educated human being from Miami, Florida—could come and beat them with this race car that they thought couldn't outrun a kiddie car.

"Nobody has stepped back and looked at what we accomplished. Some of those Charlotte racers had it tough, but man, we were in Hueytown, Alabama, with a home-built race team. Most of the Charlotte guys at least had factory-reject cars. They didn't have to build the car like we did. How many did we win in a car we bought out of a backyard in Hueytown? Nobody else has done that. Nobody. It took lots and lots of persistence and desire and feel—and work."

CHAPTER 12

Bobby: Bud, Cotton, Harry, and Ol' Ralph

"You're going to get a phone call in two minutes, and the answer is yes. Good-bye."

—**Ralph Moody**

After Bobby won three races in his little Chevelle in 1966, the racing world had no choice but to pay attention to him, not as an up-and-coming driver, but as a driver who had made it—and how. The next step would be to go from independent status to a factory team driver. But Bobby wasn't like most of the drivers. He had been successful doing things his way in his own car, and he came with an attitude. If someone wanted him, it would have to be with the understanding that he called the shots.

One car owner with a factory ride willing to let him was Bud Moore, whose shop and Ford team was located in Spartanburg, South Carolina.

In 1966 Sam McQuagg had driven Moore's number 15 Mercury. In 1967 Moore wanted to expand his operation, and invited Bobby to drive car number 16.

Moore also asked Eddie to join his team. When he was asked to work on Bobby's race team as a mechanic, it was an easy decision. Eddie, now divorced, no longer had a reason to return to Miami. He moved into the trailer of one of Moore's other mechanics and shared the rent.

Meanwhile, Bobby sold his Chevelle to Woody Bracken, whose intention was to hire a driver and go race. But Bracken also agreed to make the car available to Bobby should he need it.

Moore, like many factory team owners, was not interested in entering the many low-paying short-track races, races needed if the team wanted to win the driving championship. What was the point of risking a crash and three or four thousand dollars worth of repairs to the car in an attempt to win a $1,000 purse? The reward for winning the driving championship, moreover, was perhaps $10,000 to the driver, good money for him, but not much of an incentive for the car owner.

For Bobby, winning that Grand National racing championship was his singular goal in life, his reason for breathing. Moore even agreed in their contract to allow Bobby to race his own car in the races he himself did not enter. Bobby won the short-track race at Bowman Gray Stadium in Winston-Salem on March 26, 1967, in Woody Bracken's car.

Bobby should have been happy with the arrangement he had with Moore, but it wasn't a month before he left him. In late April, David Pearson quit the race team run by Cotton Owens, the owner of a Chrysler-backed team. Owens not only offered Bobby a more lucrative deal, but he also promised that he would run in all the races so Bobby could compete for the driving championship. Another factor Bobby considered was that Moore was having serious trouble with his engine program. His engines kept breaking.

Bobby asked the always-decent Bud Moore what he should do.

"I can't offer you a deal anywhere as good," said Moore. "Take it."

Eddie Allison left as well. Through the years Bobby and Eddie Allison always held Bud Moore in high esteem.

"Bud Moore was a good guy," said Bobby. "At the time, he was also running Trans Am cars, and those cars were dominating on the Grand Am circuit. His Grand National cars were not. The engine wasn't bad, though it didn't seem as good as the Chevrolets or the Plymouths.

"In those days we didn't sign anything. We had an agreement, and he graciously let me out of it."

Bobby joined the Cotton Owens team on April 30, 1967, at Richmond.

"I was so enthusiastic," said Bobby. "Nothing was ever a major problem. Until I went with Cotton, things were just bumps in the road that we had to figure out, go over, or go around."

Where Bud Moore was happy to let Bobby and Eddie work on the car and set it up his way, Bobby discovered quickly that Cotton Owens said no, absolutely not, we are doing things *my* way.

Before the Richmond race, they locked horns immediately. Bobby wanted to choose the car he would drive and insisted on setting it up the way he and Eddie had been used to doing. The year before, Bobby and Eddie had won three races, and Bobby knew that with better equipment they would have won more. Now they were racing on a team with top-notch equipment, but the highly successful Owens was incensed that the brothers wanted to set up his car.

When Bobby chose to run a Dodge Coronet, a small car like his Chevelle, Cotton told Bobby, "The car won't run, because it's a Coronet." Bobby and Eddie brought the Charger to the shop, and Bobby, Eddie, and a couple of Cotton's men lowered the body onto the frame.

Owens also refused to let Bobby and Eddie work on the motor. Eddie told Owens, "Cotton, the horsepower is in the tailpipe. Listen to the motor run." When

Owens finally relented, Eddie did his magic, putting the camshaft and the motor in "the right place." When they put it on the dyno in fifteen minutes, the engine had gained thirty-seven horsepower.

Despite all the difficulty, at Richmond that day Bobby finished second.

"I struggled and struggled that day," said Bobby, "and I finally ended up second. And Cotton Owens's remark to me was, 'David Pearson would have won.'

"I thought to myself, *Well, wait a minute. David Pearson quit and went somewhere else. Why are we talking about David Pearson?*"

Bobby said to Owens, "Cotton, NASCAR has allowed everyone to lower these cars two inches, and you haven't done it."

Cotton replied, "You can do it if you want to, but you have to pay the bill for any money you spend or anyone you hire."

Bobby agreed. He and Eddie went to Owens's shop in Spartanburg. They rented a room at the Pine Street Motel, and they rebuilt one of Owens's car in the week before the next race at Darlington.

They ran the next event, and finished fourth behind Richard Petty, David Pearson, and Dick Hutcherson.

"The remark again," said Bobby, "was that Pearson would have won."

Thought Bobby, *Part of the reason I didn't win is these cars aren't ready to win, but we're working on them.*

Bobby told Cotton, "We'll massage this car this week, and we'll go win next weekend's race."

Cotton said, "We're not going to run this car. We're running that car over there, and you can rebuild it or run it as it is. Your choice."

Eddie and Bobby stayed in the shop and worked on the second car along with a couple of Owens's own mechanics, including his son.

Again Bobby ran well at Beltsville, but he didn't win. He was third. Bobby was exhausted from his dual role of mechanic and driver.

Bobby told Cotton, "Man, we're worn out, but we'll get a little rest this week and really get after them next week."

Cotton said, "We're going to run this third car next week, and you can rebuild it or run it like it is."

Said Bobby, "Cotton was getting free car rebuilds at my own expense. I was working night and day, at night, up the next morning."

The next race was the World 600 at Charlotte, a race won by Jim Paschal. Pearson was second, Bobby third. Once again Owens taunted Bobby, "Pearson would have won."

"I couldn't really figure him out," Bobby said of Owens. "He wasn't friendly to me at the shop. He came across very businesslike, but it was a tough deal for me. David Pearson quit because Owens's cars had been allowed to become uncompetitive. I don't know what their personal relationship was, but they won a championship together, and then David quit. That has to say something."

Meanwhile, despite how he might have felt about Cotton Owens, Bobby ran with distinction. He ran second at Richmond, and two weeks later at Darlington, he ran fourth. He was third at Beltsville, second at Hampton, Virginia, and third in the World 600 at Charlotte. Anyone else might have been pleased, even happy. Bobby Allison was *very* unhappy. And the genial Cotton Owens was furious.

Part of the problem was that Owens had had a long, honorable history as both a racer and a car owner. Bobby Allison at the time was a nobody. Though he had won three races the year before, Owens didn't view Bobby Allison as anything special.

"All these Grand National/Winston Cup people think that they are God's answer to the racing world," said Eddie Allison. "So they didn't listen to Bobby Allison. They wanted it the way *they* wanted it. None of them guys knew how much race car driver they had. And they wouldn't listen to what he said. Bobby Allison was always Bobby Allison, and he knew that when the car got to the end of the straightaway, it had to turn, and that with Owens it didn't. They all loved horsepower. That was always their big deal. And that's why he would end up with his own car. He couldn't drive for anyone else, because they wouldn't do the car the way he wanted it."

The next blowup between Bobby and Cotton Owens came at Birmingham, Bobby's home track, for a Wednesday night show on June 10. Bobby ran some practice laps during the day, and they were among the top cars, but Bobby wasn't satisfied.

Bobby said to Owens, "Firestone has the wrong tire on the car for this track. I happen to have ten of the code-number 103 Destination tires at my shop in Hueytown." Bobby sent Chuck Looney back to his shop, a trip of about a half hour, to retrieve the new tires.

Looney returned with all ten 103 Firestone tires, and Bobby mounted four of them on the car. Bobby went out, and he ran so fast he knew no one could touch him. It was going to be a runaway.

Unfortunately for Bobby, Richard Petty had been paying attention.

"All of a sudden," said Bobby, "I was a second faster than I had been. Richard was very, very aware of everything going on around him. He was so good at so many things. He drove good, had the best stuff, and he paid attention."

After practice, as Bobby leaned against the car, grinning, a Firestone factory representative came over and said, "Jack that car up and take those four tires off and give me all ten because I'm giving them to Richard Petty, because when he wins tonight, I want him on Firestones instead of those dang Goodyears."

The Goodyear tire company was back in racing, though they hadn't had much success up to then.

Bobby said, "Whoa, they're mine. I brought them from home."

"We didn't give them to you," said the Firestone rep. "We *lent* them to you. Get them off."

Cotton said to Bobby, "Give them the tires. Firestone helps me some."

"Cotton, this is wrong," said Bobby.

"Give them the tires," he said.

"Give him six, and let me keep four," Bobby begged.

"No, he said. "Richard wants them all."

Richard Petty, who had tremendous amount of clout with the parts and tire manufacturers, got the tires. As they wheeled them away, Bobby seethed. He told Cotton Owens, "That was a real dirty deal."

"Shut up," said Cotton. "Don't bother me."

Chuck Blanchard, the field engineer and a factory representative for Goodyear, saw what was going on, and he said to Bobby, "If you run my Goodyears, I'll give you everything you need for free." To Bobby "everything you need for free" was a really big deal.

He said to Cotton, "We need to run Goodyears."

"No," said Cotton, "I don't ever run those dang Goodyears."

"Cotton," Bobby said, "Firestone did us wrong. We need to do it."

"You do whatever you want to do," said Cotton. "I'm leaving." And Owens got in his car and left the racetrack.

Bobby mounted the Goodyears, and he won the race. And Bobby's Firestones finished third on the Petty car.

The tire issue came up again at the Firecracker 400 on July 4. Owens was running Firestones, which were giving everyone problems, blowing out too often and too quickly. Bobby pleaded with Owens to let him run Goodyears, but again Owens's answer was, "I ain't running no dang Goodyears. I never ran them. I don't like them."

Bobby had a fast car, and he was leading the race when a tire blew. He saved the car, drove back to the pits, and got a new tire. The pit crew was talented and fast, and Bobby went back out, and after a caution or two, he was back in the lead when another tire blew.

It rained, and the red flag came out. Bobby was in the top ten, and during the break, he went to the restroom. When he came out, he was met by driver Sam McQuagg, who asked, "Bobby, are you okay? Are you going to be all right?"

"What are you talking about?" asked Bobby.

"Cotton Owens just came and got me," he said. "You're sick, and he wants me to get in the car for the restart."

"Whhaaaat?" Bobby said.

"Yeah," McQuagg said. "Cotton said for me to get in the car, but I said I wouldn't unless he put Goodyears on it, and so they're out there putting Goodyears on it right now."

"Whoa, wait a minute," Bobby said. "Sam, let me beat you back to that car."

Bobby climbed in the car and strapped in. Meanwhile, the mechanics took the Goodyears off and put the Firestones back on.

"What is this deal?" Bobby wanted to know. He didn't get a response.

Cale Yarborough won the race. Bobby finished seventh.

The next race was at Oxford, Maine, which started the summer northern tour. Owens called Bobby on the phone and said, "I need you to do me a favor. I need you to take your Chevrolet on the northern tour, and I'll have a good car ready to win Bristol when you get back."

Bobby said to Owens, "I sold that car. It isn't mine. And you promised me we'd go to all the races if I quit Bud Moore and came over to drive for you."

"You get that car from your friend," Owens said. "The Brackens really like you. Take that on the northern tour, and I'll have you a car to win Bristol."

When Bobby called Bracken to say he needed the Chevelle for the northern tour, Bracken readily agreed to let him use it.

Bobby didn't know it, but Owens was greasing the skids for Bobby's departure from his race team.

Bobby was in a time crunch because the car wasn't prepared to his satisfaction. He put one of his own engines in the car and took it to Oxford, the site of his first Grand National win the year before. He was staying at the home of his friend, Bobby Walker, a young kid who did PR for the Oxford track. Bobby was in a guest bedroom when about ten at night there was a knock on the door. He had a telephone call.

Bobby thought there might be an emergency back home. He went charging for the phone. It was Frank Vehorn, a reporter for the local Spartanburg newspaper. Vehorn was a close friend of Cotton Owens.

"I'm doing an article," said Vehorn. "I want to know why you quit Cotton Owens."

"What are you talking about?" asked Bobby.

"Where are you?" asked Vehorn.

"Where did you call?" asked Bobby.

"Oxford, Maine," said Vehorn. "What car are you driving?"

"I have the Chevrolet," said Bobby. Years later Allison said, "I realized it was a setup right there."

"I didn't quit him," said Bobby. "Cotton asked me to do this." Commented Allison years later, "That was like telling Frank Vehorn that the sun was going to come out of the west tomorrow."

Cotton Owens would tell Bobby he was fired because the Chrysler people were upset he was driving a Chevrolet and that was the reason he was being let go. Bobby suspected that had little to do with it.

Bobby Allison won the Oxford race in his Chevelle. Afterward, Cotton Owens distributed a press release announcing that Sam McQuagg would be his new driver.

Eddie Allison, meanwhile, had returned to Owens's shop in Spartanburg to work on the Charger. While Eddie was working there, he got a phone call from Bobby, who told him of Frank Vehorn's phone call informing him that Owens was replacing him with McQuagg,

"Hey, you're working on Sam McQuagg's car," Bobby told Eddie. "Go over to Jim Hylton's. I'll be down tomorrow or the next day."

And without missing a beat, Bobby Allison went back to driving the Chevelle. And Eddie Allison went back to working for him.

"Bobby just upped and got in the other car and raced some more," said Eddie Allison. "I mean, we have a long family history of endurance. My mother's maiden name is Katherine Patton. General George was her daddy's second cousin. And my daddy's side of the family is from Belgium, strong people, and so genes do work. You got to work them, but they work. And like I said, our daddy taught us from day one, 'The only way you get ahead is you work.' So work was never a problem. The only problem we had was keeping our eyelids open."

On July 11, 1967, Bobby, driving his Chevelle, setting up his car with Eddie the way he wanted it, tuning the motor to his specifications, this one-man band, defeated all the hot dogs, including Bud Moore, Cotton Owens, and Richard Petty to win the Maine 300 in Oxford, Maine, the site of his very first Grand National win the year before. Bobby finished second to Petty at Fonda, sixth to Petty at Islip, fifth to Dick Hutcherson at Maryville, and, after he blew an engine at Nashville, didn't win until Rockingham in late October in a season in which Richard Petty won a never-to-be-beaten record of twenty-seven races, including a never-to-be-beaten ten races in a row, earning himself the nickname the King.

On August 6, 1967, Bobby drove the K&K factory Dodge in the Dixie 500 at Atlanta. He finished eleventh, and he then went back to driving his Chevelle, with little success. Richard Petty, meanwhile, was dominating as no driver had ever dominated before.

Bobby had a one-ride deal to drive a second K&K car at Charlotte on October 15. Bobby Isaac, who would go on to win the driving championship in 1970, was the primary driver for K&K.

What made the K&K team special was the presence of crew chief and car builder entraordinaire Harry Hyde, who was the prototype for Tom Cruise's crew chief in the movie *Days of Thunder*. Like that stubborn, hard-ass character played by Robert Duvall, Hyde was a successful racer with a world of experience who liked to have things done his way without discussion.

"Harry was really hard to communicate with," said Bobby. "He was going to do his stuff the way he was going to do it. I'd go to him for a request to adjust something on the car, and he might say, 'No, we ain't doing that.' And that meant, 'We're not going to do that, period, end of conversation.' Or he might say, 'We'll give that a try.' What he never would say was, 'That was good,' or 'That wasn't good.'

"I was pretty comfortable with him, but I knew it was just a part-time deal, and I was still trying to figure out what to do next. I wanted to go to all the races, and Harry wasn't going to do that."

Before going to Charlotte, Bobby, Eddie, and Harry Hyde took the car to Atlanta to test. When the car wouldn't go around the racetrack to his satisfaction, Bobby told Eddie what it needed, and Eddie began building a spring for the car. Hyde didn't believe the new spring would make a difference, but, surprisingly, he let

Bobby and Eddie have their way. When Bobby went out, held the gas pedal to the floor, and ran significantly faster, Hyde couldn't believe it.

"We talked about that until the day Harry died," said Eddie. "But Harry had to have things his way. That's probably why we didn't stay there. And nothing wrong with that. To each his own. Harry was smart."

Harry wasn't interested in hiring Bobby full-time, and Bobby wasn't interested in working for Harry full-time. But Bobby was running out of money and running out of hope.

Bobby was in his shop in Hueytown when the phone rang. He was sweaty and the call was interrupting his work as he and Eddie attempted to build a car to go to Rockingham.

The caller didn't identify himself, but Bobby recognized the voice of Ralph Moody, the mechanical genius behind the Ford factory team of Holman and Moody. Bobby remembered Moody when he raced in Florida in the mid-fifties. Once his dad did some repair work at the gas station where Moody kept his car.

"I got within fifteen feet of it and almost touched it," said Bobby. "I got to shake his hand."

The voice said, "You're going to get a phone call in two minutes, and the answer is yes. Good-bye." And he hung up.

Bobby said to himself, *Why is that SOB Ralph Moody aggravating me?*

"I was totally dumbfounded," said Bobby.

He started to go back to work when the phone rang again. Bobby picked up, and this time the caller said, "This is Fred Lorenzen. Ford gave me a car to take to Rockingham. Will you drive it?"

Lorenzen had been one of Holman and Moody's best drivers, but he suffered from ulcers and retired from boredom to become a team manager.

"As you well know, Richard Petty's beating the socks off of everybody, and Ford wants to put a stop to it," Lorenzen told Bobby. "We feel you're the only driver to beat him outright this year."

Moody had told him to say, *The answer is yes.*

Bobby said, "The answer is yes."

"Okay, I'll meet you at Holman and Moody tomorrow," said Lorenzen.

Bobby told his crew, Eddie, Don Lawrence, and Chuck Looney, "You guys go home and get some rest. We got the break. I'm going to drive for Holman and Moody."

It was Monday afternoon. Bobby climbed into his Mooney airplane, a single-engine plane capable of speeds of up to 175 miles an hour, which he had bought so he could get from his Hueytown race shop to the Carolina racetracks without having to drive all night. The Mooney had cost him $8,500. He soloed on May 5, 1967, and he got his pilot's license on June 15.

He met Fred Lorenzen the next day, as requested. Lorenzen and Allison stayed at a motel on the west side of Charlotte and commuted each day to the Rocking-ham track in Bobby's airplane, landing on the dirt strip behind the south grand-stand. A pioneer, Bobby was the first racer to use a plane for standard, everyday transportation.

This time, Eddie was not invited to join the race team, so Eddie returned to Huey-town, where he lived in Bobby's home and built the Chevelle for the races that Hol-man and Moody chose not to run. Eddie did join the pit crew on the weekends.

"It didn't take a lot of money for me to live," said Eddie. "I lived at Bobby's house. All I had to pay was child support."

According to Eddie, Fred Lorenzen didn't have as much input in the team as did Ralph Moody, a mechanic and man Eddie and Bobby both revered.

Ralph Moody told Jake Elder, the chief mechanic, "I'll take care of everything that has to be done. You just work on the car, and we'll go from there."

"Moody was smart," said Eddie. "Moody was so intelligent. And what the intel-ligence does is let you figure out why this does that. And this is what we have lost so much of today. They have so much money, they just keep throwing parts at the car until it runs fast, but they have no idea *why* it runs fast, so tomorrow they can't make it run fast again. And that's worse in the chassis, because nobody has enough money to throw at the chassis the way you can go at it in the motor.

"The crews today get more money to cook lunch than we had to race with. It's true. They have more money to eat lunch with than we had to race."

The team of Bobby Allison and Fred Lorenzen won the last two races of the 1967 season at Rockingham and Weaverville, despite everything NASCAR and the Pettys did to try to stop him. From the time he began racing on the Grand National circuit, Bobby Allison had the feeling that he was resented for trying to topple the King. To Bobby, the Weaverville race on November 5, 1967, was proof.

Allison had dominated the race. He was two laps ahead of the entire field when a caution flag came out with but twenty laps to go. Petty had been back in the pack, but when Bobby led the cars single file behind the pace car, he noticed Petty passing a string of cars behind him and pulling in on his back bumper for the green flag restart.

"NASCAR let him do it," said Bobby. "I don't know why he was allowed to do that. It was a really, really tough deal for me. I didn't understand any of it, and I still don't. The writers who were there could tell you about it, but they are very sensitive to hurt Richard Petty's feelings.

"So I can't understand how NASCAR has allowed this, but they have, and now they're throwing the green flag, and as soon as they do, Richard Petty pushes me sideways, which made me slide down through the pit area."

In those days on the shorter tracks the cars pitted along the inside edge of the straightaway. There was no guard rail. Bobby slid down through the infield, and when he reached the pit area, he ran over teams' equipment as crew members scat-tered out of the way.

Richard passed him as he fought to regain control of the car. Even though he didn't wreck, the yellow flag came out again. When the pace car came out, Bobby resumed his spot at the head of the long line, but this time Petty was only one lap behind, and Bobby was mystified to see Petty once again pass all the other cars under the caution and sit on his back bumper.

"I figured I was going to win the race anyway," said Bobby, "because I'd beaten him all day long."

The green flag dropped, and as soon as it did, Richard Petty for a second time pushed Bobby sideways, and in a repeat performance he once again skidded through the pit area without smashing up his car. The yellow flag dropped again, and though Bobby was still the leader, now the other seven cars left in the race were on the same lap, and for a third time Bobby could see Richard Petty making his way past all the rest of the cars under the caution to sit on Bobby's back bumper.

"For a third time," said Bobby. "Yes, for a third time."

After one pace lap, seven laps remained in the race. The cars came around, and this time Bobby was determined not to let Petty spin him out again. To keep that from happening, Bobby drove up against the wall, knowing if Petty hit him, the wall would keep him going straight.

"That way he can't spin me around," said Bobby. "All I got to do is beat him into one corner, and I'm fast enough to go on and win the race."

They came to the green, and Bobby went up high, and Petty ran into his left side, pushing him up into the wall, but failing to spin him out. But Petty, as fierce a competitor as anyone, held Bobby's car up against the concrete wall of the Weaverville Speedway, knowing well that an opening and another concrete wall were approaching. Bobby would have to lift or face running into the corner of the wall.

"He's holding me tight against the wall, and I'm going to hit really hard on the other side of this concrete opening," said Bobby, "so I jammed the brakes on, and Richard took the lead."

Driving into turn one, Bobby was determined to retake the lead. When he dropped down in turn one, Richard saw what he was doing and blocked him. Richard then braked hard, and Bobby ran into the back of Richard's car.

"I didn't run into him because I wanted to," said Bobby. "I ran into him because he surprised me by putting the brakes on harder than I expected. Okay, so I hit him, and I wiggled the car. Now everyone thinks I'm mad at him because he's run into me. But that ain't what I was doing. I was trying to get back by the guy. So now I'm behind him, and we get the white flag, and he's going to win the race."

The cars went into turn one, and Bobby could see Richard looking in the mirror, wanting to bottle Bobby up. Bobby went high, and Richard went up to block him, and when he did, Bobby dove low, but Richard didn't quite get over in time. The two cars, side by side, went down the back straightaway like in a Joie Chitwood daredevil show, with the two cars turned into each other with Bobby's right side wheels off the ground and Richard's left side wheels off the ground.

"But when we came to turn three," said Bobby, "it's a left turn, and I was on the left. Adios! So I dropped him, and I went and took the checkered flag. I won the race.

"When it was over, NASCAR didn't do a thing about what went on out there, and once again Maurice Petty wanted to fight me, just like after the race at Islip, Long Island. The whole thing was really hushed up, and nobody ever spoke again why any of it happened. Why did the guy pass me with twenty laps to go and get me on a restart? When did he pass everyone again on the first yellow and get me again on the restart? Why did he get on my back bumper again a third time?

"I was driving for Ford, and I couldn't figure out why Ford wasn't saying anything. Jacques Passino and John Calley of Ford thought Richard Petty was *the* King. They held him in great esteem, and here I was beating him with a Ford, and I guess I shouldn't have been doing that. Later I found out Fred Lorenzen knew Ford was going to hire Richard, but he was sworn to secrecy. But at the same time Fred was impressed with what I did out there, because he made a remark, 'Wow, you got a job forever with me.' "

There were two more races to be run in November of 1967, races that would count in the 1968 standings. The first was held at Macon, Georgia. Bobby dominated the race, beating Richard by a lap.

The second was held at Montgomery, Alabama, a two hundred lapper, one hundred miles. For this race Jake Elder, Bobby's crew chief, was shifted to the number one car of Holman and Moody driven by David Pearson. Bobby didn't know it, but John Holman favored local boy Pearson over carpetbagger Allison, and he couldn't stand the fact that Bobby was beating his top race team.

Halfway through the race Bobby was leading in what would certainly have been his fourth victory in a row when he sought to lap Pearson. As he went to pass him, Pearson stuck Bobby into the fence. Whether Pearson did this deliberately Bobby has no idea, but the damage to his car kept him from winning a race that Petty ended up winning. Bobby finished second. It was Petty's seventy-sixth career win.

"When the race was over," said Bobby, "David was gone. Typical David. He had his little group. David did not confront anybody about anything in those days. But it gave Petty the win, and it lessened the embarrassment I was putting on all the other Ford drivers."

It would not be long before Ford and John Holman would hit Bobby hard on the blind side, almost derailing his career.

CHAPTER 13

Bobby: An Independent Again

"The car has to fit the driver, no matter how smart the mechanic is."

—**Eddie Allison**

When Bobby Allison began his career in NASCAR, one of his car owners had been Ed Parton, who had threatened John Holman for selling him a defective carburetor. Bobby didn't think twice about the incident. John Holman never forgot.

Holman was the one who dealt directly with Ford, and when Ford wanted something, even if it wasn't best for the race team, Holman would jump and Moody would resist. It made for a lot of tension. Since Holman took his orders directly from Ford, what Holman said usually went. At the end of the '67 season John Holman, still sore that Ed Parton, and by extension, Bobby, had humiliated him, sent Bobby packing.

Holman told Moody, "Ford says Bobby can drive a factory car, but he can't drive ours."

Moody, unable to buck Holman, placed Bobby and Fred Lorenzen on Bondy Long's factory Ford team based in Camden, South Carolina. Bondy Long was an heir to the DuPont fortune. His mother had married a DuPont. The Longs also owned racehorses. And they were dedicated stock car racers.

But as a result of Holman's directive, Bobby no longer would be involved with Ralph Moody, who had to stay back in Charlotte and continue to run the mechanical part of the Holman and Moody operation. Freddy Lorenzen, who no longer had the stomach for racing, was supposed to be his crew chief. The move would turn out to be a disappointment for Bobby.

"Holman got rid of me at the end of the 1967 season," said Bobby. "I was really disappointed that I didn't get the number-one Holman and Moody ride. David Pearson got it. But not only did I not get the number-one ride, Holman announced to me that I would be driving for Bondy Long.

"I went to Bondy, told him I would be driving for him, and he said, 'That's great, but Freddy and I agreed we'd only run about ten races for the year.'

"I said, 'Bondy, Bondy, hold it. We need to go race.'

"Bondy, whose mother was a DuPont, said, 'I'm going to play with my sailboat, and Freddy doesn't want to go to but a few races.'"

Bondy Long was young and carefree, and had a race team that created havoc away from the track like few others. Bobby preferred accountability and order. He also wanted to race a lot more often than Bondy Long wanted to race.

Said Bobby, "The first race [in 1968] was at Riverside, and I did decent, way ahead of a lot of other guys, and then at Daytona we didn't do as well as I wanted to, and the third race they stayed home, and boy, I didn't want to do that. And this was a Ford factory team, and I couldn't run my Chevelle."

John Holman, it turned out, had really stuck it to Bobby, but good.

When Long refused to let Bobby race his Chevelle at Birmingham, on June 8, 1968, Bobby quit the team and went back to working on his own car with brother Eddie.

A week later, on June 16, 1968, Bobby went to Rockingham and finished second to his brother Donnie. To this day Eddie is convinced Bobby would have beaten Donnie if he had let him set up the car the way *he* wanted to set it up.

"We dang near got to him," said Eddie Allison. "Our problem was the same thing: We weren't prepared well enough to race a five-hundred-mile race, and Rockingham was a racetrack then. It was flat, and boy, you could race, and we had the best race driver. So I was spoiled. I was spoiled rotten in that respect. I don't like to think it, but as the years progress I'm thinking I may not have had to do as good as I could to win a race, because I had the best race car driver. And I didn't have the same relationship with Bobby that I had with Donnie.

"Bobby wanted it like he wanted it. He wouldn't let me do it like I wanted to do it. And as the mechanic, that's what you've got to do. The car has to fit the driver, no matter how smart the mechanic is. He can't make the car go fast if it doesn't fit the driver. If the driver's asshole draws up, he's going to come up off the gas pedal. When the driver feels his butt relaxing, when both cheeks of his ass feel good, he can hold the gas pedal down. So whatever Bobby wanted, he got. We had enough input with each other that he would listen to what I said so we could fix a problem, but he wanted the car like he wanted it, so we had to do that. That was the deal. I never could get across to him why what Donnie and I did together would make us turn better than what he was doing. And Bobby was capable of turning a bad-turning car better than anybody in the world. As ill as it was, Bobby could make the car go as fast as it could go. The other driver who could do that was Dale Earnhardt. Many times the only reason Dale didn't win was that the car didn't turn. The car would be a piece of shit, and they'd say to Dale, 'How's it feel?' and Dale would say, 'Fine.'"

It was Donnie's first win, but afterward the racer Ralph Moody couldn't stop talking about Bobby.

Moody said, "Look, he goes and gets his backyard race car, and he goes and beats everybody but his brother!"

On July 7, 1968, Bobby proved his showing was no fluke when he won the Islip 300 in his little garage-built Chevelle with no factory support.

"The reason we were able to win," said Eddie Allison, "was that our car turned. We were able to make the back wheels chase the front wheels. The other cars had more horsepower, but when their tires got hot, their advantage went away, and their drivers would be dead tired when the race was over."

During the race, as happened in 1966, Richard Petty came up on the back of Bobby's car and signaled for Bobby to get out of his way, and like in '66, Allison refused. And again, Petty ran up on the back of the little Chevelle and whacked him, but this time King Richard bent his front fender. You'd have thought Petty would have learned his lesson. His long stay in the pits to fix the damage cost Petty the race.

The crew of the Richard Petty Plymouth were even more incensed than they had been two years earlier after a race in which Bobby refused to move out of the way of the King. This time there was physical violence when Maurice Petty and Dale Inman attacked Bobby. Maurice Petty knocked him to the ground, and it was alleged that Dale Inman kicked him in the back.

"We were settling an old score," said Maurice by way of explanation, referring to Weaverville and Montgomery. Maurice Petty was fined $250 and suspended for two weeks. Inman was fined $100.

Bobby's Aunt Myrtle, his Dad's eighty-five year old aunt, was a "delightful ole feisty country gal," said Bobby. She was in the pits for the race, and she joined the fray when she saw Bobby being attacked. She swung her pocketbook at Maurice Petty and whacked him in the back of the head with it.

"I don't hold grudges," said Bobby afterward, not meaning a word of it.

Eddie Allison's two young sons were traumatized with fear as they saw the Petty crew come over and begin swinging. They began crying and screaming. Little Eddie, who was six, fell in the trailer and busted up his mouth, and Papa Eddie had to run over and take care of his son. By that time, the fight was over.

Bobby wanted to call the police and have Maurice Petty and Dale Inman arrested for assault and battery, but NASCAR officials talked him out of it.

CHAPTER 14

Bobby and Eddie: Mario

"Rossi was scared that if we won, Bobby and I would get the credit, not Bobby and him."

—Eddie Allison

Chrysler was looking for a new premier race team because Richard Petty had shocked the stock car racing world by leaving Chrysler and becoming a part of the Ford Motor Company race team.

"I think what happened was that Richard and them felt they weren't the fair-haired Chrysler people per se, and they couldn't handle that," said Eddie Allison. "So they went to Ford and said, 'We'll do this for you, do that for you.' They left Chrysler to make them understand how mad they were. And when they went back to Chrysler a year later, they were the number-one team again."

When Chrysler chose to go with engine builder Mario Rossi, so did Bobby Allison. Rossi had contacted Bobby the year before to ask him to switch to his team. Bobby wanted to see who would get the Chrysler deal.

"Mario was incredibly good on the engines," said Bobby. "He was reasonably good on the basic car stuff. He was a guy who had a car, and I needed a ride.

"He said, 'Come drive my car.' So I did. He had worked for Bud Moore and for Smokey Yunick a little bit."

Rossi had started his race team the year before. In 1968, with Darel Dieringer as his driver, he had had five top-five finishes and five top tens in eighteen tries.

To take the ride, Bobby had to promise Chrysler he would not drive short-track races in his Chevelle. When Rossi refused to add brother Eddie to his race team, that again put Eddie Allison out in the cold.

"Rossi didn't want me to work on the car," said Eddie Allison. "He was scared that if we won, Bobby and I would get the credit, not Bobby and him."

Eddie told Rossi, "What's wrong with having six or seven Leonard Wood–type mechanics working on one car? If you have all the brains, as long as the egos stay in line, you can get things done."

The problem was, as it is today, that egos *do* run into each other. Eddie took a job with a Pennsylvania businessman who wanted Eddie to build a Sportsman car to run at Heidelberg and Beltsville, Maryland. When Eddie told his girlfriend Penny what he was doing, she begged to go along with him. Penny had lived in the house adjacent to Bobby's garage, and when they met, sparks flew. But Eddie did not want to live in sin, and he told Penny, "You're not going unless we get married." So they got married and moved to Pittsburgh.

As it often turns out in racing, the job didn't pan out. Eddie and Penny returned to Alabama and lived at Penny's mother's house in Hueytown. Beginning with the Darlington race in September, Eddie joined Rossi and Bobby as a member of the pit crew. The next year when Mario Rossi relented and hired him to work on Bobby's race team, Eddie and his wife moved to Spartanburg.

In 1969, Bobby ran in 27 of the 53 races, winning five, finishing in the top five thirteen times, and earning $69,483 in purses.

His most improbable win that year came at Richmond on September 7. He blew an engine during practice, and the new engine didn't arrive until ten on race morning. Bobby had to start in the back, and he roared to the front to beat Richard Petty by four laps!

The next week the new Alabama International Motor Speedway at Talladega was scheduled for its first race.

Alabama governor George Wallace had sold the property on the former air force base to Bill France for a rock-bottom price. France had been the head of Florida's Wallace for President campaign in 1968, and Wallace was repaying his loyalty. Wallace threw in the cost of building the access roads as a bonus. Getting the new Talladega track off to a fast start was vital for Bill France.

Almost two months before the inaugural race was scheduled on September 14, 1969, Bobby, who lived nearby, drove his passenger car onto the track's surface to see what it was like. At only eighty miles an hour, Bobby noticed how rough it was.

Several months later Bobby was invited to test Chrysler's new wing car at the brand-new Talladega race track. Bobby didn't know it, but this would be the experience that proved conclusively to him that he was being discriminated against because he was an Alabaman and a Catholic, while the good ole boys were Carolineans and Protestant.

The test was scheduled to run from Tuesday until Saturday. The invited drivers, from the Dodge and Plymouth race teams, included Buddy Baker, Charlie Glotzbach, Richard Petty, Pete Hamilton, Richard Brickhouse, James Hylton, and Bobby. The test was run by Frank Wylie and Bob McDaniels, the top two PR men from the Dodge division, and Larry Rathgab, Dodge's chief engineer.

On Tuesday everyone got to test but Bobby. Whenever Bobby would ask to run, Rathgab would tell him, "Sit over there and shut up. You'll get your turn."

Every day Bobby would land his Mooney plane in the middle of the big track, and every day he would sit idly by while everyone else practiced, bringing their speeds up to the mid-197s by Friday afternoon.

Saturday was to be the last day of testing, and finally after a week of pleading, Bobby was given his chance to test the wing car.

The speeds were electrically timed, and for his four laps Bobby was timed at 199.1, 199.2, 199.4, and 199.9. Though he only ran once, Bobby had the fastest time of all the drivers by a good margin. He had come within the blink of an eye from becoming the first driver ever to complete a lap at 200 miles an hour. The next best times were in the 197s from Buddy Baker and Charlie Glotzbach.

The schedule had called for the testing to end Saturday afternoon, but the Chrysler execs changed it. Larry Rathgab called the drivers together, and so Bobby could hear, he said, "We have the car instrumented really good, so my assistant, George Wallace, is going to take this data back to his hotel room and study and see how this jerk from Alabama can beat our hot shots."

Unable to believe his ears, Bobby replied meekly, "Hey guys, I just drove the car around the track."

Said Rathgab, "We're going to come back tomorrow, but tomorrow is church day, so we can't run until after noon. So we'll meet at noon and run tomorrow. Allison, you too."

Buddy Baker and Charlie Glotzbach also were asked to return on Sunday when Rathgab called everyone together and said, "Let me show you how Bobby Allison went faster than you guys."

Thought Allison, *I didn't know I was being dragged into this to be somebody's personal trainer and get no credit.*

Rathgab asked his assistant, George Wallace, to give his findings.

"I studied these tapes," said Wallace, "and here's the deal: Bobby Allison holds the steering wheel straight, and everyone else saws the steering wheel back and forth."

Then Larry Rathgab said, "Okay, Buddy Baker, take the car out and hold the steering wheel still." Baker ran 199 miles an hour. Charlie Glotzbach went out and he ran 199 miles an hour.

"Let me make another lap," said Bobby.

"Oh, no, no. We're busy," said Rathgab. "Buddy, you go again." Both Baker and Glotzbach ran laps, but they could not break the 200-mile-an-hour barrier. Only then did Rathgab let Bobby try again.

"I went out," said Bobby, "and I came by the first time at 200.001, came by the second time at 200.009, and the engine blew up as I entered turn one."

The oil went all over the windshild and the track, and Bobby did an amazing job to keep the car from hitting a wall and being destroyed. Not that Rathgab or the two PR men noticed. After Bobby coasted in to the pit, Frank Wylie told everyone,

"Nobody is to let Ford know we went 200. We don't want Ford to know, so if anyone says they went 200 miles an hour—Allison—you're fired."

Said Bobby, "I went home with my tail between my legs. Now I've done this, and I feel good about going 200, but I'm forbidden from telling anyone. I went home thinking, *I'm not going to get the credit*. But I needed my ride. I wanted to drive the thing."

The next day they put a new engine in the car, and Buddy Baker drove 200 miles an hour. And that day they announced to the racing world that Buddy Baker had been the first driver to run a lap 200 miles an hour.

"Buddy was their poster child," said Bobby. "He was a great big guy, good-looking. Everyone thought he was such a neat guy, and his dad, a past champion, was a neat guy. When I was eighteen I had worked for him. I liked his dad a lot, but still, if you do something, you do it, and if you don't do something . . ."

Bobby added, "Last year we had a reunion of the drivers of the Dodge wing car at the International Motor Sports Hall of Fame, and Buddy said, 'Everybody went faster than 200, but I was the first official one.' Well, everyone didn't. Nobody went over 200 but me."

When official practice began August 4 at Talladega, it was clear to the drivers that the tires were not going to hold up at the high speeds everyone was running on the bumpy track. Tires were exploding at an alarming rate whether they were Firestones or Goodyears. Fortunately, no one was seriously injured.

Firestone, deciding it's tires were unsafe at speeds close to 200 miles an hour, pulled out of the event. Goodyear continued, but its tires weren't faring any better. On the Saturday before the big race Bobby Allison went out to practice in his Mario Rossi wing Dodge. Running at high speeds, his front right tire tore apart and badly damaged his right front fender.

Bobby and his crew returned to the garage area to fix the car. He had every intention of running, tire problems or not. Around him stood several other drivers, including LeeRoy Yarbrough, who was in a Ford, James Hylton, and Richard Petty, "who was tagging along, but he wasn't in the front of the group," said Bobby.

LeeRoy said to Bobby, "We need to stop this thing, because there's a lot of damage, and your car is really torn up. You need to say something to Bill France."

Bill France, meanwhile, was waiting for the other shoe to drop. About a month before the Talladega inaugural a group of drivers, including Bobby and Richard Petty, were standing around moaning about the lack of decent insurance. They also discussed the fact that none of them had any kind of retirement program.

Somebody said, "We ought to do something for ourselves. Professional football's got it, baseball, basketball, all the professional sports."

Bobby said, "I'm for that," and he agreed to join. Of the fifty drivers who attended the meeting, forty-five agreed to join.

It was Richard Petty who came up with the idea of flying up to New York City to talk with lawyers who knew how to form a union for sports competitors so the drivers at the least could get a better rate on insurance and start a retirement fund.

"At the time I couldn't afford good insurance," said Bobby. "If I had gotten killed, Judy would have gotten $100,000. NASCAR would have given her $7,500. But my insurance was really expensive, and it wasn't right. And so our big deal to start the PDA (Professional Drivers Association) was for us to be able to buy decent insurance. Secondly to try to develop a proper retirement plan where we could pay into a fund so when we got out of the cars we wouldn't be working in a gas station for $1.19 an hour."

Allison, Petty, and a few others met with a New York lawyer, who also made the comment, "There's an awful lot of money out there, too." Meaning, the drivers weren't getting their fair share of the purses either.

That was as far as the PDA had gone. No one had made an overture to any existing union. But Bill France, whose antennae were always out, knew about the meeting, and he was determined to stop them—again. In 1961 Curtis Turner had made an attempt to enroll the drivers in the Teamsters, but France had stopped him cold in a meeting when he pulled his gun and threatened to ban any driver who joined up. After everyone backed down, France then banned Turner and Tim Flock for life. To France, union talk was treason. As far as Big Bill was concerned there wasn't anything wrong with the Talladega track, and he wasn't about to put up with any guff from his drivers.

When Bobby, Richard Petty, and LeeRoy Yarbrough approached him with an idea how to make the upcoming race safer, Bill France was in a defensive state of mind

"Mr. France, sir," said Bobby, "why don't we take a representative from Ford, a representative from Chrysler, and a representative from the independents, and we'll disconnect everyone's back barrel from their carburetor, making everybody have a two-barrel carburetor, and we'll go 185 miles an hour and still have a great race."

"You guys can back off the throttle," France replied.

But Allison knew that was impossible. Said Bobby years later, "How can a race driver just back off? No race driver can back off. But if we had had a two-barrel carburetor, we could have run wide open. We were going 200 when the tires were flying apart. We'd have run 185 and been fine."

Bobby continued to argue.

"You guys are trying to start a union," growled France. "If you're scared, go home."

When France said that, LeeRoy Yarbrough, a tough old bird, lunged from behind Bobby and decked Bill France with a hard right hand.

As France was getting back on his feet, Bobby, Petty, LeeRoy, and Hylton headed for their trucks, loaded up, and left.

Thirty-seven of the other top racers, including Donnie, packed up and left as well. Bobby Isaac, a bullheaded, independent cuss, was the only NASCAR regular driver to enter the inaugural Talladega race. Isaac had tire failure and didn't win. Richard Brickhouse won his only Grand National race. No one crashed, and no one was injured, because every 25 laps a caution came out so the crews could change tires.

France may have won the battle, but he didn't win the war. Reports of the tire problem and the subsequent boycott in the local papers hurt France, as attendance at the inaugural race was disappointing. Without the top drivers, so was the race. France gave rain checks to each of the 62,000 fans in attendance.

The experience, moreover, disgruntled all participants, including the drivers, the auto factories, and the tire companies. Firestone left NASCAR Grand National racing and has never returned.

It was a disaster for NASCAR. Though he refused to acknowledge that Bobby was right about the high speeds, in the end Bill France acted on his complaint. After reversing his original position that the track didn't have a problem, he asked Paul Goldsmith, a former racer, for a solution to slow the cars, and Goldsmith came up with the restrictor plate.

Said Bobby, "It's the best, most fair thing NASCAR ever did."

Toward the end of the 1969 season, in one of the first sponsorship deals, Bobby made a deal with officials from Coca-Cola to sponsor his race car.

"There was a young fellow who hung around racing some, a Canadian by the name of Mike Bailey," said Bobby. "He had became a fan of mine and a friend. 'Hi, Bobby. How you doing? Good to see you this week.'"

Mike, who was in PR, knew a young Coca-Cola executive by the name of Vic Meinert. Mike said, 'Why don't you put Coca-Cola on Bobby's race car?' Somehow Vic Meinert made his case, and Coke sponsored four races at the end of the 1969 season.

"Not a lot of money," said Bobby. "A few thousand dollars. But it was a lot of money for Rossi at the time, and big dollars through my eyes."

The next year Bobby reworked his deal with Coke that gave his race team $50,000 to put the Coca-Cola name on the car for the entire 1970 season. Most of the money went to Rossi.

Junior Johnson, with Holly Farms, was another team owner who went out and got himself a sponsor. No one knew it at the time, but Bobby and Junior Johnson were two pioneers who were changing the face of stock car racing in America.

Bobby would have left the Rossi team, but Mario Rossi, who well knew how unhappy Bobby was with the restrictions placed on his outside driving, worked hard to make Bobby happy. Rossi told Allison he had gotten backing from Chrysler to make a run for the 1970 driving championship. And if Rossi didn't go to a race, he said, Bobby could race his own Dodge, which Chuck Looney was working on back in Hueytown.

In 1970 Bobby Allison was finally able to realize his dream, entering all forty-six races and making a serious run for the driving championship. He was also able to get brother Eddie back on the team.

As for Eddie, once he started working on the car, he couldn't believe it when he saw that the Chrysler factory engineers had "no clue" how to make a race car turn.

"Larry Radgaff, who used to work for Chrysler, he was so far out in left field for what it took to turn the race car, you couldn't imagine," said Eddie. "He could get enough parts under the car to finally make it turn, so people thought he knew what he was doing. But it didn't turn like that car I took to Charlotte for Harry Hyde.

"Rossi was a good guy," said Eddie. "He didn't know me from Adam to start with. He never realized how much talent I had until I started working for him. Then he appreciated me."

Eddie liked Rossi well enough, but he had less than fond memories of his workweek.

"In addition to Rossi, there were four of us who worked in that shop on the race car, Don Lawrence, Jimmy Madison, Lee Hurley, who did the engines, and myself. We would work around the clock, twenty-four hours, seven days a week. And Rossi had a really bad habit: he liked to work the night before we left to go to the racetrack—all night long. We'd either change something on the car that took us all night or we'd do this or do that, and then we'd go home and get a shower and get in the truck and go to the track for inspection. So everyone was always tired, and the thing never panned out."

The second season with Mario Rossi in 1970 wasn't quite as good as the first. Bobby won one race and finished second six times, and he was third four times. The win in Rossi's car came in the Atlanta 500 on March 29 at the home of Coca-Cola.

"Vic Meinert was there," said Bobby. "I don't remember anyone else. But Vic Meinert was trying to convince his people this was a super good deal. I have to say, Vic was attuned."

Despite the $50,000 from Coca-Cola, Bobby Allison ended up spending a lot of his own money.

"Aw yeah. Aw yeah," Bobby said. "But all my life, whatever I could earn to do what I wanted to do was just part of the cost of doing what I wanted to do."

In other words, Bobby Allison wasn't in it for the money as much as he was in it for the pure joy of racing.

In 1970, Bobby won two other races—driving his own car. He had a total of twelve top-five finishes, and finished second to Bobby Isaac for the racing title.

For Bobby and Eddie Allison, all that counted were the wins. It would be the first of four frustrating seasons that Bobby would finish second in the points for the championship.

As it turned out, Bobby lost the title because he missed one race. He didn't have his Dodge ready for the Richmond 500. Had he finished twenty-fifth or better at Richmond, he would have won the title.

Bobby was optimistic that 1971 would be *his* year, when in November 1970 Chrysler, caving in to the demands of Richard Petty, made a shattering announcement: Beginning in 1971, Richard Petty would switch back from Ford to Chrysler and he would be the *only* race team Chrysler would back. Petty had complained he was getting secondary treatment from Chrysler. Now there would be no one else in the Chrysler picture despite the fact that the two top cars in Grand National in 1970, Bobby Isaac and the K&K Insurance car and the team of Mario Rossi and Bobby Allison, drove Chryslers.

For Bobby, this was one more egregious example of Richard Petty pushing his weight around. It was bad enough Petty had taken his tires a couple of years earlier. That strong-arm act had endangered his livelihood.

Rossi had survived as a car owner only because of his support from Chrysler, and so when Chrysler dropped Rossi, Rossi dropped Bobby and hired Dick Brooks.

"Mario was out of money, and he owed me a lot of money that he couldn't pay me, didn't have any more money to go race with, so he signed Dick Brooks, who was going to bring him a little fresh money."

Bobby took no steps, legal or otherwise, to recover the money Mario Rossi owed him.

"I just went on my way and did my next deal," he said. "I had to be at the racetrack. If this guy wasn't going, I was going to find someone who was."

By June 1971 Mario Rossi was broke and dropped out of racing.

"I find it financially unfeasible to independently support a car on the Grand National circuit," said Rossi.

A few years later, Mario Rossi died when his small plane disappeared. Federal officials said that he was using his plane to smuggle marijuana into the country. Mario Rossi's remains were never found.

"Rossi raced to have his airplane," said Eddie Allison. "It gave him enough money for him to have an airplane, because that was his thing. His love of stock cars let him enjoy his love of airplanes."

"The airplane was found in the Bahamas with three dead bodies and a load of marijuana," said Bobby. "Two of the bodies were identified. The third was not. But Mario has never been heard from. I'm sure he was the third body."

Said Eddie, "That's the last I heard. His love of his airplane did him in. He had to have the money to keep his airplane going. They could get the marijuana across the Florida line in the air easier than by boat."

CHAPTER 15

Bobby: Outsmarted by the Pettys

"Why don't you park that pile of shit and drive a real race car?"

—Ralph Moody

Bobby Allison, and any driver who wanted to remain independent in 1971, had a serious problem: Racing was getting very expensive. In the past a driver who wanted to run his own car could afford to do so if he could run up front. Those days were gone: No independent driver could foot the bill by himself and remain competitive.

The days of a neophyte building a competitive race car in his garage à la Bobby Allison were over. Independents could continue to run, but they would have to resign themselves to becoming strokers, riding in the back, waiting for a big crash so they could crack the top twenty. Bobby vowed to quit before resorting to stroking.

To help him pay the bills, he had become one of the first to attract a corporate sponsor. By 1971 Coca-Cola was paying him $75,000 for the racing season, but even the Coke money was insufficient.

In 1971 Bobby was titularly a Chrysler team, though when Bobby and Eddie went to Detroit to ask Chrysler for some help, because of the Petty deal they didn't get any. Bobby had to spend some of the $75,000 from Coke money to buy a couple of Dodge bodies from Chrysler. He and Eddie then returned to Hueytown to build their car.

Bobby began the 1971 season well, finishing second at Riverside to Ray Elder. But at Daytona in the 125-lap qualifying race, he finished twenty-fourth, and in the Daytona 500 he was eighteenth, thirteen laps behind winner Richard Petty.

In March and April he had a couple of fourths, but most of the time finished in the back of the field.

The year before, when he was running his own car in races Mario Rossi didn't run, he had gotten some help from Ray Nichols, who ran the Chrysler parts depot for the Chrysler teams.

"Ray liked me and he helped me," said Bobby.

Then, in November 1970, when Chrysler announced that Richard Petty would have the only Chrysler factory team, it also announced it was taking the parts concession away from Ray Nichels and placing it in the hands of the Pettys.

"I thought it was unfair to Ray Nichels, because he had done a really good job for all the people who needed Chrysler products," said Bobby.

Maurice Petty, whose race team was still engaged in a feud with Bobby Allison, wasn't inclined to be nearly as helpful as Nichels had been.

Before the Darlington race on May 2, 1971, Bobby called Maurice Petty to order a cylinder head and a set of eight pistons.

"Here's the deal," Maurice told him. "You pay list price, and you pay shipping. And you pay me a fifty-dollar shipping fee to have my people take it over to the airport and put it on the airplane to you. Because what you should have done is order two hundred of those things six months ago and ordered another two hundred six months from now, instead of buying one set."

Bobby was trapped but had no solution. He bought the cylinder head and the eight pistons at retail and paid the freight and Maurice's added handling fee. When Bobby opened the box, there were only seven pistons inside.

Bobby called Maurice and told him he was a piston short.

"When can I get another piston?" Bobby asked.

"The box had eight when it left here," Maurice said. "If you need another one, I will sell you one piston for fifty dollars, and it will cost you another fifty to get it to the airport, plus the air freight."

Said Bobby years later, "That one piston cost me one hundred twenty-five dollars. But I had to have it."

Bobby complained to the Chrysler people but got little satisfaction. He worked through the night to get the engine built, and then put the car on the trailer to drive it to Darlington. When he tested the car, it ran well.

All the work on the engine was for naught, as it turned out. A representative from Chrysler came up to Bobby at the track and told him, "We have arranged for you to run a Petty engine in this race, so get your engine out, and put his in. Maurice will come over and make sure you guys don't do anything wrong installing it."

"It was a slap at me and my people," said Bobby, "but I had to go along. The next week I had to have Chrysler's support. So we took our engine out and put Petty's in. And the car was five miles an hour slower than it was with my engine."

"Your car is no good," the Chrysler execs then told him.

It was a scene out of the novel *1984*. Big Brother was not only watching over him, but giving him a good screwing as well.

"Wait a minute," Bobby protested. "How can our engine go this fast, and your engine go that much slower if my car is no good?'

"Don't argue with us," the Chrysler exec said. "This is the deal. And you can't touch anything. You can't adjust the timing. You can't adjust the carburetor jets. Nothing. Maurice does everything."

The race began, Bobby's car did poorly, and the Petty engine blew up. Bobby coasted in, and when approached by a TV reporter, Bobby announced, "That's it. I'm broke." He was out of money.

With the cost of running on the Grand National circuit too great, the only option was for Bobby and Eddie to run their Modified car at Birmingham, Montgomery, and other short tracks around the south.

"Our plans were to build a car to run Saturday night races," said Eddie.

Done in by Chrysler and the Pettys, for a brief, sad moment, it looked like Bobby Allison's Grand National racing career had come to an end.

Bobby began to walk dejectedly down to the family area past the old garage stalls at Darlington. Ralph Moody was there in his little Winnebago motor home.

Ralph called Bobby over. Bobby, angry, thought to himself, *What the hell are you bothering me for?*

"You need to park that shitbox and drive my car," Moody said to him.

"All you've got to do is give me one," Bobby replied.

Bobby didn't think Moody would give him one. He had driven once already for Holman and Moody, and John Holman had exiled him to Siberia. Moreover, Moody had just won two championships with driver David Pearson.

The next weekend Bobby had to make a trip to Indianapolis, where Donnie was driving an open-wheel IndyCar for A. J. Foyt. Bobby and Donnie had jointly bought a Beechcraft Baron. Because Donnie didn't have a pilot's license, Bobby had to be the pilot. Bobby agreed after the Darlington race to fly Donnie to Indianapolis.

"Here I am, really feeling bad and dejected," said Bobby. "My whole NASCAR career is upside down. And I have to take Donnie to Indianapolis."

Bobby, seeing his career going down in flames, became ill on the flight, throwing up again and again. That night in his motel room in Indianapolis, Bobby got a message to call Ralph Moody. Curious, he woke Moody out of a deep sleep.

"Can you come back to Charlotte tomorrow?" Moody asked him.

Bobby said he could.

"What's your deal with Coke?"

"I'm not sure," said Bobby. "I told them I was out of business. I'll call them tomorrow and ask. But I thought David Pearson was your driver."

Moody told him, "Not anymore."

On May 2, 1971, the day Moody approached him at Darlington, David Pearson had quit Holman and Moody in a huff. Before the race the Holman and Moody crew had changed everything in the car, including the shocks and springs, without telling Pearson. After he scraped the wall on the thirtieth lap, he parked the car and walked away from Holman and Moody for good.

"How do you feel about driving for me?" Moody asked.

"Yes, yes, yes," Allison replied. "That would be great."

The deal was for Bobby to drive the remaining superspeedway races for Holman and Moody. He could race his own car in the others.

Ralph thought Bobby Allison was his best option, even though Moody's partner, John Holman, had never stopped disliking both Bobby and Donnie, for reasons no one could quite figure out. Moody hired Bobby for a second go-around even though he knew Holman wouldn't be happy about it.

"I'm going to run the Mercury for Moody," Bobby said to Eddie.

Eddie stayed in Hueytown to build the Dodge to run in the short-track races Holman and Moody didn't enter. On the weekends Bobby sent his plane to take Eddie to the races as a member of Ralph Moody's crack pit crew.

Bobby had a handshake agreement with Moody. He called Vic Meinert to see if Coke would continue to sponsor him. Bobby continued to be one of NASCAR's matinee idols, and Coca-Cola was only too happy to shift over its sponsorship to the prestigious Holman and Moody car.

Bobby returned to Charlotte to test. The Holman and Moody Mercury drove horribly.

"I now saw why David Pearson got out of it," Bobby said. But as Bobby watched the Holman and Moody mechanics finish their preparation of the chassis, he saw they had done something to cause it to run so badly.

"They had cut the center of the frame structure out to make room for a different style of oil pan," Bobby said. "It allowed the frame to flex so bad. When the frame would flex, the steering linkage would not flex, so the wheels would steer in and steer out, go all over all by themselves. They had been running the car like that since Daytona."

Bobby, who had that sixth sense, that incredible feel for his race car, knew not only what the problem was, but just how to fix it. He flew back to his shop in Hueytown, and he made a little part that he bolted under the chassis of the car.

"After I fixed it," he said, "I could drive that car with one hand."

Bobby went to Talladega in the Holman and Moody car. Donnie was in the Wood Brothers car. Donnie won the pole. Bobby Isaac was on the outside pole. Bobby was in the second row, third-best in qualifying.

The race started, and Bobby was the race leader by lap 6. His primary opponent was brother Donnie, who earned $31,000 by winning the race. Bobby earned $19,000 for second, thanks to the thousands of dollars he earned by leading a lot of laps. The Donnie-Bobby finish was the fourth time Bobby had finished second to his younger brother.

Eddie was on the pit crew on the day Ralph Moody invented a quicker, novel four-tire change using two jacks.

"I was the left-side tire changer," said Eddie. "I loved to change tires. Moody had put that pit deal together where we used two jacks. Instead of the right-side guys coming around and changing the left, we had a left-side tire guy—that was me—

and I took off the left front lugs and went to the back and took the rear lugs off, and by the time I got the tire off, the other tire was there, and I put the left rear on, and the right front guy came around and put the left front on. We smoked them in the pits all year!

"We didn't get to use it long because NASCAR kept critiquing it until they ruled that the same guys had to change the tires. They ruled you could only use one jack.

"The Glen Wood team got all the press for their pit crew, but we constantly beat them."

The Talladega race in May 1971, as it turned out, was the one that made the Alabama Gang nationally famous. The two brothers from Hueytown, Alabama, competing at their home track, became statewide icons overnight when after a one-lap shoot-out, Donnie won the race, six lengths ahead of Bobby.

Two men, Don Naman, the track promoter, and Jim Hunter, the track publicist both played a role in making the Alabama Gang of Bobby Allison, Donnie Allison, and Neil Bonnett into national heroes.

"Don Naman was the promoter for Talladega," said Bobby. "Don had had a short track at Merryville, Tennessee, that I went and raced at for him, so Don Naman was a fan of mine. Donnie had had success around Alabama, and had the personality to fit into the race slot there, so for us to be openly labeled 'the Alabama Gang' was an honor to us."

Humpy Wheeler, a prolific promoter himself before taking over the reins at the Charlotte Motor Speedway, well knew why Naman wanted to create instant local heroes for his track, which at that point lacked its own identity and history.

"Bill France had been thwarted in his attempt to build a track somewhere around Greenville, South Carolina, and he ended up in Alabama because he got free land in the middle of nowhere," said Wheeler.

"The first time I went down there and looked at [Talladega]," said Wheeler, "I questioned Bill France's sanity to his face. 'You can't get here from there,' I said. There were no Interstates at the time, and without I-20 or I-465 it was hard for the mother lode of race fans from the Carolinas and Virginia to get there without having to go through Atlanta, which no one wanted to do. And then you had to get on these back roads and somehow find the Talladega Speedway, where there weren't any motel rooms. And west of there? After you went west past Birmingham, there weren't any race fans all the way to Hawaii, so they couldn't pull much from the West."

But between free land and lots of promises by Alabama governor George Wallace, Bill France succumbed to the lure. According to Wheeler, after a promoter builds a new speedway, he understands the unwritten rule that you can borrow other tracks' ready-made fans, but in five years you better develop your own fan base.

"That was a tough deal in the early days of Talladega," said Wheeler. "There was more favor toward NASCAR in the Northeast than in Alabama, because Alabama tracks tended to be dirt, primitive."

The driver boycott in 1969 didn't help things. When the factory drivers pulled out of the inaugural race, Bobby and Donnie stayed out, too. By 1971, Talladega needed all the positive publicity it could get.

When the brothers, two Florida transplants now living in nearby Hueytown, finished one, two, the track suddenly had just the local attraction it needed.

"The Allisons are faux Alabamans," said Wheeler. "They are from South Florida, the Miami area. But Jimmy Hunter, the publicity director of the speedway, realizing the need to give Talladega some local heroes, had Bobby Allison, Donnie Allison, and Neil Bonnett living in the Birmingham suburbs. It was Jimmy who fostered the mystique of the Alabama Gang."

CHAPTER 16

Donnie: Banjo

"Donnie was a good race driver, but it wasn't easy for him to be in Bobby's shadow."

—**Humpy Wheeler**

Before Donnie Allison entered Grand National racing, he had won two hundred races on short tracks in the South. Part of the reason he had been successful was that most of the time he had only to deal with brother Eddie, with whom he got along. Once Eddie left, racing became harder for Donnie because it took a tough man to put up with Donnie's tough-guy personality. Where Bobby was friendly and affable, Donnie could be suspicious, distant, and difficult.

"Donnie came along in 1967, and he had a completely different personality than Bobby," said Humpy Wheeler. "Donnie was feisty. He was a fighter. If he'd been around boxing clubs, he'd have ended up a welterweight. He'd fight somebody in a minute, where Bobby would keep his cool pretty good.

"Donnie was a good race driver, but it wasn't easy for him to be in Bobby's shadow."

According to Eddie Allison, Donnie could drive a car just as well as Bobby.

"Bobby, Donnie, and I could be at Birmingham testing," said Eddie, "and Bobby would get out of the car, and Donnie would get in, and you'd be watching the stopwatch, and Donnie would make the car go faster around the track."

What hurt Donnie, says Eddie, was his tough-guy behavior.

"He wasn't as personable as Bobby, and he could be *very* belligerent," said Eddie Allison. "You cross Donnie Allison, and you're likely to see a fist in your face. And it didn't have to happen at the racetrack.

"A perception came about because of his personality, and when that's you, you don't understand that. Donnie thought the way he was was what made him win races. And he wasn't going to change. And Donnie could drive a race car as good as anybody in the world. But Donnie is not rated in the same category as Bobby, because he raced so much less in Winston Cup."

One reason Donnie didn't race in Winston Cup as much as Bobby was that no one was as driven as Bobby. Back when Donnie was first starting out, he boasted to his wife, Pat, "I'm going to race at Daytona one day." That was his goal. Bobby had a loftier goal: to win the NASCAR racing championship. To do that, he knew, he had to run the full slate of races. His whole career Donnie was satisfied just to be racing, winning, and making money. But to win a racing championship, you had to have a hard-charging personality, had to keep moving from team to team until you found the right one to get you there. In short, you had to be highly driven. It wasn't in Donnie's personality. As a boy, Donnie had enjoyed riding motorcycles, riding horses, wrestling alligators, and hunting and fishing with his friends. Bobby had no hobbies. All he wanted to do was race. Looking back, Donnie's only regret was that he wasn't a bit more ambitious.

In 1966, the year Bobby broke into Grand National racing with three wins, Donnie entered two superspeedway races, finishing twenty-seventh at Rockingham and ninth, twenty-two laps behind winner Freddie Lorenzen, at Charlotte. The next year he entered twenty races, didn't win, but broke into the top five four times and earned $17,613. His best finish was a second to Jim Paschal in the Asheville 300 on June 2. Donnie was voted Rookie of the Year.

Based on that, Ralph Moody offered Donnie a tryout in the 1968 Daytona 500. Though he crashed early in the race and finished fortieth, Moody assigned him to a Holman and Moody car run by Banjo Matthews, the top car builder of his day and a feisty guy who had once been a driver on the circuit. Moody, who was supersmart when it came to matching personalities, found just the right crew chief for the combative Donnie. As feisty as Matthews might have been, Matthews knew how to get along with his drivers.

"Banjo had an affinity with race drivers that few people I've ever known had," said Humpy Wheeler. "Being a former driver himself, he knew what to say to them. He knew what not to say. He knew when to say it and when not to say it. He wasn't as demanding as some of the car owners."

Banjo Matthews had cut his teeth under the tutelage of Harold Wilcox, the man who had also taught Eddie. Matthews drove for Wilcox on the Miami tracks, earning a reputation for being a tough guy, a bumper. If you didn't get out of Banjo's way, he'd push you aside.

Matthews had a fierce competition with Bobby Johns, for whom Bobby Allison rooted as a kid. As a result, Bobby didn't much care for Matthews.

"Banjo won a reasonable percentage of the time, but he was not my favorite competitor," said Bobby. "I was a Bobby Johns fan, not a Banjo fan. Banjo was a rough driver. He bumped a lot. He was somewhat husky in build, and so he would get out of the car after bumping somebody and say, 'I'm going to whip your ass.'"

But unlike Johns, Banjo dreamed of racing on the NASCAR Grand National circuit. He would race on the beach at Daytona and on the Carolina tracks.

"When Ralph Moody got things going in the mid-sixties," said Bobby, "Banjo was first a Holman and Moody driver, and then he became a crew chief. He ran a car financed by Ford that Banjo ran out of his shop as a team owner. He owned the tow truck and the tools.

"Banjo and Donnie really respected each other," said Bobby. "What they liked about each other was their similarity in personality. Donnie wasn't real fond of me for a while there, and Banjo certainly wasn't real fond of me. But they found each other."

When Banjo hired Donnie he was at the bottom of the Ford totem pole. Before Donnie, Banjo had taken a liking to Cale Yarborough and hired him as a driver. When Cale became a force, he moved up to the Wood Brothers race team. When Banjo left the car racing business to concentrate on building cars, his best customer was Junior Johnson, with whom he had a close, personal friendship.

On March 31, 1968, Donnie proved that he and Banjo were going to be a force when he finished third at Martinsville to Cale Yarborough and LeeRoy Yarbrough and then on April 28 finished third again, behind Cale and David Pearson. Then there was a second-place finish in the World 600, worth $12,975, followed by twenty-eight-year-old Donnie's first Grand National win on June 16, 1968, at Rockingham. At one point he had a four-lap lead over the rest of the field. He won a purse of $16,675.

In 1969 Donnie scored a victory and two second-place finishes. One of those seconds was at Charlotte in May, and the win also came at Charlotte in the fall race when Donnie and Bobbie finished one, two in the National 500. His other second-place finish came at the inaugural race at the Michigan International Speedway, an event won by Bobby Isaac.

The Banjo-Donnie team in 1970 only entered nineteen races, running more for the prize money than for the racing title.

"Banjo saw it was expensive to run the short tracks, and the income wasn't good, even if you won," said Bobby. "At the time the championship was only worth a few bucks. So that didn't offset the burden of entering the race.

"The Wood Brothers didn't run all the races either, because, once again, if you went to Winston-Salem, it took four or five employees, an engine that cost $750 from Holman and Moody and at least twelve to sixteen tires that were $40 each at the time, but then you talk about $800 or $1,000 first-place money, you were a loser before you showed up, and if you came in second, you were really, really a loser."

"You did it," I said to Bobby.

"Oh yes, yes, sir," he said. "I went to various places and begged and borrowed and ran on used tires. Because I wanted to do it so badly. Donnie wanted to do other things. He wanted to hunt and fish, and, you know, whatever. Donnie didn't want to spend his entire life racing. I did."

Banjo Matthews was satisfied to run a limited schedule of only the best-paying races. He was too much of a businessman to waste his time going to races which cost him money to run.

"When he went into the business of building cars and producing parts for people, he did it at a profit or he didn't do it," said Bobby. "He built one of the cars I drove for Roger Penske, and it wasn't discounted a penny. Later I got a couple of car parts, a chassis myself, and I got no discount and no warranty. You took it as it is, and you paid the full price before you touched it. 'If you don't like it, go buy something somewhere else.' A few people had a better relationship with him than me."

In 1970 Donnie won three races, Bristol, the World 600 at Charlotte, and the Firecracker 400 at Daytona. The team earned $96,000 that year.

What made his winning the World 600 even more remarkable was that he also entered the Indianapolis 500 the same weekend. (Donnie was the only driver ever to do that until 1993, when Jeff Gordon did it.)

Donnie was asked to drive at Indy by racing legend A. J. Foyt, It has been argued that Foyt may have been the greatest racer ever to get behind the wheel. In addition to winning four Indy 500s, he won the Daytona 500 (in 1972 with the Wood Brothers) and the 24 Hours at Le Mans in 1967 with Dan Gurney. In all, he won 12 racing titles and 172 major races in winning in NASCAR, USAC, midgets, sprints, IMSA, and at Le Mans.

Foyt was as crusty as Donnie was, maybe more so. He was another man who was quick with his fists. Supposedly he once joked to a friend, "When I was younger I would wait to hear what a man had to say. Then I'd hit him. I no longer have the patience to wait for him to speak. I know what he's thinking."

In addition to his driving skill, there was another reason the outspoken, egoistic Foyt picked Donnie.

"Donnie idolized A. J.," said Bobby. "At least that's the way I saw it. He really idolized A. J. Foyt. He thought everything about him was great. A. J. was a good driver and a good mechanic, and also a promoter's dream. He bragged a lot, but he backed it up. Anyway, A. J. hired Donnie, and they went to Indy, and Donnie did really well."

Donnie drove a Ford, and though he was lapped by winner Al Unser, he managed to finished fourth and earn himself IndyCar Rookie of the Year.

"Donnie was one of the few stock car drivers that went up to Indy and did well," said Humpy Wheeler. "Because of his size, he would have done better as an Indy driver than a stock car. That was when Indycar racing was beginning to falter a bit. The American public just didn't accept the rear-engine car, not the way they did the old Watson roadsters. He got Rookie of the Year the first time he went up there."

In that race he even beat Foyt, who finished tenth.

"My version of the deal is that the next time Donnie drove for him [in 1972] he gave Donnie a worse car, because Donnie had done better than A. J., and you don't do better than A. J. And when they went back for the second year, Donnie still finished sixth, and A. J. finished twenty-fifth. But I felt like Donnie still got short-changed. That's my opinion."

Eddie Allison, for one, is convinced that Donnie could have become an IndyCar legend had A. J. Foyt been less combative.

"Donnie Allison could have won the Indianapolis 500 eight or nine times," said Eddie. "Circumstances prevented that. At the time there was a rift between Champ cars and NASCAR. When Donnie beat A. J. as bad as he beat him the last time they raced, A. J. told him, 'You can't drive my car any more.'"

Said Bobby, "A. J. didn't want him around because how can this little kid from Alabama take A. J.'s car and do better than A. J.?"

Unfortunately for Donnie, his great finishes in his two Indy 500 races didn't help get him a full-time NASCAR ride. And because he didn't have a full-time NASCAR ride, he didn't get any other offers for the Indy 500.

Said Eddie, "Donnie was trying to make a living in Winston Cup, but he still couldn't get a Cup ride to run every race. He was with teams that only ran in the big races. And so the people at Indianapolis never came and asked him to drive, as far as I know, or anybody else. Which was a real mistake.

"Like I say, Bobby, Donnie and I could be at Birmingham testing, and Bobby would get out of the car, and Donnie would get in, and you'd be watching the stopwatch, and Donnie would make the car go faster around the track."

In late 1970, NASCAR suffered a financial crisis when first Chrysler announced it would support only the Petty team, followed by an announcement by the Ford Motor Company that it was getting out of racing entirely. Banjo Matthews had a Ford team, and now he had to race without Ford's (and Holman and Moody's) financial help. When Donnie crashed his car on lap 170 of the 1971 Daytona 500, Banjo's team crashed, too. It was Donnie's final race for Matthews, who would run two races with A. J. Foyt and four with Bobby Isaac before getting out of racing as a car owner. He would spend the rest of his life building cars for others.

CHAPTER 17

Bobby:
Allison Versus the Pettys

Two weeks after finishing second behind Donnie at Talladega, Bobby raced at Charlotte in the World 600. This time Bobby won and Donnie came in second. The next weekend, June 6, 1971, Bobby went to Dover and won the race in one of his most impressive performances. On that day in 93-degree heat, the car turned the corners perfectly, and Bobby defeated Fred Lorenzen, who had returned to racing, Richard Petty, and the entire field by over a lap. Lorenzen, Petty, Bobby Isaac, and a number of other drivers had to ask for relief help. Allison was one of only four men who drove the whole way in that oppressive heat. He kept his foot on the gas and dominated the day.

"The race car is made to run wide open," said Eddie Allison. "You don't baby a race car. These other guys say, 'You have to back off to conserve the race car.' That's crazy. You run wide-open. You lap the field fifty times if you can. Then you can coast. You can coast if you're not upsetting your applecart. We did that at Dover in '71. We lapped the field. The other drivers got out of their cars. It was unbelievable.

"We put on four tires and didn't lose the lead, so nobody else could do anything but put on two, and we just ran away from them, lapped them.

"And when the race was over, Bobby got out of the car, and he wasn't even sweating. That was his forte: not sweating in a race car. He didn't lose any water, so he didn't get weak driving. Like I say, he got that stamina strain from the Patton gene."

Bobby drove his Holman and Moody Mercury to his third victory in a row on

June 13 at Brooklyn, Michigan. Bobby Isaac led until the second-to-last lap, when Allison flew by him.

When Richard Petty and his crew began to complain that Allison had an unfair restrictor-plate advantage with his Mercury, Bobby replied by recalling the 1967 season in which Petty won 27 races and didn't look back. And in 1971 Petty would go on to win 21 races, advantage or no. Bobby answered acidly, "Some people go crying around when they're not in front."

When Holman and Moody chose not to enter the race at Riverside, California, Bobby raced his Dodge. One reason Bobby kept Eddie at home working on his own car during the week rather than having him work at Holman-Moody was that Bobby figured, based on his past experience, that his ride with Holman-Moody would not be a long-lasting one.

He could see that the relationship between John Holman and Ralph Moody—bad when he ran for them in 1968—was deteriorating even further. Bobby knew that the Holman and Moody partnership could end at any moment. Holman, the tough one, had the power. Moody, the sensitive one, had the brains. Bobby figured that anytime Holman wanted to, he could force Moody out—and Bobby along with him. It was only a matter of how much crap Moody could stomach. Holman had shipped him off to Bondy Long in '68. The gruff Holman was capable of pushing Ralph Moody over the brink and forcing him to quit just as easily.

What made the June 20, 1971, Riverside race notable was that Bobby had arranged with Motorola to put a two-way radio in the car so that during the race he could talk directly to Eddie. It was the first time a driver didn't have to rely on a chalkboard, and it wasn't long before all the drivers were doing it. During the race Eddie would listen to the trackside radio, and using that information, he could relay to Bobby what was happening on the track. At least once he warned Bobby of a crash way down the track, and Bobby was able to avoid trouble.

Late in the race Bobby passed Ray Elder, the only other car on the lead lap, and he took the checkered flag going away.

"People talk about secrets in racing," said Eddie. "There are no secrets in racing. If you do something different, people are going to see it. There are no tricks. You make the car turn the corner, and you get a driver who can turn the steering wheel. I was talking with Junie Donlavey. He said, "If one race team changes the mirrors in their trailers, everyone does it, too."

On June 23, 1971, Bobby went to Houston, Texas, in his Dodge, and he won his fifth race in a row. In earlier races the Dodge engine had blown. On this day it somehow held together.

Said Bobby, "It's strange how your luck can turn around."

His five-in-a-row streak, tied for second-most in NASCAR history, was one of the highlights of a spectacular racing career. Petty, who had won ten in a row in 1967, would tie him in July and August 1971. In the fifth win at Atlanta, on August 1, Petty would nip Bobby at the finish line.

But it was Bobby who stopped Petty from winning a sixth in a row. It was in a race that Petty didn't win, but neither did anyone else, thanks to an odd ruling by Bill France.

The next race was at Bowman Gray Stadium, and instead of driving his Dodge, Bobby drove a Mustang owned by Melvin Joseph, the owner of Dover Downs and a close friend of Bobby's. The Mustang was a Grand Am car built by Holman and Moody. The Grand Am series had closed at the end of the 1970 season, but Bill France was allowing Grand Am cars to run in 1971, because France wanted to allow the Grand Am car owners to try to recoup on their investments in the equipment.

Before the season France ruled that any Grand American car that won would be credited with a Grand American series win. Any Grand National car would get a Grand National win. The ruling would have historic consequences.

Bobby loved the little Mustang. He chose it over his Dodge, because, as Eddie Allison explained it, "the Dodge was a big ole lump of iron. The Mustang was a race car."

Against Grand National and Grand Am drivers, Bobby won the race on August 6 at Bowman Gray going away.

"We didn't have to race anybody," said Eddie. "It was so good. The thing had plenty of motor, and it turned. And it had the driver. It shook the Pettys up, but we loved to shake the Pettys up. And NASCAR never gave Bobby that win in the Grand National books. We got the money, but we didn't get the win."

When it was announced that no one was awarded the win, neither Bobby nor Eddie blinked. If Bobby had cared enough, he could have protested, and maybe he'd have gotten his win, because a race without a winner doesn't make a whole lot of sense. But Bobby and Eddie were busy racing, and they didn't have time to do what they had to do to get their win on the books.

"Bobby never thought it would be a situation that would cause any problems. Because all we wanted to do was win," said Eddie.

And so, according to the official NASCAR records, Darrell Waltrip has 84 wins, and Bobby has 84, and that irks Bobby to this day. (*The Stock Car Racing Encyclopedia,* which I wrote with Greg Fielden, gives Bobby an 85th win and so at least in our book Bobby is ahead.)

For the remainder of the 1971 season, the races came down to a win either by Bobby or by Richard Petty. At the West Virginia 500, Petty slammed Allison out of the way to win, and then at Brooklyn, Allison outran Petty. On August 22 at Talladega, Bobby won after he slammed and banged Petty out of the way for the win.

Said Petty after the race, "I've been racing thirteen years, and the only cat I've had trouble with is Bobby Allison. He came along and won some races a couple of years ago. He's been charged-up ever since. There's an awful lot of red paint on the side of my car."

Allison refused to apologize. "We both had the desire to win" was all he said.

"Bobby just loved to beat Richard," said Eddie Allison. Bobby even competed with Petty when it came to signing autographs.

"I was competitive with Richard Petty on the small tracks no matter what I drove," said Bobby. "Here I was, an outsider who had come into racing under unusual circumstances—my first win was in a little Chevelle. One of the things that was very conspicuous to me early on, was that after a race would finish, there would always be a big crowd around Richard Petty, and he would sit and sign autographs for hours. And everyone else would be hiding and getting out of there.

"I thought, *Well, this is dumb, because these people are all happy about what they've seen,* so it was a real thrill for me when people came over and wanted mine, and pretty soon I had a big crowd like Richard Petty. Everywhere I went, I signed autographs.

"Richard doesn't write fast. He puts all the curlicues in, and so his signature takes a while. I could write fast, so I would get rid of my autograph seekers faster than he could his. I can say I signed as many or more autographs than he did, because I got done quicker. So I have to smile to myself about that. I beat him at something. You know? Even if it's signing names. Everything's competitive."

I mentioned to Bobby that he never got the credit for signing autographs and being friendly to the fans like Richard did.

"He was the homegrown family hero rooted in the Carolinas," said Bobby. "Baptist. They didn't practice their faith in front of the racing crowd, but they were good people. Lee and Elizabeth Petty did an incredible job, and so did Richard. Maurice tried to drive and didn't succeed, and he then changed to the engine department, and he became one of the outstanding engine builders.

"I was an outsider who came from Miami through Alabama, a Catholic, and that was even mentioned from time to time: The comment would be, 'And he's Catholic, too.' Because I would go to Mass no matter what. It was part of my deal. They would say, 'Sunday morning we are going to have a meeting . . .' And I'd say, 'I can't meet you.' So I was the outsider from early on."

"Did you ever get inside?" I asked.

"Never did," Bobby said. "You know, some things I did annoyed people, and that was okay with me. And sometimes I annoyed people and wished I hadn't. But the main thing was, I was getting to do what I wanted to do, and I was succeeding a lot. Not as much as I wanted to, but a lot. And so I went on my way."

Said brother Eddie, "Because of the past history, Bobby hates Richard Petty the racer, but he doesn't hate Richard Petty. Bobby always felt strongly that his competitors had more than he had. That never bothered me. I like to beat people who have more than I have.

"Bobby felt that Richard always had, and that we *never* had. We had to work to get anything, and that part helped make the rivalry.

"For Bobby, even when he was making more than $300,000 in purses in 1971, he didn't have the security Richard Petty had. Petty, of course, had a lifetime job with the best race team in the game. Bobby felt that as good as he performed, the factories should have helped him the same way they were helping Richard Petty, and it never happened.

"Richard Petty is a race car driver, but he ain't *the* race car driver. He was good, but the minute anybody caught up with him with equipment, then he was history. Richard Petty couldn't tote Bobby Allison's little finger driving a race car.

"Richard's advantage was that he knew his car wasn't going to break, so he could drive it different from a driver who worried his car wouldn't make it. And that goes not only for the engine, but for the wheels and the hubs, the whole car. For a long time when we started out racing, we had to break pieces, which knocked us out of races, to find out what we needed so finally we had what the Pettys had. And when our pieces stopped breaking, it was Katie, bar the door. I mean, in 1971 Bobby could run that Holman-Moody Mercury until his tongue hung out. He knew it wasn't going to break."

The Allison-Petty rivalry caught the imagination of the racing public. Here were two tough competitors who raced clean but didn't give an inch. The two men were as popular as any sports figures in America at the time. They would race side by side, trading paint, gaining advantage, without crashing each other. It was as close to motorized ballet as NASCAR ever presented.

"It's history, and it's gone by, and nobody seems to care anymore, but it was Bobby's and Richard's integrity that brought stock car racing out of the dirt roads and into the present," said Eddie Allison. "Nobody in the world has beat and hammered and banged on each other like Bobby and Richard, but they never, ever knocked each other out of a race intentionally. Never. They always got to the checkered flag.

"I never worried about Richard crashing us, and they didn't worry about Bobby crashing them, because we trusted each other. Bobby is a *good* person, and Richard is a *good* person. We knew they could knock the fenders off the car, because the cars were good enough with the fenders off they would still get to the end of the race. They beat on each other to get where they were going, but they never wrecked each other.

"Their ability to race each other cleanly made the fans go nuts, something the drivers today don't believe in.

"Richard and I talked about it a bunch. Like at Islip, Richard made a move, and Bobby was in the way, and Richard bent his car bad enough that he couldn't finish the race, and that happened a couple of times. Once Richard stuck Bobby in the hole at the end of the fence at Asheville-Weaverville, and if Bobby had been a lesser driver, he never would have saved it and gone on to win the race. Racers are racers, and at a point their integrity leaves them in order to win a race, and probably the least that happened to was Bobby and Richard."

One peak of Bobby Allison's spectacular career came during 1971. In addition to winning five races in a row, Bobby led in the last nine races of the season. The Holman-Moody Mercury was as well made a car as he ever drove, and his pit crew—Jake Elder, Dan Ford, Eddie Allison, Waddell Wilson, and Bill Holman—was second to none.

"Ralph Moody saw to that," said Eddie Allison.

In 1971, driving most of the year for Ralph Moody, Bobby Allison finished the season with 11 wins, 27 top-five finishes, and 31 top-ten finishes. That he did not win the driving championship says a lot about the success Richard Petty achieved that year. Richard won 21 races, had 38 top fives, and 41 top tens. What was even odder was that Bobby didn't even finish second in the points, though James Hylton and Cecil Gordon, two drivers who finished ahead of him, never won a race.

But Bobby won $351,000 in purses in what was his finest season in racing. After getting dumped by Chrysler in 1970, this was one of the more remarkable comebacks in a career filled with remarkable comebacks. Bobby felt like his career was back on track and that he would keep on winning like this forever.

"I was so pumped up," said Bobby. "If I had died, it would have taken the undertaker two weeks to get the grin off my face."

Bobby Allison loved driving for Ralph Moody. It was a pairing made in heaven. What Bobby Allison anticipated but still didn't quite see was that John Holman was at the breaking point. Holman was becoming ever more jealous and angry over the recognition Ralph was getting for his automotive genius and Holman and Moody's success on the NASCAR Grand National circuit.

Because the firm was called Holman and Moody, outsiders thought they were equal partners, but when Holman, the money guy, and Moody, the automotive brain, signed the agreement to work together, Holman reserved for himself the power and control.

Holman was business smart, but relationship foolish. For the race team to succeed on the track, Holman desperately needed Moody, who not only could build and fix a car as well as anyone, but who had the personality to work with the drivers and the crews.

The racers loved Ralph Moody. They barely tolerated John Holman, who would pull dirty tricks on Moody and his drivers. Often if Holman and Moody entered two drivers in a race, one driver would list John Holman as car owner, and the other would list Ralph Moody. If Moody's driver was winning, Holman was not above ordering Moody's driver to pit, even when he didn't need to, just so his driver could take the lead.

For years Ralph Moody put up with John Holman's interference and pettiness, because the relationship allowed him to do what he loved most: build championship race cars.

At the end of the 1971 season John Holman and Ralph Moody had a serious blowup. Waddell Wilson, the famed engine builder for the Holman-Moody team, was working in the shop on a Saturday afternoon. John Holman was up in the office, which was high up in the new hangarlike building overlooking the complex, talking on the telephone. Ralph came in and, unaware John was on the phone, fired up a race car.

Holman came out of his office, ran down the steps to the ground floor, got behind a giant forklift which the employees nicknamed "Big John," and with that forklift he lifted up the race car and drove it outside the hangar.

Then he walked back in and began to scream at Moody.

"They ran through the office," said Wilson. "One of them ran through the screen door, tore the door off the hinges, and that was the end of it. John fired Ralph."

The way Ralph Moody told the story, he had held back from Holman the fact that he had raised almost $2 million in sponsorship money for Bobby to race in 1972.

When he met with Holman, Holman told him, "We aren't running Bobby Allison. We aren't running any goddamn race car. I'm going to work on trucks."

"I have a big chunk of money going into next year with Bobby," said Moody.

"I whipped the checks out and showed him," said Moody. "He said, 'Well, that's different.' I grabbed them back and put them in my pocket. He said, 'What are you going to do?' I said, 'I'm going to give them back.' And I did."

Bobby had no idea about the schism when Holman called him into his office and told him himself.

When an innocent Bobby Allison, Ralph Moody's boy, went to see John Holman, the portly Holman asked him, "So how do you feel you've done this year?"

"I'm pretty pleased," he said, and he should have been.

"And Coke is pretty happy?"

"Yes, sir. Coke is really happy. They are talking about next year and talking about a raise for next year."

Holman shocked Allison when he said, "You and your buddy [Moody] have a silver spoon up your ass, that's why. You can take your sponsorship and your buddy and go up the road some place and get something to drive because you're not driving for me anymore. Now get the hell out of here."

Said Bobby years later, "I was so floored. I mean, I almost went to my knees. It was like I was hit with a ton of bricks. I went over to Ralph and said to him, 'I don't know which way to turn.'

"He said, 'Go to my house and try to unwind a little bit. We'll figure out what to do.'"

But it would not be that easy.

Moody had $3 million in sponsorship money, but Moody ripped it up rather than have to deal with John Holman for another day.

"It would have been a fantastic deal," said Eddie Allison. "It would have saved Holman and Moody. It would have saved their business. And John couldn't understand it. The sad part was Ralph Moody was a good enough person he could have put up with anything, until it got so bad he couldn't stand it any more.

"And Moody was getting sick, too. He was going to have a problem anyway. When you're ill, you can't navigate like you can when you're healthy. He had a medical problem, which ended up being cancer. I don't know what the illness was at the end of '71, but that played on his ability to concentrate on the car."

Ralph Moody took Waddell Wilson and several of his key employees and opened an engine shop. Without Moody, Holman was finished in racing. He ended up selling his equipment to Banjo Matthews and to Eddie Pagan, who became two of the top car builders in the business. Without Holman, and by extension Ford, Ralph Moody didn't do much better. His career, too, was about over. It was one of those breakups that badly injured everyone concerned.

"If only Moody and Bobby could have stayed together," said Eddie Allison. "Richard never would have finished with 200 wins if they had. If we could just have run John Holman off, we could still have been racing Fords."

CHAPTER 18

Bobby: Junior

"Sponsorship is the thing."

—Junior Johnson

The day after John Holman kicked him out of his office, a shocked Bobby Allison went to see Ralph Moody. They were shooting pool in Ralph's basement when the phone rang. It was Richard Howard asking if Bobby could meet him at his furniture store in Denver, a sleepy town north of Charlotte.

"What do you think he wants?" Allison asked Moody.

"Looks like you'll be racing a Chevrolet next year," Moody said. "Boy, do it. Go."

John Holman's hatred for Ralph Moody would change the course of NASCAR history as the power base would switch from Holman and Moody to the race team owned by Richard Howard and run by Junior Johnson. As fate would have it, Bobby Allison would be in at the start of that transition.

Howard not only was Junior Johnson's partner and the titular owner of the race team, he was also an owner of the Charlotte Motor Speedway. Bobby had bought some furniture from Howard for their home in Hueytown, so he knew Howard. He also had dealings with Johnson. Three years earlier Bobby had asked Johnson to put him in his car.

"I begged him," said Bobby. "I got turned down flat. He said what amounted to 'Get away from me, and don't come back.'"

Bobby Allison was greeted by Richard Howard at Howard's furniture store. Howard ushered Bobby into a little office room. Junior Johnson was sitting there.

Junior got right to the point.

"You got that Coke money?" he asked Bobby.

"Yeah," said Bobby.

"We'll make a deal then," he said. "I want you to drive my car next season."

"Charlie Glotzbach's driving your car, and he's a friend of mine," said Allison.

"He's not going to drive my car anymore," said Johnson, "so you can if you want to, or not."

"If he's out, I'm definitely interested," said Bobby.

Bobby couldn't help but notice how cool, almost unfriendly Junior Johnson was to him.

"I don't know why he wasn't friendly," said Bobby years later. "Part of his attitude at the time was that he felt the boss had to be separate from the employees. He told me, 'I want to run my business with a chain of command. I will talk to Herb Nab, and Herb Nab will talk to you. When you want something, talk to Herb Nab, and Herb Nab will bring it to me.'"

Bobby had a hard time with that.

"I never could figure out how to verbalize," said Bobby. "If I could have figured out how to verbalize with him, we could have stayed together, because I really wanted to do it."

When Junior said, "I want you to drive my car," Bobby, blunt as always, said to Johnson, "A couple of years ago I begged you for a ride. Why are you giving me one now?"

"Because you proved you could win on the superspeedways," said Johnson. "Before, I didn't think you could."

"Good enough," said Bobby. "I'll drive for you."

With the car companies no longer footing the bill, race teams needed to find another way to pay the freight. Bobby and Junior were two racers to figure out that companies would pay money to put the firm's name or logo on the car as an advertisement. By 1972, the superspeedways were drawing upward of 100,000 fans, big enough crowds for a few companies to consider spending close to six figures to become sponsors.

"How much does Coke want to put into the deal?" Junior asked.

"Their top dollar was $75,000 for the season," Bobby said.

"No, I want a hundred thousand," Johnson said.

"They made a big increase, and they're offering $75,000," Bobby told him.

"You go back and tell them I want a hundred," said Johnson.

Allison said he would talk to his people in Atlanta. He called Vic Meinert and told him about Junior Johnson's offer for him to drive. He also told him Johnson wanted a hundred thousand dollars from Coca-Cola.

Meinert knew Johnson had a pretty spectacular car. He also knew that Johnson hadn't won that much with Charlie Glotzbach behind the wheel. The year before Glotzbach had led some and qualified well, but he had only won one race, at Bristol, with Friday Hassler driving in relief. Meinert was excited by the prospect of a Johnson-Allison team.

Meinert came back to Bobby and told him, "We can go to $85,000. That's the limit."

Bobby called Junior and told him the figure.

Junior, as tough a businessman as he was a driver, told Bobby, "It's a hundred or they're not on the car." This was Johnson's take-it-or-leave-it offer.

Said Bobby years later, "I wanted that deal to go together so badly I wrote Junior a check for $15,000."

"Okay, we got the deal put together," said Johnson. "Coke is on the car." And it was at this point that Johnson told Bobby if he wanted to discuss the car only to talk to his crew chief, Herb Nab.

"It was disappointing," said Bobby, "but I have to say I was still very enthusiastic."

Junior Johnson was not only a driver who won fifty races, he was the man who brought a corporate influence and structure to racing. It would not be long before a race team no longer could win if it didn't have a deep-pocket corporate sponsor. Johnson was one of the first to recognize how important this was.

Would the ride have been available to Bobby if Glotzbach had had a sponsor? Perhaps not.

"Sponsorship is the thing," said Junior Johnson. "You've got to have it to race, and we'll have it this way."

Junior Johnson knew that with the automobile factories no longer sponsoring teams, he had to do something, and quick. His last sponsor, an auto parts dealer from Detroit, had died in a plane crash.

As a historical figure, Johnson's importance in NASCAR is immense. It was Johnson, after all, who in 1970 visited the R. J. Reynolds tobacco company's main office in Winston-Salem, North Carolina, with the idea of talking the makers of Winston cigarettes into sponsoring his race team. Johnson went to see Ralph Seagraves, a Reynolds executive who had become a huge Junior Johnson fan. Johnson asked Seagraves if Reynolds would put up that same $100,000, which would pay for his cars, engines, and parts for the season. In exchange Johnson would advertise Winston cigarettes or any other R. J. Reynolds product on the hood and sides of the race car.

The deal made sense. Even though the races were not yet televised nationally, attendance was growing at Grand National events. The farsighted movers and shakers in NASCAR, including Bill France and Johnson, saw that sponsorship from wealthy corporations looking to hawk their products to the NASCAR Nation would give the sport a financial underpinning it desperately needed. France, for one, was hoping that corporate advertising would loosen the grip of the manipulative car companies. If each car owner could attract its own private sponsor, France knew, they would not have to rely on financial support from the quixotic, manipulative car companies.

What Junior Johnson didn't know when he went to meet with Seagraves was that the tobacco giant wasn't interested in spending a piddling hundred grand to run a car. Because the U.S. attorney general had ruled that smoking was so dangerous to one's health that it could no longer be advertised on television or in newspapers, the R. J. Reynolds people were desperate to find an alternative way to induce masses of people to buy Winstons. NASCAR seemed a perfect avenue. In 1971 there were few NASCAR moms. There were mostly NASCAR dads, and most of them smoked. Reynolds wanted them all to smoke Winston.

When Ralph Seagraves told Junior Johnson what they had in mind, Johnson replied, "Well, hell, why don't you just sponsor the whole show then?"

A month later the company made an agreement with Bill France to do just that. As part of a multimillion-dollar sponsorship arrangement with R. J. Reynolds, NASCAR crafted a new schedule and a new format to determine the driving champion.

In one of the last deals Bill France made before he retired and turned the industry over to his son, Bill Jr., he outlined a new format to determined the schedule and the driving championship. Because Reynolds was only interested in advertising at the large tracks before large crowds, NASCAR eliminated many of the small bull-rings, the fairground tracks where stock car racing began. Gone were tracks like Islip, New York; Bowman-Gray Stadium in Winston-Salem, the small tracks in Ona, West Virginia; Columbia, South Carolina; and Hickory, North Carolina. They would be used for NASCAR's second tier of racing, which would be called Grand National racing and later would be called the Busch series.

The premier series, soon to be called the Winston Cup series, was reduced from 47 races to 31, all over 250 miles. Winston Cup drivers would be awarded points for their finishing position in each race. The driver with the most points at the end of the year would win the Winston Cup, and $100,000 in bonus money that would be shared by the top teams in the standings. As part of the deal, France made Winston the exclusive cigarette of NASCAR. No other cigarette maker could sponsor a NASCAR race, though tobacco company logos including Camels and Skoal later would be seen on the cars themselves.

To further encourage race teams to enter every race, France announced that the tracks would pay appearance money to the top teams. It was announced that teams who aligned themselves with top sponsors would have first crack at the appearance money. With Coca-Cola on board, Richard Howard and Junior Johnson stood to gain from the new program that rewarded the top teams for just showing up.

When the 1972 season began, NASCAR announced that four teams would get the extra appearance money, including the Richard Petty's STP Plymouth team, Bud Moore's Ford team, Nord Krauskopf's K&K Insurance Dodge team, and Junior Johnson's Coca-Cola Chevrolet team. The four teams would get $2,000 for any race 400 miles or longer, and $1,500 if the race was less then 400 miles long.

All because Junior Johnson had the foresight to take R. J. Reynolds to see Bill France.

If a new NASCAR Hall of Fame were to open tomorrow, Big Bill France would be the first inductee, and unquestionably Junior Johnson would be the second. As a driver Johnson raced with a tenacious, hard-driving style. Like Bobby Allison, he was also a superb mechanic. Unlike Allison, the tough but soft-spoken Johnson was also a sharp, multibranched businessman who became wealthy from farming and road construction.

In the early 1950s one of the most lucrative Johnson family businesses involved making and hauling moonshine. In an early-morning trap, revenue agents caught him red-handed with a tractor-trailer filled with the clear liquid that sets your lungs on fire. He was incarcerated from mid-1956 through 1957.

After serving his sentence, Johnson returned to racing a bigger hero than ever. Tom Wolfe immortalized him by calling him "the Last American Hero." Johnson won 45 of his 50 wins after returning from prison, and his best season came in 1965, when he won 13 races and 10 poles. Johnson quit as a driver at the end of 1966, and for the next thirty years won over 132 races as a car owner and 21 more under the ownership of Richard Howard. Only Petty Enterprises has won more.

Johnson made an arrangement in 1972, which lasted for four years, giving Richard Howard ownership of his race team. That year Bobby Allison would win 10 races that would not be credited to Junior Johnson's total. But make no mistake about it, Junior Johnson was the heart and soul of the racing operation.

One of Johnson's greatest strengths was in his ability to identify talent. He hired the best, and when they went to work for Johnson, they only got better.

At the end of the 1971 season, engine builder Bob Allman quit because he felt the Ford engines were inferior. (Johnson must have agreed with Allman's assessment, because in 1972 he decided to switch to Chevrolets.) Johnson replaced Allman with a young man by the name of Robert Yates. Yates, who had worked at Holman and Moody under Ralph Moody, had the reputation for building powerful engines that lasted.

In 1972 Junior Johnson had a Hall of Fame race team. Along with Yates, there was crew chief Herb Nab, who was one of the best in the business, crewman Turkey Minton, and, of course, Bobby Allison behind the wheel. In 1972 Allison set a record, like Joe DiMaggio's 56-game hitting streak, that will never be broken. He had finished 1971 leading at one point in the last nine races of the season, and in 1972 he led the first *thirty* races! Thirty-nine in a row! The Allison-Johnson team was superb, though it failed to win the championship, much to everyone's disappointment. Richard Petty, supported and nurtured by Chrysler, won that honor, his fourth driving championship.

In addition to his ten wins that year, Allison would finish in the top ten in 27 of the 31 races, and earn $348,939 in purses. That Richard Petty won eight races and finished in the top ten in 28 of the 31 races only partially explains the Hatfield-McCoy feud that Allison and Petty had started in 1971 and continued throughout much of the 1972 racing season.

From the first race at Riverside to the last at the Texas World Speedway, everyone's eyes were on the red number 12 Coca-Cola car that some called "the drink box," and the Petty-blue number 43 STP car. They rarely were far apart all season long.

Behind the scenes, the relationship between Bobby and Junior Johnson was strained from the beginning. Right after Christmas they went to Daytona to test. The car was fast but didn't handle well.

"It was a handful," said Bobby, "and it was really hard on tires. Immediately."

Bobby said to Herb Nab, "We need to make a change on this chassis."

Bobby saw that the rear track bar on the car, the alignment bar for the rear wheels to the frame—was on the wrong side of the frame and was attached to the wrong side of the rear housing.

He told Nab, "It needs to be hooked right frame to left housing."

"That's the way Junior always had it when he drove," said Nab. "And it ain't changing."

Allison tested for three days. His times were fast, but he was alarmed at how terribly the car handled. He drove sideways around the huge Daytona track, something he would not be able to do safely with other cars racing around him close by. Moreover, Bobby saw that the tire wear was terrible the way the car was set up.

"When the tire gives up, you can't stop when you want to and get another one," said Bobby. "So here I am, and Junior won't talk to me. Junior would walk up to Herb Nab and say, 'Tell Bobby, we're going to do such and such . . .' He'd act like I wasn't even talking. And I couldn't deal with that very well."

Bobby, who in 1972 had upgraded from a Beechcraft to an Aerostar, flew from the Daytona test back to Junior's shop in North Wilkesboro. Riverside was the first race of the year, and Bobby wanted alterations made on the car.

Bobby said to Herb Nab, "Riverside is an important race, a road course with primarily right-hand turns, not left-hand turns. We need to take the Riverside car and mount the bar in the rear so it's pushing."

This time Nab didn't say no. He said, "Let me get Turkey Minton." Turkey was Johnson's fabricator. ("A neat guy," said Bobby.) Nab brought Minton over.

"Turkey, can you make a set of mounts where it's exactly opposite, so the bar can go click-click one way or the other like sliding the bolts out and back in?"

"Sure I can," said Minton.

"We really need this thing to be fast at Riverside, and pushing is fast," said Bobby. "We need it like that."

So they agreed to fix the car the way Bobby wanted it for Riverside. But when it was time to test, the bar still had not been changed. Bobby asked Nab if he would change it.

"Yeah, I will."

"Good deal."

But Nab hadn't lifted a finger to make the change. Nab told Bobby, "Run another lap. I want to try another tire."

Bobby ran another lap. The time was good. They would be close to the front, along with Richard Petty and Bobby Isaac.

When he came in, Bobby said to Nab, "Herb, swap that bar."

"I'm gonna," he said. But he didn't do anything.

Practice ended. Only then did Nab slide under the car and change the bar.

Years later Bobby explained, "What he was going to do was embarrass me, because this thing was not going to be as good, but it was going to be my deal, and that was going to shut me up forever.

"I was really unhappy about this. I didn't say anything to him. Junior wouldn't talk to me. Turkey Minton was doing what Herb told him to do. And so here we were."

The next day Bobby went out to qualify with the bar the way he wanted it. After driving the first lap, no time was announced.

Ordinarily at Riverside, the time of the first lap was usually the best, because the tires began to wear from the start. Bobby drove a second lap, came around, and it was announced he had established a new track record and would be the pole sitter.

Bobby came in. Everyone was happy, patting him on the back. Bobby was pleased to know his adjustment on the car worked very, very well.

"What was my first lap?" he asked the crew.

"Oh, they never called it," he was told.

"Why?"

"We don't know."

Bobby was not the type to leave well enough alone. He knew Joe Rector, an Alabaman who was an assistant to head scorer Morris Metcalf. The scoring was done in the aircraft control tower mounted in the infield at Riverside. Bobby climbed the steps of the control tower, and when he got to the top, he saw Rector, who motioned for him not to come any closer. Rector held his finger up to his lips for Bobby to keep quiet.

Bobby waited for Rector at the door, and when Rector finally emerged, he told Bobby, "You're on the pole. Shut up and don't say anything more. Please. Get out of here."

"Joe, what happened?" Bobby persisted.

"When you came by the first time," Rector said, "the time was so fast, Morris thought the clock malfunctioned. When the time was printed out, he tore it up and threw it into the wind. He's embarrassed, so don't say anything because there is nothing that can be done about it."

"Okay," he said, and he climbed back down. Once the race started, the car had an engine problem.

"It had a wet sump, and something went wrong with it," said Bobby. "We didn't win the race, which we should have won so easy."

It was time to go to Daytona.

When Bobby arrived at Daytona, he was gratified that Nab had changed the bar over to the way he wanted it, but was puzzled to see that Junior continued his practice of not talking to him about the car.

"He would say, 'Hi,' said Bobby, "but he wouldn't say, 'Hi, how are you?' I'd say, 'Junior, I went fishing and caught a bass the other day.'

"Oh yeah, how big was it?"

"Fourteen inches long, two and a half pounds."

"Oh great, must have been neat."

"Junior, how about changing the valve cover on the race car?"

Not a word. He wouldn't answer.

"Junior, let's change the rear wheel."

Silence.

Said Bobby, "I mean, he absolutely would not talk to me about the race car, period.

"And I had another big problem as I look at it now. I never thought then it was a problem, but I would help a competitor get his car better, because I was so confident I could beat them anyway.

"So I would be over at Buddy Baker's car, and I'd be helping him, and the professional racers all had the same thought: *Why are you helping your competitor?* So."

At Daytona, Herb Nab fixed the car the way Bobby wanted it, and Bobby couldn't have been happier. Bobby was fourth-fastest qualifying, and even though he didn't win one of the twin 125-qualifiers, he was pleased by the way things were going.

"By Saturday we were really ready to go," said Bobby. "We finished Happy Hour, and I was happy with that car, and we're going to beat them on Sunday."

Bobby arrived at the track Sunday.

"Herb said hello," said Bobby. "Even Junior said hello. I checked in and got ready to get in the car. Everything felt fine. Everything was working.

"I put the car in low gear and started. We came around, did the pace lap, and got the green flag. I revved the engine, pushed the clutch in, the clutch pedal stuck to the floor, and I damaged the engine."

Nab told Bobby, "Keep going. Get the best finish we can." Bobby drove the race with the damaged car and still managed to finish sixteenth.

"The thing was so rugged you could go on with a damaged engine and finish," Bobby said.

After the race was over, Bobby went over to Nab.

"What in the world did you guys do to me?" Bobby asked.

"Well," said Nab, "last night we decided to change the pressure plate to a new one that General Motors gave us, a diaphragm style."

Said Bobby years later, "The diaphragm style was famous for sticking in the disengaged position when the engine was turning rpms. Had I known they had put it in there, I would have been careful of it, because I was totally familiar with it. With the normal coil-spring pressure plate, you could push it turning 10,000 rpms and it still worked. With the diaphragm plate, if it was at 3,000 rpms, it was going to stay on the floor.

"So here we were with a poor finish."

Success was right around the corner, however. Richmond was next, and Bobby finished second to Richard Petty when his tires wore out. Then at Ontario, California, he finished second to A. J. Foyt.

At Rockingham, Bobby won the outside pole. But Herb Nab decided to pull what Bobby called "an Indian trick." He put the right-side tires on the left, and the left-side tires on the right. Which the NASCAR officials detected. As a penalty, Bobby had to start in the rear of the field.

The race began, and Bobby's car was so fast by lap 68 he was in the lead. Bobby led the race through lap 345, when his engine blew.

"So now here we were," said Bobby, "failure, failure, finish, finish, failure."

On March 26, 1972, at Atlanta, Bobby and Junior Johnson showed the racing world that they were going to be a force. Bobby made up a seven-second deficit in the final thirty laps and caught A. J. Foyt before 50,000 screaming fans. It was the first win for a Chevrolet on a superspeedway since Junior Johnson himself won at Charlotte in October 1963.

"We were a little bit redeemed," said Bobby, "and that was Coke's home ground, and they were pretty happy. Things smoothed out a little bit."

Allison, whose car sported a wedge engine with a large opening in the restrictor plate, went to Bristol and blew out the field to make it two in a row. Bobby Isaac finished second, four laps back, and Petty was third.

Petty bitched, "NASCAR has jacked the rules around so much to help that Chevy. Just once I'd like to be even with them."

Answered Bobby, "We win two races, and everyone says we have an advantage. I guess that's to be expected."

NASCAR refused to change the rules.

After a seventh-place finish at Darlington, on April 23, the next stop was North Wilkesboro, Junior Johnson's home track, where Richard Petty beat Allison by just two seconds in what Petty described as a "wing-doolie of a battle."

"I was leading that race, winning that race so easy," said Bobby, "and a caution flag right at the end put Petty right on my back bumper. Petty got into me and turned me sideways and got by me. And it made me really mad, so I put Petty *on top* of the fence in turn one on the white flag. I mean *on top* of the fence, but I didn't push him far enough.

"My car was bent up and full of smoke, but I was sure he was stuck up on the fence, and while I was going slow, he came past me to take the checkered flag, and he won the race, and I finished second.

"I was really mad at myself about that, but at least it was a decent finish, and at least I had stood up for myself.

"Petty was tough, boy. Early on he believed he was the King, and part of the privilege of the King is that nobody gives you a tough time. Nobody should mess with the King. He still feels that way a little bit today. He is still the King in his own mind. And he does a really good job at being the King. He's really kept the fans in his palm, and that's neat. And I give him a lot of credit for that. And I forgive him for some of the other stuff that I didn't like about him."

Bobby won his fifth race of the 1972 season in the Northern 500 at Trenton, New Jersey, on July 16, beating Bobby Isaac and Petty in 95-degree heat. Behind the scenes Bobby and Herb Nab fought over how to set up the car.

"I had run Trenton myself and won it both as a mile race and as a mile and a half," said Bobby. "I told Junior, 'Trenton has a right-hand turn in the front straightaway. That track has a dogleg in the back straightaway, a right-hand turn, and a wetsump oil pan will not survive there.'

"Richard Howard had bought a car from me from Alabama that had a dry sump. It was a homemade rig I had come up with, and it was really, really good. The car was leading Charlotte late in the race when Junior's engine had a failure, a valve spring or rocker arm or something. That car was pushed over to the side, but it was a front-steer-style car, where Junior's cars were the Holman and Moody rear-steer cars, which was okay with me, but I was confident the front steer would be better.

"I said, 'Herb, we really need to run the car you have from my shop at Trenton. We need to run the dry-sump engine. All you have to do is put that equipment on any one of the engines.'

"I had been doing some short-track racing somewhere up there, making appearances along the way, and when I got to Trenton they brought the Alabama car."

Bobby qualified for the Trenton race on the outside pole. Bobby Isaac had the inside pole.

"I then briefed Herb on some of the other chassis maintenance on the car," said Bobby. "The front lower A-frame had a stock rubber–style bushing for the lower A-frame mount. Those bushings gave out. They would tear up as the race went on. I said, 'Herb, why don't we have new bushings on these A-frames?'

"You want to run that car," Nab said defensively. "You run that car."

He resented Bobby's interference with his job as crew chief. If Bobby wanted to change something, he would have to do it himself. Bobby was more than happy to oblige. He went to a parts place near the Trenton Speedway and bought a set of bushings. He came back, and he looked in the car manual to see how to install them.

"I won that race so easily it wasn't even funny," said Bobby. "And Junior's remark was, 'He drove his own car so he drove it harder.' Which floored me. But we won the race, so I just gritted my teeth and went on.

"They never would run that car again. There were a couple of tracks where I wanted to try it, because I felt the chassis was better. But they refused to run that car anywhere else after that."

Bobby then went to Atlanta and won his third race in a row, beating Petty and David Pearson. Allison led the final eighty-eight laps.

At Talladega on August 6, 1972, Bobby finished third behind Remo Stott and James Hylton, and two weeks later he finished second to David Pearson at Michigan. Behind the scenes, Junior Johnson's silent treatment of Bobby was beginning to grate. At Michigan, Bobby wanted to make an adjustment to the car. Bobby was standing with Herb Nab when Junior walked by.

Junior said to Nab, "Tell Bobby we're going to change a gear and we'll also make a chassis change."

And Bobby replied with, "Herb, tell Junior to kiss my ass."

Johnson, who all along had refused to talk to Bobby about the car, did not respond. He just turned and walked away without saying a word.

"It really was subtracting from my sanity," said Bobby.

It was not, however, affecting his success. In the next race, at Nashville, Bobby beat Richard Petty in a controversial finish marred by a disputed official's call.

Once the race started, Allison and Petty ran away from the field. Three-quarters of the way through, Petty stopped to take on right-side tires, and when he headed back on the track, NASCAR official Bill Gazaway saw the traffic coming around, and he threw up the stop sign. Petty either didn't see it or ignored him. Gazaway black-flagged an enraged Petty, who pounded on the steering wheel in anger. He lost a lap, and it cost him the victory.

On September 10 at the Richmond Fairgrounds, the Allison-Petty paint trading, which had first broken out in 1966 and occurred again in 1971, resumed. Once again, the two drivers were the class of the field. With just over a hundred laps to go, Petty started things by tapping the back of Allison's car and passing him. As they reached the third turn, Allison smacked Petty's rear bumper. Petty's Plymouth headed up the track, hit the outside wall, and bounced back on the track. Petty managed to keep control and the lead.

Said Petty from the winner's circle, "I'm surprised the car still had wheels on it."

"The guy was good and the guy was tough," said Bobby years later. "He was good on pavement, and he was good on dirt, though by then there was no dirt left. I had admired how good he was on dirt in earlier years. A lot of guys are good on dirt *or* pavement. He was good on both."

Two weeks later, on September 24 at Martinsville, there was yet another controversy. Petty and Allison had lapped the field twice, with Bobby leading 432 of the 500 laps. Toward the end Allison was a car length from putting Petty a lap down. NASCAR ordered Petty to move over so Allison could pass him, but Petty ignored the flag. Allison had blocked him in the same situation often enough. Petty figured he'd give Allison some of the same medicine. He held his ground—and NASCAR didn't penalize him for it. When a caution came out, Petty was able to catch up.

For fifty laps Petty sat on Allison's bumper, hoping Bobby'd make a mistake. Petty moved inside him, climbed the curb, and hit the side of Allison's car, knocking off Allison's fuel cap. NASCAR then ordered Allison to come in and put it back on, and Allison ignored that order. When a caution came out, he went in and had it put back on.

In the end, Petty beat Allison by six seconds. NASCAR fined Allison $500 for ignoring the order to pit. Petty was not fined even though he had refused the order to move over.

"If you can ignore one flag, why can't you ignore them all?" asked Bobby. "If you must obey one flag, why shouldn't you have to obey them all?"

He added, "The other competitor [he didn't mention Petty by name] wrecked me and tore off my gas cap. Yet I get fined for ignoring the black flag."

At the end of the race, in his fervor to catch Petty, an enraged Allison wrecked two cars driven by Ben Arnold and Ed Negre, who were unlucky enough to be in his way. After the race a contrite Allison agreed to pay Negre $3,000 to fix his car out of his own pocket.

Said Bobby years later, "I was the outsider. I was the villain. The deck was stacked. Richard did stuff he got away with that other people couldn't, because he was the King. Here I was trying to win Martinsville, which I never won."

The next week, at North Wilkesboro, Allison and Petty staged one of the most exciting races in NASCAR history. Once again, the two drivers ran away from the field. They were four laps in front of everyone else when, with sixty laps to go, Petty sat on Allison's bumper. During the last forty laps, the two swapped leads ten times.

Trading paint has always been part of the game, but when a driver deliberately tries to wreck another driver, the game takes on a markedly darker tone. With three laps to go, Petty took the lead and was trying to hold off Allison. Bobby moved inside on the backstretch. He tried to pass a lapped car driven by Vic Parsons even though there wasn't enough room. Instead of backing off, Bobby tried to find a lane to get by Petty. There wasn't enough room, and the collision sent Petty into the wall as Allison took the lead.

Petty, who was a master at controlling his car after getting hit, recovered and sought revenge. As the cars went into turn one, he rammed into the side of Allison's car, bending the sheet metal of Allison's car into his tires. When Bobby's tires began to smoke, the white flag waved, signaling one lap to go.

Petty's front and back bumpers were lying on the track, and Bobby had to go around the debris or risk a flat tire. Allison suddenly swerved up the track while Petty kept his foot on the gas, passing Allison, taking the lead, and winning the race by two lengths.

After the race, the words weren't quite as civil as before. Petty accused Allison of "trying to put me in the boondocks."

Said Petty, "There's not going to be any trouble until he hurts me."

"I got under him fair and square, but he hit me so hard he bent my fender in," said Bobby. "When he did that, I just ran back into him."

Petty had the last word. "If I had films of this, I could sue him for assault with intent to kill, or something close to that."

It was a good thing they weren't feuding.

"They raced each other tooth and nail every race," said Eddie Allison.

There were no more incidents the rest of the year.

Bobby excelled at Charlotte on October 8 and beat Buddy Baker by two car lengths. It was Bobby's ninth win of the year. He made it number ten in the second-to-last race at Rockingham, when he beat Petty. Allison would have to finish ahead of Petty in the finale at the Texas Motor Speedway to win the points championship.

At home in Hueytown the week before the Texas 500, Bobby got a call from Ralph Moody. Holman and Moody had disbanded, but Ralph Moody was itching to go racing again. He told Bobby, "We got a deal put together. Come back and drive for me next year."

"Okay," said Bobby, who was fed up with Junior's silent treatment all year. "I'm with you."

Somehow, Junior Johnson found out what Bobby intended to do. Junior called Bobby on the phone at six in the morning.

Junior said to him, "Bobby, yes or no. Are you going to drive for us next year? If you're not, we have a chance to get the best driver in NASCAR right now." He was talking about Cale Yarborough, who had spent the last two years driving IndyCars. The fact that Junior didn't think *he* was the best driver in NASCAR hurt Bobby deeply.

Bobby, awakened from sleep, tersely replied, "Get him."

And with those two words, Bobby Allison walked away from Junior Johnson's race team. Had he not, there is no telling how many races the two would have won together.

I asked Bobby whether Junior wanted him to quit.

"Yeah," he said. "Yeah."

"He was as mad at you as you were at him apparently," I said.

"Apparently. And I never thought of it exactly like that until you said that, but yeah."

There was still one more race to go, at College Station in Texas. According to Bobby, Junior did what he could to make sure Bobby ran poorly that day.

"I had led every race all year long," said Bobby. "We go to College Station, and that car was so detuned, it was pitiful."

"Detuned?" I asked.

"They detuned the car so I wouldn't lead. Herb Nab was determined I wasn't going to get the credit for leading every race all year long. And when it looked like I was going to lead, he had me pit."

The Allison-Nab-Johnson feud cost Bobby the driving championship. When Petty finished third and Allison fourth, it was the third time Bobby would finish second in the points race. The Texas race, moreover, was the only race all year that Bobby didn't lead.

I asked Eddie Allison whether Bobby was disappointed he lost the title that year.

"It was, 'We'll get 'em next year,' said Eddie. "Bobby kept his disappointments pretty much wrapped inside himself. Even as close as brothers as we were, the disappointments were not external."

What Bobby also kept to himself was how angry he was at Junior Johnson.

One might have thought that the Junior Johnson–Bobby Allison team was so successful that each man would have put away his differences to stay together through the next decade. They were the perfect team, and they would have rewritten NASCAR history. But unfortunately for both of them, Bobby had a problem with authority, and Junior liked to call the shots all the time.

"Bobby wanted the race car like he wanted it," said Eddie. "And Junior was enough of a racer, he thought he could make the car go fast, and all Bobby had to do was drive it. That's more what broke the thing up than the money."

Which also was an issue. Bobby had brought the Coca-Cola sponsorship to Junior, and Junior kept all of the money in 1972. Junior felt that since he had to bear most of the costs—salaries, engine, cars, tires—the sponsorship money should go to him, the owner. The two also argued about the distribution of the winnings. After wins at Charlotte and Rockingham, and before the finale at Texas, they had a screaming match over who got how much. Bobby was feeling cheated, and so he made up his mind to take his Coca-Cola sponsorship with him and leave Junior.

When Junior Johnson sold his race team at the end of the 1995 season, after 139 wins with various drivers, including an eight-year run with Cale Yarborough, Johnson told his employees, "If we'd been able to keep Bobby Allison, we would have won 200 races, and Richard Petty wouldn't have."

Brother Eddie begged Bobby not to leave Junior. He said, "Bobby, please, stay in the car. At least let us get our cars built before you quit."

"Nah," Bobby replied, "I can't stay there no longer."

"Junior was as hard-headed as Bobby was," said Eddie. "Junior may have been harder-headed than Bobby. I begged him. I said, 'Gosh, Bobby, you can't do no better than this.'"

"Naw, we can do it better ourselves." Bobby said.

Bobby never regretted his decision, but Eddie sure did.

Said Eddie, "We were just trying to figure out what kind of cars to build for the next season, and then we got a crash course. And 1973 was a fiasco, and it got so bad in '74 that I said, 'I'm done.'"

CHAPTER 19

Bobby: IROC and Indy, 1973

After leaving the powerful Junior Johnson race team, Bobby Allison thought he would continue to have a strong race team when he reconnected with Ralph Moody, now an independent after he split from John Holman two years earlier.

"When Ralph called me to race with him," said Bobby, "I got the impression that he was somehow going to get his friends together to buy Holman and Moody away from John Holman. With a good general manager directing the business and Ralph directing the racing operation, that could have been *the* absolute top-of-the-line racing team, better than anything that came along at that point."

The problem, one that very few people knew, was that John Holman's jealousy of Ralph Moody was so great and his ego so huge, there was no way Holman would have sold out to Moody, no matter how much money he was offered.

Moody had started an engine-building company with Waddell Wilson, his head engine builder at Holman and Moody, but with the Ford Motor Company no longer behind him, Moody didn't have any of the resources he once had had.

Bobby decided he would drive a Chevy. He had raced Monte Carlos for Junior Johnson the year before, but Bobby saw in '73 that the new Monte Carlo was going to have a big square grille that looked very unaerodynamic. When Bobby looked at the Laguna, the next size down, he saw a fish-mouth front end that didn't appeal to him either. He decided to go with the even smaller Chevy Malibu.

"It had a nice smooth little curved header piece in the front," Bobby said. "So I chose that."

Ralph Moody wasn't connected to the auto executives the way John Holman had been at Holman and Moody. Bobby had never spent any time cozying up to the car executives in racing, either. When Bobby went to the Chevrolet people, he asked if they would give his race team a Laguna nose.

"No, we'll sell you one," he was told.

Years later Bobby said, "Let me figure out how to position myself." He paused. "I got zero help from Chevrolet."

Moody had told Bobby he had a sponsorship deal, but the deal had fallen apart, leaving Bobby little better off than if he were running the team himself.

He began 1973 in no shape to run for an entire season. Bobby had $100,000 coming from Coca-Cola, and he had money in the bank, having made a lot of money driving for Junior Johnson. In 1973 he would have to spend a significant amount of that money just to run.

Said Bobby about the money he made in 1973, "It allowed me to borrow even more."

Bobby built the chassis, and Ralph built the engines, but the engine program for Bobby's car often was behind, and more often than not the motor would blow up.

Bobby and Ralph Moody went to Riverside to begin the 1973 season. The week before the race, Allison, who loved to race regardless of the course or the type of car, drove in the inaugural running of the International Race of Champions series. The IROC president was Roger Penske, who came up with the idea of pitting the best drivers from the various race circuits—Grand National, Indy, United States Auto Club—against each other. Each driver was given an identical Porsche 911, and all the mechanics came from Germany. The idea was to make every car the same so that the skill of the driver would be the sole determinant of the outcome.

After Bobby was invited to participate, he went out and bought himself a Porsche 911 so he could become accustomed to driving it. Bobby tested at Riverside, and only Mark Donohue, a veteran Indy driver, was faster.

A raffle determined which driver was assigned to which car, and when Bobby went out to test his, the gearshift didn't work properly.

Bobby said a German mechanic told him, "It can't be the car's fault. It was made in Germany. It must be your fault."

In the race Bobby ran last. When Bobby Unser was assigned that car in the second race, he, too, finished last.

For the third race, Bobby had the misfortune of drawing his original car. When Bobby complained to Penske, he was told he was stuck. He would have to drive it anyway.

"Well, on the first lap it started smoking, but I wouldn't come in," said Bobby. "The longer I went, the more it smoked, and I knew it was making the Porsche people mad, but I was mad, too, so I just kept driving around and around with smoke pouring out. I proved what I'd told them all along, that that one car was lousy.

"I went right home and sold my Porsche as fast as I could."

Penske would get another opportunity see what Bobby could do in an open-wheel car. Also before the February Riverside race, Peter Brock hired Bobby to run at Riverside in a Datsun 510 Trans Am car. Bobby was on vacation, and he thought it might be fun to enter a different kind of race. Bobby was very fast in the car, and everyone there noticed.

Bobby was walking through the garage area talking to people, having a fine time for himself, when a stranger called his name, came over and shook hands.

"My name is Don Nichols," the man said, "and I run the UOP Shadow cars. I'd love you to race in my car." Bobby was under the impression that Nichols owned the cars or at the least was the general manager of the race team.

The UOP Shadow, which ran in the Can Am series, looked beautiful, but it didn't go very fast in competition compared to the German Porsches and British McLarens. Jackie Oliver, from Great Britain, was the Shadow team's primary driver. There was a second car, but no one who drove it ever went as fast as Oliver.

Nichols asked Bobby to drive the second Shadow. Bobby went out and ran, and when he came in, Nichols said to him, "Boy, we have to get you signed up. You were the third-fastest qualifier. You were seven miles an hour faster than Oliver."

When Oliver came in, he was furious. He started cussing at Nichols, who, it turned out, neither owned nor ran the race team. Nichols was the chief mechanic. Oliver was his equal.

"You sabotaged me, you rotten SOB," Oliver said to Nichols. "Allison is *not* driving this car."

Allison, who didn't want to get between the two of them, said to Oliver, "I'm here on vacation. You drive the car yourself." And he started to walk away.

Standing within earshot was Roger Penske, who even back in 1973 was one of the most influential figures in motor sports in the world.

Penske had watched the ease with which Bobby drove the Shadow around the Riverside road course.

"Hey, Bobby," he said, "you were really fast in that thing."

"It was kind of fun," said Bobby.

"I gotta get you in an IndyCar," said Penske.

"I don't want to be in an IndyCar," said Allison.

Bobby didn't know it, but the persistent Roger Penske was someone who refused to take no for an answer. He kept insisting, as Bobby kept refusing.

"I want to race stock cars," Bobby kept saying.

Then Roger Penske said the magic words.

"If you come to Ontario on Wednesday to test," he said, "just run a few laps. I'll pay you to do it."

Bobby was going into his NASCAR season with precious little money. Penske had hooked him.

"How much?" asked Bobby.

"I'll give you ten thousand dollars to test the car."

Talk about an offer Bobby couldn't refuse.

Said Allison years later, "I had won NASCAR races that didn't pay ten thousand dollars, and he's going to give me ten thousand to test his IndyCar."

"What time do you want me there?" Bobby said.

Bobby flew home to Alabama in his Aerostar Saturday night. He returned to California Tuesday night with his friend Tom Gloor.

When he arrived at the Ontario track to test, Bobby was surprised when Teddy Mayer, the McLaren team manager, expressed his anger over having to work with a driver who had never raced in an IndyCar before.

"I arrived at Indy," said Bobby, "and here comes this guy with a heavy brogue who used terrible, terrible language." Mayer, who lived abroad, was actually American, not British. He was born in Scranton, graduated from Yale University, and had gone to the Cornell School of Law, and he introduced himself to Bobby with the line, "I'm goddamned tired of being Roger Penske's goddamned baby-sitter."

Why does this person have to express himself so vulgarly? Bobby thought to himself.

At one time Teddy Mayer had been the right-hand man to Bruce McLaren, the genius behind the car that bore his name. When he died in a testing accident in June 1970 at the age of thirty-three, he left Mayer in charge of everything.

To anyone else, Teddy Mayer would have said, "I'm not going to do this with a rookie driver," but Roger Penske had chosen Allison, and Mayer wasn't about to offend him. (It was a smart move. In 1986 Mayer joined Roger Penske as vice president of Penske Racing.)

Penske, himself a racer in the 1960s, came to the realization that the day would come when racing would sell products like no advertising could. Racing, Penske visualized, would lead to big business. It was not long before Penske Enterprises became the multimillion-dollar conglomerate he had envisioned. Mayer, not about to make waves with Penske, was left to mutter and rave at the fact that Bobby had never been in an IndyCar.

"A front-driver, rear-engine car was totally new to me," said Bobby. "The car was totally open except for little wings in front of the front wheels. In my mind they were my front fenders. But I had never driven that car."

Bobby had driven Super Modifieds, similar to the IndyCars, around the South and had been very successful.

"I was curious," said Bobby. "And I was getting paid a lot of money to do this. I needed the money to go back to my NASCAR team to pay bills."

Mayer said to Bobby, "Get ready to run that car right there."

Said Bobby, "I put on my driving suit, climbed over in the car, and this little English guy, this little Limey, said to me, 'You gotta go slow in this car. Do you understand me? This car is going to kill you. In fifteen minutes I'm going to be calling your wife and telling her that you just killed yourself.'"

"Hey, I'll go slow," Bobby said.

Mayer hammered on. "You can't go fast. You can't arm-wrestle this car. You can't jerk the car around."

Bobby sat there listening.

"All right," said Mayer, "Go out and go a few laps."

Bobby went out and cautiously ran around the track several laps. He could actually see both front tires, and his mirrors allowed him to see the back ones as well. He mashed the gas, let up, mashed the gas, let up. He wiggled the steering wheel to see if there was any play. Then he drove into the pits.

"Boy," said the hauty Mayer sarcastically, "the big stock-car driver does one hundred thirty miles an hour in an IndyCar. Is that all you can do?"

Bobby did his best to hold his temper.

"You spent fifteen minutes telling me to go slow, so I went slow," Bobby said. "Now, if it's okay, I'll go out, and I'll go a little faster."

"Oh no," said Mayer, "we can't let you back out now. We're testing."

"Am I done then?" asked Bobby.

"We'll let you run this afternoon," said Mayer.

It was 8:30 in the morning.

"This afternoon?" asked Bobby

"This afternoon."

Bobby and Tom Gloor got in their rental car and drove away for a little sightseeing. They returned to the track around 2:30 in the afternoon.

"I came back in," said Bobby, "and the little Limey came walking up and he said, 'Okay, you'll run the same car again. Go and get ready.'"

Bobby put his driver's suit back on, and he got back into the McLaren.

"How fast can I go?" Bobby asked.

"You go as fast as you want," said Mayer. "Just be careful."

Bobby went out on the famed Indianapolis track and ran about ten laps. He was impressed with the machinery.

"The McLaren car at the time was really *the* A-number one piece of equipment," said Bobby.

Bobby came in. He took off his helmet. He was sitting in the car still wearing his head sock and full driving suit when Teddy Mayer crawled across the nose of the car screaming at him.

"You lying SOB," he said. "I hate a liar." Mayer grabbed Bobby by the shirt collar pulling Bobby toward him as he waved his other fist in Bobby's face.

While Mayer continued ranting how Bobby was a "lying SOB," Bobby unclipped his seat belts and grabbed Mayer's hands.

"I haven't lied to you about anything," said Bobby. "What are you talking about?"

"Mark Donohue and Peter Revson are the two best in the world in these cars," said Mayer. "Their best lap has been 192 miles an hour. You say you've never been in one of these cars, and you go out and do 191? You liar, you."

Bobby stood up in the car, brushed away Mayer's hands, and he said, "This morning is the first time in my life I ever sat in one of these cars, and I just earned my pay." Since Penske was paying him $10,000 just for the test, his obligation was over.

Eddie Allison had gone to Indy with Bobby to put the pit crew together for the race car. He had never seen an IndyCar race, and he noticed how difficult a time the drivers had driving those cars.

"I went with Bobby in '73," said Eddie, "and I got the biggest surprise of my life. I was out there on pit road. Cars went out and raced for two laps, and the drivers would come in, and here were these guys who we call hot-dog racers, and after they stopped in the pits, they couldn't remove their hands from the steering wheel. They would have a death grip on the steering wheel that they literally could not let go of the wheel. I asked myself, *How do these guys drive these cars?*

"I knew it wasn't easy, because Bobby couldn't just jump out of the car. But when he came in, he was at least able to take his hands off the steering wheel, and he laid it on the cowling of the car. For the rest of the guys, their veins were sticking out the backs of their hands as they held onto the steering wheel."

What Eddie Allison noticed immediately was that Bobby Allison, had he chosen to, could have competed and won on the IndyCar circuit. Eddie saw that Mark Donohue was outrunning everyone because he had the fastest car, but he also saw that because his car couldn't handle in the corners, he gave up a lot of that advantage.

"Bobby did not have that problem," said Eddie. "Bobby had fixed it. If only Roger Penske would have listened to Bobby and let him have what he wanted and needed, he'd have smoked the field. He could have beaten Gordon Johncock with one hand tied behind his back. Instead, the motor blew up on the first lap, and Johncock won the race.

Said Eddie Allison, "There are two great race car drivers in the world, Bobby Allison and A. J. Foyt. Foyt could drive anything. Didn't make any difference what kind of car it was. If he drove a two-wheel bicycle, he'd beat your butt with it.

"I told Foyt, 'You can drive any kind of race car on any kind of racetrack at any time. Take it out of the truck, put it on the track, and the first time you mash the gas pedal that race car is going to go as fast as that track will let it go.'

"The first time Bobby mashed the gas with an IndyCar was at Ontario, California. Bobby Unser was sitting on the wall watching, and his teeth fell out. He said, 'No man alive can drive a race car like that.'

"Bobby Unser was God's gift to the race car, and he couldn't even tote Bobby Allison's little finger driving a race car."

After Bobby tested for Roger Penske, he and friend Tom Gloor returned to Alabama to resume his Winston Cup preparation. Back home the next morning, Bobby received a phone call from Roger Penske.

"Man, you were fast in that thing," Penske said.

"The car went really fast," Bobby had to admit.

"I gotta get you to Indy," said Penske.

"Roger, I don't want to go to Indy."

But Bobby, still needing money badly, was easy prey for Roger Penske, who unbeknownst to him had a $10 million sponsorship deal.

"I'll give you $25,000 and half the winnings," said Penske.

"Wow!" said Bobby years later. "This was so much more than I had ever seen in NASCAR. The man was paying me $25,000 plus half the winnings, and that could have been really big."

"Okay," said Bobby, "what do we do next?"

Bobby signed a two-year contract with Penske to drive his Offenhausen 1-4–powered McLaren in the Indianapolis 500. Part of the deal was that Bobby would have to skip three NASCAR races, including the World 600 at Charlotte, that weekend to run at Indy in 1973.

Bobby went back to Indy to test. His crew chief was a fellow by the name of Earl McMillan. In the movie *Stroker Ace,* the mechanic's name was "Lugs." Bobby called McMillan "Lugs."

McMillan, who mutually respected Bobby, in turn called him, "Stroker."

Roger Penske attended the test.

"Run the car," Penske told Bobby. "If you want to make an adjustment to the car, you can do that, but if you do, Gary Bettenhausen has to test-drive the car before you're allowed to run it, because Gary understands these things, and he'll make sure you don't hurt yourself."

Bobby went out and ran a few laps, and his lap time was around 187 miles an hour. Gary Bettenhausen clocked 188 miles an hour. Mark Donohue, who was around 199, would be on the pole by a big margin.

Bobby told Lugs he thought if he could adjust the casters on the car, he could make it go faster.

"Lugs," he instructed, "put the left front caster to less than what you have in the car."

They jacked up the car, and Lugs made the adjustment. Then as Bobby requested, he reduced the caster on the right by a degree. They then reset the toe-in.

"Okay, Gary, drive this car for me."

Bettenhausen went out, and on the first lap he ran 194 miles an hour. On the second lap he ran 194, and the third lap he was at 194. Not only was he six miles an hour faster, but typically with the Indy cars, the first lap was fastest, the next lap a little slower, and the third lap even slower. With Bobby's adjustment the car maintained its speed.

"Wow," said Bobby. "What a difference!"

Bettenhausen came in all smiles.

"Man, what did you do to that car?" he asked.

"I changed the caster," Bobby said. Bettenhausen looked at him like he had seen a ghost.

"Oh, you can't do that in these IndyCars," Bettenhausen said. "Don't do that to my car."

"Gary," Bobby replied, "we won't do it to your car."

Gary left, shaking his head. Bobby went back onto the track and did a lap at 193 miles an hour.

Bobby was the rookie with the fastest lap time. He qualified twelfth at 192.308 miles an hour.

Bobby had a few days off, and then came Carburation Day the following Thursday. Bobby got back in the car, and he drove a slow lap. When he came back in, he noticed the caster had been put back the way it was originally.

"When we did the inspection," said Lugs, "we put the car in the standard set-up." It was their standard way of doing things, and they didn't want to upset the inspectors.

"Put the caster back for me," said Bobby. Lugs did as he was asked.

After a month of practice, the race was postponed a day because of rain. On Monday, Bobby started his car, got up to speed, and as he came out of turn two on the pace lap, his engine blew.

"What a bummer," said Bobby. "Except I got a lot of money, another $10,000 to add to my $25,000."

Driver Art Pollard had gotten killed on the first day of practice at the Brickyard, and in the 1973 Indy 500 race Swede Savage, who had driven for Holman and Moody, was killed in a fiery crash. Judy and Bobby both knew Swede and liked him.

Judy, who accompanied Bobby at Indy, was sitting in the family grandstand during the race with Bobby's dad and with son Davey, and she was forced to watch the whole race because she wasn't allowed to leave her seat until the very end.

She was horrified when Pollard was killed, shocked when Swede Savage was killed, and she watched once more in horror as the safety truck, rushing to try to rescue Savage, raced the wrong way on pit road and hit and killed a crewman, who landed twenty-five feet from where she was sitting.

"It was so bad," Judy said years later. "You spend weeks and weeks with these people, and you get to know them. It was really, really bad."

When that happened, Judy, who could be strong-willed and insistent when thwarted, insisted she be allowed to join Bobby in Gasoline Alley. She joined Bobby in the garage, really upset about the whole experience. She didn't like the dangerous nature of the cars, didn't like what had happened. She was in shock over having witnessed three deaths.

When the race ended, Roger Penske came over to say, "Well, we'll get them next year."

Judy said, "I don't ever want to come back here again."

"If you don't want to," said Penske, "you don't have to." Bobby had signed a two-year contract. Penske took the contract out of his briefcase, ripped it up, and handed it to Judy.

"I've always admired the man for that," said Bobby.

"Penske treated us really well," said Judy. "He paid Bobby very well, and I had a really good relationship with his wife, Kathy. I still love her to death."

"Let me tell you something everybody misses when they write about this business," said Humpy Wheeler. "The guys who raced in the 1960s and 1970s were put through it mentally and physically. It was the most terrible time in racing, a period when horsepower far exceeded safety. Bobby not only got through this period, but he got through it driving two very dangerous race cars, both the NASCAR car, but even more dangerous, the IndyCar.

"I was involved in a lot of tire testing in those days. We thought we knew how to set up and run cars at superspeedways. We didn't. What we were doing in those days was so primitive, it's a wonder more people didn't bite the dust."

CHAPTER 20

Bobby:
The Roger Penske Years

"I was hurtin' pretty good, but I couldn't pass it up."

—**Bobby Allison**

As the 1974 season began, racing in America was under the dark cloud of a gasoline crisis. Motorists had to wait in long lines to fill up, and sometimes filling stations ran out before noon. Bill France Jr. was looking to silence critics who thought stock car racing should be shut down during the nation's gas shortage. As one measure France Jr. declared that the distance of each race would be reduced ten percent.

In 1974 Bobby again entered the IROC competition at Riverside. This time everyone drove Chevrolet Camaros, and in the first of the three IROC races, Bobby collided with Bobby Unser and was seriously injured.

He was taken to the hospital in Riverside. Attendants removed his clothes and gave him a front-side only smock. X-rays were taken, and he was told to lie down and wait for a doctor. But Bobby hurt more lying down than sitting up, and after two hours of waiting, he became impatient. When friends came to see him, he asked them to go out in the hall and retrieve his clothes. He got dressed and left the hospital at around five in the evening.

He was back in his motel room about an hour later when the doctor called.

"Where are you?" the doctor asked.

"You know where I am because you called me," Bobby said.

The doctor said, "You have to come back to the hospital. You have a broken back. We didn't release you."

"You had me and you lost me, and I ain't coming back," Allison told him.

The doctor told him it would take about thirty days to heal and that he'd better take it easy.

Each IROC Camaro was a different color, and Bobby knew the black one was best and that he had been assigned the black one for the next day's race. He also knew he was scheduled to qualify first and that with the black Camaro, he'd be sitting on the pole.

"I was hurtin' pretty good, but I couldn't pass it up," said Bobby. "I showed up the next day and won, wire to wire.

"It was hurting so bad that I couldn't fly home for four or five days, but it would have hurt a whole lot more if I hadn't won the race."

Bobby Allison still had his Coca-Cola sponsorship, but by 1974 the $85,000 wasn't close to what he needed to run an independent race team on the Winston Cup circuit and be competitive. In 1974 the racing title was fought among three powerful, well-heeled race teams: Richard Petty's Dodge (10 wins), Cale Yarborough and Junior Johnson's Chevrolet (10 wins), and the David Pearson–Wood Brothers Mercury (7 wins). Those three cars took the checkered flag in twenty-seven of the thirty races in 1974. Bobby won two of the other three. He won at Richmond in his own Chevrolet, and he won in the final race at Ontario in a Roger Penske Matador.

Bobby hadn't had much luck with Penske's engines in the past, but Bobby took the Penske ride because he liked Roger Penske, and more important, he had no other option. Racing was expensive enough, but NASCAR was making things *a lot* more expensive by constantly changing the rules related to the size and power of the engines. Every rule change meant car owners had to buy new equipment and discard the old, and when NASCAR changed the rules three times during the '74 season, the financial drain was such that Bobby didn't have the means to keep up.

At the time Penske phoned Bobby in mid-June at Michigan, he was struggling, tearing out his hair, frustrated at his lack of success. At Michigan his car had mechanical failure. Once again he was resigned to having to quit Winston Cup racing to concentrate on driving in Sportsman races, something his brother Donnie and buddy Red Farmer had been doing for years.

After the Michigan race, Roger Penske came over to Bobby and told him, "Gary Bettenhausen got hurt in a spring car race, and I need you to run the Matador at Daytona on July 4. If you run it for me, I'll pay you and give you a percentage of the winnings."

Bobby needed the money desperately. Worse, his physical and mental health were deteriorating. When his car ran bad, he felt worse. He needed the opportunity to be competitive again.

"Whatever I run I need to have Coke on it because they have stuck with me through thick and thin," said Bobby.

The deal Penske had with the American Motors Corporation was that AMC was the only decal.

"The car is red, white, and blue," said Penske. "I'll see if we can have Coke on the car."

Bobby went to Vic Meinert at Coca-Cola and said, "We really need to run the AMC car. We'll put a big Coke patch on the hood, and we'll put the white Coca-Cola script on both the red quarter panels. It will look proper for Coke."

Meinert got the Coca-Cola brass to agree. Penske got AMC to go along as well.

Bobby went to Penske's race shop in Reading, Pennsylvania, to study the strange-looking car. Bobby took a liking to it. When Bobby studied the car, he could see that Penske's basic setup was quite different from his own.

The crew chief was a young fellow by the name of John Woodard, who everyone called Woody. Bobby asked Woody to make the changes he wanted, and Woody did them all.

"He did everything I asked of him," said Bobby. "The car got significantly changed from what they had prepared. We went to Daytona, and I was going to be on the pole by a respectable number.

"Here I was getting paid a driving fee and a percentage of the winnings," said Bobby, "and they are paying lap money, and I got about every dime of the lap money, because it was easy to lead. All of a sudden I'm getting some money to pay my bills.

"They are doing their deal, I'm driving the car," said Bobby. "I'm talking to Woody about how we adjust the car. And boy, this thing is really flying."

Suddenly, with fifteen laps to go in the Firecracker 400, the engine began missing. Bobby radioed his crew, "The engine blew up."

"No, it didn't," he was told. "Keep going. It won't fly apart. It'll finish. We've had this trouble before."

Despite the impaired engine, Bobby was able to finish a respectable fifth.

Penske's AMC engines were prepared in California by a company called Traco, which was owned by Jim Travers and his partner "Crabby" Coons.

Travers and Coons knew of Bobby's reputation for always wanting to tinker with the car and the engine, and when Penske signed Bobby, Traco issued a demand to Penske that Allison not be allowed to look under the hood.

"It was just ego," said Bobby. "I wasn't allowed to look at the spark plugs, the valve fittings, nothing. They said I couldn't look under the hood, period."

At Dover Bobby led and finished thirteenth. Bobby went to North Wilkesboro in his own car, and he didn't even qualify.

He was in the depths of despair when Roger Penske called him and said, 'Bobby, we're running an IndyCar test at Michigan with some new engine stuff we're doing. We got to put miles on the car. We need you to come drive the car. I know I told Judy you'd never have to drive one of these things again, but I'll pay you good if you come. I need you to run this test for me, because Mike Hiss, our current driver, can't stay. He'll be there Monday morning, but then he has to leave. You don't have to go fast. You just have to put laps on the car for me."

Bobby, needing the payday badly, flew his Aerostar to Michigan Monday morning. He landed on the back straightaway of the Michigan track, taxied the plane, and parked on the grass on the tri-oval on the front straightaway. Bobby walked to the garage area and met driver Mike Hiss.

"The only way to go fast in these cars is to hold the gas pedal wide open and drag the speed down with the brake using the other foot," Hiss told Bobby.

"Mike, I don't have to go fast," Bobby replied.

"Okay," said Hiss, "I'm gone. See ya."

Hiss had qualified in the car the week before at 179 miles an hour, which wasn't very good. Bobby got in the car.

"Go out and when you feel comfortable, we'll do five timed laps," Lugs told him.

Bobby went out and rode around. The McLaren felt good, and so Bobby held his hand up, signaling he was going to run for time. He mashed the gas, and after he came by after the second lap his time was 179.1 miles an hour. Bobby was pleased he had gone two laps and already was faster than Hiss. After another lap, the speed rose to 179.2 miles an hour. Bobby was patting himself on the back.

He came in, and Lugs said, 'Stroker, you know how fast you went?"

"I went 179.2," said Bobby.

"No," he said, "192. If you'd have been here yesterday, you'd have won the race." Then Lugs said, "I have to call the Captain," meaning Roger Penske.

Bobby did everything he could to stop him, but Lugs slipped away, found a phone in the Union 76 building, and called Penske with the news.

Penske called Bobby.

"Man," Penske said, "you love that thing."

"I told you I'd run a test for you," said Bobby, "and then I'm out of here. Goodbye." And he hung up the phone. Bobby gave Lugs grief for going behind his back and calling Penske, and Lugs apologized.

After breaking for lunch, Bobby took the McLaren out for one hundred-mile runs. He finished the first run, they refueled, and he went out again, when the engine blew. He came coasting in to a stop in the pit area, when Roger Penske put his left foot on the left front tire.

"Man," said Penske, "I gotta get you back in these cars. You were fast!"

"Roger, I don't want to run these cars," said Bobby. "Let's fix the Matador."

"Nah," said Penske, "We need to get you back in the IndyCar."

It was a battle of wills. Bobby wanted to look under the hood of Penske's Matador to find out why it kept failing at the end of the NASCAR races. Penske wanted Bobby to race his IndyCar. It was a stalemate.

Bobby continued to race Penske's Matador, but the engine problem kept repeating itself, and it was costing Bobby a lot of money. Finally, he said to Penske, "I have got to look at that engine. I'll take my engine guy with me from Alabama." His engine man was a Canadian by the name of Dave Vaselneiuck.

Penske gave in, and he called Traco to tell Travers and Coons that Bobby was coming to see them on Monday to look at their engines and figure out why the engine dropped a cylinder every race.

On Monday morning, Bobby went to Traco. He walked into the engine shop, and as soon as he walked in the door and saw the engine, he diagnosed what the problem was. Bobby was as brilliant diagnosing cars as the fictional Gil Grissom is with crime scenes long before the show *CSI* was ever put on TV.

"They were using an after-market aluminum rocker arm that will break if you put it on your mother's station wagon to get groceries," said Bobby. "It was a part that had a really bad reputation in the industry."

Bobby looked at it, and he said to Travers and Coons, "Those rocker arms are no good. Why are you using them?"

"We bought a case of those things," he was told, "and we're using them until they are used up."

Thought Bobby, *If they break and are no good, I don't care if you bought two cases.*

Bobby liked a rocker arm made by a company called Norris, and he went and bought a set of stainless steel rocker arms. Bobby had his assistant, Dave Vaselneiuck, install the new rocker arms and massage the engine a bit. At the time a good NASCAR engine achieved 525 horsepower. The Traco engine was pulling 505 horsepower.

"After Dave did his stuff," said Bobby, "the engine pulled 540 horsepower. Man, we were really doing okay."

Bobby took the engine to Ontario, and he won the race. According to Bobby, someone at Traco got even.

"Before the race, while the engine was apart," said Bobby, "I saw they had installed roller tappets, which were illegal. I had seen roller tappets in Darrell Waltrip's car the week before. The ones he had were conspicuous, and NASCAR ignored them. I told Crabby that the roller tappets were illegal, and Crabby said, 'I'm not going to waste my time with a flat-tappet camshaft. These are okay.'

"We put the engine in the car, we went to Ontario, and I won the race. I don't have proof, but I am sure that [one of my crew members] told NASCAR that the roller tappets were in there. Because you had to take one out to see it, and normal postrace inspection did not remove a tappet. Who else could have known it was there?

"I went to the press box, smiling and laughing. Roger had asked me not to fly my own airplane to Ontario, so I flew a commercial airliner home. I flew through the night, and I got off at Atlanta to change to go to Birmingham, and here was the *Atlanta Journal* with a headline on the front page of the paper. It said, "Allison Fined $9,100." They didn't take the win away, but $9,100 was almost as much as the race paid."

Allison was torn between quitting and staying. The year before he had raised a stink that led to inspectors finding oversized engines in Junior Johnson's and Richard Petty's cars. Allison had threatened to quit NASCAR if the cheating continued. He considered himself scrupulously honest, and here his reputation was being questioned in an episode of cheating. Bobby was angry, but practical. Since he knew he no longer could afford to race on his own, he decided he had to stay with Penske. But he vowed to keep a closer eye on what was being installed under the hood.

It would take the golden eye of television to give the car owners the exposure NASCAR racing needed to survive and thrive. In 1975 the American Broadcasting Company announced it would televise live the end of the Daytona 500 and the Atlanta 500. It would also tape five other races and play them on delay. With the races on TV, a corporate sponsor no longer would reach just the thousands in the stands. It would now reach millions of viewers all over the country.

And once TV could reach millions of viewers, it made financial sense for corporate sponsors to pay race car owners big bucks to put their logos and names on the race cars for all to see.

Holly Farms began its long association with Junior Johnson in 1976. Pepsi, Nitro 9, Cam 2, Armor-All, Gatorade, and Norris Industries all announced they would sponsor race cars for the season. In the past the Big Three car companies paid race teams money, and the only way a race team would lose support would be if the car company got out of racing. The corporate sponsors changed all that. Corporate executives did not want to be associated with losers. Also, the more the car ran up front, the more TV exposure the brand name would get. Corporations even hired people to time how much tube time the brand received. If you wanted to keep your sponsor, you had better win or at least run up front a lot.

The change in the way team owners raised money also meant that they had to be effective businessmen as well as have racing savvy. They needed to be like Pablo Picasso, who could not only paint a mean picture, but also manage the marketing, promotion, and salesmanship that getting rich in the art game required.

Roger Penske would turn out to be just such an artist-businessman. Born on February 20, 1937, Penske began as a racer, competing at the Akron Speedway. In 1961 and 1962 he entered the U.S. Grand Prix. He was named Sports Car Club of America (SCCA) Driver of the Year by *Sports Illustrated*.

The next year he was offered a chance to open a Chevrolet dealership in Philadelphia. He hesitated, because he wanted to race at Indy. He was told he had to choose, and he chose business over sport.

After founding the Penske Corporation in 1969, his car- and truck-leasing companies and 136 car dealerships today generate $14 billion annually. He owned the Michigan Speedway, the Nazareth Speedway, the North Carolina Motor Speedway, and the new California Speedway.

The Detroit-based car owner has won thirteen Indianapolis 500s with nine different drivers and nine Championship Auto Racing Teams (CART) titles. His Champ car team has won a hundred races with driver Gils deFerran. In NASCAR, he has won 64 Winston Cup races, including 55 by Rusty Wallace.

"I've been able to hire drivers better than me," said Penske about his decision not to drive in the Indy 500.

Bobby Allison was one of those drivers. At Riverside in 1975 in Roger Penske's Matador, Bobby led all but eighteen laps, and won the race handily. In the Daytona 500, he was beaten by Benny Parsons. Bobby had a faster car than Parsons, but Parsons was helped by Richard Petty, who, though far behind, wanted to make sure rival David Pearson didn't win. After Petty hooked up with Parsons, Benny wasn't catchable. Parsons beat Bobby by over a lap.

Though Bobby was leading in the points standings, Penske chose not to enter the Richmond race because of the lack of sponsorship. Allison wanted to run every race, but Bobby no longer could afford to run his own car on the Winston Cup circuit, so he announced he would run his own car on the Sportsman circuit any weekend Penske wasn't running Winston Cup.

Bobby went to Darlington on April 13, 1975. He was two laps behind the leaders with only forty laps to go, but when David Pearson and Benny Parsons collided toward the end, Bobby, rookie Darrell Waltrip, and Donnie Allison roared to the front.

Darrell led, when with eight laps to go, Bobby passed him and won by a single car length. It was Bobby's forty-sixth career win. Donnie finished third. Bobby then took time off to run five Indy races for Roger Penske.

"He totally . . . He was very persuasive about wanting me to run those Indy-Cars," said Bobby.

"He twisted your arm hard," I said.

"Yes," he said, "He used money, and he would say, 'Bobby, you gotta do it for me. You gotta do it.'"

"Roger wasn't used to people saying no to him," I said.

"I'm sure he wasn't," Bobby said. "He still isn't."

As talented as he was behind the wheel, Bobby's success at IndyCar racing was negligible. At Ontario he was running sixth, but after only 30 of the 200 laps, his engine blew. Allison nursed the open-wheel car to the infield before getting out in disgust. When he started to walk away, an official on a motorcycle rode over and told him that under Indy rules, the driver had to stay with the car. Bobby had other ideas.

"There's a snake wrapped around the pedals," he told the official. Come see." When the official got off his motorcycle to look for the imagined snake, Bobby jumped on the bike and roared into the garage area. He got a ride to his plane, and he listened to the rest of the race on the plane radio.

"I laughed the whole way home," Allison said.

A couple of weeks later Bobby went to Indianapolis with racer Tom Sneva to test. Bobby had complained about the setup, and Penske agreed to let Bobby have the final say. Bobby had to leave for a couple days, and when he returned, he found the setup changed by the crew chief. After an argument, Bobby put it back. After that, strange events began to plague the race team, enough to make Bobby wonder if somebody on his race team wasn't deliberately sabotaging the effort.

Allison was leading the Indianapolis 500 on lap 23, when he pitted. During the pit stop, a fuel valve vent broke, bathing him in methanol. A spark would have turned the car into an inferno.

"I was thinking, I'm going to burn up here," said Bobby. "How could I hold the throttle way open?"

Bobby fell back in the pack and was lapped. He pitted, and the crew plugged the hole, but on his third stop, the plug handle broke and would not allow more fuel to be added to the car. Allison got his lap back, but when a flywheel broke, his transmission was cooked, and his day was over.

Bobby coasted into the pits, and he shut off the engine. The crew pushed the car into the garage.

Commented Bobby sarcastically, "My best [Indy] finish was second—to last. Penske had an engine deal with some outfit back then. They were good engines, unless you wanted to drive fast. The first time I was there, the engine blew after a half lap. The second time it blew at the end of the first lap."

At Pocono in an IndyCar race, Bobby was fast enough in practice to sit on the pole, but the car was acting funny, and Bobby was informed that someone was tampering with the car. Bobby thought it best to quit, but Roger Penske talked him into continuing. In the race he blew another engine.

At Michigan Bobby drove both the IndyCar race and a USAC stock car race. In the IndyCar race Bobby was in the lead lap just before the end when the engine blew.

An angry Allison took off his helmet, his driving uniform, pulled off his driving shoes, and he threw them in a garbage can. He told Roger Penske, "I won't be needing these." Walking in his underwear and socks, he stormed out of the IndyCar garage area, changed uniforms, climbed into his stock car, and went out and won the USAC race.

At Rockingham Bobby escaped serious injury when three-quarters of the way through the race, he and Cale Yarborough brushed fenders on the backstretch. Bobby's car hit the outside wall, flew up into the air, and landed upside down. Bobby had a cooler of Coca-Cola positioned just behind the driver's seat, and when the car flipped, Coke spilled all over him.

When rescuers approached, he told them he couldn't see. "I'm hurt, and I'm blind," he said. He suffered from a badly cut eyeball. After three days in Memorial Hospital, he returned to racing. At Richmond he finished third to Dave Marcis and Petty.

Through April and May Bobby had a series of top-five finishes, but he didn't win a race. On July 10, 1976, he went to Elko, Minnesota, to drive in a Modified race.

"In 1976 Roger Penske only had me racing for him in the major races," said Bobby, "so I wasn't going to any of the NASCAR short-track races like I really wanted to, so reluctantly he allowed me to run my little short-track program where

I could make some spending money. I had an AMC Hornet with an AMC engine that really performed well.

"In July I went to Elko," a racetrack in Minnesota. Judy went, too, along with all four of the children, plus a nephew of Bobby's and a friend of the boys by the name of Greg Campbell. Judy brought the six children because she had begun going to Dr. David Morris, who specialized in curing people with allergies.

"Dr. Morris was way ahead of his time," said Judy. "He would test you by putting drops under your tongue, and a couple of hours later he'd know what was wrong. I sent a lot of people to him. Ned Jarrett even went to him."

Judy, another couple, and the six kids were sitting high in the grandstands. Bobby was leading the race, when he came off the fourth turn and hit some oil on the front straightaway. He lost control of his AMC Hornet, and the car hit an abutment, where the pit gate was located, head-on.

When Bobby crashed, Judy said to her friends, "Oh my God. Can you keep an eye on them?" And she took off, climbing right over the wall and the fence on top of the wall. She reached Bobby's car before the ambulance arrived.

A track official was trying to keep her from getting too close, but Judy could see Bobby slumped on the wheel, and blood everywhere. The ambulance came, but Bobby lay bleeding and unconscious for thirty minutes before rescue workers could free him from the crumpled wreckage. He suffered a broken nose and ribs, chest injuries, torn ligaments, and both feet were broken.

Judy went with Bobby in the ambulance. Bobby was in the emergency room all night long. He needed forty stitches to his face. He kept complaining about his feet, but when the doctors looked at them, they looked normal.

The next morning, the doctor came in, and Bobby was conscious. He said, "Doc, please look at my feet. They're really hurting me."

Judy was standing there when the doctor pulled back the covers. She could see his feet were black.

Right away, the doctor ordered X-rays. Twelve bones in both feet were broken.

The doctors put his feet in plaster casts and made special shoes for him.

"We don't want you to take these casts off for a while," he was told.

He also suffered a blow-out fracture of his right eye socket, causing double vision. This time he was hospitalized for four days. Two friends, Tom Gloor and T. D. Howton, flew him home in Howton's plane. Judy and the four children accompanied him.

Despite his injuries, Bobby was determined to race at Nashville the next Saturday night.

"NASCAR agreed all I had to do was start the race and run the pace lap, and I would get credit for the points," said Bobby.

When Bobby arrived in Nashville, he cut off the plaster casts and put on the shoes.

"He didn't break his ankles," said Eddie Allison. "He broke his feet. If it had broken his ankles, he couldn't have driven on Saturday. But it wasn't going to stop him from driving, because he was driving for Penske then.

"When he got in the car and raced at Nashville, I know he was hurting."

"It was painful, but not incredibly," said Bobby. "My whole attitude was, You do what you gotta do. Not running wasn't in the equation."

Neil Bonnett, his friend and protégé, qualified for him and won the pole. Bobby drove the pace lap, came in, and Bonnett went out and finished seventh in the race.

The big test of a driver is what happens to him after the first time he is badly injured. The racing world learned what Bobby Allison was made of after Elko.

"A lot of drivers might have kept racing after that, but you wouldn't see the spark anymore," said Humpy Wheeler. "Bobby busted his feet up, and he just showed the absolute, unbelievable toughness he had as a driver."

In the summer of 1976 Bobby, who thought of himself as something of an entrepreneur, decided to try his hand at promoting races at the Birmingham International Raceway. One move he made was to boost purses higher than at other tracks.

The promoting game is always a risky proposition because the one variable no one can control is the weather, and Bobby was incredibly unlucky. During the two years he put on races, twenty-three of the forty-four dates were rained out.

"I can help farmers, even today," says Bobby. "If farmers are in a drought, hire me to be a race promoter. I will get rain."

Bobby decided to enter the races he was promoting, figuring his presence would lead to bigger crowds, but that just angered the other drivers, who thought it a conflict of interest.

"The deal was fair," said Bobby. "You can look at my car anytime you want to. You can buy my tires anytime you want to."

Bobby saw that Goodyear and Firestone tires were very expensive for the drivers, more than $100 apiece, and because they wore so quickly and there were two feature races, drivers needed two sets of tires for every race date.

And so, for the 1977 season, Bobby made a deal with the Hoosier Tire Company to supply all his drivers with tires that were not only fifty bucks cheaper but lasted a lot longer.

When Bobby mandated that every driver run on Hoosiers, he had a rebellion on his hands. Most of the drivers, including good friends Neil Bonnett and Red Farmer, chose to boycott his races rather than run on Hoosiers.

As at many smaller tracks, Bobby had a rule that after each feature, the winner had to sell his tires for the price of a new tire if any competitor wanted to buy them. This rule was made to assure everyone that the tires were stock off the Hoosier company truck.

"It really floored me," said Bobby, "because I thought it was such a smart idea. What happened instead, the competitors not only refused to buy his tires, they boycotted the racetrack. They either had Goodyear or Firestones, and they criticized me very heavily."

Bobby finally was forced to admit defeat and allow everyone to use whatever brand of tire he wished. He also did away with the rule that allowed competitors to buy the winner's tires.

So they showed up with the tires they wanted, and Donnie Allison kept winning with the Hoosiers. Donnie won eight of the first nine features on the same set of tires! Bobby won the one Donnie didn't win. When Neil Bonnett finally put on Hoosiers, he won his first feature.

Bobby did not make money as a race promoter.

Bobby had a series of top-ten Winston Cup finishes in August and September, but still he didn't win a race. Toward the end of the 1976 season Roger Penske offered Bobby a very lucrative contract to drive his cars in ten NASCAR and ten USAC events. Bobby would earn a salary of $125,000 plus another $25,000 and 50 percent of the winnings if he entered the Indianapolis 500. After Bobby's crash at Elko, Penske wanted to protect Bobby from getting hurt, and so Bobby was not going to be allowed to drive in any other races.

Bobby had finished fourth in the NASCAR points race and had won $230,000 in purses, but it ate at him that he hadn't won a race. He also didn't think it right that he would not be allowed to race where he wanted to race on weekends Penske didn't schedule him to drive. Before the final race at Ontario, Bobby announced he was leaving the Penske race team.

The announcement surprised everyone, including Roger Penske. But Bobby felt trapped because Roger Penske was putting together an IndyCar for yet another try for Allison, and Bobby couldn't figure out any other way to get out of it.

"When I tried to discuss it with Roger," said Bobby, "he was totally fixed in his position, so I felt it was better not to say anything until the end of the season, to make the best effort I could for the stock car program.

"I felt I was too old to start a career in a different form of racing. I had devoted my life to Winston Cup racing, and I really wanted to do that. I had finished second in the points a few times, and I really wanted to compete in NASCAR. I felt you couldn't do both NASCAR and Indy properly, so my choice was NASCAR.

"Roger wanted to do it his way, and I didn't want to do it his way. He was so incredibly persuasive. I could go to a meeting with him and have all my ammunition ready, and he'd just totally disarm me. I'd be smiling and saying, 'Roger, you're right. We'll do it your way.' And I'd walk out of the meeting and say to myself, *What did I just do?*"

Despite his best effort, Bobby didn't win a single race in 1976.

"That was heartbreaking for me," he said.

CHAPTER 21

Donnie:
Outsmarted by the Gardners

"They were strange people. All I can say about the whole deal is, What goes around, comes around."

—**Pat Allison**

In 1971, Donnie Allison got a ride with the famed Wood Brothers after Banjo Matthews folded his team. Leonard and Glen Wood won almost one hundred races over a fifty-year career with such drivers as Cale Yarborough, David Pearson, and Neil Bonnett. It would be Donnie's best opportunity for success, but unfortunately part of one season would be all the chance he would get.

After A. J. Foyt and the Woods parted company, they hired Donnie for the rest of the 1971 season, a total of eleven races. Donnie made the most of his opportunity. He won five poles, won at Talladega, beating brother Bobby, and had four other impressive top fives. He would have won at Martinsville, but blew an engine late in the race. At Darlington, Donnie had the lead with just eleven laps to go, when his car began to smoke. Buddy Baker won, and Donnie finished fourth.

On May 16, 1971, Donnie drove for the first time on the Talladega track. He had boycotted the race in 1969 and hadn't entered either race in 1970. With one lap to go, the race came down to Donnie or Buddy Baker. Donnie was in the lead, and when Baker chose not to try to pass him, Baker was passed by Bobby, who just did get past him for second place. It was the fourth time Donnie and Bobby ran one and two.

"I had the other two races won, but we didn't finish," said Donnie. "I was determined not to let this one slip away."

"I finished second," said Bobby. "My car was better in the long run, but the Wood Brothers were able to get their car to respond to pit stops and fresh tires.

There was a restart at the end where Donnie beat me. Leonard Wood had selected a transmission that accelerated way better than the regular stuff."

After Donnie finished the Indianapolis 500, he flew back to Charlotte to enter the World 600. On May 30, 1971, at Charlotte, Bobby, in his second start for Holman and Moody, finally beat Donnie in head-to-head competition.

This was the season Bobby and Richard Petty won most of the races during the second half of the year. When the season ended, A. J. Foyt came back to the Wood Brothers, and Donnie was let go.

"A.J. had a lot of clout," said Bobby. "Purolator was their sponsor, and Paul Cameron, the CEO of Purolator, was really infatuated with A. J. Foyt. Even though Donnie had done really well, he didn't dominate, and when A.J. wanted to come back, Donnie was let go."

An independent once again, Donnie entered but ten Grand National races in 1972. He had two top-five finishes and otherwise wasn't a factor. One of those top fives was a third-place finish in a Roger Penske Matador at Riverside. Donnie drove a couple of races for Bud Moore, but didn't finish. In all, Donnie earned $16,000 on the Grand National circuit. He was looking for a race team that would embrace him.

Unfortunately for Donnie, his desire to continue racing made him fair game for a team that called itself DiGard. The three principals were a man named Mike DiProspero, and two brothers named Gardner. They were from Connecticut—Yankees to say the least. In 1973, Donnie was invited to become a partner in the new race team.

"The leader of the group was Bill Gardner," said Bobby. "His brother Jim was actually older, but Jim worked for Bill. Bill was the operator of the deal. He got ahold of Donnie. Donnie had some equipment and some tools, and so he signed over all of his racing equipment, including his pickup truck, to the Gardners in exchange for stock in the company.

"Bill Gardner told a good story. 'I'm going to get sponsorship money, and we're going to race, and we're going to have a first-class race team, and I'm going to hire good people . . .'"

Say what you want about the Gardners, they knew talent. Robert Yates, the engine builder, and Mario Rossi, Bobby's old crew chief, led the team.

"Bill Gardner was the main player in DiGard, a big businessman," said Pat Allison. "After talking with him, we put everything we had, all our racing equipment, into DiGard. We had everything you needed to run Late Model, trucks, equipment, engines, a car, whatever. We were thinking big. We felt we were part of the DiGard team. We heard wonderful promises, which never came about. We were given shares in DiGard, which were basically worth nothing later on.

"We still own a little house in Hueytown, and that's where DiGard was started, in Donnie's garage."

In 1973 Donnie and the DiGard team entered fourteen races and didn't win any. His best run came on May 6, 1973, at Talladega, when Donnie finished second to

David Pearson, the Wood Brothers' new hotshot. The race was marked by a crash involving twenty-one cars.

Midway through the first season, the Gardners told Donnie they wanted to move the race shop closer to NASCAR's Southeast roots. The choice was between Charlotte and Daytona, and the Gardners chose Daytona.

Donnie rarely finished races the second half of the year. His cars suffered engine failure, a cracked windshield, and a broken wheel.

In 1974, the team improved, as Donnie had five top-ten finishes and five top fives. The constant changes in the rules concerning the size of the engines made Robert Yates's job extremely difficult.

It looked like Donnie would win the Daytona 500 in 1974, as he led the race with only eleven laps to go. Ahead by thirty-eight seconds, he ran over debris after Bob Burcham's engine blew up, and he blew out his two front tires, and finished sixth.

"I was running so good, I was beginning to feel sorry for Richard," said Donnie. "Then, before I knew it, I was feeling more sorry for myself."

Donnie's best finish in '74 was a second to Richard Petty at Nashville on May 12. The race was stopped by rain and resumed the following day. The second half of the '74 season was very much like the second half of the '73 season, a series a blown engines and crashes. A third-place at Rockingham didn't move the Gardners to want to keep him.

A third-place finish at Darlington on April 13, 1975, was Donnie's only decent performance the following year. Failed brakes, blown engines, and fighting among the crew marked the end of Donnie's days with DiGard.

After Donnie finished fifth in the Daytona Firecracker 500 in July 1975, the Gardners told the press that Donnie was as good as gone.

"The doors were locked at the shop, and that was it," said Pat. "We packed our stuff and came back to Hueytown."

At the end of the '75 season, DiGard hired Darrell Waltrip, with whom they feuded for the next four years. According to Pat and Bobby, Donnie never got back the two hundred thousand dollar investment he had personally made in the race team. Donnie and Pat had to start over from scratch.

"Gardner had his own special contract," said Bobby. "I know, because I drove for him later on. He had a clause in the contract that said if Donnie left for any reason, he had to forfeit all of his equipment to Gardner. I'm sure he signed a contract that said he would forfeit everything if he left under any circumstance not one hundred percent to Gardner's liking and choosing."

"After DiGard fired Donnie, he came back to Hueytown," said Eddie Allison. "Heck, that was hard for Donnie. If he hadn't had some good friends here—he and his family got to move in with an elderly gentleman and his wife, a friend of his, and basically they saved his life. It gave him an opportunity to get started again without it costing any money."

"We were foolish," said Pat Allison. "We should have kept our equipment. We were very trusting, and we didn't have the business know-how to get our own lawyer and listen to him.

"They were strange people. All I can say about the whole deal is, What goes around, comes around. You learn by your lessons, and you have to look at it like it was a lesson.

"It was the absolute worst mistake we ever made in racing. It set us back about twenty years."

Said Eddie, "I helped Donnie in 1975 after his deal with DiGard fell apart. He came back home, and we went short-track racing. We built this little Camaro in the garage down the street, and he and I had ideas about what we wanted to do, and as we got the car put together, it really started to look good, we took it out to Opp, Alabama, a little bitty track, a nice little track to race on, not high-banked, but just enough bank that you could really drive the thing in the corner, and if the car handled, you could drive outside of somebody and drive it home.

"We got there and unloaded, and Donnie said, 'Boy, does it feel good.' We were a second faster than any other car there. "The next week we went to Birmingham, a Saturday night race, and we took the car out on the track and ran it three laps, and the car that night was unbelievable.

"We came in and Donnie said, 'If I don't keep my foot on the gas, this thing runs in the dirt.'

"'Donnie, you've had a car like that before,' I said. "Remember that little Crosley? That's what it did.'"

"When we got done with that car, I didn't fool with anybody anymore. It was too much aggravation, until 1999, when I helped Ken McFarland with his Legacy car."

Eddie suffered physically and mentally while he was involved in racing, and even afterward.

"Eddie was a very nervous type," said Bobby. "He was very, very involved in everything he went to do. He would get totally involved. He never could get his emotions down to the point where he could deal with the everyday problems or with the big things that often came along in racing. He wasn't equipped to handle the pressure."

"For years and years I went to ulcer doctors," said Eddie, "and I never had an ulcer. But I thought I did. It would get to the point where I couldn't navigate a lick. I had to stop and stay in bed for three days to refresh my body. I didn't get to refresh my mind, because I couldn't fix that part."

It took the right psychological help to get Eddie well.

"My body stopped hurting when I happened to get to the right man, and he's my pride and joy today. We haven't talked in years, and I haven't needed to."

As for Donnie, he hooked up with a veteran racer by the name of Hoss Ellington. Hoss had never won a race, but Donnie needed a ride. Kindred spirits, their relationship would last for five full seasons.

CHAPTER 22

Neil Bonnett: Susan

"The more Neil got involved with racing, the less he wanted to be involved with his pipe fitting, which put food on the table."

—**Sue Bonnett**

The three pioneers of the Alabama Gang were Bobby Allison, Donnie Allison, and Red Farmer. The fourth member of the gang, Neil Bonnett, began racing in the Birmingham area in 1963, when he was seventeen. Before too long Bonnett was winning regularly in the Sportsman division, and it wasn't long after that that he had visions of competing in Winston Cup racing. By 1970 Bonnett moved to Hueytown to live closer to Bobby, Donnie, and Red, who had become fans and patrons of the well-spoken, hard-charging Bonnett.

In 1962 Neil went out on a blind date with Susan McAdams. The two were in high school. Susan's closest friend, Diane Vallely, was dating a guy named Bill Green, and Bill was best friends with Neil. Bill and Diane had been trying to get together, but Bill didn't have a car. Neil did. So Bill and Diane arranged for Susan to go out with Neil, so they'd have transportation. Under the cloud of such deviousness does love blossom.

When Diane told Susan about Neil, Susan asked her what he was like.

"He's a great guy. You'll love him," Diane said. But Diane didn't know him, and Susan suspected that, and it made her very uncomfortable.

"I had heard some things about Neil," said Susan. "I heard he was wild. I was very leery about the whole thing. He was probably the fourth person I ever dated."

The plan was to go to the drive-in to see the movie *The Pit and the Pendulum*, a horror film based on the Edgar Allan Poe short story. By the end of the evening Susan and Neil were partners for life.

"I don't know," said Susan. "It was kind of an instant thing. We just hit it off, and we were never apart from then on. We never dated anyone else."

"What was it about Neil that caused the attraction?" I asked her.

"I wish I knew," she said. "I don't really know. It was just instant knowing? You know?"

At the time they met, Neil wasn't involved in stock car racing except as a spectator. His father had always loved the sport, and he had taken Neil to the old Iron Bowl out at Irondale, Alabama, to watch the races. Neil couldn't afford to go to the races at Birmingham International Raceway, so on Sunday afternoons he and Susan would drive up a hill two blocks from the track where they could see the third and fourth corners, and they'd watch.

"Neil always wanted to race," said Susan. "He hadn't had a car very long before I met him, and once he got his car, he started slipping off and going to the drag races at Lassiter Mountain and Cherokee Beach in a little place below Bessemer, tearing up the transmission and telling his dad it happened on the street."

Susan didn't go with him because her parents didn't let her stay out late. Susan says Neil's dad would believe his story and buy him a new transmission.

"Neil was an only child, and they pretty much doted on him," said Susan.

But after two blown transmissions, Neil's dad figured out what was going on. Not that he was disappointed. Neil's dad himself loved racing. He would take his speedboat out on the river and run it as fast as he could.

Neil and Susan married when they were seventeen. Neil was working as a bagger at Hills Grocery.

"He wasn't making much money, and we were struggling, and his mom and dad helped us out quite a bit," said Susan. "We lived with them to begin with, and then they got us an apartment over in Fairfield, and we moved in, and Neil started checking around about getting into some kind of career."

The career he chose was pipe fitting, and for five years he went to school to study it two or three nights a week. Though members of the pipe fitters' union were selected because they were relatives, Neil managed to pass the test and get in even though he didn't have any pull.

Neil worked long hours as a pipe fitter, making $12 an hour. But it was dangerous work. He would work high in the air on skyscrapers, walking across narrow beams with no nets in the cold and the heat.

"What scared Neil Bonnett most was having to walk twenty stories up on a six-inch beam," said Susan. "When you look down, you are staring death in the face. He lost three close friends to falls."

Bonnett decided to go into a profession that was safer: stock car racing.

Years after he quit as a pipe fitter, he would say, "When your best friend fell, you didn't wonder if he made it; you knew what happened to him. When somebody crashes [in a race], I can go to the hospital the next day and sit up with him."

Said Sue Bonnett, "He was way up there, and most of the jobs were out of town, and he was working six days a week, but whenever we got the chance, we'd sit on top of the hill and watch them race [at Birmingham International Raceway]."

"Was that romantic?" I asked her.

"Not for me," she said. "But it was what he liked to do, so I was okay with it."

While Neil was living with his parents, occasionally from his bedroom he would hear the roar of a race car engine being cranked up.

"Someone has a race car," Neil told Susan.

He kept searching until he found where the noise came from. Three blocks away lived a racer by the name of Lee Hurley. Neil started hanging out at Lee's garage, watching him work, picking up tips around the shop.

"He just made himself at home," said Susan.

Lee Hurley raced at Birmingham, at Montgomery, at Huntsville, and at the Rocket Speedway at Dothan, Alabama. One day Lee took Neil with him to practice at Birmingham. Lee had broken his leg in an accident and couldn't drive, and he asked Neil if he wanted to try driving.

"Neil had been hanging around for so long," said Susan, "and that was right up Neil's alley."

Two friends of Hurley, Anthony Artoli and Bob Guined, had built a Cadet car, and they were looking for someone to drive it. Hurley suggested Neil.

Bonnett began racing on the short tracks around Birmingham at age seventeen. He won a couple of races that first year driving Cadet cars, and the next year he and his two car owners moved up to the Sportsman division, where he won 19 of 26 races.

"He did excellent," said Susan. "I can remember Anthony saying he was just such a natural. If you saw him back in those days, you just knew it was what he was supposed to do. Which was not too exciting for me. Because the more he got involved with it, the less he wanted to be involved with his pipe fitting, which put food on the table. The wife and the kids worry about that."

Neil Bonnett would fit pipes by day and race by night.

"In other words," said Sue, "we didn't sleep a whole lot. We traveled on the weekends, and he worked during the week."

Neil's grand plan was to drive on the Grand National circuit. He got his first taste of superspeedway racing when he drove at the big Talladega track in the Sportsman division.

"When Neil was driving a Sportsman car for Artoli and Guined," said Sue, "the person who sponsored them was Butch Nelson. Butch is a longtime friend who later went into business with Neil in several ventures. Butch was the sponsor when Neil drove his Sportsman car at Talladega. He had to run a last-chance race to get in, and so to make the car go faster, they put in some type of fuel [additive], and it caught on fire and blew up.

"Then he went to Daytona and wrecked there."

Fire and wreckage, rather than being a deterrent, only whetted Neil's appetite for more. Artoli and Guined didn't have the financial means to race on the Grand National level, so Neil decided he needed to hook up with someone who did.

He knew he needed to start hanging around shops that were building cars that ran the Grand National circuit, and down the road in Hueytown there were three racers doing just that, Bobby Allison, Donnie Allison, and Red Farmer, who themselves couldn't help but notice how dominant Neil was on the local tracks.

Neil, Bobby, Donnie, and Red Farmer quickly became fast friends, and Neil decided to move his family to Hueytown so he could work more closely with Bobby and Red.

"He was forever in and out of those places trying to find out everything he could," said Sue. "At that time Neil would have paid to drive. He just loved doing it.

"The next thing I knew, Neil was helping Bobby and traveling with Bobby to the Grand National races. Even though he wasn't employed by Bobby, he left his pipe-fitting job. He just wanted so badly to get his foot in the door, so me and our two children had to make a sacrifice for this to take place."

"Did you ever say to him, 'This is a terrible price to pay?'" I asked.

"It wouldn't have made any difference," she said. "But no, it wasn't terrible, because I knew it was what he wanted to do. He had it in his heart to do it. How could I tell him he couldn't do it?

"And Neil was a person, if he believed he could do something, he was going to do it. Also, I could see when he started hanging around with Bobby how his attitude about life changed: he was happy. And finally, eventually, Bobby got so involved with his own car and all the things he was doing that he needed extra help, so one day he said to Neil, 'I'll build you a car, and when I can't make an appearance somewhere, I'll send you.'"

Neil was thrilled. Bobby gave him part of the winnings, so finally Neil was earning some money racing.

One wouldn't think a promoter would accept a substitute when the driver they wanted in their race was the renowned Bobby Allison, but Allison would tell the promoter, "Look for a country hick with his nose in the air and his cold blue eyes on the victory cup."

Bonnett once said, "I was like a bounty hunter. Wherever I went, I loaded my gun and shot people down. I'd blow in, then blow them out of the weeds."

Said Sue Bonnett, "When people would call Bobby and say, 'We need you. Can you make an appearance and drive at Trenton, New Jersey?' Bobby would say, 'I can't come, but I will send my protégé, Neil Bonnett.'

"They would say, 'Neil who?' So that's what he put on his car. 'Neil who?' And the couple of years Neil drove for Bobby, he won something like forty-nine or fifty races, so he was getting known. He would go and run and put on a really good show, and they would remember him."

"In 1978–79, Neil entered eighty races and won sixty of them," said Bobby Allison.

Bonnett won so much that when a promoter asked how much he wanted for a race, he would say, 'Forget about that, my man. What's your trophy look like and how much are you gonna give me for winning it?"

With the winnings, Bonnett built himself a Grand National car.

"Bobby helped him," said Susan Bonnett. "Bobby told him he could slowly take the time and build his own car in his shop. And that's what he did."

In 1974 Bonnett entered two Grand National races. In May he went to Talladega and finished forty-fifth. At Daytona he failed to qualify. The two tries cost him whatever extra money he had, but the thrill of racing at the Grand National level made him more determined than ever.

"He didn't want to go back to Sportsman racing once he did that," said Susan Bonnett. "He wanted to move on up."

CHAPTER 23

Bobby: Bud Moore Saves Him

Leaving Roger Penske almost cost Bobby his career. Bobby announced that in 1977 he would run his own equipment. He asked his fans which car he should drive. Not surprisingly, the answer came back: the funky-looking Matador.

"The fans came strong for the Matador," said Bobby, "and that was good for me because I had maintained a friendship with the AMC folks. I called them up and said, 'Let's go run.'

"They said, 'Okay, let's do it.'"

But the best AMC could do financially was to pay Bobby to build a car to go to Riverside. AMC sent him the parts he needed. Bobby signed First National City Travelers Checks to be his sponsor after his Coca-Cola sponsorship went away.

In 1976 Vic Meinert, Bobby's connection to the Coca-Cola brass, was transferred. His replacement, Henry Brandees, loved soccer, and took Bobby's Coke money and plowed it into World Cup soccer.

Citicorp had been an associate sponsor on his car when Bobby drove for Roger Penske the year before. Bobby called Fred Stecker of Citicorp and said, 'We need sponsorship money.' Stecker, a fan of Bobby's, obliged.

But in 1977, driving on his own, Bobby Allison had the worst season of his career. After a winless year in 1976, he had no wins and only five top-five finishes in 1977. He blew more engines than he did finish races, and it was beginning to look like his racing career might be coming to an end.

"I had a real problem," said Bobby. "I had hired some engine guys, and they and my mechanics took the attitude that the AMC Matador wasn't as worthy of their best efforts as the Ford, Chevrolet, or Chrysler products.

"That's when Neil Bonnett came in and gave me a hand.

"I was working on the AMC engines by myself in Hueytown one afternoon when Neil walked in. He had been to his regular job as a pipe fitter until quitting time, and then he came to see me. He wouldn't take any pay. He was the best employee I had, and beside that, he was free. Of all the guys, he was my most productive worker."

From the middle of the 1976 season through February 1978, Bobby Allison didn't win a single race, a skein of sixty-seven races. His health, meanwhile, deteriorated. Worried and stressed, his weight dropped from a robust 200 pounds to a scrawny 145 pounds.

"It was fatigue and a lack of personal care," said Bobby. "Worry was part of it, but just a part. The other part was my disappointment in my inability to achieve success. It was so disheartening. I knew I could go good in a car. But I could hear the hangers-on who said, 'You need to quit. You're too old. You've lost it.' And I certainly didn't feel like I had. All those things contributed to a decline in my personal health."

In June, Bobby flew to Disney World in Orlando to celebrate his parents' fiftieth wedding anniversary. During the evening he became nauseous, and his friend Chuck Stallings had to fly him home to Birmingham. Tests results indicated fatigue. Bobby was sure it was something far worse.

After the '77 season he received a phone call from Bud Moore. "I know you've been doing lousy," said Moore, "and I've been doing lousy, and I think we ought to see if we can get together."

Bobby, hopeful he could bring back the magic, agreed.

"His cars had done pretty good from time to time," said Bobby, "but inconsistently. He had won races with Buddy Baker as late as 1977. What happened, Buddy got an offer to go to M. C. Anderson, who looked like he was putting together a stronger, newer, fancier team. So Buddy was gone, and Bud called me up and said, 'I need you to drive my car.'

"I don't know because I'm feeling so bad," Bobby told Bud. When Bobby came to drive for Bud Moore, the two had a mutual admiration that allowed them to work together as a team.

Bud Moore ran a Ford with the Banjo Matthews front suspension, a configuration Bobby knew very well. Bud respected Bobby's ability to make a car better, and so when Bobby suggested some changes to the car, Bud was happy to let him go to work.

Bobby, honest to a fault, wanted Moore to know before he signed on that he was suffering from spells of nausea.

"Don't worry about it," said Moore.

The team went to Riverside and qualified well, but the engine blew up early in the race. At Daytona, the car was running well in the twin 125s when Buddy Baker ran into Bobby and wrecked him. He finished an ignominious thirtieth.

After the race Bobby was ill, sick to his stomach.

"I didn't know what it was," Bobby said. "I knew I was weak, and I felt bad. I couldn't eat, and if I ate, I'd be nauseated."

At Daytona, Bobby drove two warm-up laps in practice when the engine blew.

"Don't worry about it," said Moore. "We'll fix it and get it going again."

"Don't hurry," said Bobby. "I'm going back to the hotel to lay down. I'm not feeling good."

Bobby was physically ill, and he was depressed. He feared he would have to go through another season like the last one. At age thirty-eight he was concerned that maybe, just maybe, he was washed up.

The next day the car had a new engine, and Bobby's times were respectable. At Daytona in one of the preliminary races, Bobby was wiped out by Buddy Baker halfway through the race. His nausea returned while he was riding in the wrecker. He returned to his hotel room to rest and hide.

He hadn't won in 1977, so he wasn't entered in Saturday's Busch Clash.

On Saturday Bobby felt worse. He went into driver Marvin Panch's camper to sleep on the sofa all day. He was feeling so ill he decided to skip the Daytona 500 and return to Alabama. All day he moped around, seriously considering quitting racing altogether.

"I finally decided I was going to tell Bud I was going home," Bobby said. "That I had quit."

Later that Saturday afternoon Bobby headed for the garage area, intent on giving Bud Moore the bad news. When he arrived in his stall, he saw that his car, crumpled by Buddy Baker on Friday, was its shiny, new self.

"These guys had fixed it up gorgeous," said Bobby. "They put a fresh engine in it, and it was ready to go for Sunday."

Bobby would not be able to test the car during Happy Hour late Saturday afternoon, but he was so impressed with the hard work put in by Greg Moore, crew chief Doug Williams, mechanic Harold Stott, and the rest of the gang, that he decided to put off his decision to quit.

Bobby and the Bud Moore Ford began the 1978 Daytona 500 in 33rd position. Early in the race he caught a break. He was in traffic, trying to avoid a fender bender, when race leader Cale Yarborough began moving up, ready to lap him, and a caution came out.

Bobby pitted. The Bud Moore pit crew did a great job, and crew chief Doug Williams adjusted the car and made it run faster.

"From then on," said Bobby, "I was competitive, and pretty soon I was up near the front."

Then on lap 60, three of Allison's top competitors, A. J. Foyt, Richard Petty, and Darrell Waltrip were involved in a pileup.

"They all crashed through the tri-oval," said Bobby. "Petty was leading when that happened. I missed all the debris."

Toward the end of the race, Allison fought valiantly to catch race leader Buddy

Baker, whose ride he had taken in Bud Moore's car. Allison had been able to pass Baker on lap 168, but Baker had passed him back. Bobby chased Baker the rest of the race and caught him with fourteen laps to go. Bobby passed Baker on the low side in the tri-oval to take the lead. Baker's engine began to sputter and with only five laps to go it finally blew.

If Buddy Baker had a weakness, it was that he overtaxed his engines so badly that too often they'd blow up before he could finish the race. Richard Petty once told Baker, "If you had finished the last fifty miles of the races you were leading, you'd have some record."

Replied Baker, "That's why they said I was the official dyno for NASCAR."

When Baker's engine blew up behind him, Bobby was assured of victory. He finished 33 seconds ahead of Cale Yarborough. It was Bobby's forty-eighth career win, perhaps the most important in Bobby Allison's long career.

"It was incredible," said Bobby Allison years later.

Said Baker, "I was going through the dogleg and *pooof*. I watched the number 15 Ford I had left the year before win the Daytona 500. If you don't think that don't make you feel like the tiger bit you. Oh, wow."

Commented Bud Moore, "We had good pit stops, and Bobby drove as good a race as he'd ever driven. It was just our day, and when it's your day and everything falls and clicks, you're bound to win."

As Bobby drove into the winner's circle, he was hit with the worst bout of nausea he ever felt. As he came to a stop, he felt sick.

Bobby didn't let on. He told the racing world, "I'm so tickled, I can't see straight. I've been coming here since I was a little boy, and after twenty-one years of trying, it's really a thrill to win this race."

Bobby won four more races in 1978, including Atlanta, Dover, Charlotte, and Ontario. After winning at Atlanta, nausea attacked him the same way it had at Daytona. Making things more painful, the crew pushed the car after the race and Bobby didn't see it coming; the spoiler of the Thunderbird caught Bobby's heels and sliced them. His shoes filled with blood. Only Judy knew. Bobby didn't tell anyone.

After Atlanta on March 19, Bobby was so weak he couldn't get out of the car. Bobby had refused to see a doctor. Once again, his wife Judy was the only one who knew something was wrong.

"I had a really bad habit of not listening to her," said Bobby. "This was one of those times."

In late June, Bobby finally agreed to get medical help. He went to the Mayo Clinic in Rochester, Minnesota.

"The main doctor wanted me to quit racing," said Bobby. "This was a great, big fat guy, sitting behind a desk, saying what was wrong with me was that I was unhappy with my choice of occupation. He's telling me this, and he's a 450-pound guy telling me how much he hates the Mayo Clinic, hates the people there. I said, 'You're the one who needs to change occupation, not me.' And I got up and left.

"They called it a hiatal hernia, but it wasn't that. It was just pressure. Once I started winning again, it went away.

"I had to be careful with what I ate, and Judy really helped me with that. I began to get my strength back. Things with Bud Moore were going good, and I could run off and have fun with my short-track program. I was having fun again."

On October 8, 1978, Bobby won the fall race at Charlotte, the Napa National 500. The day before, he also won the Grand National race in his Matador.

"Everyone was saying I was done," Bobby said, "and I went on to have an incredible year with Bud Moore. I won five times in 1978, and I finished second in the points to the team of Cale Yarborough and Junior Johnson." His purse winnings amounted to $411,517.

"I really liked Bud Moore personally. He was an old codger. He was the 'Last American Hero' of the old guys. And he's still there."

CHAPTER 24

Donnie: Hoss

"DiGard was a down, and we had to start climbing the hill again."

—Pat Allison

When Smokey Yunick had a fallout with the France family in 1976, Smokey decided to quit NASCAR and run at Indianapolis. Humpy Wheeler, who was one of the great promoters in the history of the sport, knew that Hoss Ellington had an extra race car, and so he called Smokey and made a deal with him to make a comeback at Charlotte in the 1976 World 600.

Donnie was out of a ride, so Smokey painted the car black and gold and hired Donnie to drive it.

"It was a pretty good promotion, because everybody had known Smokey's difficulties with NASCAR," said Wheeler.

Hoss Ellington was a businessman, a frustrated race driver from the east coast of North Carolina. Hoss had decent equipment, but his best asset was his engine builder, Runt Pittman.

"Hoss did not have a top team," said Bobby. "Their reputation was they would go to the racetrack and prepare by having a few beers. I can't say I ever saw that, but that was their reputation.

"Runt was more serious than Hoss. I liked Hoss, and I still do. Hoss was good at putting the race team together, but he wasn't good at doing all the little things it took to have a consistently competitive race car. I always felt he wasn't serious enough about the effort to go racing."

Donnie finished sixth in the World 600, a great finish for both Donnie and Ellington. Donnie didn't run for Ellington again until October 10, when they teamed together to enter the National 500 at Charlotte.

Donnie drove Ellington's second car. The first was driven by A. J. Foyt, who pulled into the pits after 59 laps.

"It's the same old story," Foyt told reporters. "Every time we came to the track—the car is never prepared. I'd rather build my own car than run in a pile of hogwash like this car. I couldn't keep it in a ten-acre briar patch."

If Ellington took umbrage with Foyt's remarks, he was mollified greatly when Donnie went on to win the race, making Foyt's remarks sound like sour grapes.

Then, during inspection, Bill Gazaway ruled that Donnie's engine appeared to be oversized. When Cale Yarborough, who drove for Junior Johnson, finished second, crew chief Herb Nab screamed bloody murder.

"Everybody wanted to fight," said Humpy Wheeler. "I went over there to try to referee what was going on and calm everybody down, 'cause it appeared there that the engine was too big. And of course with Smokey involved in it, who knows? He might have had a little engine in each of the rear wheels for all we knew!

"They let the car cool off, and it got back to a reasonable cubic inches. But I could tell, Donnie was getting madder and madder and madder, 'cause he worked hard, and he had a chance to come back. Here he won a big race, and it was going to get taken away from him.

"Donnie was pretty hot," said Wheeler. "Everyone wanted to fight. I finally got the protagonists, Donnie and Herb Nab, in my car. Herb was sitting in the backseat, because Herb was working for Junior, and he was as feisty as Donnie. This was in a Dodge Charger, and there wasn't much room in the car, so I figured if there was going to be a fight, it wasn't going to be much of one. 'Cause it was the closest thing I could find to a phone booth!

"They knew if they started fighting, I was going to punch somebody, too. I wasn't taking sides. I figured if I could get them to talk, maybe we could calm them down, and it actually did have that effect. I said, 'You'll just have to wait to find out what's going on.'

"It all came out okay."

Four hours later Donnie—and Hoss—were awarded their win. The win in the Charlotte World 600 was Hoss's first since he began racing in 1968 and Donnie's first since 1971—a five-year hiatus.

"There were a couple of reasons Donnie didn't win during this period," said Bobby. "One, he didn't pursue the racing schedule like I did. He only went to selected races. The other reason was that he would get into what looked like a good car, and they'd have misfortune, bad luck. There were a lot of guys who didn't win. Donnie fell into that category. When he raced, things didn't go like they should have."

Donnie entered seventeen races in 1977, won twice, and finished in the top ten ten times. Donnie won poles at both Daytona and Rockingham. He had the third-fastest time at Martinsville. His best finish was fourth at Talladega on May 1 in a race won by Darrell Waltrip.

On August 7, 1977, Donnie entered the Talladega 500, and with 23 laps to go, he was leading the race. But because of heat exhaustion, he took ill and could not continue. Darrell Waltrip, who had blown an engine and was out of the race, took over. When Waltrip crossed the finish line first, Donnie had his eighth Winston Cup victory.

"Donnie had gotten sick, and I relief-drove for him," said Waltrip. When the race was over, the press asked Hoss what were they going to do for me relieving Donnie and winning the race?

"Hoss said, 'I think I'll buy him a bottle of Gatorade.' I was sponsored by Gatorade at the time."

Though Waltrip had taken Donnie's ride at DiGard in '75, Donnie didn't hold it against him, said Pat. "I might have said something to Donnie about Darrell, but Donnie'd always say, 'Now that's not the way it is. Don't be like that.'"

On October 23, 1977, at Rockingham, Donnie beat Richard Petty and Darrell Waltrip for his ninth Winston Cup win. He led the final 72 laps.

In 1977 Donnie won two races and $146,000 in purses. Only ten other drivers had done better. As low as he had sunk when DiGard fired him midway through 1975, that's how quickly Donnie rebounded to get back on top.

"He recovered," said Pat, "but it was still a struggle for a while. Like I said, ups and downs. DiGard was a down, and we had to start climbing the hill again."

Donnie won his tenth and final race in 1978, at Atlanta, on November 5. The ending was similar to the race he won at Charlotte the year before. With seven laps to go, Dave Marcis led Richard Petty by a small distance when there was a five-car pile-up. On the restart, Donnie, who at one point had been two laps back, flew out of the pack to pass everyone. After Donnie took the checkered flag, Petty beat Marcis by two feet at the finish line.

After Donnie drove on to Victory Lane, it was announced that Petty had won the race and that Donnie had been a lap back in third place.

When Donnie left the track he was furious, figuring he had been robbed.

"I guess NASCAR needs for Richard to win a race more than they need me to win," said Donnie. "I'm going home."

Then after the official scorer checked all the cards, he decided that Donnie had won, not Petty. Night had fallen when Bill France Jr. made it official: Donnie was the winner. He didn't hear the news until the following morning.

The next year Donnie would be involved in another controversial race, one for which he would be indelibly remembered.

CHAPTER 25

Bobby and Donnie: The Fight at Daytona

Bobby was involved in two highly publicized incidents in 1979. The first came at Daytona. Bobby slugged Cale Yarborough at the end of the 500, while Donnie stood there poised to brain him with his helmet. The incident became indelibly etched in the minds of millions that day because it occurred during the first Winston Cup race ever televised live nationally from beginning to end.

CBS wasn't sure people would sit for three-plus hours and watch a car race. When Bobby duked it out with Yarborough, the event became the stuff of legends.

The trouble between the Allisons and Yarborough first occurred early in the race. On lap 31 Bobby, Donnie, and Cale did some beating and banging, and everyone spun out.

"Both Donnie and Cale blamed me for the spinout," said Bobby years later. "I still say I didn't cause that spinout, either. It was just something that happened. But in that spinout, I lost two laps, and Cale lost two laps, and Donnie didn't. Donnie got back going, and he went on to lead the race."

Donnie was the class of the field on this day, though Cale's car was just as good. Donnie was under the misapprehension that Cale was three laps down, and so when Yarborough twice tried to pass him back to the flag to get a lap back, twice Donnie let him go, figuring that as long as Cale was a lap behind, he didn't have to worry about him.

With just twenty-two laps to go, Donnie discovered his error. All of a sudden Cale was hot on Donnie's tail, and he was in a race. The two hooked up and ran away from the rest of the field. When they took the white flag signifying there was only one lap to go, they were a full lap ahead of A. J. Foyt, Richard Petty, and Darrell Waltrip.

With the race on the line, Yarborough ducked down low to pass Donnie. Donnie knew Cale had the faster car on the straightaways, but it was the last lap of the Daytona 500, and the unwritten rule was that on the last lap, anything goes. Donnie, seeing Yarborough attempt to pass, moved down a lane to block him. Yarborough, to get by, moved even closer to the infield. Donnie moved again to block him. To win Yarborough was going to have to go right through him.

"Cale could only draft Donnie," said Bobby. "He could not pass Donnie. The only way Cale could beat Donnie to that checkered flag would be to wreck him. So he did. But he was caught up in the wreck. He thought he could get rid of Donnie and not be out of it himself, but he got tangled up with Donnie."

Before he knew it, Yarborough was going almost 200 miles an hour in the dirt. He began to lose control, and when he steered back onto the track, he hit the left side of Donnie's car. The two cars separated, and then they came together again. Out of control, the two cars slid together into the third-turn wall, and after a long slide, both cars came to a halt in the infield. Yarborough's aggressiveness and Donnie's intransigence had put them both out of contention.

Eddie Allison was home in Hueytown watching the race on television.

"I kept cussing the television set," he said. "In the middle of the race Donnie was two laps ahead of Cale, and I said, 'Donnie, don't let him pass you.' Well, Donnie didn't want to race Cale because he had the race won. But Cale made the laps up, and I knew Cale was going to wreck him when he got to him.

"I don't know what was wrong with Cale's car, but Junior did something, got it fixed—and the car was flying. So Donnie didn't want to try to race him, but he should have kept him at least a lap down. Donnie should have made him earn the lap back.

"They had the camera in the cars going down the back straightaway. Not inside, outside the car. It came through the windshield, and Cale was right on Donnie's door, and I could see Cale's hands go right, and I said, 'Wooooooo.'

"They hit the wall. I remember when Lee Petty did that to Johnny Beauchamp at Daytona in 1959, and Beauchamp went sailing. Luckily, they didn't get out of the back straightaway. If they had, Lord knows where they'd've ended up. Halfway down the airstrip.

"And it's a shame, because Donnie never did get to win Daytona, and so many times he was in good shape to win it. One time he had a big ole lead, had the thing won, and he ran over something and blew out his two left-side tires.

"Because when Cale Yarborough turned the steering wheel to the right going down the back straightaway at Daytona Beach, he said, 'I want to kill you.' That's what it means. There is no other way you can interpret it. Because when you're running 180 miles an hour and you intentionally wreck somebody, you're going to kill them. There is no way around it."

When the caution flag that the wreck caused came out, A. J. Foyt slowed, but Richard Petty and Darrell Waltrip never let up. After they passed the crash site, they sped across the finish line, Petty first, Waltrip second, and Foyt third. Donnie was awarded fourth place based on his 199 laps completed. Yarborough was given fifth. It was Petty's first win in forty-five races, going back to the 1977 Firecracker 400.

Bobby Allison, three laps down, finished eleventh, and after he crossed the line, he drove over to Donnie's car to make sure his brother, who was standing outside his car, was okay.

"Here's what happened," said Bobby. "Donnie and Cale were ahead of me by two and a quarter miles when that happened. My crew radioed me, "Cale and Donnie are really going at each other. Give them plenty of room."

"I will," Bobby said, "but I won't catch them."

"I went through [turns] three and four, and they have gotten the white flag," said Bobby, "I'm coming to the white flag, and the yellow lights come on, the caution, so I raced back to the flag. My job was to finish the race."

He saw that neither Donnie nor Cale had made it to the finish line.

"I went by the wreckage," said Bobby. "Donnie's car was torn all to pieces, but Donnie was already climbing out of his car, so I knew he wasn't hurt bad, if he's hurt. Cale's car was also torn to pieces. The two cars were probably seventy-five feet apart down in the infield grass.

"I went on and took the checkered flag, and I put the brakes on, slowed down, and I pulled up near Donnie to see whether he wanted a ride back to the garage area. I was directly off Donnie's car, maybe forty feet away. I was maybe 125 feet from Cale's car.

"I hollered to Donnie, 'Do you want a ride?'"

"No," he said. "Go on. I'll get a ride."

"With that Cale started yelling at me that I caused the wreck, that the wreck was my fault.

"How could it be my fault? I was a quarter mile in front of them (or two and a quarter miles behind them.) But earlier in the day, there had been a spinout that both Donnie and Cale blamed me for. I still say I didn't cause that spinout, either. It was just something that happened. But in that earlier spinout, I lost two laps, and Cale lost two laps, and Donnie didn't. Donnie got back going, and he went on to lead the race.

"Cale could draft Donnie, but he couldn't pass him. That's the way the thing had gone all afternoon.

"So they got together, Cale got into Donnie, and they ended up both wrecked, and here I come around, and Cale said to me, 'The wreck was your fault.' His thinking was that if I hadn't caused the earlier wreck, he and Donnie wouldn't have gotten together, and they wouldn't have had the wreck.

"Everybody's defense of his own position is individual.

"Cale had his helmet in his hand, and when he came yelling at me, I'm sure that I questioned his ancestry. [Bobby's exact words were "You SOB."]

"That didn't do anything to calm him down, so he ran at me further, and he got fifteen feet away still yelling and screaming and cussing at me. I was sure he was going to stop right there.

"I had my car in low gear, had the window net down, but I still had the belts on, and I had my helmet on.

"Cale came closer to the car. So I questioned his ancestry a little further.

"By then I'm annoyed at him, and he's in a rage. He doesn't want to go beat on Donnie, because Donnie has always been a little scrapper. Donnie would have hurt him bad.

"Cale was always a scrapper, too. He was a Golden Gloves champion, a skydiver, did all kinds of athletic things, and he was always a tough little guy.

"We'd be at a drivers' meeting, and NASCAR would call the roll, and they'd say, 'We had a little problem last week,' and Cale would point to me and say, 'If you do that today, I'm going to whip your butt and wreck you and take you out of the car and beat your ass.'

"So Cale was five feet away from me, and he was yelling at me, and so I said, 'The hell with you.' With that he lunged at me and hit me in the face with his helmet. I mean, *whap*. I looked down, and my nose was bleeding, and my lip was bleeding, and I was dripping red blood on my blue uniform.

"I said to myself, *I have to get out of this car and address this right now or run from him the rest of my life*.

"So I climbed out of the car. This is my version of the next part: He started beating on my fist with his nose.

"Donnie came over. He had his helmet in the air, and the pictures showed this, so people thought Donnie was beating on Cale.

" 'I have a helmet, too, if you want to fight with helmets,' Donnie said to Cale. Donnie never hit Cale, never touched Cale."

Bobby had punched Yarborough three times in the face and drew blood.

"How Bobby got out of that car that fast I'll never know," said Donnie. "But I knew what was going to happen. I'd seen that look on Bobby's face before. Bobby beat the shit out of him. Hit him three good times right in the face. Cale tried to kick him, and Bobby grabbed his foot and turned him upside down.

"I guess Cale didn't dream Bobby would come after him," said Eddie Allison. "And Bobby's not a fighter. But you got to do something in that circumstance. You become a fighter when you have to. Especially as competitive a person as Bobby Allison is."

As Eddie Allison saw it, Cale was lucky he went after Bobby and not Donnie.

"You don't get in front of Donnie when he gets angry and emotional, because he'll kill you," said Eddie. "Donnie is strong. If Cale Yarborough would have raised his fist to Donnie, Cale Yarborough wouldn't be here. Donnie would have killed him.

"I was watching TV, and Dave Despain was talking with Ryan Newman, and they were talking about 'the fight between Donnie and Cale,' and I wanted to call up so badly and say, 'Donnie didn't fight Cale. If Cale had wanted to fight Donnie, Cale would have been dead, and Donnie would be in the penitentiary.'"

After Bobby punched Cale, several of the safety workers grabbed them and pulled them apart.

"I climbed back in Bud Moore's car with my bloody nose and cut lip," said Bobby, "and drove back to the garage area."

Les Richter, who was in charge of keeping order, wasn't focusing on the fight's impact on the viewing public. He was NASCAR's top cop, and he was sure that Donnie and Bobby had set up Yarborough for a beating. He fined all three of them $6,000 each and placed them all on six-months probation. He ruled that by making Yarborough drive onto the grass, Donnie had "acted in a manner contrary to the best interest of the sport."

Bobby and Donnie requested a hearing that was held in a hotel near the Atlanta International Raceway. Yarborough didn't show. Donnie told Richter he was racing for the win like he did every week. He said he didn't see where he did anything wrong.

Richter backed away from his conspiracy theory. But to make sure the bad blood between the Allisons and Cale didn't go any farther, he said he would retain $1,000 a race for five races so long as nothing else happened. The other $1,000 would go to the point fund.

"NASCAR fined us $6,000 apiece," said Bobby. "I had finished eleventh in the race, and my share was not enough to pay the fine. I had to write out a check on Judy's and my personal account in order to compete the next week. The rule was, if I didn't pay my fine, I couldn't race.

"In the end they gave Donnie all his money back, and they gave all of Cale's back, but they kept some of mine, and I don't know why. I don't have any explanation because NASCAR traditionally does not explain anything. Because of some pain-in-the-neck like me."

When Donnie and Yarborough wrecked in the very next race, at Rockingham, a race that Bobby won, both drivers went out of their way not to blame the other. But Donnie remains convinced that the incident in the 1979 Daytona 500 prevented him from ever again getting a top ride.

"For all practical purposes, that ended my career," said Donnie.

He would drive three races for Hoss Ellington before being replaced by David Pearson. Donnie would never be offered a first-class ride again.

The other memorable incident involving Bobby Allison in 1979 occurred on October 14 at North Wilkesboro. His antagonist this time was Darrell Waltrip, who had blasted onto the scene in 1974, boasting and bragging that he, not Richard Petty, was going to rule NASCAR's roost.

"I was at a gathering at Daytona one night," said Buddy Baker, "and Darrell was on the stage, and he walked up there to do a radio show, and he said, 'I know you don't know me. I'm Darrell Waltrip from Owensboro, Kentucky, and I'm here to take Richard Petty's place. I went, 'Boooooo,' and everybody sat there for a second and went, 'Booooooooooo.' It didn't take Darrell but a second to turn the racing world against him. They used to say when he drove down Interstate 77, people booed him here in Charlotte."

Waltrip, handsome and garrulous, so angered Cale Yarborough with his big talk that Cale gave the brash newcomer the nickname "Jaws." But what made the drivers most angry was the same thing that caused the veterans to despise Bobby Allison when he came up to stay in 1966: The guy was just too damn good. He could back up what he was saying, and he reveled in beating the old-timers.

Said Bob Tomlinson, who was on Darrell Waltrip's DiGard race team, "He ran his mouth a lot. Darrell opened his mouth and would say something against these Gods like Petty, Pearson, Cale, and the Allisons. And he backed up what he said. It was sort of like paying admission to see Babe Ruth hit a home run and the pitcher would keep striking him out. You start booing the pitcher. And so the fans turned against Darrell because he would win races and say things like 'It isn't that hard. You just have to drive your butt off, but you can win races.'"

Somebody had to teach the young, cocky Waltrip a lesson. Bobby Allison decided he would take on the job.

The to-do began innocently enough on lap 308 of the Holly Farms 400 at North Wilkesboro when Waltrip twice bumped into the back of Allison's car, in effect demanding that Bobby get out of his way. In turn three, Waltrip tapped Bobby's car again, turning them both sideways. They recovered, and after Waltrip completed the pass on the front straight, Allison sent Waltrip into the wall head-on.

After a nine-minute pit stop, Waltrip went back out onto the track. The caution flag came out. Waltrip, looking for revenge, wedged himself in front of Allison in an attempt to block him and keep him from victory. Bill Gazaway, the competition director, ran down from the control tower and personally black-flagged Waltrip.

After the race, Waltrip told reporters, "Bobby intentionally wrecked me, and I won't forget it. I can't believe he'd do something like that knowing the points race I'm in."

"It started when he hit me three times going by me," said Allison. "He has to learn that when you want to pass someone, you go around him, not through him."

The incident would cost Darrell Waltrip the driving championship in 1979. Richard Petty won his sixth title, beating him by a scant 11 points. After the race Waltrip told reporters he was heartbroken.

Few, however, were sympathetic. Said former teammate Bob Tomlinson, "Before Bobby wrecked him, Darrell's crew chief had come on the radio and told him, 'Don't beat on Allison any more. Let off the thing. You don't need to do that.'

"And Darrell said, 'He'll take it. There ain't nothing he can do about it.' And about that time Allison let off, let him go underneath him, and just put him right into the wall.

"Those drivers will tell you, if a guy can beat on my back bumper, he can pass me. So don't hit me in the back. It's one thing a driver cannot stand. Somebody, somewhere down the line, is going to pay for it. And so Bobby took care of Darrell. Bobby said to himself, *I've taken it and that's all.*

"Darrell wasn't the kind of person to listen to his crew chief. That's what I mean about Darrell being cocky. But when he first came up, Darrell took on the establishment, and so the press and the fans started jumping on him and calling him 'Jaws' and other names.

"Darrell Waltrip was the one who succeeded in breaking the monopoly of the established drivers, and so all at once it went from six or seven competitive teams to twelve and fifteen, and now it's to where twenty or forty cars might end up the winner."

This race would be the start of an ugly, decade-long feud that would last even after Bobby retired.

Bud Moore and Bobby had another successful year in 1979. They won five races, finished in the top five eighteen times, were third in the points, and won $428,800 in prize money.

In 1980, Bobby won four races and $378,969 in the Bud Moore Ford, but he was unhappy because he had determined that the Ford engines were inferior to the Chevys, especially on the short tracks.

After his win at Dover on May 18, he told reporters, "A Ford is capable of winning only at Atlanta, Charlotte, Dover, and Rockingham. We still need two Chevys for the other tracks." Bobby begged Bud Moore to change factories, but Moore had worked with Ford for twenty years, and he refused to leave them.

By the end of the 1980 season, Bobby had convinced himself he needed to drive for a Chevy team. He and Bud Moore had had a nice run, but once again, it was time for Bobby to move on to a team where he felt he would have a better chance to win.

"I was in a rut with the Bud Moore operation," said Bobby. "We were doing good, better than Bud had ever done, but I wanted to do better. I wasn't convinced Ford was the best competitor. Bud and his sons were doing a really good job, but they hadn't gotten the last bit out of that motor. I didn't think it was available, but Bill Elliott would prove me wrong. When the Elliotts came on strong with their Ford, all the other Ford teams went back to work. But I had to make a move to find out that I was wrong."

CHAPTER 26

Bobby: Butting Heads

"I had really, really bad communication skills, and he had worse."

—Bobby Allison

After the 1980 season Bobby left Bud Moore and signed a lucrative three-year contract to drive a Chevy Monte Carlo for Harry Ranier, one of the first millionaire car owners to invade the sport in the 1980s. Now Bobby had an owner with money, and he had the make of car he was seeking, but, to be successful, he also had to get along with the crew chief. When Bobby arrived at the Rainer shop, he discovered that his crew chief, the great engine builder Waddell Wilson, was the sort of man used to giving advice, not taking it. Like Harry Hyde, Wilson saw himself as the boss of the race team. His driver was supposed to listen and shut up. Bobby, who was used to having major input in every decision affecting his car, saw from the very first race that he and Wilson were not destined to work together for long. Part of the problem, as Bobby saw it, was that Wilson didn't know as much about setting up a car as Bobby did. He should have built the engines and let Bobby decide the rest. But Waddell wouldn't do that, and it led to strife all year long.

The first race of the season was at Riverside. It was to be the final race of the big cars, and Bobby was driving a Chevy Monte Carlo. Bobby went out for the pace lap, and he felt a vibration.

"It was obvious the driveshaft wasn't connected right," said Bobby. "The thing was vibrating so bad it was unbelievable."

On the radio Bobby said to Waddell Wilson, "I have a bad vibration. The driveshaft is not in the socket where it belongs."

According to Bobby, Wilson told him, "Shut up and keep driving."

"No, no, no," Bobby replied, "This thing is really bad. I'm pitting. You go under this car and take a look at it."

During the first of two pace laps, Bobby came back in, knowing it would put him back to the rear.

Jimmy Cavalcheck, whose nickname was Zoomer, volunteered to go under the car and take a look. He jacked the car up, stuck his hand under there, and said, "I see the problem. I'll have it fixed in just a second."

Cavalcheck fixed it, dropped the car back down, and sure enough, the car ran smooth as silk. From his position at the back of the field, Bobby went on and won the race.

"The rest of the preparation for the car was good," said Bobby. "Waddell's engines were so good, and that day the engine ran really good. The rest of the stuff worked, and I had the best car out there that day. But when I drove into Victory Lane, Waddell was mad at me, and he refused to come to Victory Lane."

Bobby said, "What's the deal? We won the race."

"By some deal that you did," replied Wilson.

In hindsight Bobby says he should have sat down with Wilson right then and there and talked out their differences. But Bobby was not into sharing feelings. He was into having things done right, and if your feelings get in the way, too bad.

"I never, never stopped a second to say, 'What's wrong here that maybe I can fix things with Waddell.' I never addressed that. My attitude was: I'm giving one hundred percent to this team, and the rest of you better, too. Row the boat, or get out.

"My attitude was really good, and really bad. I didn't give people the consideration of saying, Why do you feel this way?"

The next race was the Daytona 500. It was the first race of the downsized, 110-inch-wheelbase cars. Every car owner had to scramble to find the best little car to race. Among the most popular choices for Daytona were the Buick Regal, Chrysler LeBaron, Dodge Mirada, Ford Thunderbird, Mercury Cougar, Oldsmobile Cutlass, and Pontiac Grand Prix. The Ranier team didn't have factory help, so it was free to pick whatever car it wanted. Though the Buick appeared to be the best of the General Motors models for racing, Junior Johnson had the primary Buick team, so Harry Ranier and Waddell Wilson decided to try running an Oldsmobile. The rules called for a small three-inch spoiler.

When Bobby took the car on the track, the new square-backed car was loose at high speeds. After two days of testing, its handling improved only from "horrible" to "bad."

Said Bobby, "I was hoping to draft with Darrell, but right now I don't even want the seagulls out there with me."

Bobby wasn't the only driver with problems finding the right car. Richard Petty selected a Dodge Mirada, but when he saw it ran eight miles an hour slower than the GM cars during testing, he switched to a Buick Regal.

Said Petty, "This is a whole new ball game."

Back home in Hueytown a few days earlier, Bobby's son Davey had gone looking for a street car, and he became enamored of the Pontiac LeMans. The kid, who had just graduated from high school, knew cars like his dad, and he liked the lines and thought it would be fast on the racetrack. Davey suggested to his dad that he consider switching from the blocky Olds to the LeMans.

"Davey had gone to summer school, and so he had graduated early so he could get busy with his short-track racing," said Bobby. "His mother said he had to have a high school diploma before he could race. Here Davey was, out of high school, and all the young boys had to have new cars. Since I had been involved with AMC, I had gotten him a Hornet, which was a putdown as far as he was concerned. He was into girls and fancy cars, and he told me about this LeMans he had been looking at."

Bobby, Davey, Harry Ranier, and Waddell Wilson drove over to Lamb Pontiac on Volusia Avenue in Daytona Beach a few blocks from the speedway. The dealership didn't have a LeMans. They only had a picture of one. The men noticed that the car had a sloped rear window, a little inverted V in the middle of the hood, and "a gorgeous nose."

"Everything about this car grabbed all four of us," said Bobby. Bobby said he thought the car might run faster even than the Pontiac Grand Prix. Bobby didn't want anyone to know what he was planning, and he paid for the car out of his own pocket.

Bobby had a close relationship with a car builder by the name of Mike Laughlin. Banjo Matthews was still the top dog in the car-building business, and Holman and Moody, minus Ralph Moody, was still building a few cars. Laughlin was the little guy. He had built cars for Butch Lyndley, and after they went their separate ways, he went into the car building business. Bobby had given Laughlin some tips how to make his chassis better, benefiting Laughlin's burgeoning business.

When Harry Ranier asked Bobby what the next move should be, Bobby suggested he get Mike Laughlin to build the car for them and that they do it in secret. When Bobby ordered his car, he told Laughlin to put the words "Sportsman Car" on the work order.

"If we had an advantage," said Bobby, "we wanted to keep that advantage and spring it on them."

Bobby particularly didn't want the Pettys, who had *the* Pontiac factory deal, to know what he was up to. Just to be sure, Bobby visited the NASCAR offices in Daytona and asked for a copy of the current rules and specifications.

Laughlin built the car in a matter of days. Since it was labeled a Sportsman car, nobody paid much attention to it.

When the car was finished, Waddell Wilson and Harry Ranier decided to raise the deck lid an extra inch at the rear hoping the inspectors wouldn't notice. Bobby tried to talk them out of it, but was outvoted.

Bobby and Harry Ranier took the LeMans to Talladega to test it, and the car was very fast. It was aerodynamically very stable because of its sloped rear window. The first lap around Talladega, Bobby drove six miles an hour faster than anyone had ever gone before. Most cars went in the high 180s. Bobby was clocked at 196 miles an hour.

"Of course, you have safety crews to run the test," said Bobby, "and they were sitting up there with stopwatches, and I ran this blistering lap, so in fifteen minutes NASCAR knew it."

Ranier told Bobby, "No more fast laps. We know the car is good. Let's get out of here before we get penalized. NASCAR isn't going to like somebody being *way* faster than everyone else."

They took the car to their shop in Charlotte, painted it black and silver, and put on the Tuf-Lon decal. Tuf-Lon, an oil additive, was sponsoring the car for the first few races.

They went to Daytona. When Bobby brought the car for inspection, his was the only LeMans entered. No one else thought the car was eligible.

"I don't know why nobody else came up with it," said Bobby. "I sure wasn't going to call anybody and tell them."

When they arrived at the speedway, the inspectors told them, "We have never seen this car before.. We don't have templates. You guys can't go out and practice until we get templates."

By then Lamb Pontiac had a street model, and NASCAR took it and quickly made templates. But the delay kept the car off the track most of the first day of practice.

The Ranier car didn't fit the templates. The inspectors had caught on to the fact that the deck lid had been raised higher than the specs allowed.

"I was disappointed, and I felt like it had been a foolish thing to do," said Bobby, "but as soon as I said, 'Mike, we don't want this,' I got outvoted quickly. I didn't realize it, but I was quickly becoming an outsider to the Ranier effort.

"Here I was, full of enthusiasm, but if I said the sky is blue, they would say, 'No, it's gray.'"

To this day Bobby does not understand what it was about him that caused others to react to him that way.

"You know, I lost people," he said. "I was putting in what I felt was my ultimate effort, and I would lose people. Going all the way back to Cotton Owens. I broke my back for him, but I was never smart enough to take a step back and say, *Woooo, what happened and why?*"

When the NASCAR inspectors finally approved the car, Bobby went out on the track and was pleased to see he could still drive the car "with one hand."

When the other teams saw how fast Bobby was running, they began to complain about his car.

Said Waddell Wilson, "They *hated* the idea we were down there with a Pontiac LeMans, although they couldn't say anything because it was okay by the rule book. They made the rules; we didn't."

Bobby entered the Busch Clash, and finished sixth after he had to make an unscheduled pit stop. He then won one of the twin 125-mile qualifying races and was the class of the race. Darrell Waltrip won the other prelim in a Buick Regal.

In qualifying for the Daytona 500, Bobby won the pole at a speed of 194.624 miles an hour. Going into the Daytona 500, the only car that handled well was the Le-Mans. Everyone else had to lift going around the turns or risk hitting the outside wall.

Before the race, Waddell Wilson, on the advice of Harry Ranier, told Bobby, "We're not going to lead this race. We're not going to show our hand, because if we do, NASCAR is going to take our car away."

"Wait a minute," said Bobby. "We're here for this race. They're not taking it away for this race. And if we can win this race, we should."

Before the race the team was arguing.

Said Bobby, "My argument was, They drop the green, the easiest way to win is from out front."

"We're not going to lead," he was ordered. "Don't you lead."

Bobby, on the pole, led the first three laps then dropped back.

"I was running back third or fourth," said Bobby, "and Buddy Baker, of all people, started drafting on me, and he rubbed on the side of the car. He put wheel marks all the way down the side of the car. Now I really like Buddy, but I don't want to race side by side with him around the track, because he was on the gas sometimes when he shouldn't have been.

"I got on the radio and said to Waddell, 'We're going to sit here and wreck this car when we could win this race.'"

"Do whatever you want to do" was Waddell's reply.

"He was mad at me," said Bobby. "Oh yeah. Because I'm not following the race plan."

Bobby went out to the front and dominated the race. He had the lead on lap 173 when he ran out of gas.

"The car was programmed to go thirty-nine laps on a tank of gas," said Bobby. "I wasn't counting, and as I came off turn four, I ran out of gas. I was going too fast to turn into pit road, so I had to go all the way around. The engine had stopped. I coasted, and I lost the lead and some time, and I came into the pits.

"We had nineteen laps to go, which is essentially one can of gas. We'd have a teacup left, but we could make it.

"We stopped. Waddell said, 'Put two cans of gas in that thing and change the tires.' At that point I wasn't allowed to open my mouth. There was no debate. If we had put in one can and no tires, we'd have won, because, as it was, I finished just a few feet behind Richard Petty. I came all the way from the back. We had gone from two-thirds of a lap ahead to three-fourths of a lap down, and in nineteen laps came all the way to within a few feet of the leader.

"We lost the race, and Waddell said, 'His lousy chassis used up all my gas.' When I looked at the race chart, we had gone forty-three laps on that tank of gas. So then I had to take the attitude that he ran me out of gas on purpose. I was getting credit for this car, and he absolutely was really anti that deal."

Bobby Allison after winning the Charlotte World 600 in 1971. *(All photos courtesy of International Motorsports Hall of Fame)*

Pop Allison waits for Bobby to pit.

Another one for Bobby—he had eighty-five in all.

Eddie Allison (center) turned wrenches on his brothers' race cars when they regularly campaigned on the short tracks of Florida and Alabama. They are Donnie Allison (left) and Bobby Allison (right).

Neil Bonnett, Donnie Allison, and Bobby Allison.

Bobby holds up his belt buckle for winning the racing championship in 1983.

Bobby finished first and Davey second in the 1988 Daytona 500, the first time since 1960 that father and son finished 1, 2. It was Bobby's final victory.

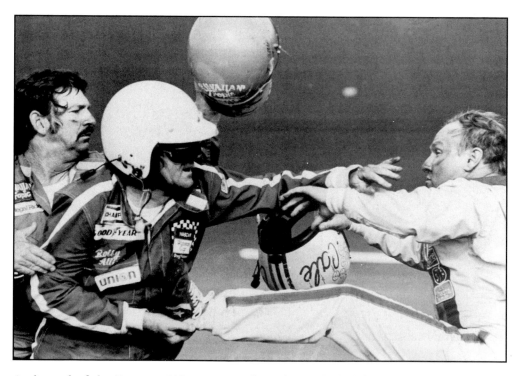

At the end of the Daytona 500 in 1979 Cale Yarborough (right) attacked Bobby Allison, striking him with his helmet. Bobby jumped out of the car and hit back as brother Donnie backed him up. The event became the stuff of legends.

Bobby with his DiGard winning car.

Bobby Allison exults with one of his eighty-five trophies.

Donnie Allison.

Donnie Allison had the reputation for being a hard charger.

Eddie Allison (right) was a member of Bobby's race team in 1967.

Ralph Moody, one of Bobby's strongest supporters.

Davey is presented with the keys to the city by Talladega mayor Larry Barton. Davey died a week later.

"He had a really good feel for a car," said Bobby of younger son Clifford.

By 1991 Clifford had really blossomed into a good driver.

Red Farmer in car C-97 said, "You went out there, and you got run over, until you learned to get out of the way."

In 1955 Red Farmer and John Fitzgibbons bought this '37 Ford for Red to race.

Red Farmer has run a car with the number 97 on it for almost fifty years.

Red Farmer was inducted into the International Motorsports Hall of Fame in 2004.

Pam Allison, Donnie's daughter, told Hut Stricklin, "I hate your guts." They married not long afterward.

When he and Davey first started out racing each other, Hut Stricklin won all the time.

Bobby and his protégé Neil Bonnett.

Neil Bonnett (left) had been one of the first to appreciate the skills of Davey Allison (right).

Neil Bonnett signed with the Wood Brothers in 1979.

Those who knew Neil Bonnett best knew he was miserable when he wasn't behind the wheel of a race car.

After a serious crash, Neil Bonnett returned and won at Richmond.

It was Richard Petty's 193rd win. He was still the King, but his domination was coming to an end.

An observer who was even angrier at Wilson than Bobby was his brother Eddie.

"As I've said," commented Eddie, "if you have enough money, you can bolt stuff onto the engine until it runs, so you don't have to know anything about it. And there are very few people who know why a motor runs like it runs. Very few. Most of them bolt parts on. They know if they put a certain part on, they go fast. But they don't know why.

"The only one I knew in the whole bunch who really knew engines was Waddell Wilson, but Waddell Wilson had a screw loose in his head. See, when Bobby drove that car for him, they could have won every race—if he had listened to Bobby. But he didn't, because his ego was too big.

"They had the race won at Daytona Beach the first time they ran that Pontiac. And Waddell let him run out of gas. 'Cause his ego was so big.

"And when Bobby did something Waddell didn't want him to do, and Bobby won as a result, Waddell would not show up at the victory party. 'Cause his ego was too big. It was one of them marriages that could have been made in heaven if the thing would have flowed.

"Bobby had that problem so often.

"Waddell never should have been a crew chief. Waddell didn't know how to run a race car. The mechanic cannot make the race car like he wants it, and the driver not. You cannot say, 'We're going to run it this way because I say so.' Because the driver may say, 'I can't drive it like that.' Waddell did the same thing when he teamed up with Darrell Waltrip on the Dream Team. It didn't work out because Waddell kept telling Darrell how to set up the car.

"The difference between Darrell and Bobby is that Bobby can drive an ill car way better than anybody. He can make an ill car go fast where other people can't drive it. It was Bobby's forte."

After Bobby finished sixth at Rockingham, NASCAR cracked down on the Le-Mans, as Ranier and Waddell Wilson feared. It lowered the LeMans's spoiler two full inches from 3.5 inches to 1.5 inches, making it dangerously unstable. Every other car was allowed a 3.5-inch spoiler but the LeMans.

Ranier, outraged, threatened to boycott the Atlanta race on March 15. He and Bobby flew to Montgomery, the state capital and seat of the federal court, where the Saturday night before the race they tried to get an injunction to stop it. Their efforts failed.

Before the race, Ranier told Bobby, "You have to act like this thing is really loose."

Said Bobby, "The truth was the car was really okay. But I couldn't say that."

In an attempt to get NASCAR to modify its ruling, Bobby refused to qualify. He loaded his car back onto the trailer and threatened to go home.

"We want Bobby" was scrawled on windows and walls of the Atlanta track by Bobby's fans.

NASCAR, not wanting to see a boycott by the Ranier team, announced in the spirit of compromise it would add an inch to Bobby's spoiler

Though Bobby only qualified thirtieth, he ran fourth in the race as Cale Yarborough won the Coca-Cola 500 at Atlanta.

Allison drove the LeMans in four more races, finishing third at Bristol, second at North Wilkesboro to Richard Petty, ninth at Darlington, and thirteenth at Martinsville.

According to Bobby, the disappointing finish at Darlington was less the result of the spoiler than the deteriorating relationship between Bobby on one hand and Harry Ranier and Waddell Wilson on the other.

"By now I have zero communication with Harry and Waddell," said Bobby. "I hate to criticize Harry, because I like the man, and the man put some effort for me, but Harry would tell me one thing, and he would tell Waddell something else. If he was talking to me, he'd say, 'Yeah, Bobby, you're right,' and if he was talking to Waddell, he'd tell him, 'Yeah, you're right.'

"Not only were we not communicating, but our engines weren't running as well as I thought they should have. In my exuberance, I discovered two boys in the Miami area, Bob Rahilly and Butch Mock, who were in the cylinder head modification business. I had put a set of their heads on my short-track car, and that was incredible. Boy, I mean, I zoomed."

Bobby took a second set to Waddell and asked him to put them on the LeMans for the Darlington race. Bobby had spent $2,000 on the new heads, figuring he would recoup his money with a victory in the race. Bobby told him, "They really, really worked on my short-track car."

According to Bobby, Wilson took one of the two heads out of the box, held it up to the light, twisted it around as he studied it, and threw it down onto the floor with a "bam."

"I'm not putting that junk on my engine," said Wilson.

Bobby turned around and stormed out of the shop.

The next race was at Martinsville, and before the race Wilson told Bobby that under no circumstances was he to look under the hood of the race car. It was a repeat of the Roger Penske experience when Traco was building his engines.

Allison went out onto the track, and the car ran remarkably well.

I'm going to win this thing easy, Bobby told himself.

"Waddell," said Bobby, "what did you do to this thing?"

"Don't worry about it," he said. "I built you a new engine."

"Man," said Bobby, "that thing is really good."

Bobby, being naturally curious, was dying to see what Wilson had done to the engine. Bobby decided he would get one of the other crew members to call Wilson on the phone so he could look under the hood while he was called away.

Before the Martinsville race, it was announced on the loudspeaker, "Waddell Wilson, please come to the announcer's tower for a phone call."

Wilson left the shop to field the call, and as soon as he left, Bobby lifted the hood and saw the cylinder heads. At the spot where the Rahilly-Mock stamp should have been was a blob of stylistic. Bobby reached in and scraped it off, and sure enough, underneath was the Rahilly-Mock name.

Bobby closed the hood and didn't say a word. When Wilson returned, he must have realized that the call was a ruse, because he immediately raised the hood and saw that the stylistic had been scratched off.

When the race began, Bobby noticed, the timing was way off.

"Immediately, I felt the car had been detuned," said Bobby. "Of course, I got blamed when we finished thirteenth. Waddell said, 'These cylinder heads were no good.'"

There was nothing more for Bobby to say. His relationship with Wilson was over. He would discuss what needed to be done on the car at the track with Zoomer. During the week Bobby stayed away from the Ranier shop altogether. Bobby Allison felt like an outcast on his own race team.

There was still two thirds of the season to go. Bobby convinced Harry Ranier that it made sense to dump the controversial LeMans and to opt for the car that not only seemed by consensus of the drivers to be the most stable, but which had won seven of the eight races: the Buick Regal. Mike Laughlin made them a Buick Regal.

Bobby went to Talladega on May 3, 1981, surprising everyone with his new car. Waddell Wilson built a strong engine, and Bobby not only sat on the pole, on the final lap of the race he passed Buddy Baker to take the checkered flag.

During the race Bobby had suffered a broken windshield, lost his rear bumper when he was hit from behind by Morgan Shephard, and a flat tire had cost him a lap. Allison, Baker, Darrell Waltrip, and Ricky Rudd raced in a pack to the finish line. Bobby was first by a tenth of a second. Despite the dysfunctional nature of the race team Bobby had a big lead in the points race for the driving championship over Rudd and Waltrip.

Bobby finished third at Nashville behind Benny Parsons and Darrell Waltrip, then traveled to Dover. Bobby was leading the race, when the lugs on the right front studs of the car broke. Bobby made a ten-lap pit stop while his crew changed the hubs, and then in the final 150 laps of the race made up nine of the ten laps and finished second to Jody Ridley, who was driving for Junie Donlavey, the only race Ridley and Donlavey ever won.

"Jody and Junie did a good job," said Bobby, "but we were much faster. We'd have won if it hadn't been for those hubs. After the race I saw that somebody had used a different material for the lug studs."

Was someone sabotaging his efforts? I asked.

"Yeah," said Bobby. "We definitely weren't a team."

At Charlotte Bobby was in for more aggravation. He was leading the race when he called in on the radio, "My feet are burning." The installation of the floorboards hadn't been done properly.

"Don't worry me about your little problems," said Wilson. "Drive the car."

Bobby won the race over Harry Gant and Cale Yarborough. At the end of the race Bobby's lead over Waltrip was 249 points and seemed insurmountable. When he arrived in Victory Lane, his feet were burned so badly, he couldn't stand up.

Bobby sat on the hood of the car while Bob Spangler, a close friend who ran his souvenir program, took off his shoes and socks. Bobby was in agony.

Spangler turned to Waddell Wilson, who was standing with Harry Ranier five feet away, and said, "Waddell, you should take better care of him. His feet are burned up."

According to Bobby, Wilson's answer was, "Fuck him. He makes plenty of money."

Said Bobby, years later, "What can you do?"

In the middle of that World 600 race, Donnie Allison was T-boned and seriously hurt. After the ceremony at Victory Lane, Bobby went to the hospital to see how his brother was doing. His feet needed medical attention, but he decided they could wait until he returned to Alabama the next day. At the hospital, Bobby was assured by the doctors that they were doing everything they could for Donnie.

Bobby got in his Aerostar and flew home to Alabama. His personal physician had him lie facedown on a table while he cut the burned skin and blisters off both his feet and dropped the dead skin on the floor. The right foot was burned worse than his left.

The doctor bandaged him up and put him on crutches. The pain was so great Bobby couldn't put any weight on his heels. For three weeks he walked on his toes using crutches while the burns healed.

Despite the pain, he drove in the next race on June 7 at College Station and finished third. Bobby Allison should have been a lock to win the elusive racing championship in 1981. The tour moved on to Riverside.

Right before they called for the start of the engines, Waddell Wilson told Bobby, "Please don't blow up the engine. It's a really hot day." Wilson felt there would be a lot of engine trouble, and he was right. Bobby didn't run long before he blew up his engine. He finished twenty-ninth. Bobby and Wilson were furious with each other. Wilson was sure Bobby had mashed on the gas too hard and blown the engine. Bobby was sure Wilson had built a lousy engine.

At Michigan on June 21 Bobby and Wilson had another ugly confrontation. Because Bobby had blown up the engine at Riverside, before the Michigan race Wilson installed a rev limiter in the car as a precaution against engine failure.

When Bobby pitted with fifteen laps to go, he told Wilson that if he didn't unhook the rev limiter, he'd pull out the wires himself.

Bobby came from seventh to first to win the race. Kyle Petty blew an engine, and oil leaked all over the track. Cale Yarborough hit the oil and spun, causing a multicar crash that collected him, Dale Earnhardt, Harry Gant, Buddy Baker, and Benny Parsons. Bobby passed all six and reached the line first under the caution. The race ended without going back to green, and Bobby was the winner.

"With five laps to go, I was running eighth," said Bobby, "and then there was a giant wreck coming off turn two on the back straightaway. Cars were wrecking, and lapped cars got tangled, and I wiggled in, wiggled out, and I was just lucky—I missed everything and came around.

"The caution lights came on, and in those days you had to pit and put new tires on for a restart, because new tires were two seconds faster than old tires for a lap or two.

"With only four or five laps to go, they were not going to clean the thing up, plus I saw that every good car was already in the wreck, so when Waddell came on the radio, he said, 'Pit.'

"Waddell," Bobby said, "We just won the race."

"I said pit," ordered Wilson.

"I ain't pitting," Bobby said. "We just won the race."

Wilson was screaming into the phone as Bobby drove past pit road. Bobby continued driving under the caution, took the checkered flag, and won the race.

When Allison came to Victory Lane, Wilson refused to go to the celebration.

I asked Bobby how it was that the two of them didn't get into a fistfight.

"A big reason we didn't," he said, "was that I was wimpy, and Waddell was muscular, and he would have hurt me bad in a fistfight."

With fourteen races go, Bobby seemed sure to win the racing title in 1981, but Darrell Waltrip, in one of the strongest finishes in NASCAR history, won seven of those races. In the final thirteen races he dominated, with seven firsts, five seconds, and a third, while Bobby was saddled with dysfunction from his race team.

"There was never any communication," said Bobby. "I was totally committed to this, but if I said something, the opposite got done. There I was hanging by my neck.

"A friend of mine, Bo Fields, started going to the race with me. I had met Bo really early when I came to Alabama. He let me use his shop to work on my car, gave me a hand. He had been a good competitor, a good mechanic, and we struck up a friendship, and now Bo was traveling with me. If I needed to talk, I could talk to Bo.

"I was trying to figure out how to give a better effort, but what I should have been doing was asking, *How can I communicate with Waddell?* That's what I needed to do. Was it possible? I don't know?

"Before the final race I told them I was leaving. We struggled along and did poorly."

Going into that final race at Riverside, Bobby could still win the title with a win, but Darrell Waltrip would have to finish far back for that to happen.

Once again Wilson put the rev limiter on Bobby's car in an attempt to keep the engine from overheating and blowing up. In the latter part of the race, Allison was leading Joe Ruttman when, with thirty laps to go, the caution came out. Bobby came in to the pits, and the crew put four tires on the car. At the same time Wilson reached in and pulled the wires of the rev limiter.

"You've got it all now, Bobby," Wilson told him. "The rev limiter is off, and you have four brand-new tires."

Bobby outran Ruttman the last ten laps to win the race. Waltrip, running a safe race, finished sixth, which gave him the championship by a scant 53 points.

"I felt some anger we lost that year," said Bobby, "but I was more disappointed than anything. I lost what I was sure had been a really good friendship with Waddell. He had been the engine builder in 1967 at Holman and Moody when I ran for them. When I went back there in 1971 he built the engines, and then in 1972 he became the engine builder for my Alabama race team, and we had some problems. Maybe our problems started because of that. You never know. What a shame! Because the guy did have incredible talent on the engine end of it.

"I had really, really bad communication skills, and he had worse."

CHAPTER 27

Donnie:
T-Boned and in a Coma

"He should have just gotten out of the car and said, 'I'm not driving it,' but he didn't."

—Pat Allison

Donnie Allison in 1981 was hired to drive by John Rebham. His crew chief was Harry Hyde, who was trying to recover from bankruptcy after working for car owner J. D. Stacy. According to Hyde's nephew, Tommy Johnson, Stacy and Hyde fought a prolonged legal battle over equipment. After getting the sheriff to padlock the doors to Hyde's race shop, thirteen times Stacy sued Hyde, and thirteen times Hyde beat him, according to Johnson. But Hyde and Johnson had to spend $235,000 defending themselves to keep property that was already theirs.

"It broke Harry," said Johnson. "Broke both of us." They borrowed money from friends and relatives, and when the case finally was heard in federal court, Stacy lost.

In 1979 Harry and Johnson, desperate for work, were hired by Tighe Scott's father, owner of Scotty's Fashions in Pennsylvania, to run a race team with young Tighe as the driver. It was run on a shoestring, and the kid had a couple of decent runs at Daytona and Talladega, but they couldn't compete against the more powerful Winston Cup teams.

Tighe ended up leaving Cup racing and going back north, where he ran Modifieds for a while before fading from the racing scene. Hyde then was hired by John Rebham, a builder of coal-mining machinery. The driver they hired first was John Anderson, a very good driver from the Midwest. But Rebham was impatient, and the pressure on Anderson too great, and nothing clicked, and at the end of the 1980 season he was fired, and Donnie was hired.

"Donnie was a worker-driver," said Tommy Johnson. "He worked hard on the car along with us."

"Donnie was a *really* good driver," said Jimmy Makar, a crew member on the team. "He had been around a long time, but he really never got going very well with Harry."

The poor communication between Donnie and Hyde led to disaster on May 23, 1981, at the Charlotte Motor Speedway.

"Donnie admired Harry Hyde's record," said Bobby. "He had had some success with Neil Bonnett. I'm not sure Donnie agreed with everything Harry chose to do in the preparation of the car. He was unhappy with the car that day."

"The car didn't have any downforce," said Tommy Johnson.

"Donnie said his car was not handling well," said Pat Allison. "Harry Hyde was old school, had been around racing forever.

"After practice, Donnie was concerned the car was handling so poorly. He should have just gotten out of the car and said, 'I'm not driving it,' but he didn't. He lost it, then hit the wall, and Dick Brooks hit him."

"Donnie was hurt very badly," said Bobby. "He had broken bones, a broken left leg, which had already been broken on the motorcycle when he was a kid. He had broken ribs. And he had a head injury—he was unconscious for a while. Some days later we transported him home in my airplane. He was gravely injured and not fully conscious."

"The thing that happened to Donnie was so tragic," said Humpy Wheeler, who was at the race that day. "It was one of the most unique wrecks we've ever seen on a superspeedway. He and Richard Brooks hit each other up at the third turn, and they hit each other sideways as flat as you could get. You could not get a stunt driver to duplicate that wreck. Of course, Donnie's head hit something. We don't know what it was.

"Dr. Jerry Petty saved his life that day," said Wheeler. "Because we got a three signal, indicating he was unconscious and unresponsive. When they brought him in the trauma center, one diagnosis was that he had a ruptured aorta, not completely, but a tear, and obviously they would have had to have gone in right away to stop that.

"Dr. Petty said, 'No, it's blunt head trauma. Let's get him to the hospital.'

"That's precisely what it turned out to be. If he had been at another track or another doctor had been at ours, and if they had invaded him, he would have died."

Dr. Petty saved him by making the proper diagnosis.

"When Donnie got to the hospital, they put him in intensive care," said Wheeler. "I got to the hospital that night, and he was in a coma, wasn't moving, and I thought, *It just doesn't look good*. Eventually he got better, but it was touch and go. That was a tough, tough deal."

"What happened," said Eddie Allison, "Donnie's brain banged the side of his skull and bruised it real bad. So it paralyzed him. The side of his face was all drooped. The left side of his face was paralyzed, and his left arm, and he had trouble talking. He would have trouble thinking of things to say. He had trouble making sentences."

"That was very, very scary," said Pat Allison, "because I didn't know whether he was going to live or die. I had the twins, Ronald and Donald, with me. They were young, not yet teenagers. We had some friends up from Alabama, and they got Ronald and Donald, and I went to the infield hospital. I knew it was bad, but I did not get to see him there. To see him, I had to go to the hospital.

"When I got there, they didn't really tell me a whole lot of anything. Humpy Wheeler's wife, Pat, came to the hospital, and she was very comforting and nice, telling me that Charlotte Memorial was a teaching hospital. There were a ton of fans trying to get into the elevator to come up, and I still had not seen Donnie.

"Finally, I was allowed to go in, and when I saw him tied to the bed and his eyes looking in two different directions, I just hit the floor. Because then I knew something was drastic wrong, bad wrong. The race preacher, a big guy, was there and very good. The fans were all concerned. Everyone was going crazy."

"Donnie didn't get back here for a week," said Eddie Allison. "He was in the hospital in Charlotte, and Dr. Petty was taking care of him. I was going to meet Bobby at the airport to help him out of the plane, but they were two hours late, and I had to go back to work, so I didn't see Donnie until that night in the hospital. And he looked way more dead than Bobby did the next morning after his crash at Pocono.

"Donnie was in a coma—out of it—for about three days," said Pat Allison. "I stayed in his room with him, very positive. Humpy made it very comfortable. We didn't really know the consequences of his head injury, how bad it would be. They were doing CAT scans.

"Donnie came to, and he knew some things, but he also was saying some crazy things. Someone asked him, 'How many kids do you have?' He named five kids. We only have four. I figured something was really wrong.

"It was a horrifying event to go through. A brain injury can be far worse than death.

"At this point I didn't know whether he'd be a normal person. I didn't have any idea what the future would hold, and that's scary. We were all praying. I tried to keep the details from the rest of the family."

It took about a year for Donnie's speech and everything else to return to normal.

After Donnie's hospital stay in Charlotte, Dr. Jerry Petty sent him to a Dr. Davies in Birmingham. One of Donnie's first questions to Dr. Davies was, "When can I start racing again?"

"I can't tell you that," said Dr. Davies. "You will know. There are a lot of things we don't know about the brain."

Even though it took Donnie a full year to recover, he was back driving again three months later. Despite serious injury, Donnie had bills to pay. He needed to go back to work. Donnie didn't make a salary. He earned a percentage of the purse. No racing, no purse.

"In those days if you showed up at the racetrack, you pretty much could get in a car if someone would let you in one," said Bobby. "You didn't have to go through the physical inspection that's common now, where you have to get some sort of clearance. And Donnie had done well enough through his career that people had confidence in him. I'm not sure he was ready to get back in the car that quick, but they let him back in."

As time went on, Donnie's driving skills improved until he was totally recovered from his injuries. But people were aware of how serious his head injuries had been, and no one wanted to risk hiring and having him die in another crash.

In 1982 Donnie ran Late Models around Birmingham.

"Donnie, to say it properly, retreated to the short tracks, where he could make a good living, didn't have to run all the time and didn't have to win," said Bobby. "The pay was decent down through the ranks, and he could run good enough to be near the front and be competitive no matter what."

"He had his own car," said Pat, "and he would run different places. We were living on the farm near Demopolis, Alabama. He had bought it in '78 when we were making good money. He needed a place where he could go and relax away from the fast, high-pressured races. It was our getaway place. We had cows and horses. It's in the country. You can't even get to an airport from there."

Said Eddie Allison, "He healed a hundred percent, but the sad part was nobody would trust him to drive a race car again. And I don't really know why."

"The bad thing about this business," said Humpy Wheeler, "when a driver gets really, really hurt, where he has to spend a lot of time in rehab, people begin to shun him. It's no different from a football player with a terrible ACL injury or a quarterback with twelve concussions. He might have a few games left in him, but people don't want to take the chance."

Donnie drove other races after that, but nothing of consequence, according to Wheeler. "Not that I can remember."

"After Donnie got hurt, he and his son Kenny had to build whatever he was racing," said Eddie Allison. "He ran a lot of Sportsman Busch races after that, but Kenny built the car. Kenny today builds the Legacy cars. A man named Collins, a Toyota dealer in Cape Coral, Florida, owned the car. Collins ended up giving Kenny all his equipment, because Kenny was starting to be a car builder."

Donnie entered only two Winston Cup races in 1983, and he didn't race on the circuit at all in 1984 and 1985.

"He was Late Model racing," said Pat, "and our son Ronald got a Late Model car, and he was racing at Montgomery, and Donnie was helping him with that."

Then in the 1980s it became too expensive for Donnie to run a Late Model car without significant sponsorship. Tires alone were costing $1,000 per race.

"If he didn't have to buy tires, he would have been okay," said Pat.

In 1986 Donnie took a job working with driver Eddie Bierschwale in Texas, all the while waiting for the phone call that would bring him back to Winston Cup racing. Bierschwale's father, Don, owned funeral homes in Texas, and Don wanted his son Eddie to be the next great, young racer. They made races, but never won. Eddie Bierschwale won one fourth-place finish in forty tries.

All the while, Donnie's equipment bag, with his helmet, driving suit, and shoes was packed and ready for use. A few times he took it with him, he was going to drive, but no offer came.

In 1987 and 1988 Donnie drove in a few Busch races and generally did very well. In 1988, he qualified fourth in the Goody's 300 at Daytona.

On August 21, 1988, Donnie Allison drove in his final Winston Cup race at Michigan. Joe Ruttman had walked away from Bob Clarke's race team. Clarke, who needed a last-minute replacement, asked Donnie to drive. The engine died early in the race, and Donnie's Winston Cup career was over.

"Eighty-eight was his last race," said Pat. "Since then he has had a knee replacement stemming from the motorcycle crash he had when he was sixteen and from the wreck at Charlotte in 1981.

"Last month [August 2004] someone called him and asked him to drive in a Busch race in Kentucky. They were looking for a driver over sixty. Donnie told them to call Red Farmer. The guy called back and said he didn't want Red, but we didn't need anyone else hurt in this family.

"I tell Donnie, 'You don't need to get in a race car.'"

In 1990 Donnie got a call from Joe Nemechek, asking if Donnie would be interested in moving to North Carolina to become a crew chief. Did Donnie want to try his hand again at running a car?

He did, and Donnie, Pat, and the Allison family moved away from their beloved Alabama to the town of Salisbury, North Carolina.

No new driving opportunities arose.

"Nobody knew much about a head injury back then," said Pat. "They pretty much said they didn't think Donnie could drive anymore. And the thing he didn't do, and he says now he wishes he did, he didn't go to the races and be at the tracks and in the garages where he could be seen. That's real important if a driver loses a ride. He needed to be on the scene, and Donnie did not do that. He kind of became a recluse for a while.

"Then he went short-track racing, because he needed to make some money, and it became a struggle. He raced until 1988, and then he started to do some crew-chiefing. That's when his career turned again, and now he does consulting, and it's not that bad. When all is said and done, racing has been up and down, but it's ending up pretty nice. That's good, because it could have been a whole lot worse."

CHAPTER 28

Bobby:
A Championship—at Last

"He said to me, quote, 'Someday you assholes from Alabama will learn that we executives don't have to tell you the truth about anything.' Unquote."

—**Bobby Allison**

Bobby Allison's first priority was to find a race team that could win. Otherwise how else could one explain why Bobby would sign up with a team headed by Bill Gardner, the man who outwitted his brother Donnie out of about $250,000 worth of cars and parts?

Bill Gardner was the most active partner on the DiGard team, and while he had a reputation for overpromising, he did have a great eye for talent. His engine builder, Robert Yates, would rate among the best ever, and his crew chief, Gary Nelson, would be placed in the same class with Ralph Moody and Smokey Yunick.

After cutting their teeth with Donnie, DiGard won with Darrell Waltrip, until Darrell got tired of Bill Gardner's shenanigans and left with each threatening to sue the other. After Waltrip, the Gardners then ran off a young Ricky Rudd. Bobby knew of their reputation for being difficult, but he was sure he'd have less aggravation and greater success than he had with the Ranier-Wilson team.

Bill Gardner, the consummate salesman, called Bobby to offer him the ride.

"I want to meet with you," he said. "Come to Connecticut, and I'll make you a deal. I've seen my bad ways. I totally want to amend my way of running the race team. I want to have a good team. Come to Connecticut."

Bobby and his brother-in-law, Tom Kincaid, flew in Bobby's plane to Bridgeport, Connecticut. They met with Gardner and his chief lawyer.

"After what Gardner did to Donnie, I was pretty sure I was reasonably protected because I had my lawyer go through the contract. Also two guys connected with the team, Gary Nelson and Robert Yates, assured me they would go to bat for me and protect me one hundred percent," said Bobby.

"I had known Gary from the short tracks around California. He was from San Bernardino. He had worked for Ivan Baldwin, a guy I really liked out on the West Coast. Gary was a youngster who was very enthusiastic but also was sharp. He was a good people handler, a good boss. He could organize good, could direct whatever the operation was without having to do the work himself, though he was also good at doing the work itself.

"I knew Robert from Holman and Moody, and later Robert was my engine builder at Junior Johnson's. Early on Robert got recognized as one of those guys who knew the right choice of equipment, who made the right adjustments to engines to get the best performance out of them. Most of the guys at Holman and Moody built the engines the way the Ford book said to do it. A couple of guys, Robert and Waddell Wilson, could make the engines just a little bit better."

When Gardner handed Bobby the contract, he was glad he had brought Tom Kincaid along to analyze it. The contract was eighty-eight pages long!

"I had never seen an eighty-eight-page contract in my life," said Bobby. He had his chief lawyer there with him, and they're going to do this deal, and I'm going through it, and Gardner is saying, 'Come on. Come on. Sign it. Let's get this signed, and we'll go out to a restaurant and have a big meal and a few drinks."

"Wait a minute," Bobby said. "Let me look at the thing."

Bobby found a clause that said, "In the event of a rainout, Allison agrees to surrender all proceeds from the race to DiGard."

"We have a few rainouts," Bobby said to Gardner. "This says if we have a rainout, even if we come back and race the next week and I win, you get all the money."

"Oh, don't worry about that," said Gardner. "I'll just take the clause out of there. Call the girl."

He called his secretary and said, "We have to reprint this." Gardner left the room with the contract, and he returned several minutes later. He put it down and said, "It's out of there. Okay, now sign it." He had it open to the page where the offending clause once had been.

Bobby continued looking, and three pages later he found the same rainout clause on a different page. Bobby swore. Gardner again promised to take it out. He went out, came back, and for a third time Bobby found the offending paragraph.

It was eleven at night, and Bobby said to Tom Kincaid, "Come on. Let's get out of here. We can't make a deal with this SOB."

"Ah, come on," said Gardner. "I had to try. You beat me. You got it. Let's make a deal. We'll go page by page."

By two in the morning they had gone through the contract, and both parties signed it. Bobby and Tom Kincaid returned to the airport and flew back to Alabama.

The year 1982 was the first year that the opening race was going to be at Daytona. When Bobby arrived at the track, he was asked about his chances of winning the driving championship. Refusing to set himself up for more disappointment, Bobby said, "Let's just say that I'm going to run all the races. We'll just have to see how it goes." He paused. "I'm going to win some races."

With Robert Yates building the engines and Gary Nelson building the car bodies, Bobby showed early that DiGard was going to be a powerful team. It was not often that a driver could leave a team and contend the next year with his new team, but Bobby looked to be as strong, if not stronger, than he had been in 1981. His competition once again would be the Junior Johnson–Darrell Waltrip race team.

At Daytona, Bobby's car passed inspection before he won the pole for the Daytona 500, and the car passed inspection before he won the Busch Clash, and it passed inspection yet a third time before he won the 125-mile preliminary, but just before Bobby was supposed to go out and practice on Saturday afternoon during what is known as Happy Hour, Joe Gazaway, the inspector who for years seemed to have it in for Allison, ordered the car off the track.

"Your bumper is a quarter inch from where it's supposed to be according to my measurements," said Gazaway. "You have to cut it off and move it before I let you on the track for practice."

It was a pain for the crew, and it made the team miss last practice. Bobby's crew cut the brackets and bumper off, and when they put it back on, they didn't weld the bumper on as snugly as they might have.

"Gary Nelson was very good about saying, 'Let's do it,'" said Bobby. "We only had a little 110-wire welder, which was too light for the job. It was good for sheet metal but inadequate for fine welding. We welded the brackets back on the frame, and we put it all back with the pop rivets on the aluminum trim.

"Gary was disappointed we didn't get to run Happy Hour, but he knew he had me as the driver, and I was going to bring a lot of scrutiny to this race team, because Joe Gazaway didn't like me. I had beaten Joe's Modified car in the Peach Bowl in 1959, and he never got over it. His comment at the time was 'You brought that blankety-blank cheater from Miami and stole our money.'

"I knew Joe Gazaway didn't like me, because he would say so. I'd walk into the garage area, and he'd greet me with, 'You SOB, why did you bother showing up today?'"

After Gazaway approved his new bumper, Bobby started the Daytona 500. He was driving in a pack in the fourth lap when Cale Yarborough got into him and almost put his car into the wall. Cale had Bobby's car turned, and he wasn't letting it go. Cale's bumper hooked Bobby's bumper, and tore it completely off the car.

"That was lucky for me," said Bobby. If it hadn't been for that, I'd have been in the wall."

It wasn't lucky for the rest of the field. When Bobby's bumper fell off, it sat in the middle of the track. The three or four cars that ran over it started a huge wreck.

Bobby ended up crossing the finish line out of gas and won the race. Bobby won fifty percent of the $120,630 winner's share after gaining his sixty-eighth career victory. Cale Yarborough came in second. Tim Brewer, Yarborough's crew chief, charged that Nelson had affixed that rear bumper with Scotch tape so it would fall off at the slightest tap because Bobby's car ran faster without its rear bumper, and that Bobby had slowed down on purpose to get Cale to hit him. It seemed far-fetched, and no one gave the charges much credence.

Nelson, who had a reputation for working up to the edges of the rules, was furious at his accusers. He was also in possession of the four-foot-tall trophy.

After the race Bill Gardner called Bobby up on the phone to thank him.

"I appreciate you," said Gardner, "but I have to ask you a favor."

"What's that?" Bobby asked.

"I'm really in a tight financial bind for race-team money. I need to keep all the proceeds from Daytona for a few days to get some of my bills paid. Will you okay that?"

Because of what had happened between Gardner and Donnie, Bobby had put a clause in their contract that Gardner had to pay Bobby within a certain number of hours after receiving his check from the track. Now Gardner was asking for an exception, and Bobby, flush from having won the biggest race of the year, gave it to him.

Bobby claimed that he did not get paid for the Daytona race until five months later, in early July.

"What about the Rockingham, Richmond, and Atlanta money?" Bobby asked Gardner.

"I'll get it," he said. "I just need a little time."

Throughout the year Gardner would send Bobby checks, some rather large, but they never quite caught up to what he was owed.

"He always stayed months behind," said Bobby.

Bobby's main competitor, Darrell Waltrip, won five races in the spring, including a win at Nashville on May 8. In that race, Bobby's crew chief Gary Nelson installed power steering in his car for the first time. Bobby finished sixth.

The next week at Dover, Bobby became the first driver ever to win a race with power steering. Though Bobby said he felt embarrassed to be using it, because it made his job so much easier, his embarrassment had faded by the next week at Dover when he led 486 of the 500 laps and won the race by three full laps over Dave Marcis. Darrell Waltrip blew his engine late in the race to make the day even grander.

At Charlotte the next week, Neil Bonnett won, and Bill Elliott was second. When Darrell Waltrip spun out three-quarters of the way through the race, many in the crowd cheered. Waltrip was furious. He invited all the fans who were cheering to "meet me in the parking lot of the Big K, and we'll duke it out." He added, "I am embarrassed for the sport."

Bobby won at Long Pond on June 6, thanks to some Good Samaritan help from Dave Marcis. With 41 laps to go and rain on the horizon, Bobby chose to stay out on the track rather than get gas. Four laps later, he was gasless. His car would have rolled to a stop short of his pit, but Marcis, an independent driver who was a friend to all, pulled in behind Bobby and pushed him the rest of the way. Marcis's good deed won Bobby the race. Five days later, his car owner, J. D. Stacy, fired him.

What the naive Marcis didn't know was that Stacy was also the owner of Tim Richmond's car, and Richmond, who finished second, would have won if Allison had been left stranded. Marcis, one of great people on the tour, would have helped anyone. In this case, it happened to be the race leader.

"Mr. Stacy never told me that Richmond and I were teammates," said Marcis. By the end of the next year Stacy, whose race teams had run short on cash at the end of the 1978 season, was in such financial trouble that he was out of Winston Cup racing for good.

Bobby won the second-to-last race of the season at Atlanta, beating Harry Gant and Waltrip. It was Allison's seventy-fourth career win, tying him with Cale Yarborough for third place all-time. Going into the final race at Riverside, Bobby, the winner of ten races that year, trailed Waltrip by 22 points.

The Riverside race began, and without warning, as he drove down the back straightaway, Bobby had a mysterious flat tire. He drove into the pits, got his tire changed, and lost a lap. After his crew took the tire off, Bobby went to inspect the tire to see what had caused the flat, but he had driven it long enough that it had shredded. What caused it remained a mystery.

Bobby went back out onto the track, and as he drove along the back straightaway, once again his tire went flat.

This time Bobby slowed down immediately, seeking to protect the tire from further damage in order to determine what was causing the flat tires.

"When I got to the pits," said Bobby, "the tire had an odd-looking puncture in the outer sidewall. That's all I know about it. If I had to guess, I would say that somebody shot at the car with a gun. I couldn't find the bullet, but I believe to this day that it was a bullet hole."

I asked Bobby where someone could have been standing to shoot a bullet at his car.

"At Riverside, they parked cars all the way around the racetrack," he said. "There were a lot of places somebody could have discreetly fired a gun."

In addition to the two flat tires, Bobby also had stripped lug nuts during a tire change that cost him a lap. He finished the race sixteenth.

Darrell Waltrip suffered with a bad gear box, but he had it changed, and the Junior Johnson Buick recovered to finish the race third. Waltrip beat Bobby in the points race by 72 points, the second such crushing disappointment in a row. It was the fourth year that Bobby had finished second in the points race. The one consolation was his prize money. His car earned $795,077, not a bad year's work.

But at the end of the year, Bobby and Gardner were again fighting over money.

"I made a lot of money that year," said Bobby. "I was running my short-track car and making appearance money, so I had income. I got checks, and they were marked, "proceeds for so and so races," but I never checked it against the accessory sponsorship money I was supposed to get. He was always months behind in what he owed me."

But Bobby wasn't in it for the money. He was in it to win races, and he was comfortable with Robert Yates and Gary Nelson, and so even though he wrangled with the Gardners over what they owed him, he stayed.

Bobby's sponsor had been Gatorade, but in 1982 he got a call from the folks at Miller Beer.

"Miller wanted to go into NASCAR racing," said Bobby, "and they had the money to do it right. But they didn't want to go with Bill Gardner.

"The Miller people said, 'Quit DiGard and come over to M. C. Anderson, and you drive for M. C. Anderson.'

" 'No, no, no,' I said. 'You have to talk to DiGard.' " Bobby gave the Miller representatives Bill Gardner's phone number.

"I wasn't smart enough to figure, Wait a minute. This is generating income," said Bobby.

After Miller called Gardner, Gardner called Bobby to ask if he would allow a beer sponsor on his car. Bobby didn't tell Gardner that he himself had sent Miller to him. Gardner asked Bobby to jump in his plane and meet with the Miller representatives.

When they were done, Miller and Gardner signed a deal for $2 million a year. Bobby didn't make a penny on the deal.

"I didn't do the business part of the deal very well," said Bobby. "I was out there racing, and I was going fast and winning and people were patting me on the back, and my short-track program was good, and I was winning on the short tracks and flying my airplane around the country, just having a ball. So here I was: Gardner made this deal with Miller, and away we went racing with Miller High Life in 1983."

In 1983 Bobby got a call from Walt Sprinkle, who represented the Chevrolet division of General Motors. Sprinkle called to talk Bobby into getting DiGard to run a Chevy rather than the Buick he had run the year before. Sprinkle told him that a guy named Akers, who ran the wind tunnel in Detroit, could show him how to configure the Monte Carlo so it would be as aerodynamic as the Buick. Bobby was skeptical, but he agreed to meet Akers and Sprinkle at the wind tunnel.

Bobby and Gary Nelson put the Monte Carlo on the wind tunnel skid pad, and after they cranked the fan up, the wind started to blow the car off the skid pad. It was clear to everyone that the Buick was not going to be able to perform.

It was eleven o'clock at night, and Sprinkle said to Bobby, "We have a drawing for a new nose for the Chevrolet, but our guys say they can't have it for two years."

"Can I see the drawing?" asked Bobby. Sprinkle showed it to him.

"I have a guy in Alabama named Grady Humphries," Bobby said. "He works for me in my little Sportsman shop. We can make this thing for you in one week and have this car back here in the wind tunnel one week from today."

Bobby was given the green light to build the new nose for the Monte Carlo. The nose, an add-on, was bigger than the original nose. Back in Alabama, Grady

Humphries and the race team crumpled newspaper to fill the area and make this fiberglass nose for the Chevrolet Monte Carlo.

As promised, the car was back in Detroit for the wind tunnel test in a week. And not only was the car better than the Monte Carlo had ever been, but it was also more aerodynamic than the best Buick.

Adding to the performance was the improvement Bobby had made to the back window. Bobby's new design had more slope, making it slightly better on drag, but *way* better on lift.

The Chevrolet executives were ecstatic, so they called Robert Stemple, vice president of General Motors, to tell him about the test. At about eleven at night on a Monday evening, Stemple came to the wind tunnel to inspect the car.

"Wow, I see what you've done," Stemple said to Bobby. "I really like that nose. But I don't like that back window, so I'll give you the nose, but you're going to have to learn to drive it without the back window."

Bobby agreed.

On the way out, Bobby was told, "You have to leave the nose here so we can copy your nose exactly." Bobby's men cut off the front of the car and left them the entire nose so they could make their model.

Bobby went home, and the DiGard team got busy building their Monte Carlo for Daytona. About a week later Bobby attended an autograph session at a car show at Burke Lakefront Airport in Cleveland. Bobby had a large crowd of autograph seekers around him, when one of them said, "Bobby, have you seen Junior's new car down there? Boy, does it really look nice."

In 1982 Junior had run a Buick. Bobby said to himself, *Buick isn't making anything new. What the heck is he talking about?* After a break, Bobby walked down to the display of Junior Johnson's new car: It was a Monte Carlo, and it was sporting Bobby's nose built in Hueytown, Alabama!

"I was absolutely beside myself about this," said Bobby. "We've done all this work. I haven't charged General Motors a penny. I paid my own way.

"Then I found out that the guy who had been the field rep for the Buick division of General Motors, Herb Fishel, had been transferred to the Chevrolet division. So now Fishel is in charge of Chevrolet—he ranks above Walt Sprinkle—and Fishel is Junior Johnson's buddy. He thinks Junior Johnson hung the moon, and so he's made a deal with Junior. He has made Junior the Chevrolet factory deal to the point that when it's time for us to get our noses for Daytona, we have to get them from Junior! Yes, from Junior!"

When Bobby went to Junior to get his noses, Junior told him, "You can only have one nose."

"Junior, we have cars we have to make ready," said Bobby.

"Right now we don't have enough," said Junior. "We'll give you two so you'll have one for the Busch Clash and one for your backup. That's all you get for now."

The DiGard team went to Daytona, where Bobby crashed the Busch car *and* the backup car. The only car left was a short-track car that was getting readied for Richmond. Bobby almost won the Daytona 500 anyway.

"We were way, way up front at the end, when something went wrong," said Bobby. He finished ninth behind Cale Yarborough.

After the race Bobby went to see Herb Fishel.

"Herb," said Bobby. "What's the deal? I thought we were supposed to be the Chevrolet connection.

"And Herb Fishel said to me, quote, 'Someday you assholes from Alabama will learn that we executives don't have to tell you the truth about anything.' Unquote.

"I was floored," said Bobby.

At Richmond, Bobby won the race in his Monte Carlo with Dale Earnhardt on his back bumper. Then he finished tenth at Rockingham, pushing his career winnings over $4 million. Only Richard Petty had won more.

But after Herb Fishel had told Bobby off, it was decided that DiGard needed to switch to Buick, even though the Monte Carlo had a better body style.

"We needed to be somewhere else," said Bobby. "By then a fellow by the name of Ray Smith was the Buick field representative, and Ray was very easy to work with. Don Hackworth had become general manager of the Buick division, and Don also was really good for me and to me."

After Rockingham, DiGard switched to a Buick, a switch that didn't slow the DiGard team a bit. Bobby had a top ten at Darlington, leading the race but falling back, then was second behind Darrell Waltrip at North Wilkesboro, Junior Johnson's home track.

Waltrip and Bobby then resumed their mano a mano. At Martinsville, Bobby led with 15 laps to go. As Bobby headed for pit road, he was sure Waltrip was following behind him, but then, at the last moment, Waltrip stayed out on the track and took the lead. Waltrip won that day, and Bobby finished third.

At Talladega, Richard Petty won, and both Bobby and Waltrip had problems. Bobby had bad tires and mechanical problems and finished tenth, two laps down. Waltrip suffered a blown right tire, then crashed into Phil Parsons, who had a horrific crash, flipping and rolling.

At Nashville on May 7, Bobby and Waltrip fought for the lead. Waltrip had the better car, and Bobby was second. He was upset he hadn't won, because the race was named for his close friend, the country and western singer and stock car racer, Marty Robbins. Bobby had to look on as Ronnie Robbins, Marty's son, presented Darrell with Robbins's driver's uniform and copies of some of his gold records.

On May 17 at Dover, Bobby caught a break. Waltrip was a fender ahead with five laps left when it began to pour. Bobby stuck his nose in front of Waltrip just as the race was red-flagged. The win gave Bobby the points lead.

After the race, Bobby told reporters that one of the members of Junior's crew had been telling his race team everything Bobby's team was doing.

Bobby finished fourth at Nashville and third at Pocono, and then at Talladega on

July 31, Waltrip was leading Dale Earnhardt when Bobby slid in behind Earnhardt. The two drafted together, as Earnhardt passed Waltrip for the win. After the race Waltrip was furious, accusing Bobby of doing everything he could to cost him the victory.

Years later Bobby could not hide his pleasure. "If I helped Earnhardt draft by Darrell," said Bobby, "I'm sure I got a kick out of that."

After the race Bobby accused the Junior Johnson–Darrell Waltrip team of cheating.

"Darrell got away with engines that were the wrong cubic-inch size," said Bobby. "Darrell had gotten away with that since he came into Winston Cup. Bill and Joe Gazaway, the inspectors, loved Darrell. They decided he was the best young man who had come along. They were always incredibly fond of him. And I always resented him for it."

As July moved into August, Bobby and Waltrip continued to battle. At Nashville, Waltrip was second, Bobby fourth. At Richmond, Waltrip was second, Bobby third. After the race, Waltrip accused Bobby of blocking him so he couldn't pass Dale Earnhardt and win the race.

Bobby accused Waltrip of making up excuses. Said Bobby, "We look out for ourselves. There were money and points involved."

At Bristol, Waltrip won, and Bobby was third. Waltrip won when his last pit stop was faster than Dale Earnhardt's. Waltrip beat him out, and then the rains came, ending the race early.

At Darlington on September 5, Bobby won his fifth race of the year despite a grueling 97-degree heat. He was forty-six-years old, the oldest driver ever to win at Darlington. Two months before, son Clifford's wife had given birth to a daughter, Leslie Kay. The writers were taking to calling Bobby "Grandpa."

At Richmond, Bobby won his second race in a row. Ricky Rudd was second, Waltrip fourth. When Bobby won again on September 18, and Waltrip had mechanical trouble, Bobby's point lead blossomed to 101.

"We were working together really good," said Bobby. "I had a really good relationship with Gary Nelson and Robert Yates all through 1982 and 1983. Gary Nelson had the great attitude of *What's the problem? Let's address it. Forget yesterday, and let's go and do the best we can.* As a result, yesterday's disappointments had nothing to do with what we were going to do today. We were able to go on from there, and that really worked well with my attitude and temperament."

Waltrip, as was his nature, refused to quit. At Martinsville, Ricky Rudd won. Bobby was second, Waltrip third. Then Waltrip finished second at Charlotte, while Bobby was seventh. The lead fell to 67 points. In this race Richard Petty's win created a scandal. Maurice Petty had installed an oversized engine, and NASCAR caught him. Petty was allowed to keep his win, but Petty Enterprises was fined $35,000. Richard Petty would leave the family business at the end of the year.

At Rockingham, Bobby blew a tire and finished sixteenth, losing more points to Waltrip, who finished fifth. Bobby was leading the Atlanta race, looking to pad his points lead, when he drove down pit road and ran over sharp debris that caused a tire to blow and his car to hit the pit road wall. Though the setup was lost, Bobby was able to recover and finish third. Waltrip finished ninth.

With the Riverside race left on the schedule, Bobby had a 64-point lead over Waltrip. Bobby needed to finish thirteenth to clinch it.

Darrell Waltrip won the pole for the Riverside race, and Bobby qualified sixth. Gary Nelson, Bobby's crew chief, sat with Bobby, and they decided to be conservative. As the race began, Bobby looked at his gas gauge, and the indicator said he was low on fuel pressure.

"I'm out of gas," Bobby yelled to Nelson.

"You can't be out of gas," said Nelson. "Keep going."

"Gary, I'm out of gas," said Bobby. "Something's wrong."

Said Bobby, "He's telling me to keep going, but I came into the pits and they put gas in the car. The tank held eight gallons.

"I ran for several laps, and the car ran pretty good, and then it did it again."

"Gary, I'm out of gas again," Bobby said. "Something's wrong."

"Come on. We'll fill you back up," said Nelson. "But we don't see anything wrong."

Bobby came in, and Nelson topped off the tank. Bobby was beside himself. His engine wasn't running right, and he knew he was going to lose points and blow the championship once again.

"The car is really running bad, and it's a shorter number of laps before it starts to run bad again. I was picturing that the pickup hose was broken off inside the tank," said Bobby. "Something was wrong in the pickup fuel system, making the thing not able to get gas to the carburetor.

"We were struggling, losing the championship. There was enough distance between where we're going to finish and where Darrell's going to finish that he's going to win again."

This time, the Gods were smiling down on Bobby Allison. Waltrip and Tim Richmond came together, and Richmond spun Waltrip out, sending him through the infield on turn nine. Despite the fuel problems, Bobby was able to finish the race in ninth place. Despite the collision, Waltrip finished sixth.

"That allowed us to win the championship," said Bobby, who finished the 1983 season 47 points ahead of Waltrip. Finally, Bobby Allison was the Winston Cup driving champion.

Despite this, Bobby was beside himself after the race.

"What could have gone wrong? I wondered. I wanted to look at the car, but Gary Nelson said to me, 'Bobby, we won. Forget it. Forget everything. We won. We're champions. Be happy.'"

Bobby and Judy celebrated for over two hours. After the race, they flew home on a commercial jet. When they arrived at the Birmingham airport, Bobby received a hero's welcome. A hundred fans gathered with banners and signs and cheers. When they arrived home, more people were there to greet them.

Meanwhile, Bobby's car traveled on a PR tour and didn't return to Charlotte for a couple of weeks. Bobby, obsessed with what could have gone wrong with his engine, met Gary at the shop at Charlotte.

"Look at the car and see what's wrong," said Bobby.

Nelson demurred.

"We won the championship, so be happy," he said.

Several days later when Nelson took the car apart, he discovered a huge amount of sugar had been poured into the gas tank of Bobby's Buick. Since the car had never been left unsupervised, Nelson figured that someone had to have sabotaged the gas can at the race track.

Bobby had no proof, but for years he's held a strong belief that a rogue member on the Junior Johnson race team went off and sabotaged his car—with bullets and then with sugar—at the Riverside race of 1982 and again in 1983. Recently, Bobby says, he was told that a former member of the Johnson race team was heard bragging about the sugar incident.

"It was a guy who worked for Johnson at the time," said Bobby. "Anyway, we somehow scraped on through and finished with that sugar in our gas tank and won the championship, and then it wasn't important to anybody but me why it happened and how it got by us. How did somebody get away with doing this? Who did it? For a long time no one admitted anything. People accused me of being paranoid. Darrell always said that my problem was that I felt everyone was out to get me. But I didn't think *everyone* was out to get me. Just a few. Only a few. But they were really good at getting me."

CHAPTER 29

Bobby: It Gets Ugly

"I'm doing this whether you like it or not. Get your best lawyers, and we'll fight it out in court."

—Bill Gardner

Winning a championship one year is no guarantee of success for the next. If an owner is in it for the money more than for victory, there may be a temptation to use victory to expand the race team's sphere of influence. In the case of DiGard, owner Bill Gardner, flush with success, decided he could earn even more money by using Robert Yates's skill as an engine builder to supply engines to other teams—even though he had explicitly agreed in his contract with Bobby Allison two years earlier not to do just that.

When Bobby Allison signed his contract, he inserted a noncompete clause that specifically barred the DiGard team from helping any other race team.

"Throughout my career I was willing to help people," said Bobby, "and I did that an awful lot. But I began to see it was pretty much a one-way street. The people who benefited from my help rarely came back to return the favor when I needed help. Most of the time, it was, 'We're competitors. I can't do that for you.' "

Bobby wanted DiGard helping him and him alone, and this clause was designed to insure that.

But Bill Gardner was too clever for Bobby Allison. According to Bobby, the contract said DiGard couldn't help any other team. To get around it, in 1984 Gardner started a whole new company, calling it the Research and Development team. He made himself president and named Gary Nelson vice president. If Gardner wanted to run a second car, so his thinking went, he could, because it wasn't the DiGard team, but the Research and Development team. By extending the logic, if Research and Development wanted to supply engines to a competitor, using the same leg-erdemain, he could do that, too. It was all perfectly legal—unfortunately for Bobby.

When the 1984 season began, Gardner informed Bobby that he was going to supply engines to the new Mike Curb racing team with Richard Petty behind the wheel. It wasn't bad enough that Robert Yates would be building engines for one of his fiercest competitors, but under their deal, if Petty wasn't satisfied with his en-gine, the morning of any race he could drive over to the DiGard garage and take Bobby's engine and give Bobby his. For Bobby, it was more a punch in the mouth than a slap in the face. Bad enough Gardner was doing it at all. But to build engines for Richard Petty, the rich guy who over the years used his clout to beat him time and time again? The only way this could have been worse would have been if Gardner had signed a deal to build engines for Darrell Waltrip, whom he despised even more.

"They made the deal with the Pettys," said Bobby. "Here was the seven-time champion who DiGard Racing had a chance to do business with. And they made a deal, if Richard was unhappy with his DiGard-supplied engine, he could take my engine out of my car on Sunday morning and give me his. The bottom line was I was furious.

"Here the man owed me all this money, and after we win the national champi-onship with a lot of credit to Gary Nelson and Robert Yates and a little bit of credit to me, now he's made a deal to build the engines for Petty and not for a big profit but for the political credit of furnishing engines to the great Richard Petty."

Bobby didn't want Robert Yates building engines for a chief competitor. In fact, Yates didn't want to do it, either. But his contract with DiGard let the Gardners dic-tate his duties.

When Bobby confronted Bill Gardner, the car owner told him bluntly, "I'm do-ing this whether you like it or not. Get your best lawyers, and we'll fight it out in court."

When Bobby looked into hiring counsel, his family lawyer didn't have the expe-rience, and the hot shots in Birmingham wanted more than he was willing to pay up front to contest it. Ultimately Bobby decided he didn't have the time or the energy to sue. He was a racer, and he needed to concentrate on what he needed to do: win races.

"I paid a big price for trying to do the best I could with my career," said Bobby. "A lot of times I took guff from people when I should have said, 'That ain't the deal.' I did two things wrong. One, I was too enthusiastic about what I was doing and what I was trying to accomplish even under these screwball circumstances, and two, I wasn't a good businessman. I never once sat down and said, 'The cost of achieving this victory, which is worth $100,000, is $150,000.'

"Other drivers were so much better at the business part of racing. If somebody else did it well, I should have, too."

———

If Bobby Allison hadn't become a stock car racer, he could very easily have become a mechanical engineer in airplane design. His greatest joy away from the track was flying and working on airplanes. Unlike many of the drivers who enjoyed hunting in their spare time, Bobby much preferred the thrill of going into the wild blue yonder.

He had bought the Aerostar 601P, which came with two 290-horsepower engines, for $300,000, in 1981, and had Machen do a conversion to improve the speed of the plane at the cost of another $175,000 to install twin 350-horsepower engines. They called the plane the Aerostar Superstar.

It was not a frivolous investment, because Bobby used the plane to fly himself to short-track races and personal appearances, making him a lot of money he could not have earned without the speed and convenience of flight.

In 1983 Bobby lent his 1981 Aerostar 601P that had been converted to a Superstar to the Piper Aircraft Corporation, so they could use it as a prototype of Piper's new 700 version of their top-of-the-line corporate twin. After Piper built the 700, Bobby bought one of the first ones off the line for $400,000. (He then sold his other Aerostar to a friend, Roy Hess.)

"Judy wasn't fond of my fleet of airplanes," said Bobby, "but she knew it was what I wanted to do and knew I was making the money to do it. My airplane investments usually did not turn out to be unprofitable. I could buy a plane and sell it and make a profit."

Bobby's son, Davey, also began flying. Bobby had a single-engine Grumman that Davey flew before he even got his flying license. When Davey began to have success and make money, he bought a single-engine Beechcraft Bonanza, one of the most reliable planes in the air. Like his dad, Davey wasn't happy with the performance of his plane. His comment was, "I want my plane to be able to go faster than my race car." The Bonanza didn't do that, and so he traded it in for a Piper Cheyenne, a much bigger airplane with two Pratt and Whitney turbine engines.

Piper completed the construction of its 700 just before the 1984 Daytona 500. The Wednesday before the race Bobby landed the plane on the backstretch at Daytona, taxiing it into an area of track equipment out of sight of the front grandstand.

Bobby won the second of the 125 qualifying races, and after going to Victory Lane, he walked onto the grass of the tri-oval where his new plane sat waiting. As the fans were leaving the track, Bobby got in the plane and took off down the back straightaway and landed at the nearby Daytona Beach airport. The next morning he flew to Vero Beach for a big delivery ceremony at the Piper plant.

Bobby's only disappointment was that Piper made a few changes at the factory, and as a result it was more reliable, but wasn't quite as fast as his Aerostar.

"It wasn't as good as it could have been," said Bobby, "but it was still way better than anything else in the sky."

During his tumultuous years with DiGard, Bobby flew to rid himself of his bad feelings for Bill Gardner.

"I could put all that behind me," he said. "I could go to a short-track race, have a big old time, maybe win the race. I would go to about thirty short-track races a year, and I'd make five grand, seventy-five hundred, or maybe even ten thousand for an event. In those days that was big money."

At Daytona, Bobby started the 1984 season badly when he had to exit the 500 with a faulty camshaft, and a blown engine ended his day at Richmond. His mood was black, but at Rockingham Bobby won his eighty-first Winston Cup victory, passing Terry Labonte with fifty laps to go.

On May 20 Petty won his 199th race at Dover with one of Robert Yates's engines. In that race Bobby finished twelfth, eight laps down.

The next week Bobby won his eighty-second race in the Charlotte World 600. His Buick had outstanding gas mileage, and chief competitor Darrell Waltrip's engine quit with seventeen laps to go. It was his 600th start, a milestone, and the $88,500 he won made him the second driver after Petty to win $5 million in purses.

According to Bobby, on July 3, 1984, the day before the Firecracker 400, Robert Yates went to the Curb transporter with the intention of retrieving the engine. Curb hadn't paid for it as well as for others Yates had built. Yates was the sort of person who didn't borrow money and didn't like to be owed money.

But NASCAR, knowing that President Ronald Reagan would be attending, was fearful that Yates would cause a scene and embarrass the sport in front of the president. NASCAR asked Yates to back off.

July 4, 1984, was a day of wonder, as Richard Petty won the race with Robert Yates's DiGard engine. It was Petty's 200th and final victory, a memorable day in NASCAR history. During his whole career. Bobby had resented Petty's financial and political advantages. Bobby had to sit by and watch as the Pride of the Carolinas seemed to get every ruling NASCAR could give him while he, Donnie, and Neil Bonnett were viewed by the NASCAR inspectors as illegal aliens from Alabama land. It was only fitting, Bobby thought wryly, that Petty should win this race with one of his engines and that NASCAR would refuse to inspect it after the race. Bobby was seething, mad at Gardner, jealous of Petty, and furious with NASCAR, but as always, helpless to do anything about it.

Bobby first had been suspicious of Petty's winning engine the week before the race. From time to time he would walk through the DiGard engine room to go see Robert Yates, who built his engines as well. Bobby regarded Yates as "one of the neat guys in racing," and he "wanted to keep this personal friendship and also keep his best efforts." Said Bobby, "I felt I could only do that by accepting this deal I didn't like and still spend a little time with him."

When Bobby viewed the engine that he was sure Yates was building for Richard Petty, he thought that it looked significantly oversized. When he asked who it was for, he was told, "Don't worry about that. It's for a customer. Get out of here."

Allison, suspicious, went back and scratched a little mark on the engine block with a sharp object in a "very inconspicuous place."

Said Bobby, "I knew where to look, and before the race, I looked under the hood of Petty's car and saw the mark on the block."

When Allison fell out of the race early and Petty went on to win, it was perhaps the lowest emotional point of Bobby Allison's long career.

"Here was Richard Petty winning with a DiGard engine, and here I am, the defending champion, and I felt like such an outsider you could not believe it," said Bobby. "Here Bill Gardner still owed me this incredible amount of money, and that was what he *said* he owed me."

Adding insult to injury, according to Bobby, NASCAR skipped the postrace inspection, an indication to Bobby that NASCAR was turning a blind eye to what he believed was an oversized engine.

"Somebody in NASCAR definitely knew about it," said Bobby, "but I don't know who. By then, the Gazaways were gone. Joe got fired, and Bill was moved to an office job at Daytona that was comparable to checking the latrine. So he retired. They brought in Dick Beaty, who was better for me. Beaty at least didn't single me out for unfair scrutiny."

Said Bobby, "There were a couple of reasons why they didn't have an inspection after the 1984 Firecracker 400. First of all, Richard won. Second, it was in front of the president of the United States, and there was the king of racing and the president, and it all made for such a good story.

"Had I won the race, I'm sure there would have been a postrace inspection. But being that Richard won, that was fine."

Bobby decided to keep his mouth shut. Bobby got to meet President Reagan after the race. An associate sponsor, Quaker State, made a racing jacket especially for the president, and Bobby presented it to him as he walked through the garage area.

By the summer, DiGard was in financial trouble. How the Gardners were spending their money became an issue when Miller Beer, Bobby's sponsor, began to ask questions.

Tensions between Bobby and Bill Gardner were growing. In late July Bobby had engine problems at Darlington and more engine problems at Richmond. Then at Dover a blown tire sent his Buick out of control. He broke a collarbone and cracked his right shoulder blade.

Bobby went to the local hospital, where the doctor told him he was scheduling surgery on his shoulder. Bobby told the doctor he would take care of his shoulder back in Birmingham. The doctor asked how he was going to get there.

"Fly," he said. The doctor said it would be dangerous to fly because he also had a bruised lung.

"I'll chance it," Bobby said.

In the air, Bobby had to fly with his left arm in a sling.

The pain in Bobby's lungs became so great he had to land in Knoxville.

Meanwhile, financial problems for the team were growing. Hotels were not letting Bobby and the team register, citing unpaid bills. Gary Nelson sometimes paid hotel bills on his personal credit card. Payroll checks were being cut after 4:00 p.m. on Friday so they couldn't be cashed until the following Monday. Meanwhile, Bill Gardner called a press conference to announce he was going to build a new multi-million dollar industrial park in Charlotte.

Nelson, who was plagued by a shortage of adequate parts and by the Gardners, wanted to quit. So did Robert Yates. So did Bobby. But Nelson, Yates, and Bobby all had contracts with DiGard through 1985, and they remembered how tough the Gardners had fought Darrell Waltrip when he tried to leave prematurely, so they stayed, despite the financial problems and the unhappiness.

In 1984, a year of turmoil, Bobby won just two races. Injuries from his crash at Dover in August added to his woes. That year the 1983 Winston Cup champion earned $641,048 but finished sixth in the points. Terry Labonte didn't win a single race but became the new racing champion.

In January 1985, the Gardners hired Paul Giltinan as a chassis engineer and promoted one of the crew, Robin Pemberton, to be crew chief. The year before, Pemberton had worked for Richard Petty.

"Gary Nelson called to see if I was interested in joining DiGard," said Pemberton. "I was leaving a team [Petty Enterprises] that had gone through five drivers during the year, and they didn't have a sponsor. So even the Gardners appeared to be more stable. That should tell you something.

"When I joined DiGard, they were winners. They were a year removed from a championship. I thought I was going to the top. Little did I know— The saying we used was 'We're getting into a hot air balloon with holes in it.' We thought we were going up, but no matter how hard we tried, it wouldn't stay up."

Bobby asked Gary Nelson what his job was.

"Bill has some special things he wants me to do," he replied.

The "special things" was to start a second race team under a separate company called Research and Development with Greg Sacks as the other driver. Gardner correctly figured that if Allison wasn't going to sue over the Petty engine deal, he wouldn't sue over the second race team, either. And yet at the same time Gardner used the wording of the contract to keep Bobby from quitting the team.

"Gardner was incredible," said Bobby. "He kept saying, 'We have in the contract that if you quit, you forfeit all the earnings still owed you.' So I couldn't afford to quit."

Bobby's race team had a deal with Buick, which furnished sheet metal, engine parts, and some money. It was a significant deal, and Bobby didn't want to jeopardize it. When he learned that Bill Gardner intended the Greg Sacks car to be a Chevrolet, Bobby exploded, to no avail.

"Buick was helping us, and they were stabbing Buick in the back," said Bobby, "using Buick engines and support money and equipment to run a Chevrolet. The divisions at General Motors were stiff rivals with each other."

Daytona was a nightmare. Bobby's car didn't run well in the Daytona 500, and a faulty clutch ruined his day. Making things worse, Sacks finished sixth in a Sacks and Sons Chevrolet.

"They couldn't call it DiGard because that violated our contract," said Bobby.

Bobby finished a lame sixteenth at Richmond, and another faulty clutch did him in at Rockingham. He finished thirty-first despite Robin Pemberton's best efforts.

"Robin tried hard," said Bobby, "but there was just no harmony."

Pemberton, in his first crew chief job, could see firsthand what a terrific driver Bobby was.

"Bobby was an incredible driver," said Pemberton. "Bobby had an incredible feel for the car. He had stamina, a lot of common sense, though a lot of times he'd aggravate the mortal shit out of you. He would drag some piece in from Alabama that he needed bolted onto his [street] car—I would kid Bobby and Donnie about it occasionally—you didn't mind doing it, but a lot of times it was at four o'clock in the afternoon of the day you wanted to go somewhere. Like to the racetrack. It was comical at times.

"Bobby was into it. He tried. You try very hard for the guys who try hard. If there is something they think they need to go better, then you try to give it to them."

By this time, Bill Gardner badly wanted Bobby Allison to quit. He had had his fill of Bobby, and if Bobby did quit, under the contract Gardner would be absolved of having to pay him the substantial amount of back earnings he owed him.

Before the Pocono race on June 9, the lawyer for the Gardners approached Robin Pemberton and said, "Will you see T.R. this weekend?"

Pemberton thought he meant Tom Roberts, the public relations man for Miller Beer, their sponsor.

Pemberton said he certainly would see him.

"Would you give this envelope to him then?" the lawyer said.

When Pemberton got to Pocono, he found Roberts and gave him the envelope. The next day Roberts found Pemberton and said, "You gave this to the wrong T.R."

Pemberton asked him what he was talking about.

Roberts showed him the contents of the envelope. It was a proposed contract for driver Tim Richmond, who was a friend of Pemberton's.

Said Pemberton, "The lawyer, as ignorant as he was, he just tried to be real cute and say, 'T.R.' And this was while Bobby Allison was our driver. They were going to fire him!"

Pemberton, who was loyal to Bobby, informed him of what Bill Gardner was up to.

"Somehow—imagine this—it leaked out that Bobby was getting the skids put to him," said Pemberton.

Bobby could see that the racing game was dominated by wealthy organizations willing to spend a lot of money on their cars and on top employees. Richard Childress, with Dale Earnhardt as his driver, was putting together just such an organization. So was the Melling organization with Bill Elliott.

The Gardner brothers, meanwhile, were so behind the eight ball financially that they no longer could afford new equipment.

Prior to the June 5 race at Pocono, Bobby, Yates, and Nelson demanded a sit-down with the Gardners. Bobby said he wanted to quit. As a concession, Bill Gardner said Bobby could go back to setting up his own chassis, in effect firing Paul Giltinan.

After two top-ten finishes at Pocono and Michigan, the team went to Daytona for the Firecracker 500.

"We went to Daytona for the Fourth of July race," said Robin Pemberton. "Bobby was our driver. I was his crew chief. DiGard also had a research and development car driven by Greg Sacks. Gary Nelson was his crew chief.

"Late in the race we were running on seven cylinders, but we were still a top-ten car. If the motor hadn't blown, we'd have won the race. No one figured Sacks would run as good as he was, but he was hauling ass. It came down to a green-flag pit stop, and the Sacks team only had a makeshift pit crew, so all my guys ran down to pit his car. Well, the next lap Bobby came down pit road, and I didn't have anybody in my pit. All the Miller guys were pitting Greg Sacks in his Monte Carlo. There wasn't a single son of a bitch standing in the pits when Bobby Allison came in. Not one.

"I came over to try to change tires. He came on the radio and said, 'Don't worry about it. It's over. Just put gas in it.'

"I didn't have a gas guy. I didn't have anything. One of the guys went over and put gas in it and sent Bobby on his way. And that was the end of it.

"After the race, which Greg won, Bobby told me, 'Hey, I appreciate the effort, man. I'll be talking to you.' And he said it in a tone of voice where I knew it was not going to be good. The very next race Bobby started his own team.

"The Gardners didn't treat Robert Yates very well, either. They promised Robert part of the business." Bobby heard that as Robert was trying to pay the bills for the engine department to get the equipment paid for, one of the Gardners was mortgaging the equipment back to another bank. There's nothing illegal about that, but it just drove Robert crazy.

"Even today, Robert doesn't take on a lot of debt. He gets stuff paid off as fast as he can. He just likes to live that way. He's a son of a preacher, and he'll always be that way.

"So it got to be a little edgy. They promised Robert research and development facilities, but the same old deal, they never carried through on their promise. When I signed my contract, they showed me a drawing of this incredible facility for research and development—it was beautiful. But it was never built. They used the promise of it to attract people."

A couple of other things happened in the Firecracker 500 that convinced Bobby it was time to walk out on the Gardners.

During practice for the race, Bobby was fast in his Buick. Greg Sacks's team tried a new chassis setup, and it didn't work. Greg's car was slow, even though it still had the oversized engine Richard Petty had run in the Firecracker 400 the year before.

Gary Nelson walked over to Bobby's car, and he took note of the adjustments he and Robin Pemberton had made to the shocks and springs.

"I had a ten-and-a-half-inch-long, 2,250-pound right-front spring, and a nine-and-a-half-inch-long, 1,400-pound left-front spring, and they put the same thing in their car," said Bobby. "They copied what I had to where Greg could drive it.

"But I was still going to win the race. And then the race started, and my engine started missing. It really annoyed me. They told me on the radio to come in to the pits. I didn't answer them. I drove to the garage area, went to the toolbox, pulled the valve cover off the engine, and one of my rocker arms didn't have the adjustment-screw lock nut on it—there was *no* lock nut on the rocker arm adjuster. So I was on seven cylinders.

"It was a deal where eventually it would kick the lifter out of the hole and then kill the oil pressure and the engine. But I caught it before that happened.

"I fixed the thing, but at that point I decided I needed to be out of this thing."

Irony of ironies, Greg Sacks won that day, his only Winston Cup win in ten years of trying for the New Yorker. No one was happier about Sacks's win than Bobby, because it was obvious that Sacks was driving for the Gardners. After the race Bobby went to a lawyer in Birmingham and sued Bill Gardner for breach of contract in an effort to prevent Gardner from saying he had quit and forfeiting approximately $250,000 in winnings that Gardner owed him.

By 10:00 A.M. the next morning, Gardner said Bobby was free to go.

It wasn't until 1988, right before his near-fatal accident at Pocono, that Bobby decided to look into whether he could collect the money he believed Gardner owed him. Bobby wrote a friend who worked in one of the companies that had paid contingency-prize money. He asked his friend how much money the company had sent to Gardner.

"I wrote every company I got checks from—STP, Union Oil, Goodyear—and I got photocopies of paid checks. I contacted fourteen of the companies and got photocopies of canceled checks that they had sent him." Then Bobby called his lawyer.

Bobby was almost killed at Pocono, and he was in no condition for a legal fight. Bobby's lawyer, Tom Kincaid, was more concerned about Bobby's mental health than he was about Bobby recovering the money from Gardner. It was his opinion that Bobby shouldn't go through the trauma of a trial. There was another practical problem. It was Kincaid's opinion that even if Bobby won, he wouldn't be able to collect.

By now, the statute of limitations has run, and Bobby never did collect any money from Gardner.

"Let me tell you," said Bobby in 2004, "the man owes me two hundred and fifty thousand dollars right now."

After he left DiGard, Bobby decided that he would run his own car out of his shop in Hueytown until he could hook up with another race team. Several disgruntled members of his team, including Wayne Baumgartner, Mike Bessinger, and Pat Broyles, left with him. His friends at Miller Beer also came along.

He drove a Buick, and mostly he ran poorly. A highlight for Bobby came at Talladega, where son Davey entered his first Winston Cup race. Bobby finished twenty-first. Davey, driving for Hoss Ellington, finished an impressive tenth.

The other bright spot for Bobby after leaving DiGard came at Dover on September 15. He finished fourth in a Ford he rented from Maurice Petty in a race won by Harry Gant.

Bobby ran the Ford because NASCAR had changed the rules and made it too difficult to continue with the Buick. He had been loyal to Buick, one of the last Buick drivers left, and so reluctantly he made the switch to Ford. By then Maurice Petty had fallen on hard times. Richard had left him to go with Mike Curb, and Maurice was a car owner without a race team. In the past Maurice and Bobby were antagonistic rivals. At Dover they joined together and did well. When NASCAR readjusted the rules to help Buick after the race, Bobby returned to running his Buick.

In order to race at Martinsville the next week, Bobby rented a Buick from the Stavola brothers, two men from New Jersey who had made a lot of money in the rock and road building businesses. The father of the two men had discovered that there was a vein of excellent road-building material running from New Jersey all the way into New England. They had built a lot of the turnpikes throughout New England and also ran a very successful asphalt and paving business. The brothers were race fans, and in 1985 ran a car driven by a youngster by the name of Bobby Hillin.

Bobby finished tenth at Martinsville in Stavola's Buick.

Bobby's race shop was on Route 29 in sight of the Charlotte Motor Speedway. The Stavola's shop was on Highway 49 in Harrisburg. Ed Bracefield, who did PR for the Stavola's, came over to Bobby's shop and asked if he would stop by the Stavolas for a chat.

They met, and they agreed that Bobby would sell the Stavolas all his racing equipment, the Stavolas would hire his crew, and he would sign on as the driver of their second car. As part of the deal, Bobby agreed to help groom Bobby Hillin.

"When I left DiGard and started running my own car, I realized that the whole situation was a bigger total picture than I had previously thought," said Bobby. "Racing had grown to where you needed a lot of employees. You had the engine group, the car-building group. The days of Eddie and me working on my car were over.

"When the deal with the Stavolas came together, they were going to allow me to race. They were going to furnish me with good equipment, let me do what I wanted to do, call my shots to a large degree. The way it came together, it was going to be an ideal situation."

It didn't turn out that way. It rarely did. Bobby ran a few races for the Stavolas in 1985 with little success. He was last at North Wilkesboro when his engine failed early and fourteenth at Charlotte. Nevertheless, he signed to drive for them in 1986.

Bobby was going to be forty-nine years old. Everyone in racing figured Bobby Allison was done. Everyone, that is, except Bobby Allison.

CHAPTER 30

Davey: The Prodigal Son

"You can either be a choirboy or a race car driver."

—Neil Bonnett

Before Davey Allison could walk, he wanted to race. His first sounds were engine sounds.

"I remember the first two words out of his mouth when he was nine months old," said Bobby. "Davey stood up in the car seat next to me and said, 'Vraddnnnn! Vraddnnnnn!' It was the sound a V-8 makes when the driver hits the throttle.

While Davey was growing up, all he thought about was racing.

"I had to stay after school because I was dillydallying, drawing pictures of race cars instead of paying attention," Davey said. "Sometimes they were pictures of my dad's car, but mostly they were what I dreamed mine would look like."

Wanda Lund, Tiny Lund's widow, was a close friend of the Allisons. Wanda recalled one race when Judy asked her to watch Davey, who was six or seven.

"This was before wives and children were allowed in the pits," she said. "The wives all tried to pitch in and watch each other's kids. Davey was a little spitfire who'd dart here and dart there. He was so inquisitive, so nosy, about this racing.

"Davey got away from me and ran in front of a car, and when I caught him, I wanted to shake him. I told him, 'Your momma should tie you to a tree.' He never forgot that."

In high school all Davey thought about was stock car racing. He went out for football in the ninth grade, but the coach told him he would have to gain forty pounds to reach 130 pounds. Davey quit to concentrate on working for his dad.

"Bobby would be working on his Cup car," said Red Farmer, "and Davey would come in, and Bobby would make him sweep the floors, clean up stuff." Bobby paid him fifty cents an hour.

"It used to burn ole Davey," said Farmer, "but he was learning how to do things. Bobby taught him the right way. Davey didn't get nothing handed to him. He had to help Bobby during the day, and then he could work nights on his Sportsman car."

When Davey was sixteen, Bobby was working on his '77 American Motors Matador, and he was having trouble with the car. Bobby was doing all the work himself, and he said, "It was killing me."

Davey volunteered to help, and Bobby was so weary that he agreed. It wasn't long, said Bobby, before Davey could do a complete teardown.

"I mean he could build an engine, put it on the dyno, prep it, test it, tear it down, put it back together, everything needed to get the car ready," said Bobby.

"Davey had a bunch of kids who worked with him, and they worked hard, and they loved to race. Davey was smart enough to know experience would overcome a lot of things if you took time to learn, so he was listening pretty good.

"If you told him something, he would go back and do it, and if it worked good, he'd remember that. He learned good, and that's why he became such a great driver. He had the feel for the car. He was supersharp. You could give him two pieces of angle iron, and he could build you a chassis, build a motor, wire them up, and set the chassis."

"After everyone left the shop, I taught myself how to weld," said Davey. "I would pick up scrap metal and weld it together, practicing every night."

"He wanted to learn all that stuff," said Red Farmer. "He could do anything. There wasn't anything about a race car Davey didn't know about. That's what made him good, because when he came off the racetrack, he could talk to the crew chief. He didn't say, 'The car ain't handling.' He'd come in and say, 'We need to change the springs,' or the shocks or the sway bar, because he understood it. So he could give the crew chief more input than most drivers, and that made a lot of difference."

Davey also drove the truck that carried Bobby's race car to the track. While Bobby was flying to the race in his plane, Davey was logging 150,000 miles staying up all night to get to the races on time.

"Dad would give me a place and a time to be there, and I'd better be there," Davey said.

Judy told Davey he couldn't begin his racing career until he graduated from high school. He had to get his diploma. No GED.

Davey, who wanted to begin his racing career just as soon as he could, went to summer school for extra credit in order to graduate a term early. Such was the dedication of Davey Allison.

"Constantly Davey would say, 'I'm going to be the best racer,' said Bobby. "I'm going to do what my dad did. I'm going to do better than my Dad did.'"

Davey started in the Hobby division while Bobby was off Winston Cup racing. Red Farmer did all he could to help Davey and younger brother Clifford as well.

"I was running here in Birmingham, Huntsville, and Montgomery, tracks Davey and Clifford were running on, and so naturally I took over Bobby's place trying to help Davey and Clifford as much as I could, because they were like my kids," said Red.

Farmer took Davey to his first race on dirt. They went to the Dixie Speedway in Woodstock, Alabama.

"He was like *Ned's First Reader* the first few laps," said Farmer.

Red told him he had to throw the nose of the car ten feet deeper in the turn than he had been doing on asphalt. Within a few laps Davey set a new world record for a three-eighths-mile dirt track.

"But Davey was like his daddy and Donnie," said Red. "He never liked the dirt tracks much, either."

The day Davey turned eighteen, he showed up at the Birmingham Speedway ready to race. It was his Uncle Donnie who gave him the equipment to compete.

Donnie Allison had three boys, Kenny and twins Ronald and Donald. Ronald was a good driver, ("Ronald had big balls," says John Bailey, who raced against him), and Bobby gave him a fast car for Ronald to race at the Birmingham International Raceway.

(As a driver, Kenny was "way better than Davey," says Eddie Allison. Kenny ran Late Model. When Kenny moved to North Carolina to race, he asked John Bailey if he wanted to go with him. Bailey, who was living in Dothan, Alabama, decided not to go. Later, Kenny had to choose between racing and his girlfriend, and he chose the girlfriend. Bailey today drives Modified cars at the Desoto Speedway in Bradenton, Florida.)

By 1979, Donnie felt Davey needed more help than Bobby was giving him.

Donnie said to Bobby, "Why don't you give that boy a car he can go race with?"

Bobby said, "He'll do all right."

"And that was it," said Donnie. "That boy was at a stage where he needed help. And for whatever reason, he didn't get it."

Donnie decided that since Bobby had helped out Ronnie, he would help out Davey. Donnie gave Davey his old DiGard car, an old Nova. It had been sitting for two years.

Bobby said Davey would have to work on his car "after hours." And so after working eight to five on Bobby's car, Davey and cousin Kenny stripped the Nova down and got it ready to race evenings and early mornings.

When Davey and his crew cranked the engine up, water crickets blew out the exhaust. Once fixed, though, the car still could go fast.

"Davey came and got my car on a Tuesday afternoon," said Donnie. That night he didn't run, but a week later he made his first start and finished fifth.

Donnie helped Davey in other ways. Donnie loved to discuss how to drive with

Davey, and when he was needed, Donnie would cut and weld and bolt or do whatever Davey needed.

"Donnie loved Davey, too," said Eddie Allison. "Donnie would talk to him about how to work hard. So did I. Davey would work his ass off."

If Bobby didn't give Davey money or cars to race, he encouraged him and gave him wise advice. Bobby believed strongly that his short-track experience had been crucial to his success, and he counseled Davey to follow the same path.

"I encouraged him to go to the short tracks, to the local Late Model, Modified, and Sportsmen races," said Bobby. "And he had pretty good success pretty quick. He really wanted to do it."

Davey drove his first race at the Birmingham International Speedway on April 22, 1979. He finished twentieth. On May 5, in his sixth start, Bobby watched as Davey won. (The next day Bobby won at Talladega.) For a time, racing didn't come easy for Davey.

"Davey had to work, because he didn't have the talent," said Eddie Allison. "He got in that race car, and he grabbed hold of that steering wheel, and he said, 'I'm going to beat you.'"

But as dedicated and hardworking as Davey was working on his Sportsman car, in the beginning he didn't accomplish much because he didn't know *how* to work.

"You had to drive a leg alongside of him to see he was moving in his results," said Eddie. "But because he kept working, he finally got by that. See, he overpowered that just working. Eventually Davey knew everything on the race car there was to do.

"And Davey ended up getting the feel his daddy had. If he needed a washer in the corner of his seat, he could feel it."

One of Davey's close friends was John Bailey, whose father, Jerry, did paint and body work for Bobby Allison Racing.

"When we were eighteen," Bailey said, "we talked about girls, and we talked about booze. We were both racers, and I remember going with Davey to buy tires. Afterward we sat and talked about our futures. We were running Late Models. Davey was talking about running Winston Cup one day. I knew I'd never have the money or help to get that far.

"My daddy was a body man," Bailey said. "His daddy was Bobby Allison."

The first time Davey and John Bailey raced against each other, John won. The second time, Davey finished ahead. By the third race, Davey was winning races.

John Bailey had sought the same sponsor as Davey. Said Bailey without rancor, "His name was Allison. Mine was Bailey. Guess who got the sponsorship? He had a better car, and he had sponsorship money to buy the little extras like new tires that gave him the advantage over the others."

Davey and John would go into a bar together. According to Bailey, Davey's pickup line was, "My dad is Bobby Allison." Said Bailey, "He was enthralled that his daddy was Bobby Allison." But, Bailey said, "the line didn't mean much to those girls."

Davey didn't get new cars to race. Rather, Bobby gave him what others described as junk cars.

"My dad told me I had to prove to him my ambition, dedication, and determination before he would support me in anything," said Davey. "If he was going to supply me with a race car, he wanted me to know what was going on in that car."

Bobby wanted Davey to learn another important lesson: why it made financial sense to finish races. If Davey crashed and if he didn't have the money on hand to repair the car, Bobby didn't bail him out. He would have to sit out a few races while he earned the money to fix the car. Davey learned this lesson quickly.

Davey, his brother Clifford, and a youngster by the name of Hut Stricklin began racing at the half-mile paved track in Montgomery, one of the tracks the Alabama Gang had dominated in the mid-1960s. Before, it had been the Alabama Gang—two Allison brothers, Bobby and Donnie, along with Red Farmer. Now it was two Allison brothers, Davey and Clifford, along with their friend Hut Stricklin.

When Davey started out in the Sportsman division, Bobby never put any pressure on him. People thought he had better equipment than he had, and the fans were surprised when he crashed as much as he did.

"Driving skill is not inherited," said Eddie Allison. "You have to *learn* how to drive a car. After a while, Davey figured out how to go faster, and he became very successful in the Sportsman division."

Bobby's plan was for Davey to move up from Sportsman and Late Model racing to the higher ARCA and Busch circuits, and then work his way up to Winston Cup. First, Davey had to get out of Alabama.

In 1983 Davey began to drive on the ARCA circuit. He won the pole at Talladega, and then the race.

In 1984 Davey was ARCA Rookie of the Year. That year he won at Talladega, Atlanta, and Indianapolis Raceway Park. He lost the ARCA racing championship by 30 points because he had to miss one of the races: He was on his honeymoon with his first wife, Deborah.

By 1985, Davey had won more superspeedway races than any other ARCA driver in history, and that year he drove in three Winston Cup races for Hoss Ellington.

Davey entered his first Winston Cup race, in his backyard at Talladega, on July 28, 1985. He was twenty-four years old, and NASCAR wasn't sure it was a good idea to let him enter his first race on the fastest speedway of them all, but NASCAR also knew that a lot of Allison fans from Alabama would flock to the track to see what Bobby's son could do. All weekend Davey was mobbed by well-wishers and reporters.

He finished the race a remarkable tenth. Dad Bobby was tickled pink.

"I thought that was really neat," said Bobby. "Here was this youngster coming along, and he had this personality that people really just loved. People would meet him, and after two or three minutes, they'd really like him. I enjoyed that part of his personality, too. Every father enjoys their children when they see special parts of their personality. When people became Davey Allison fans, that was a compliment to me, too."

Based on this performance, Hoss Ellington offered Davey two more rides. On October 6 he went to Charlotte, and he was driving in the top ten when, with 30 laps left in the race, his engine blew.

His third start was at Atlanta on November 3. He only went 52 laps when his engine failed. His was the first car to be eliminated.

Davey was hired to drive for Nathan Sims, a family friend from Pensacola. But when Davey blew three engines in seven laps, he decided he needed to run better equipment and quit.

In 1986 Davey drove in four races for trucking magnate Earl Sadler and his son Check, who were from Greenville, South Carolina. Davey's best finish in 1986 was a twelfth at Richmond. Tom Pistone prepared the cars in his Charlotte shop and acted as crew chief. Davey was expecting to race in as many as twenty races, but the Sadlers weren't able to attract a sponsor. The low point of the season came at Darlington, where Davey was involved in a crash on the first lap. Critics barked that the only reason he was in the race was that his last name was Allison. He had no serious prospects for continuing.

Then, in July 1986, Neil Bonnett was injured at Pocono. Davey decided to open the door himself. He called car owner Junior Johnson and offered his services to practice and qualify the car for Neil. Junior hired him, and when doctors refused to let Bonnett drive because of an injury to his right arm, on July 27, 1986, Davey drove Junior's car in the Talladega 500.

Davey led the race several times, and when he finished seventh, no one ever questioned his ability again.

Bonnett had been one of the first to appreciate Davey's skill. "He's a good one," he said. "There's a quality that separates the good ones from the rest, and he has it. It's something people don't like nowadays: aggressiveness. But I say you can either be a choirboy or a race driver."

Davey had put in his time, paid his dues. Now he was ready. Harry Ranier had not seen the Talladega race because he was in Australia at the time, but a friend taped it and showed it to him two weeks later. Ranier was impressed and hired Davey for 1987.

Driver Cale Yarborough had left Ranier to start his own team, and took his sponsor, Hardee's, with him. Crew chief Waddell Wilson left as well. And Harry Ranier was having financial difficulties.

Harry Ranier recovered. He attracted a new sponsor, Texaco. And he made two important hires, signing Joey Knuckles to be the crew chief and Robert Yates to be the team manager and engine builder. Davey, a twenty-five-year-old rookie on the Winston Cup circuit, had exactly eight Winston Cup races under his belt.

Most rebuilt race teams take some time to make their mark. Davey's Texaco team made its impact immediately. Davey had driven at Daytona since 1991 in races in lesser circuits, so the track was not new to him. In his first attempt at qualifying for the Daytona 500, Davey outran his father and his uncle Donnie to win the outside pole at 210.364 miles an hour. He was the first rookie ever to start in the first row in the Daytona 500. Bill Elliott was the pole sitter.

"He may be a rookie in some other people's eyes, but not in mine," said Elliott.

Bobby qualified fourth behind Ken Schrader.

"Don't turn your back on the Alabama Gang," cracked Bobby. "They're liable to take your wallet."

Bobby finished sixth that day; Davey twenty-seventh.

"I think we could have won that race, but we made a rookie mistake," said Davey. "We had a jack break during a pit stop. It had never happened before, and I didn't know how to react. I got overanxious and left without the lug nuts. I didn't make it back around."

At the end of May, Davey and Bobby again were running one, two at the high-banked Dover Downs International Speedway when Bobby's car overheated three-quarters of the way through the race and he had to drop out. Davey won again. It was the first time in Winston Cup history that a rookie had won two races in a season.

Davey Allison was named Rookie of the Year.

After J. T. Lundy left Ranier racing after the 1987 season, Ranier's financial state worsened. Engine builder Robert Yates even spent some of his own money to keep the team going. Yates would turn out to be the single most important figure in Davey's racing career.

Robert Yates had begun his racing career in 1968 working for Holman and Moody as its air gauge department manager and quickly moved up to assistant engine builder. In 1971, he joined Junior Johnson's race team and built engines for Bobby Allison and Cale Yarborough. Then he spent ten years fighting with the Gardner brothers at DiGard while he built engines that ran fast and lasted. Yates had been the engine builder when Bobby won his driving championship in 1983.

DiGard wasn't stable, and just before the Daytona 500 in 1986, Yates left the team abruptly.

Robin Pemberton, the crew chief of the DiGard team, recalled the day Robert Yates left DiGard and the final days of a once-great race team.

"We made some decent runs with Greg [Sacks] in '85, but we were struggling," said Pemberton. "We made it through the year, made it through the wintertime attempting to build a car or two, but then there was big money trouble. The checks never bounced, but we knew it was close when we would get paid, because we always got our paycheck two minutes after the bank closed.

"We made it through the wintertime but some of our people left. They had been there long enough, and it didn't look like we would have a sponsor.

"We signed TRW, the automotive after-market, to be Greg's sponsor in 1986. We started the season, but we were struggling. Robert Yates was still there. In February of 1986 we were at Daytona for the 500, and Dick Beaty, who was in charge of competition for NASCAR, made the announcement at the end of the day, 'OK, guys, put your tools down and go home.'

"The night he made that announcement, Robert Yates said, 'Okay, I'm laying my tools down, and I'm going home.' Well, what Robert meant was, he was laying his tools down and going home home. He said to me, 'I got you this far.'

"I had the sense something was going wrong, and sure enough, that was his last day at Di-Gard. He was gone. He took his tools, and he went home. He had just had enough. One too many checks didn't go in the right direction. So the next day I have no engine builder.

"We went to Richmond, then we went to Rockingham. By then we were working from six in the morning until five or six in the morning every day. We didn't have enough men, didn't have enough going on. You would literally leave the shop, drive home, take a shower, turn around, and drive back to work. My wife wasn't doing real good with it. Our child was four months old. This whole thing was insane.

"It was time to leave."

Robert Yates was so disillusioned with what happened to him at DiGard that he decided to leave stock car racing completely and accept a job working on the development of synthetic fuels. His civilian career didn't last a year. In 1987 the master engine builder was hired as team manager of the Ranier-Lundy race team, which itself was experiencing hard times.

Davey expressed his concern to the hardworking Yates that if he didn't do something, there would be no race team at all in 1988. Even though Yates had been a weekly paycheck employee his whole career, Harry Ranier saw in Yates the same thing Davey saw: a bright—no, brilliant—engine man who had what it took to own and run a successful race team. At the end of the 1987 season, Ranier offered to sell Yates the team at a discount with an affordable payment plan.

Davey and Robert Yates had developed a mutual admiration society. When Davey heard about the offer, Davey told Yates, "If you buy the team, I will drive for you the rest of my life."

"What Davey loved about Robert was that he loved to win," said Eddie Allison. "Robert's a racer. Robert is sharp, and Robert *really* knew why the motor ran, so he could bolt the stuff on he knew made it run. And Robert was willing to listen. He didn't buck Davey on how to make the car turn the corner, as so many do."

His confidence bolstered by Davey's promise, Robert Yates agreed to buy the team from Ranier, though he was acting against his very conservative nature. An ethical, upstanding person, Yates firmly believed in the adage, "Neither a lender nor a borrower be," and to buy the team Yates would have to go into hock.

This was a crossroads in his life. If Robert Yates was going to be a team owner, this was his shot. Because Harry Ranier was in financial trouble, the team would go for a cut-rate price. Not cheap, but cut-rate. Yates could see it was a team with all the elements in place: good cars, great engines, and a talented young driver. And so Robert Yates sold his car and mortgaged his home and secured the financing to buy the race team.

For the rest of his career, as promised, Davey Allison would drive for Robert Yates Racing.

CHAPTER 31

Hut: Rookie of the Year

"Don't talk to anyone else. Talk to Hut."

—**Davey Allison**

One of Davey's closest friends growing up was a boy by the name of Hut Stricklin. Like Davey, Waymond Lane Stricklin Jr. was born in 1961, and when he was three or four, his dad, Waymond Lane Sr., gave him that nickname. He doesn't know why.

"I was a junior, and I guess my dad didn't want me to have the same name," said Stricklin. "I have no idea where the name Hut came from."

Hut was born and raised in Calera, Alabama, about forty miles southeast of Hueytown.

"When I was real small, we were very poor," said Stricklin. "My dad had a gas station with an old rundown wrecker. We always wanted to go to the races, but never could afford the price, until we found out if we took a wrecker and pulled the wrecked cars off the track, we could get in free. I would ride with Dad in the wrecker to the Dixie Speedway in Midfield, Alabama, a quarter-mile asphalt track, and he would do that."

Father and son had worked at the track for several years, when his dad got out of the gas station business. Dad and Mom each opened an automobile salvage yard about ten miles apart from each other. After five or six years, the businesses thrived, and Hut's dad decided he wanted to go racing. He built an old junker out of the wrecked cars and headed for the local Alabama tracks where Bobby Allison, Donnie Allison, Red Farmer, and Freddie Fryar ran.

Like Red Farmer, Waymond Stricklin didn't like the big tracks. Like Red, he preferred the rubbing and beating and banging of the quarter-mile tracks. Stricklin, helped by two of his junkyard employees who doubled as his mechanics, raced all around the Southeast, going to the Dixie Speedway, Birmingham, Montgomery, Huntsville, and Opp, a little track in southern Alabama, and the Heart O'Dixie Speedway, which was also called the Sayre Speedway, because that was the town it was in.

One of the most memorable races Papa Stricklin won was the last race ever held at the Dixie Speedway. It was 200 laps, and three cars were vying for the win. They tangled, and Stricklin won the race with his car crossing the finish line on its roof.

When Hut was ten or eleven, he went with his dad to the Heart O' Dixie Speedway in Sayre, a quarter-mile asphalt track fifteen miles northwest of Birmingham. Midway through the race Hut's dad not only hit the wall, he went through it into a dirt bank. The car was demolished, and Stricklin was badly injured.

"I was standing on top of his truck," said Hut. "We had a two-car hauler we used around the salvage yard. I remember jumping off the top of that thing and running over to him. I was about the first one to him. When you're a kid, you can run. I could run like nobody else could. When I got to him, I saw he had blood coming out of about every hole in his head. It was a pretty bad sight to see, but, luckily, it had a happy story at the end."

Waymond Stricklin had internal injuries, including a ruptured spleen. He was in the hospital for more than two months.

"He survived it," said Hut, "and he went back to driving, but he never got back to the level where he was."

In 1977 the sixteen-year-old Hut wanted to race at the Sayre Speedway. The track was starting a new division, and his dad gave him a '64 Chevelle body to work on. Hut, unlike his dad, was a mechanical whiz.

"I always wondered what made things tick," Hut said. For years, Hut had removed the parts from the junked cars, and he also worked on his dad's race cars. Hut built his race car from the ground up all by himself.

Hut was fast, right off the bat. He won his first two races at the Sayre Speedway.

"Hut was a good little driver," said Red Farmer. "He kept his car in a little barn right behind his daddy's junkyard, and he worked on that thing after working in the junkyard all day."

The next year, in 1978, Hut met Davey Allison and his younger brother Clifford.

"They were both down-to-earth," said Hut. "I was always impressed with Davey's knowledge. He ought to have been smart. He had had an incredible teacher. I was always impressed with the knowledge Davey had about the cars from one end to the other.

"Clifford at the time was just goofing around. It seemed he didn't care that much about it. Once he got older, he got the itch to do it. Bobby got behind him and started helping him out, lining things up, and he just kind of went on.

"Clifford had a lot of natural talent. I felt he had as much natural talent as anyone I've seen. Davey was good, but I didn't feel Davey was as natural as Clifford. But Davey had a desire and a will to teach himself that Clifford didn't have.

"When I began racing against Davey, Davey told the story that he won one week, and I won one week, and we'd swap weeks, but that really wasn't how it was. I used to win all the time.

"Pam, Donnie's daughter, who I later married, used to root for Davey—that was before she knew me. She used to laugh at him a lot because he couldn't beat me."

In the summer of 1979 Davey and Hut and two or three of their friends were riding in Bobby's van up and down the beach in Panama City, Florida. There were hundreds of kids on the beach. Davey was driving, and Hut was in the passenger seat. They were hollering at the girls as teenage boys are wont to do.

"There's Pam and her girlfriend over there," Davey said.

"Pam who?" Hut asked.

"Pam, Donnie's daughter," said Davey. Hut knew from Davey that Donnie had a daughter, but he had never seen or met her.

Davey pulled over, rolled down his window, and asked Pam and her girlfriend, "What are you girls doing?"

They walked up. "Nothing," Pam said. "Who you got in there?"

Davey told her the names of the boys in the back of the van, and then he said, "And I got Hut Stricklin."

Pam knew Hut Stricklin, all right, because when she would go to the racetrack to watch Davey race, inevitably Hut won and she would go home disappointed for her cousin.

"Hut Stricklin?" she said. "What are you doing in there?"

She walked around to where Hut was sitting, and she started in on him.

"You win every week," she said. "I hate your guts."

Hut, who didn't want to hear her lip, told Davey, "Let's go." Hut rolled up the window. Davey drove away.

Two or three weeks later Hut again ran into Pam Allison.

"One night I was out at a Birmingham mall where a bunch of teenagers hung out," said Hut, "and I met her, and we started talking, and basically, we've been to-gether ever since."

Pam quickly switched her allegiance from Davey to Hut.

"She sure did," Hut said. "She had a change of heart right away. Plus I started sharing my paycheck with her, and Davey wasn't sharing his, and that probably had a little bit to do with it, too."

By 1981 Hut was family, so when Donnie crashed at Charlotte in May of that year and was seriously hurt, Hut was witness to the heartbreak.

"Pam was over at my parents' house," said Hut. "We were all there watching the race on TV, and we saw the wreck and how bad it looked. Pam broke down in tears. She left immediately, heading home, fearing what the phone call would bring.

"It's the call you don't ever want to get," said Hut.

"I went to visit Donnie in the hospital," he said. "He looked like he was going to pass away at any moment. He had lines and hoses going in him and through him. His color was terrible. I thought, *He's going to be lucky to survive.*

"It look a long time for Donnie to recover," said Hut. "Like anyone with a bad head injury, his speech was messed up. He got back to where he could do most anything, though his speech was slurred for a long time. It took him four or five years to get over that."

"No one gave him a decent ride ever again," I said.

"That's the way it is in this business," said Hut. "Everybody gets scared off. You see it with a lot of different drivers. Ricky Craven was one of the few who got a second chance, and Ernie Irvan was another one. Ernie was able to come back [after a crash in which he almost died]. Not many of them do."

Hut continued to move up in racing. In 1986 he won 10 of 14 races in the Daytona Dash series driving four-cylinder, mini-Winston Cup cars. He won the Dash championship for a car owner by the name of Richard Mash.

Skip Jaehne had started a Winston Cup team in Mash's shop in Taylorsville, North Carolina, and he asked Stricklin if he wanted to run a few Winston Cup races in 1987.

"Skip lived in Venice, Florida," said Hut. "He worked for a stocks and bonds company called Prudential, Bache. He had come into a lot of money. I don't know whether it was his life savings or he inherited it, but he had a dream of being a Winston Cup car owner."

Hut ran at North Wilkesboro, Rockingham, and Atlanta. His best effort was a sixteenth place at Atlanta.

"I don't remember much about it," said Stricklin, "except it was the longest race of my entire life. Coming off being a short-track driver, it was incredibly long."

Hut won just $6,000 in purses, and Jaehne left racing.

That same year his racing buddy, Davey Allison, the kid he always beat at the Sayre Speedway, won two races and was named the Winston Cup Rookie of the Year. Davey earned $361,000.

I asked Hut if that was hard for him.

"It was," Stricklin said. "Being perfectly honest, to see him have the success he had, you feel, *If I could just get into equipment that's close to that, I feel I can do that well.*"

"Davey got in with Robert Yates, a pretty good guy," I said.

"You better bet," Hut said. "He got a big break right off, and that was something that was unheard of, a rookie to get with that caliber of team right off. Now it's the norm. Not then. You had to work your way into a premier ride. Those rides were saved for the big name drivers."

In 1988 Stricklin decided he would try to run his own Busch Grand National team. He didn't have any money, and he didn't have a sponsor to speak of.

"I ran here and there, just a handful," he said. "I didn't really have any success. I finished ninth or tenth at South Boston, but for me it was terrible. And I lost a lot of money. But that year I did a lot of promoting myself."

One owner Hut decided he wanted to drive for was Rod Osterlund, who was starting a new team. Osterlund, a San Jose, California, real estate developer, had struck gold once back in 1979 when he signed a young Dale Earnhardt to be a second driver to Dave Marcis. When Marcis quit before the season started, Earnhardt became the team's top driver. Earnhardt not only won Rookie of the Year for Osterlund in 1979, but he won the driving championship in 1980.

In the middle of the following season Osterlund, without informing Earnhardt, sold the race team to J. D. Stacy. After two races, Earhardt quit Stacy and floundered until he went to Junior Johnson to ask for a ride. Johnson didn't have an opening, but he knew someone who did. After Johnson took the youngster coon hunting, Johnson sent Earnhardt to see Richard Childress. The Earnhardt-Childress team won six racing championships.

After a seven-year absence, Rod Osterlund was back in racing, and Stricklin was hoping lightning would strike twice. He would drive by Osterlund's Mooresville shop and chat with crew chief Roland Wlodyka.

He'd say to Wlodyka, "How about coming up to watch me race?"

"Are you going to win?" Wlodyka asked.

"I hope so. But to be honest with you, I don't have the stuff to win with."

Wlodyka came to watch Hut race three or four times, and afterward he would call Osterlund and say, "This kid doesn't have anything to drive, but he sure was impressive."

Osterlund would reply, "How in the world would you know that?"

"But they saw something in me, and they gave me a chance," said Stricklin.

There was another factor in Stricklin getting the ride. Buddy Davey Allison had promised Hut that if and when he made it to Winston Cup, he would do what he could to get Hut a ride. Davey, a loyal friend, made good on his promise.

"Davey and I were very close," said Hut. "We hunted together down in Alabama. I flew with him a lot out of Alabama.

"He talked to Rod Osterlund," said Hut. "He told Rod that I beat him every week," and he said, "You need to give this guy a chance. Don't talk to anyone else. Talk to Hut."

Stricklin got to drive Osterlund's Pontiac. During conversations, Osterlund sometimes would talk about his days with Dale Earnhardt.

"Rod always had the utmost respect for Dale as far as his talent," said Stricklin. "He would talk about how weak Dale was when he started. The races were so long, and it would take a toll on his body. He about fell out of his seat. Every Saturday night before the race, Rod said, they would cram pizza down him to get him as much strength for him to drive the next day."

In 1989 Hut drove in twenty-seven races for Rod Osterlund. The year began at Daytona. Hut didn't qualify.

"It was pretty hectic," said Stricklin. "We didn't have anything. We shouldn't have been down there. We didn't have an engine program for restrictor plate racing. We were trying to do that ourselves, and it was a joke.

"To be honest, Rod didn't have enough money to do this. He got $990,000 for the full season from Heinz in 1989 to race Winston Cup."

"My paycheck wasn't a whole lot. It wasn't anything to write home about, but the money was irrelevant at the time. I felt like the money would come if I could ever get my foot in the door."

After failing to qualify at Daytona, Hut went 115 laps at Rockingham, when the car broke. He finished forty-first. Stricklin was beginning to learn just how hard it was to break into Winston Cup racing. Osterlund hired Donnie Allison and Doug Richert each to help out for a few races, and that helped.

"In 1989, Donnie came over for a few races, and we ran decent, finishing in the top ten two or three times. And then Doug Richert came over for two or three races. Rod just thought the world of Doug, and for the Michigan race we rented an engine from Randy Dornton, and we ran fourth. All I remember is the big right front spring we had in it.

"What separates your good teams from your bad teams is that the good teams put together a good race car thirty-six races if there are thirty-six races. We were putting together a good race car for four or five races. We didn't have the money. It boiled down to the money."

Though he didn't run that well, in 1989 Stricklin was runner-up for Rookie of the Year honors to forty-eight-year-old Dick Trickle, who was driving for the Stavola Brothers.

At the end of 1989, Hut was invited to come race for Bobby Allison Motorsports, where he would officially become a part of the fabled Alabama Gang.

It appeared to be Hut's big break. But as it has been with so many aspiring racers, success always seemed within reach but, because of circumstances, never quite materialized.

CHAPTER 32

Neil: In Waltrip's Shadow

"And it got me mad at Junior, because I felt he was favoring Darrell, and he was."

—**Susan Bonnett**

Neil Bonnett had raced in 1972, but it took another three years for him to take another crack at Grand National racing. In August of 1975 he raced at Talladega, and finished thirty-fifth in a fateful race in which Tiny Lund was killed. Finally, in 1976, Bonnett made the jump to stay. He drove in thirteen Grand National races in a car he owned himself. Bobby Allison made it possible for Bonnett to race when he recommended that Armor-All, which wanted to sponsor Bobby, sponsor Neil instead.

Armor-All agreed to sponsor Neil for three races. The first race was the Daytona 500, always a risk for a new sponsor, because no car is guaranteed a spot in the race. You have to qualify to make it, and to make any money, you have to finish.

It's also an expensive race to run. At the time most veteran teams used one engine to qualify and another to race. Neil only had one, and it blew, so Neil had to spend $17,000 to buy another. Neil was worried, because he knew he wasn't going to have any more money for the other races if he finished poorly, but he finished a notable fifth (this was the famous race in which Richard Petty and David Pearson crashed at the finish line), and it paid him $14,000, so he was able to go to the next two races, and after that Armor-All gave him more money. When the Armor-All deal ended, he made a deal with Hawaiian Tropics.

Even with sponsorship, Bonnett discovered how difficult and expensive it was to mount an independently run team. In thirteen races, he had only one top-five finish. His winnings amounted to $31,000. It wasn't enough to eat well or run well.

"It was really hard," said Susan Bonnett. "He had to get the car where it needed to go, had to work on it and drive it all himself, and he was doing all that. He had the expertise on how to get the car to the track and set it up. He had some people helping him, but basically all the stress fell on him. Plus he was trying to support his family. And it was pretty stressful on me, because he left all the bills on me."

When Neil burst onto the scene, people were impressed.

"He was a good natural race driver on asphalt," said Humpy Wheeler. "Outside of Fireball Roberts, Neil Bonnett probably took to asphalt quicker than any driver I knew of. He was smooth. He thought things through. When he needed to charge, he did. He was a lot like Bobby.

"Neil was the most pragmatic racer of them all. He looked at everything with a lot of logic. He didn't get real emotional about racing. You had to wake him up to tell him it was time to qualify when everybody else was sitting around with their hearts beating 150 beats a minute."

Bonnett, impressive early, caught the eyes of the Wood Brothers, who signed him to drive in 1979.

That year Bonnett blazed onto the scene, winning at Dover and Daytona in the Firecracker 400, and defeating Dale Earnhardt at Atlanta in the fall. In the process the affable Bonnett and his wife, Susan, were making friends. In addition to Bobby Allison, who had been Neil Bonnett's mentor, he also forged a close friendship with a young racer by the name of Dale Earnhardt.

"Neil raced when the competition was very fierce," said Susan Bonnett. "It was unheard of for anyone to come up into those ranks and actually win, because Richard Petty, Cale Yarborough, Bobby, and David Pearson had been so dominant for so long. Neil did well. And we got along so well with everyone. We were the closest with the Allisons, Bobby and Judy and Donnie and Pat, and as time went on, Neil and Dale Earnhardt became very close. I don't even know when they got so close. They enjoyed a lot of the same things, I guess, hunting and fishing, whereas Bobby was not into hunting and fishing. So away from the racetrack, Neil and Dale just had the same interests. They both loved to hunt and they both loved to fish."

I had been told stories of Neil and Dale each buying all-terrain vehicles and racing them at breakneck speeds through the woods. I asked Susan if it was so.

"Right," she said. "They had a lot of the same goals, and they just hit it off. And he was close to Bobby. Bobby was always there for Neil, and Neil was always there for Bobby. They were not people who would backstab each other. I remember one time people came to Neil and asked him if he was interested in driving a car that Bobby was driving. Neil was very unnerved.

" 'I think I'm just going to tell Bobby.' he said.

"I said, 'That's the right thing to do.' And instead of going behind Bobby's back, he went to Bobby and told him. And Bobby was very appreciative."

In 1980 Neil Bonnett was leading the Daytona 500 with three laps to go when he blew the engine. He was able to limp around, finish the race, and come in third.

That year Bonnett drove in 22 of the 30 races, winning two races and $231,000 in purses.

Before the race at Riverside on June 8, 1980, Neil Bonnett's first at that tricky road course, he decided he needed some expert instruction, and he attended a two-day driving course taught by the famed road course instructor Bob Bondurant.

"I remember the first time we went to Riverside, we had a rental car, and Bobby and Judy, Neil and I, all went together to the track. Bobby drove the four of us onto the track in the rental car, and he drove us around and showed us how you go through the turns. Neil didn't feel confident and he decided to take a course with Bondurant. Neil was too aggressive, and he needed to have patience. He really didn't know what to do. When he came back from the course, he did better than he had done in a long time on a road course."

Which is an understatement, to say the least. At Riverside that June, Neil Bonnett was leading the race going into the ninth turn of the final lap when Darrell Waltrip caught him on the long backstretch and won by 0.3 seconds. Benny Parsons finished third.

On July 27, 1980, Bonnett won the Pocono race over Buddy Baker, and the very next week he followed that up with a win at Talladega over Cale Yarborough, Dale Earnhardt, and Benny Parsons. The hometown Hueytown boy sped his Mercury to the lead with four laps to go and held off the trio of contenders.

"Talladega was Neil's favorite place," said Susan Bonnett. "I don't know if it was because it was so close to home, but he loved everything about Talladega, except the fact that everybody who thought they knew him came out of the woodwork that week. Everybody was calling asking for free tickets, wanting Neil to do this, do that, and we always had a lot of company, a lot of people staying with us that week, and it was pretty stressful driving back and forth the hour and fifteen minutes to the track, and you're outside in the hot sun. People pull at you all day long, and you come home and you're worn out, and you have a house full of people. It was his favorite place, and he always wanted to do well, but he always felt there was more pressure on him, but he felt it was a track where he could excel. Knowing a lot of people he knew all his life were there was important.

"Most of the time he gave the trophy to the sponsor, but after this race he did bring it home. It had a crystal on top of it. The trophy didn't mean that much to Neil. I remember when he won at Ontario, he told Jim Stacy, 'You can have it.' I was thinking, *Please don't give it away*, because it was a silver punch bowl and twelve cups, and it was beautiful. Stacy insisted we have it, and I have used that punch bowl until I have about worn it out. But Neil didn't care about trophies, didn't care about fame, didn't care about none of that.

"He had a passion to do what he did, and when you have a passion, you give one hundred percent of yourself. It doesn't matter what people think about it. You're going to do it."

In 1981 Bonnett won three more races, nipping Darrell Waltrip by a car length at the wire at Darlington, beating Waltrip again at Dover in September, and winning at Atlanta by a single car length over Waltrip two months later. In a year in which Waltrip won twelve races and earned $799,000, Bonnett did his best but was unable to keep Waltrip from beating his buddy Bobby Allison out of the racing championship.

"I don't remember Neil ever saying anything bad about Darrell," said Susan Bonnett. "They had a couple of run-ins at the racetrack, and they had a run-in at the White House. Needless to say, they were not the best of buddies.

"The feud between Neil and Darrell was more a press thing than anything else. Like with Donnie and Cale, the press hyped it up so much that in the next race the least little bump was going to be blown out of proportion. Them ya-yaying back and forth in the paper made it even bigger, and then someone said they didn't know if they could trust them together at the White House, because they didn't want them brawling on the lawn and rolling down the hill at the White House.

"We were invited by Jimmy Carter, who wasn't there. The [Mideast peace] talks had begun at Camp David with Sadat and Begin, so he was not able to be there, but Rosalynn was there. I was so impressed with her. It was an excellent time. I really enjoyed that."

In 1982 Neil Bonnett won the World 600 at Charlotte, but it was the only race he won that year, and at the end of the year Bonnett and the Wood Brothers decided it was best to go their separate ways.

"They knew when their time together was finished," said Susan Bonnett. "It was time for everybody to move on. And everybody moved on with the right attitude. That's the type of relationship we had."

In November 1983 it was announced that Warner Hodgdon would invest in the RahMoc team owned by Bob Rahilly and Butch Mock and also in the Junior Johnson team. Hodgdon had hired Neil Bonnett to drive for him at Indy several years earlier, and when Hodgdon bought into NASCAR racing, one of the drivers he wanted on one of his teams was Bonnett.

"Neil was going to drive for Junior," said Susan Bonnett, "but Junior had some contracts to fulfill for a couple of years, so Neil drove for RahMac during that time."

In 1983 Bonnett for the first time got to drive in all thirty races. Bonnett won two races, finishing sixth in the points and winning $453,000 in purses.

"RahMoc was just the last names of Butch and Bob put together," said Susan Bonnett. "Bob built the motors, and Butch was in charge of everything else. They were two guys in business, and I was—and am—crazy about them. Hardworking. Good guys. They were young, dedicated, and Neil absolutely enjoyed driving for them. They had a real good relationship."

In 1983 Bonnett won the World 600 at Charlotte for the second year in a row and late in the season won at Atlanta.

Buddy Baker, who ran second to Bonnett that day in Atlanta, recalled Bonnett's talents.

"I was running second to Bobby Allison," said Baker. "Neil was behind me when Bobby blew a tire and hit the wall. With only a few laps to go, Neil passed me for the win. I can only tell you that anytime you lose the lead at Atlanta, it's because you're out of tires. Atlanta is like a bowl. You're the rabbit that everybody has been chasing. The guys behind you are taking it a little easier getting in the corners and drafting back up on you in the straightaways. Once you start skating across the racetrack, you say to yourself, I'm out of tires. That's what happened to me when Neil passed me that day.

"Boy, Neil Bonnett was so talented, but he got hurt a bunch. He broke his leg at Charlotte, had a bad injury at Darlington, and one time leading the race at Martinsville he broke his thumb. He said it was pointing back at him. He was a good race driver, but his seventeen wins do not tell you what kind of race car driver he was. Neil Bonnett ran wide open, half-turned-over all the time. That was his style, and that takes away from you sometimes."

"If I remember correctly," said Susan Bonnett, "Neil was the only one who ever drove for RahMac who ever won a race."

She was right. RahMoc raced between 1978 and 1991, and Neil Bonnett, with two wins in 1983 and two more in 1988, had RahMoc's only victories. None of their other drivers won, not Morgan Shepherd, Joe Ruttman, Lake Speed, nor even Tim Richmond.

As well as Bonnett did, the celebration at the end of the 1983 season was for Bobby Allison, who, after narrowly losing the driving championship to hated rival Darrell Waltrip in 1981 and 1982, edged his rival for his first and only championship. Neil and Susan Bonnett enjoyed Bobby's victory as well.

"We were all excited for Bobby," she said. "He had worked so long and so hard. We had seen the ups and downs, the good and the bad, so it was absolutely just like we had won it. It was meaningful to all of us. Neil and Bobby were close, and if they were excited about something, we were excited about it. They were *for* each other, not against each other. And you don't find that much in racing."

In 1984 Bonnett—as planned—switched to the Junior Johnson team.

"Back then Junior won the biggest share of the races and sat on the most poles," said Bill Ingle, who worked for Johnson at the time. "It wasn't anything for Junior to sit on a minimum of six poles and win eleven to thirteen races a year. His cars were dominant, and I would say a big part of it was his knowledge and experience. He trained a lot of people."

With Warner Hodgdon footing the bill, Bonnett drove for Junior's second team. The driver of his other race team was Darrell Waltrip, with whom Bonnett and buddy Bobby Allison had feuded over the years. In '83 Bonnett ran thirty races, won a pole, and had two second-place finishes while Waltrip had seven wins and earned $767,000—about a half a million more than Bonnett.

Two-car teams were not new to the sport, but they weren't common because the arrangement was fraught with problems if the drivers weren't willing to accept their role as teammates on a team. On the Junior Johnson team, driver Darrell Waltrip wanted Junior's undivided attention.

Junior Johnson would discover that adding a second team when Darrell Waltrip was your driver wasn't the best move in the world.

"In 1984, I decided to add a second car, and I hired Neil Bonnett in addition to Darrell," said Johnson. "It's a problem when you've got a guy like Darrell that thinks the way he does. If he's working with a race team, he wants the race team to focus on Darrell Waltrip, and when he lost my personal attention to the car, then he wasn't satisfied. He wanted my time to be devoted solely to him. When I went to run two cars, that could not happen."

Said Bill Ingle, "Junior was running two teams, one with Neil Bonnett in the number 12 car, and the other with Darrell Waltrip in the 11 car. There was friction between the two teams. I would say the friction came more from the 11 side to the 12 side than the other way around."

Waltrip let everyone know he was the top dog and that Bonnett's team was secondary. Neil held his tongue.

"Neil's team was like research and development," said Susan Bonnett. "That's what they used to call Neil's team, the R&D team. 'Cause he was more for research and development.

"Neil was okay with it. He looked at it like it was an opportunity for him. He never got upset with anything like that. He usually just went with the flow.

"The first year Neil drove for Junior, right off the bat at Daytona his crew chief, Doug Richert, was injured. They had just gotten their team together, had been practicing pit stops, and Doug was part of that, and he was hit in the pits and broke his leg and was out about six months. That part was not a good start. Doug getting hurt set off a chain of events, and they didn't have as good a year as they had hoped for."

A bigger problem arose when Warner Hodgdon lost his racing empire after his engineering companies back in California were accused of big rigging. He was not personally accused of any wrongdoing, but faced with two lawsuits for a total of $53 million, he was forced to file for bankruptcy. He had owned—and lost—interests in the Nashville Speedway and the North Carolina Motor Speedway at Rockingham. He owned half of the Junior Johnson race team, which Johnson won back in court. By 1985 Hodgdon was out of racing, but ironically that year Neil Bonnett had one of his finest seasons. Though Darrell Waltrip won the driving championship with 3 wins and 22 top-ten finishes in 28 races and purses worth $1,218,274, Bonnett, the other Junior Johnson team, won 2 races, had 18 top-ten finishes, and earned $530,144. When I asked Susan Bonnett to talk about the relationship between Neil and Darrell Waltrip, she chuckled.

"There is no real easy way to say they didn't get along that well," she said. "Neil could get along with anybody, but there had been misunderstandings. Later we came to know Darrell and we were really crazy about him, but at that time they never got very close because Darrell was the Golden Boy and Neil was second in line.

"There was a race at Nashville [on May 12, 1984, the last Winston Cup race held at that track]. There was a caution on the last lap, and Neil won the race. Darrell just pitched a fit over that. He complained that Neil had passed on the caution—we all thought he was ahead when the caution came out anyway—and he pushed NASCAR, and the next day NASCAR took it away and gave it to Darrell, and Neil finished second. And that didn't sit well with Neil, just to be honest. It had never been done before, and he was really upset because he had never heard of NASCAR doing that before. He felt like they should have done it that day when it happened, not to wait until someone threw a fit and then change it. It didn't help their personal relationship.

"And it got me mad at Junior, because I felt he was favoring Darrell, and he was. Darrell had been with him before we ever came. Darrell had won races for him. That's just the way it was."

The last season Neil Bonnett drove for Junior Johnson was 1986. Bonnett won the next-to-last race at Rockingham in October. It had been seventeen months since Bonnett's last win. After winning that race, Neil hugged Johnson and thanked him for giving him good cars for the three years. Bonnett, taking his Valvoline sponsorship with him, then went back to RahMoc.

CHAPTER 33

Bobby:
The Oldest Winner Ever

"I almost had Davey talked into lending me some money."

—**Bobby Allison**

The Stavola brothers, Bill and Mickey, who had real estate hold-ings and an asphalt company out of Kingston, New Jersey, began in Winston Cup racing in 1984 when they bought the Bobby Hillin race team.

Hillin himself had begun his driving career in Winston Cup in 1982 at age six-teen when his father hired the legendary Harry Hyde to be his son's crew chief. Hyde took the job because he had gone broke after a bitter legal struggle with car owner J. D. Stacy. After working with eighteen-year-old Tighe Scott and John An-derson, and then crew-chiefing for Donnie Allison, only to see him crash and almost die at Charlotte, Hyde, who was broke and desperate, was glad to have someone to pay the bills. Hillin's dad and granddad had made a score in the oil business, and they were hoping that the legendary Hyde would take his son to the heights of rac-ing. Hyde did some of his best work while mentoring the young driver, who man-aged five top tens in two years of trying.

Then, in 1984, Harry Hyde was offered an opportunity to work for another new team, Hendrick Motorsports, owned by Rick Hendrick, a former speedboat racer who was slowly but surely building an empire in new-car sales. He had begun with one Chevy dealership in Charlotte, and he was expanding across the South with amazing success. Hyde was impressed by Hendrick and went to work for him. His partnership with driver Tim Richmond would be immortalized in the movie *Days of Thunder*.

Bill and Mickey Stavola had been impressed with how well Bobby Hillin had raced despite his youth, and they were sure that with some TLC he could compete with the other new hotshots like Dale Earnhardt and Tim Richmond. The Stavolas figured they were entering Winston Cup racing with the new big thing in racing, but in sixteen starts in 1984, Hillin didn't once finish in the top ten. In 1985 he had five top-ten finishes, but no top fives.

In 1986, when Bobby Allison signed with the Stavolas, for years he had refused to be part of a two-man team. He wanted everyone on the team devoted to him. When the Stavolas told Bobby he would be joining Bobby Hillin, Bobby assumed since he was the veteran with the track record of more than eighty wins, he would be top dog and Hillin the second car. He didn't realize that after his winless 1985, the Stavolas saw him as an over-the-hill has-been hired to take their wunderkind to the next level.

Bobby, not understanding his role and place, even went so far us to suggest that the Stavolas put Hillin in an ARCA car, so Bobby could teach him what he needed to know to win at the Winston Cup level.

"Oh, no," Bobby was told. "We're going to run him at Daytona, not some ARCA race. He's going to run Winston Cup, period. You can drive for us, too—if you want to."

Bobby had to eat a little crow. He went and apologized to Hillin.

The Stavolas badly wanted for Bobby Hillin to be the next young superstar in racing. They assigned Ron Puryear, who was hired as their manager of racing operations, to get Hillin to the top. Puryear, in an attempt to satisfy his bosses' desire to better Hillin, paid Allison's wants little mind, and it became very difficult for Allison to work with him.

"Let's get myself going, and for now let me not think about Bobby Hillin," Allison would say to Puryear.

"No, no, no, no," was the answer. "You've got to help Hillin."

Bobby hired Wayne Baumgartner to be his crew chief.

"I thought Wayne did a very good job," said Bobby. "Wayne tried hard to do my part of the program, with very little cooperation from Ron Puryear."

Despite the limitations, Bobby kept positive.

"I felt our team had promise for the future," he said.

The highlight of Bobby's 1986 season, one in which he finished seventh in the points and earned more than a half million dollars in purses, came at Talladega on May 4. Bill Elliott had the lead, but with thirteen laps to go, his engine blew. Dale Earnhardt took the lead, with Bobby right behind him, and right at the end Bobby got his nose in front of the Intimidator for his first Winston Cup win in two years.

Eddie Allison watched the race. He says the only reason Earnhardt didn't wreck Bobby was that he was intimidated by the Talladega fans, who favored the hometown boy.

"Earnhardt drove all the way up under him in turn three, and he knew he was going to crash into him, so he took his foot off the gas," said Eddie. "It was one of the few times he did, because he knew if he wrecked Bobby Allison at Talladega, he was in deep doo. And when he took his foot off the gas, Bobby just went away. Poof. He was gone."

It was win number eighty-three in Bobby's storied career. At age forty-seven, Bobby was the oldest driver ever to win a Winston Cup race.

At Dover, Bobby finished second to Geoff Bodine, but then the car finished out of the top ten several races in a row. He was fifth at Pocono, but then at Talladega, on July 27, on the final lap Hillin was in the lead with Bobby right behind him getting ready to slingshot past him, when Sterling Marlin hooked Bobby's bumper, and Bobby crashed into the wall. His car was destroyed, but he wasn't hurt. Hillin at age twenty-two was the third-youngest driver ever to win a Winston Cup race.

Meanwhile, whenever Bobby would return to Alabama after a race, brother Eddie would resume an argument they had had for decades.

"Bobby, fix the thing so it'll turn," Eddie would say.

"We need more motor," Bobby would reply.

Said Eddie, "If you have 859 horsepower and you can turn the corner when you get there, and another car has 900 horsepower and can't, that 900 is going to lose."

There were precious few other bright moments for Bobby that year. On August 31, 1986, he was second at Darlington when Bill Elliott hit the wall, but he couldn't catch Tim Richmond. Though the rest of the way he wasn't often a factor, Bobby still managed to finish seventh in the points and to earn $503,000 in prize money while Hillin finished ninth and had $448,000 in earnings.

The year 1987 was an exciting one for Bobby, because his son Davey was driving in Winston Cup competition full-time for owner Harry Ranier, who then sold the race team to Robert Yates. Father and son met on the huge asphalt track at Talladega on May 3, 1987. It was only Davey's fourteenth start in the big time.

Davey was just ahead of Bobby, the first time a father and son had led a race since Lee and Richard Petty had done it, when on lap 21 Bobby's engine blew. He was going 205 miles an hour, speeds that racers were saying were unsafe, when he ran over debris that dropped from his car, and his tire exploded. His 3,500 pound Buick LeSabre lifted into the air and vaulted backward high into the chain-link fence designed to protect spectators from the cars along the main grandstand near the start-finish line just ten feet in front of the first row of spectators.

Said Ed Carroll, who was there that day, "If the car had gotten up in the stands, it could have killed hundreds of people."

"Bill Elliott had qualified on the pole at 212 miles an hour," said Bobby, "and I was on the outside pole at 212 miles an hour. The race started, and early on my engine blew up, and it blew up so bad the entire front section of the crankshaft came off the engine and went under my car with the pulleys and drive gear and dry sump attached to it.

"The crankshaft broke turning 7,500 rpms, which was way at the top of the range. The force is so great, the crankshaft broke at the first journal, and it took a *big* chunk of stuff with it. This all went onto the racetrack, and I ran over it with my right rear tire, which catapulted the car into the air.

"As the car catapulted in the air, the wind got under it, the car spun around, and the wind made the car go up instead of down. I just barely missed hitting the flag stand. A little higher, and I would have killed the flagman.

"The only thing that went in the stands were pieces of concrete from the fence structure. No car parts.

"As I was flying through the air, all I could think about was, Oh, shucks, this is going to be bad. I hope nobody hits me too hard."

Bobby's car came to rest a hundred feet past the flag stand. Phil Parsons ran into the car, spinning it more and rupturing Bobby's dry-sump oil tank, which was located in the left front fender behind the tire. The collision threw oil all over the inside of the car. The oil was warm, but fortunately it wasn't hot enough to scald Bobby. He was wearing goggles, and the oil covered the glass of the goggles, making it impossible for him to see momentarily.

Davey was just ahead of Bobby when the incident occurred, and his heart stopped when he saw his dad's car in his mirror. He saw dust fly and then he could see the side of the 22 car up in the air, going around and hitting the fence. He wondered whether the car would hurdle through it. Davey screamed into his open radio mike.

Bobby's car had snagged the fence and pulled it loose, dragging it onto the track as debris flew everywhere. He tore out nine steel uprights and a hundred and fifty feet of fifteen-foot-high fencing, but the fence had done its job, keeping the car from the spectators packed in the grandstand. Several people were slightly injured by flying debris, but no one was seriously hurt. The race was stopped for two and a half hours while crews replaced the mangled fence.

Bobby sat in the wreckage, trying to rub the oil from his goggles. When the safety truck came, the attendants told him, "Come on, we have to get you to the hospital."

But Bobby was more concerned about the fans in the grandstand.

"How many people are hurt back there?" he wanted to know.

"Don't worry about them" was the reply. "We have to get you to the hospital."

They handed Bobby a cloth, and he wiped his eyes until he could see, and inside the ambulance he was aware that they were taking him the long way around the racetrack. Had the ambulance gone left, past the site of the accident, it was only half a mile. Right, it was two miles and a quarter.

Bobby said to himself, *There must be dead people everywhere. That's why they don't want me to see it.*

The ambulance drove to the infirmary area, and Bobby was met by Dr. Hardwick, the head doctor for the track. Hardwick looked at Bobby and yelled, "Okay, shut the helicopters off. We don't need them."

"That was good news to me," said Bobby, "because that meant nobody else needed them, either."

"What's the deal back there?" Bobby said to Dr. Hardwick.

"A couple of people had minor injuries," he said. "Don't worry. I've attended to them. Nobody got hurt in the crash."

Bobby wanted to leave, but Judy made him stick it out.

"Let's stay and support Davey," she said. "He's running really good."

When the race resumed, Davey went to the front with ten laps to go and won the race, beating all the hotshots, including Dale Earnhardt, Bill Elliott, and Tim Richmond, to the finish line. Bobby was the first to greet his son in Victory Lane.

Bobby thanked Robert Yates, Davey's car owner, for giving Davey such a great car. He also mentioned how hard Davey had worked to get where he had gotten.

When the Allison clan met back at Bobby's house, everyone watched the tape of the race. When Davey took the lead, Bobby joked, "Look at that cheater Ford running out front."

At the end of May 1987 at the high-banked Dover Downs International Speedway, Bobby was leading most of the way, but his car overheated three-quarters of the way through the race and he had to drop out. Davey won again.

I asked Bobby whether he had mixed emotions about his son winning races he was competing in.

"No, no," said Bobby. "I never had any feeling like that whatsoever. I don't know whether I had gotten old enough to where I was looking forward to his future and the end of my career . . . I was forty-nine years old and had had a really tremendous career with so many good times. All these wins. Good times and good times and good times. Basically, I was pleased with the way things were going for me, though you can't be happy with the things that aren't going quite so good, because it makes you try harder. But I still had the enthusiasm, still had my enjoyment. Here we were, and the best young man in racing went out and won a race."

The next two races at Pocono and Riverside were won by Tim Richmond, who had missed the first four months of the season with a mysterious illness. Bobby had always liked Richmond. He could be a tough driver, but after the race he would come over and say something like "Aw, it's going to be okay. Don't worry about it. Let's have a beer."

"So you would," said Bobby. "He came out of Indiana, ran some Indy-type cars, was very enthusiastic, had an exuberant personality. Tim was an exciting driver to watch. He was fast, and he could get his car out of shape and get it back. He took some chances and succeeded, but off the racetrack he was still very friendly. If he asked you a question, and he felt your answer helped him, he'd always come back and thank you. I liked him. We were friends."

Bobby noticed that at his tow rig, he'd have five mechanics. At Tim's tow rig, he'd have two mechanics and a girlfriend. "And she would be a spectacular-looking, spectacularly dressed young lady" said Bobby.

"Tim had a great feel for the car, and he'd take whatever Harry Hyde gave him. I don't think he did anything with the car. He'd show up at the racetrack, and he had a great relationship with Harry Hyde. He was exactly what Harry wanted in a driver. Harry wanted somebody who drove the car and shut up. Tim wouldn't tell him to change a caster or a spring or a camber or put bite in or take it out. When I drove for Harry, I told him all those things, and it kept Harry from being my number-one supporter."

After Tim missed the February through May races, only to return July 14 and 21 and win at Pocono and Riverside, everyone was amazed.

"Riverside was especially tough on Tim," said Bobby, "because Riverside was physically demanding, a long race where you stood on the gas and jammed on the brakes, shifted gears, turned to the right and left. I was impressed.

"I liked Tim personally. I knew he had been sick. The reporters were saying that he had possibly gotten into dope. I was ready to defend him on that, even though I didn't have any knowledge one way or the other. People said he got a disease through his shenanigans, but I never questioned any of it. He's over there, and I'm over here, and I'm busy."

By midsummer 1987 Bobby replaced crew chief Wayne Baumgartner with Jimmy Fennig, who had worked with him in short-track racing in the Midwest. Fennig was joined by Keith Allman. Also helping Bobby's team get better was the improved relationship with Ron Puryear, who now was fully cooperating whenever Bobby wanted parts. No one said anything, but it was obvious the Stavolas were seeing Bobby as more than just an instructor for Bobby Hillin.

The Firecracker 400 on July 4, 1987, was the first race in which NASCAR dictated restrictor plates on the small engines. As a result of Bobby's high-speed close call at Talladega in May, NASCAR decided right then and there that it had better slow down the cars before there was a terrible tragedy.

There are four barrels in the carburetor, and each barrel has a hole almost two inches in diameter. To slow the cars at Talladega and Daytona, NASCAR made each car install a plate directly under the carburetor with four holes seven-eighths of an inch in diameter to let in the air. The smaller holes took a good 200 horsepower out of the motor.

"I knew we needed it," said Bobby. "My deal was never how many miles an hour you could go, just how can you be in front of everyone else at the end?"

Davey took the early lead in the race, but then some bolts on his carburetor got loose, and he needed three pit stops to tighten them.

Bobby had fallen back a lap early in the race and drove most of it at the tail end of the lead lap. He sat in his race car and prayed for a wreck or a blown engine and a caution. He needed a caution to come out for him to win the race.

"I had been a lap down, and I had just passed the leader, Buddy Baker, to get my lap back with ten laps to go when the caution came out," said Bobby.

Rick Wilson hit the wall and left a trail of debris on the track.

"I radioed to Jimmy Fennig, 'Give me four new tires,'" said Bobby.

Bobby was the only driver to put on four fresh tires. When the green flag came out with five laps remaining, he was twelfth, but he was flying.

With three laps to go he was fourth. With two laps to go, Dave Marcis and Ken Schrader were side by side for the lead, with Bobby right behind. As they flew down the backstretch, Allison went low and the cars were now three across.

As they headed for the final lap with Buddy Baker on his bumper, racers Ken Schrader, Dave Marcis, and Harry Gant became entangled in a smoky, metal-flying crash. Schrader's T-Bird did a barrel roll, buckling his hood. When it righted itself, it smashed into Gant's Chevy. After Bobby passed everyone to take the lead, Schrader and Gant's mangled cars just did manage to cross the finish line and come to a stop.

"I looked in my rearview mirror and saw a couple of cars get together, and I knew it was trouble," said Bobby. "I just thanked the good Lord that it happened behind me instead of on top of me. I was straining as hard as I could get to the checkered flag."

Even after he crossed the finish line, most of the crowd didn't realize Bobby had won the race, because they thought he was still one lap down.

"I think Buddy Baker felt that way," said Bobby. "In fact, the scoreboard never caught up with me being back on the lead lap. On the white flag lap, as I looked up to the scoreboard, it didn't show me on the scoreboard at all. As I went across and got the checkered, Buddy Baker was still shown as the winner.

"Then they changed the scoreboard, and everybody realized I had come on and won the race. It was an incredible day for me."

Bobby Allison, at forty-nine years and seven months, bettered his record for being the oldest driver ever to win a Winston Cup race. It was his eighty-fourth win (eighty-third by NASCAR's official count) and his first win in thirty-four starts, since the Winston 500 at Talladega in 1986.

Said Bobby after the race, "I already was the oldest guy. I almost had Davey talked into lending me some money. I guess today canceled that out."

Tim Richmond finished tenth in a race at Watkins Glen on August 10, and then the next week at Michigan, the Richmond saga turned dark. He fell asleep in his motor home just before qualifying was to begin. Other drivers, fearing he was drunk or on drugs, didn't want him in the race. His engine blew up early, and Tim Richmond never raced again.

"People were beginning to say, 'Tim's on dope,' or 'Tim is really sick with some disease, and he's trying to hide it,'" said Bobby. "Once again, I was defending him. I liked him. I was for him, not against him. He secluded himself from all of us, and he carried on his disagreement with NASCAR. They wanted him to take a physical, and he refused. I began to get the impression he was trying to medicate himself for some disease he was fighting, and that he knew more about it than he wanted to let on, but it still wasn't any of my business."

After Michigan, Tim Richmond disappeared from the racing scene. By the end of the year he was dead, a victim of AIDS.

"How do you address that?" said Bobby. "Did he get AIDS from one of his female companions along the way or from sharing a dirty needle with somebody? Those questions never got answered, and here was a guy who had delighted a lot of race fans who suffered one of the worst tragedies in life imaginable."

On October 7, 1987, Bobby Allison continued to prove to everyone that despite his age, he still had it in him to drive a race car. He won the pole for the Oakwood Homes 500 race at Charlotte with a 171.636 mile an hour average. It was his first pole since September 1982, setting a single-lap record of 171.860 on the first of his two laps. His two-lap mark also was a record. Allison finished second in the race to Bill Elliott. In the race Neil Bonnett sustained serious injuries when his Pontiac blew a tire and slammed hard into the fourth-turn wall. It took rescue workers and Bonnett's crew over twenty minutes to cut away the car's roof and remove him from the car on a stretcher. Bonnett fractured his right hip and would not race again until the next season.

Said Bonnet from his hospital bed, "I can't think of anything I have ever done to myself that hurt this bad or would take this long to get over. I can't stand not racing. And after being in the top five and top ten in points all year, and now to lose a big chunk of money on that, you know that's real disappointing, too."

Bonnett had an operation on his femur, the upper bone of his right leg, and underwent therapy.

A month after his injury, he was still out of racing. He figured to be back at Riverside on November 8, but still couldn't lift his leg. He had lost a lot of blood, and he was just starting to get his strength back.

"If I could, I'd be back in the car tomorrow, but right now I'm having a hard time driving these damn crutches," Bonnett said.

Bobby finished the 1987 season with a fifth at Riverside and a fourth at Atlanta. He ended the year a solid ninth in the points. His purses of $515,894 should have guaranteed he would no longer have to worry about money.

Davey Allison, meanwhile, was named 1987 Rookie of the Year.

CHAPTER 34

Bobby and Davey: Father, Son Finish 1, 2

"Bobby won, and Davey came in second. Waltrip tried to make a mess out of it, but his car wasn't good enough."

—Eddie Allison

Every once in a while, a car company would consult with Bobby on the aerodynamics of its race car, and the car would inevitably end up sleeker and faster. In the summer of 1987 the Buick executives invited him to Detroit to look at and comment on their design for the 1988 Buick Regal.

Bobby looked at the plans and made two minor suggestions, to change the design of the parking lights, which protruded on the bumper and looked to Bobby like they would catch air and slow the car down. Bobby also asked the designers to raise the sharp slope of the deck lid.

The Stavolas built two cars to test at Daytona, one for Bobby and one for Bobby Hillin. Jimmy Fennig built Bobby's car. Ron Puryear built Hillin's. In January when the two cars tested, Bobby's car went 190 miles an hour, and Hillin's ten miles an hour slower.

Ron Puryear, who over the two years he worked with Bobby, had slowly become aware of Bobby's skill when it came to making a car go fast. He asked Bobby if he would take Hillin's car out on the track and drive it. Puryear was trying to determine whether the problem was the car or the driver.

Allison drove Hillin's car 189 miles an hour. When Bobby came in, Puryear was smiling. Bobby wasn't.

"Before I say anything," said Bobby, "let me get the hair down the back of my neck. This thing scares me."

The car was so loose, Bobby told him, it would barely stay in a lane. And that was with no other cars around him.

"First, let Hillin drive my car a lap. Then I'll make some suggestions to take care of this one."

Bobby then showed Puryear the setup he had been using since starting out in Winston Cup racing back in 1966.

"The upper and lower A-frames and steering linkage all stayed the same for years and years," said Bobby.

With the newfound cooperation on the part of everyone on the Stavola brothers race team, optimism was high before Daytona.

"My car was really good," said Bobby. "Jimmy Fennig, Wayne Baumgartner, Elvin Rector, Mike Bessinger, Len Bobo, a little bitty guy who painted bodies, all these guys were really enthusiastic. We had about twenty-four guys working on our race team. Today the same effort would take 125 crewmen."

After testing, Bobby returned home to Hueytown, where he was working on the upgrading of his Aerostar, a twin-engine plane that he adored.

Bobby was in the process of converting an old Aerostar 601P in his hangar at the Bessemer airport. He spent three or four hours with Chuck Stallings, who was supervising the conversion work. Chuck was a pilot and a mechanic involved in general service. He had been the manager of the Bessemer airport after his father-in-law had bought it. Bobby hired him full-time to do the mechanical work.

Bobby had made the engine mounts himself at his race shop in Hueytown. He made the control cables and control rods and supervised the wiring. He had the basic picture of how it all fit together, but a lot of the design was by the seat of his pants.

After four hours working on his plane, Bobby and Judy flew to Daytona, where they owned a time-share condo at the racetrack.

When Bobby went to qualify for the Daytona 500, he finished third behind son Davey and Ken Schrader. He then entered the Busch Clash, a fifty-lap sprint featuring drivers who had won races the year before.

As the race neared the finish, Dale Earnhardt held off Davey in a T-Bird and Bobby in his Buick Regal. The three cars were bumper to bumper the final two laps. Davey tried to move to the outside to get ahead of Earnhardt on the backstretch of the final lap, but Earnhardt, a wizard at controlling the track, cut him off. Without having another car to draft with, he couldn't pass him, and Earnhardt took the checkered flag.

After the race Earnhardt entertained the crowd with his version of the last lap: "I knew I'd have my hands full when I looked back and saw Davey making his way to the front pretty fast. But I didn't get real worried until I looked back with two laps to go and saw Davey's daddy pop up right behind him. It was going to be the Alabama Gang against ole Earnhardt the rest of the way."

On Wednesday before the race Bobby entered the fishing contest that was held on the lake in the track's infield. He won it by catching a couple of large bass, the third time Bobby had won. His prize was an all-aluminum fishing boat and a small Evinrude engine.

That night Bobby flew back to the Bessemer airport and continued work on his Aerostar.

The Thursday before the Daytona 500 featured the twin 125-milers, shorter races to decide who started where in the Big One. The winners of the two qualifying races were Bobby Allison and Darrell Waltrip. In his race, Bobby held off Rusty Wallace and Ken Schrader for the win. He then flew back to Bessemer, where he spent Friday in his hangar working on his plane. His intention was to fly the plane in a week, and he wanted to finish the work.

That afternoon Bobby flew back to Daytona, and on Saturday he entered the Goody's 300, the Busch Grand National race, NASCAR's Triple-A event. Piper was the sponsor, and son Clifford prepared the car and was its crew chief.

Toward the end of the race Bobby trailed Darrell Waltrip and needed some help. Son Davey gave it to him. Davey pulled behind him, and the two blasted past Waltrip. Bobby then held off Geoff Bodine to win the race.

After the race Bobby was angry with Earnhardt and other drivers who grew impatient and tried to squeeze their cars into spaces that didn't exist.

Earnhardt had tried to beat Ken Schrader to a spot and hit Schrader from behind. Schrader hit the wall, and as Schrader's car slid across the track, Neil Bonnett slammed into him, sending three other cars spinning.

"People can't go as fast as they'd like," said Bobby, "so they're driving like fools out there. These restrictor plates have inexperienced guys trying to do things they don't know how to do. Everyone's trying to take everyone else's space, and it doesn't work.

"The reason I got through those messes is that I left enough space between me and the next guy. When you're right up on a guy's rear, and he brakes, there's nothing you can do but brake and spin. That's what was happening all day."

In that race Donnie Allison, driving a Ken Allen Buick, was involved in a seven-car crash on the second-to-last lap. The crash popped the hood and bumper off his car and sent debris sailing over the catch fence and into the stands, cutting one spectator and bruising several others. The crumpled hood floated over the fence on the main straightaway just past the finish line. It was Donnie's last race. His time wasn't good enough for him to qualify for the Daytona 500.

On Saturday afternoon the Winston Cup cars came onto the track to practice, and something went wrong and Davey crashed into the wall. His crew had to make extensive repairs to his Ford, whose frame had been knocked out of line. Davey got on the radio and instructed his crew to get ready to go to work. He drove straight into the garage, put on his work clothes and helped the crew members with the repairs until nine at night when NASCAR ran everyone out of the garage.

The crew returned at four in the morning and worked until race time.

When the green flag dropped at the start of the 1988 Daytona 500, Bobby and Davey Allison raced down the front straightaway side by side. But Davey's chassis was still out of alignment from the crash the day before, and he fell back early from second to twenty-fifth.

Buddy Baker was one of the first to discover the hard way the new reality of restrictor-plate racing. He was behind Bobby and attempted to pass him for the lead, but when the other cars filled the hole behind Bobby, Buddy was hung out to dry. The line of cars passed him like he was standing still, and by the time he finally was able to nudge himself back in line, he had fallen to ninth.

For most of the race, Bobby and Darrell Waltrip had the dominant cars. With only twenty-five laps to go, Waltrip had a half-minute lead over Bobby and looked like a lock to win his first Daytona 500. Then Waltrip heard something go pop in his engine, and he quickly faded toward the back.

After a pit stop Phil Parsons took the lead, but with 18 laps to go Bobby was able to catch him. Davey, meanwhile, was getting stronger. With every pit stop, his crew would adjust the car's chassis and bodywork, and by the end of the race his car was set up perfectly.

When Davey also passed Parsons, father and son were running first and second. As they flew through turns three and four for the last time, Davey was on Bobby's bumper. When Davey tried to pull inside, Bobby cut him off. Davey almost caught him at turn four, but Bobby cut in front of him and finished two lengths in front. It was the first time father and son had finished one, two since Lee Petty outran son Richard at the Heidelberg Speedway in Pittsburgh in 1960.

Neil Bonnett, who was competing in his first race since breaking his leg in October, finished fourth. In the race Richard Petty, the King, was involved in a horrific crash. He rolled over seven times, pirouetting the car on its nose four times before landing in the middle of the track, where it was struck again. Miraculously, Richard wasn't injured seriously.

It was Bobby's third Daytona 500 win. He had won in 1978 and 1982. It was his eighty-fifth win (eighty-fourth in the NASCAR record book), third-most ever behind Richard Petty and David Pearson. He became the first fifty-year-old driver ever to win a Winston Cup race.

No one was prouder of Bobby and Davey than Bobby's brother Eddie, who watched on TV.

"That was neat," he said. "Bobby won, and Davey came in second. Waltrip tried to make a mess out of it, but his car wasn't good enough.

"When Bobby and Davey drove against each other, they were rivals. Dad-gum right. You don't think Davey wanted to beat his dad? So bad you can't imagine. And there was no way his daddy was going to let him beat him. People who don't have integrity don't understand what integrity is. Bobby Allison would not let Davey Allison beat him. Bobby Allison would not let Davey get a lap back in a race. Because he wouldn't have let anyone else. Because letting these guys get a lap back without a fight is stupid. Man, when you get someone a lap down, that's somebody you have to race. You're trying to win the race. You don't want to have to race that guy. Why are you giving him back his lap?"

After the race Bobby was ecstatic, for himself and also for his son.

"My parents were a real inspiration for me, and now I'm racing against my son," said Bobby. "It was a great race, and Davey did such a good job after wrecking his car in practice. I am very proud of him. He's a fine young man and a fine competitor.

"He drove the wheels off the car all day."

Said Bobby, "It was really good to be in front. It was a great feeling to look back and see someone you think is the best coming up and know it is your son. It's a very special feeling and it is hard to put into words."

Said Davey, "He's just so tough. If I couldn't win it, I'm just so happy that my dad did."

When Davey was asked what his father had done right to win, he said, "He had the better car." When he was asked whether he was proud to have finished second, his reply was "Never."

Davey added, "I didn't even think of him as my dad until after the checkered flag fell."

Said Bobby proudly, "That shows how much he's learned."

As Bobby walked into the press box for the postrace interviews, Davey said, "I really had mixed emotions coming around the last turn. I've dreamed about racing against my dad at the wire since I was a little kid, but the only difference is that in my dreams, *he* finished second."

Judy Allison was asked who she was rooting for.

"I would have been happy either way," she said, "but as long as Bobby won, I was rooting for him."

Added Bobby, years later, "I won the Super Bowl of automobile racing, the Daytona 500, for the third time in my career," said Bobby, "with the best young man in racing second. My son Davey. How could it get any better?"

That night the entire Stavola race team had a big party at Park's Seafood Restaurant, a family-run establishment that was one of Bobby's favorites.

The next morning in Vero Beach, Stuart Millar planned an open house to show off the Busch race car that had "Piper Aircraft" on its side. Bobby flew to Vero Beach, while Clifford drove the race car and the tow rig there. Monday morning was a joyous occasion. Bobby was the star of the day.

He then jumped in his plane and flew to Kissimmee, Florida, where he had contracted to sign autographs for one of his corporate clients. From there he flew to Fort Myers, to see his older sister Claire, who had married Robert Sundman, but who had been divorced for fifteen years and was living by herself. She had contracted pancreatic cancer, and her doctor had called Bobby.

"You're the only one in the family who communicates with her," the doctor said. "You have to come over and tell her she's dying."

The doctor told Bobby she had six months to live.

"This is something she's going to have to face up to," the doctor said.

Bobby went to the hospital and found his sister. She was conscious and alert.

"Claire," said Bobby, "you're dying."

She had one request. She wanted to see her son, Bobby Jr., one more time. Eight years earlier, when her son was nineteen, he had begun dating a two-time divorcee with two children, and Claire had objected strenuously. The boy moved out, married the woman, and adopted the two girls, ages eight and four. The two hadn't spoken to each other since.

Bobby had the boy's number in his wallet, and he called him. The boy said he had some business to attend to first, but he would come as soon as he could.

Bobby told his sister, "He'll be here to see you. I don't know when. But very soon. I have to go prepare for the Richmond race, and from Richmond I have to go to Australia."

Bobby left Fort Myers and flew home to Hueytown. The next day at Bobby's hangar at the Bessemer airport was to be the first flight of his highly awaited conversion of a Piper Aerostar.

The first flight of the unique plane was attended by around two hundred people, including representatives from the FAA and Stuart Millar of Piper Aircraft.

When Millar had asked Bobby if he could put turbine engines on a Piper Malibu, he said, "I can do it in a month."

The awed Millar told Bobby his engineers had told him it would take them two years to make such a conversion.

Bobby and Chuck Stallings began work on Millar's airplane on January 15, 1988. They pulled the Lycoming engines off, put the turbines on, and scheduled the maiden flight of the airplane for February 16.

Some of those in attendance had no idea what was going on. Some were sure they were going to need the crash truck and fire equipment. Bobby had no doubts. He was sure this would be the finest small personal aircraft ever built.

Stuart Millar brought along the engineers who had told him it would take two years to complete. The men were unhappy to be dragged along, and very negative about the project.

Bobby described this plane, one of his most important projects, as "the Corvette of private airplanes." In his own shop Bobby and Chuck Stallings took out the stock engines and replaced them with twin B250-C Allison turbine engines. (Allison, a division of General Motors, had no connection whatsoever with Bobby Allison.)

The aircraft design provided for pressurized cabins, enabling it to fly higher than most private planes, and though it flew at only 260 miles an hour, slower than the Aerostar Superstar, it had far superior climb and great performance at slow speeds. This plane, as Bobby saw it, would be quieter and smoother, and because of the turbine engines would have no piston-engine vibration whatsoever. The only vibration would come from the propellers.

Chuck Stallings had worked with Bobby to make the basic configuration of the plane work. They had had to make new front panels for the engine cowlings because the turbine engines didn't require any of the intake for cooling, but the turbine engine intake required a bigger area for the front panels.

"I knew it would work," said Eddie Allison. "This is the kind of magnificent mechanical mind Bobby has. He was the only man in the world who could have done it. Nobody really knows what kind of a fantastic mind Bobby Allison has. He was a better airplane pilot than a race car driver, and he was the best race car driver who's ever been."

Chuck tested the plane first. He flew it, raised the wheels, let the wheels down, landed, took off, flew, made a circle, flew a few miles away until the plane was almost out of sight, came back, let the wheels down and landed.

Bobby then got behind the controls. The FAA rules only allowed him to fly a small circle around the airport, but quickly the FAA expanded his range until he was cleared to fly anywhere in the continental United States and Canada.

Eddie Allison, who was working for a masonry company in Birmingham, had to go to Tuscaloosca to fix a machine on the day of the test flight. On the way back he had time to drop by Bobby's hangar in Bessemer to watch the turbine-engined Aerostar fly. Eddie was standing next to Stuart Millar as they waited to see what would happen.

"When the plane lifted off the runway," said Eddie Allison, "Millar was so happy the man about peed in his pants."

After the test flight, Stuart Millar made his engineers remain behind in his private plane while he and Bobby went out to lunch.

"The heck with them guys," Millar said to Bobby. "They can go hungry."

"It was the only time I ever saw him really openly display his feelings toward these people," said Bobby. "He had bought a company that was going bankrupt, and he had put it back in business again, gave all these guys jobs, and a lot of them resented him."

Millar flew his Piper Cheyenne back to Vero Beach. Bobby headed for the next race at Richmond in his Piper 700. He was on top of the world.

The second race of the 1988 season, held at Richmond, was won by Neil Bonnett. The forty-one-year-old passed Lake Speed to win the Pontiac Excitement 400. Bobby finished eleventh.

Bonnett chose to put Hoosier tires on his car, and they proved to be faster than the Goodyears, which at the time was working to build a radial racing tire. Radials had already become standard for passenger cars. Goodyear badly needed to make a radial racing tire as a sales tool.

Bobby, who was a good friend of Bob Newton, the head of Hoosier tires, refused to switch from Goodyear. Bobby ran on Hoosiers on a lot of short tracks around the country, but Bobby felt loyal to the Goodyear people.

The next week Bobby Allison and Neil Bonnett traveled halfway around the world to Melbourne, Australia, to enter the Goodyear 500 at the Calder Park Raceway. It was the first NASCAR event held outside the United States. It was also the first race in Australia in which the cars drove counterclockwise. There were a couple of Australian drivers, but most came from the Winston West circuit. Bobby and Neil Bonnett represented the Winston Cup series.

Clifford had done an excellent job building and tuning Bobby's car, and for much of the race it looked like Bobby would win, until very late in the race the power-steering pump failed and the car began pulling to the left. Bobby quickly realized what the problem was, but he also knew he would not be able to turn the corners quite so easily, especially at slower speeds. As long as he could stay in front of the rest of the field, he would be okay. Only a caution could beat him.

Near the end of the race a caution came out, and he was in trouble. Neil Bonnett quickly figured out Bobby had a steering problem, and with only a few laps left, Neil drove under him on the restart. Bobby couldn't race him and had to let him pass. Bobby finished third.

Bobby was surprised the track was packed with fans. In 1983 he and Judy had traveled to Sweden, visiting her parents' relatives, and he noticed that throughout the country compact cars all tricked out were sliding sidewise going around racetracks in American-style racing. With the TV coverage and satellite technology, the world was shrinking, and NASCAR-style racing was becoming popular worldwide, even in Australia.

"The interest was incredible," said Bobby. "The track was full, and the promoter was very happy. Why this thing didn't take off in Australia right then really surprised us. NASCAR was very negative toward it. I was positive toward everything. When someone was negative, I didn't understand why."

After Bobby and Neil Bonnett returned to the United States, Bonnett proved his wins at Richmond and in Australia were no flukes. On March 6, 1988, at Rockingham, North Carolina, Bonnett made it three wins in a row when he again passed Lake Speed to win the Goodwrench 500 at the North Carolina Motor Speedway. Bonnett took a 58-point lead in the race for the championship. Dave Marcis finished third. Several times during the day Bobby and Bonnett raced side by side.

"It was the same old deal," said Bobby. "We've been racing that way for twenty years."

Bonnett was winning races, but the talk of the circuit wasn't just about Neil. It was also about Bobby Allison, who was so strong in 1988 few could believe it. On May 1 at Talladega, Bobby barely lost to Phil Parsons in the Winston 500. Had Bobby won, he would have been in great shape to win the Winston Million, awarded to a driver who wins three of four major races. Allison passed Geoff Bodine with two laps left to finish second.

In mid-May Bobby did some tire testing for Goodyear at the Charlotte Motor Speedway. He and several other drivers rode on experimental radial tires. Everyone had trouble handling cars except Bobby.

"I didn't have trouble," he said. "I recognized the different feel, and I adjusted. When you went to the right place at the right time with the tire, the car went pretty fast. I went nearly as fast as on Goodyear's best bias-ply tire. I was confident Goodyear would come on and build a tire that was faster than the Hoosier tire."

The Stavolas wanted to put Hoosiers on Bobby Hillin's car. Bobby Allison told them he was going to stay with Goodyear. "This is a situation that can't have a good future," he said. Bobby figured that Goodyear, a large company with deep pockets, would do everything in its power to prevent Hoosier from succeeding, and that the Hoosier involvement quickly would go away.

On May 19, 1988, it was announced that Bobby Allison was third in the first-quarter voting for Driver of the Year behind Dale Earnhardt and drag racer Eddie Hill.

What Bobby Allison loved more than life itself was to race, and it didn't matter where. Though he was as famous a racer as there was in America, he still went to small tracks across the country to race. On June 11, 1988, for instance, he traveled to the Saugus Speedway in California to race defending Sportsman champion Dave Phipps of Simi Valley and a field of unknowns.

Another driver would have seen such a race as a lose-lose proposition. If he won, he was supposed to win. If he lost . . . But Bobby, for all his celebrity, did not have the usual racer's ego. PR literally meant nothing to him. He loved to race. So he raced.

At Saugus, where the pits were packed with spectators seeking to get a glimpse of the local hero, Phipps chased Allison for the last 37 of 40 laps, banging on his bumper and trying to pass him at every turn, but he couldn't catch him. Allison showed everyone he was just as good as ever, an amazing realization considering that Bobby had just passed his fiftieth birthday.

Said the gracious Allison after the race, "He was strong enough to keep me busy. He raced me hard at the end."

The day after running at Saugus, Bobby ran in the last race ever held at Riverside. Late in the race Darrell Waltrip spun Bobby out, sending him into the weeds and rekindling the simmering hatred against Waltrip that had ebbed and flowed over the years.

After the Riverside race, Bobby flew the turbine Aerostar to Slinger, Wisconsin, where he entered and won one of the two 250-lap feature races. In addition to the purse, he also received a substantial fee to appear in the race.

"At the time it was ASA," said Bobby, "but it was open to anybody. Wayne Erickson owned the racetrack, and he paid so well that drivers came from all over to compete. Dick Trickle had been one of the big winners there. A lot of Wisconsin drivers raced there. A hundred cars would show up for a thirty-car feature. That's a lot of cars on a small track. The grandstands held about 6,000, and he would have 12,000 people pack the place."

That night at the track a fan who knew that Bobby collected vintage Buick cars approached him and said, "I found a 1933 Buick at a little place over in western Wisconsin. You really need to see it."

Bobby was racing Buicks, and he had collected a garageful of antique Buicks. The man told him where the seller lived.

"The man has a mile-long driveway," he told Bobby. "You can land your plane on it. I'll meet you there, and I'll drive you to where the car is."

Bobby landed on the man's driveway, met his contact, and went to see the car, which Bobby purchased on the spot for $8,500.

"It was a 1933 Buick, a two-door sedan, painted tan and brown," said Bobby. "The fenders were brown, and the basic car was tan. The car looked brand-new. No dents. No scratches. The radio played. It was an original somebody had kept in a closed-in garage forever."

After buying the car Bobby flew to Flint, Michigan, for a press conference to tout the new Buick LeSabre. There he got to drive the new Buick Riata, a two-seater with a look and a feel he loved.

From there Bobby flew home to Hueytown. He was still in the process of putting more powerful engines in his old Aerostar plane in his hangar at the Bessemer airport.

He left Hueytown, and flew by himself to Pocono on a Thursday. Judy wasn't going to go, but after a phone call from Bobby, she flew up the next day in a single-engine plane owned by close friend Walter Short. As she flew north to Pennsylvania, she noticed that Short loved to fly his small private plane through the clouds, making the plane go bumpety-bump. Bobby for a long time had flown twin-engine planes, and she didn't feel comfortable in Short's plane. But what made her feel worse was something that had happened just a couple days before Bobby left for Pocono. She had a lump in the pit of her stomach. As she flew, she felt very much alone.

CHAPTER 35

Bobby: At Death's Door

"I didn't think you were going to make it."

—Dr. Harry Stevens

When I interviewed Judy about Bobby's final race at Pocono, I began by saying something insipid. "That had to be beyond comprehension."

"You got that right," she replied.

"So what happened?" I asked.

"First of all," she said, "when Bobby left to go to Pocono, we were having a little difficulty right then."

"What was it over?" I asked.

"To tell you the truth, I don't know," she said. Then she said, "I'm not sure I want to see this printed."

"Don't tell it to me then," I replied. "But if you think about it, maybe it's not so terrible."

"Well, maybe not," she said.

"It's your story, too," I said. "Tell me."

Then she said seven words which just about floored me.

"Bobby told me he wanted a divorce," she said, an irony considering that it had been Father's Day weekend. "And, see, nobody in this family knows that. Nobody. And he wouldn't tell me why. So then, of course, I was really upset. And then he left and went to Pocono.

"But then he called me and said he had left his shaving kit at home, and he told me he needed it, and asked if maybe I could send it on a Delta flight overnight. I told him our friend Walter Short was flying up in his place, and maybe Walter could bring it up.

"He said, 'Why don't you bring it to me?'"

"I said, 'I'll think about it.' Because of the circumstances. But he sounded like he wanted me to come. So I went up there and that was the first and last time I ever flew with Walter Short in that single-engine plane."

Even though Bobby had asked for a divorce, he had to be feeling ambivalent about such a drastic step, because after Judy joined him at Pocono, on Friday night through Saturday, Bobby and Judy had a great time together.

"Except he was still upset about something Darrell Waltrip had done," said Judy. "He was insistent on saying something at the driver's meeting the next day. I told him I didn't think he should do that, but Bobby was adamant.

"Plus they had painted his car gold, and for some reason I had a really bad feeling about that. I didn't feel flaunting it was the right thing. To me, gold signified high-and-mighty, a bigger-than-God type of attitude. I really didn't like that, but no one would listen to me. Who was I to say?"

The race was held at the Pocono Raceway at Long Pond, Pennsylvania, on Sunday June 19, 1988. Bobby had qualified poorly and was starting at the back of the field, angering his brother Eddie.

"He was driving junk," said Eddie Allison. "But he got into that groove all old drivers get in. They go out and qualify last.

"I was fixing to get on him. I wanted to say, 'Gosh dang, Bobby, fix the dang car so it'll turn the corner when it gets there. If it'll turn the corner, you'll qualify fifth or sixth, and then you don't have to worry about running back there in that junk and getting wrecked. You won't have to start in the back of the Winston Cup race and get to the front.'"

Added Eddie, "Once in a blue moon you might do well when you start at the back, but ninety times out of a hundred you're going to crash before you get to the front."

At the drivers' meeting before the Pocono race, NASCAR officials asked if there were any questions.

Bobby, who was still enraged after having been spun out by Darrell Waltrip at Riverside, raised his hand and said, "What are you supposed to do if some asshole spins you out?"

Michael Waltrip, Darrell's younger brother, replied, "I am not the asshole. I'm just his brother."

According to Darrell Waltrip, who had qualified ninth, a couple of Bobby's crew members came up to him just before the race started.

"Please watch out for Bobby," they told Waltrip. "He had a terrible week, and he's crazy. He says he's gonna wreck you, and he's gonna wreck you big," they told him.

On the parade lap, Darrell radioed his crew and said, "Let me know if Bobby gets anywhere near me. I gotta keep my eye on him today."

Waltrip took the green flag, drove the first lap, and when he came around, he could see what was left of Bobby's car. It had been demolished.

As Bobby crossed the starting line far behind the leaders, he had radioed crew chief Jimmy Fennig to say a tire was going down. The crew had radioed back that it was his left rear tire. Bobby then decided to head to the pits for another tire. The race was just thirty seconds long.

As he went through turn one and headed to the second corner, he was still traveling at 150 miles an hour. While the field powered up and headed for the tunnel turn on Pocono's tri-oval, Bobby pulled down low to get out of the racing groove. Behind him was a long pack of cars. It was so early in the race that the cars had not yet begun to string out.

As he entered the second turn the tire blew apart, upsetting the car's balance. The car turned sideways and slid, first going into the grass and then heading back across the track and slamming into the outside wall, nose first. Then he slid back low in front of traffic.

The caution flag came out, but the rule at the time was that the drivers raced back to the flag to establish position. It was a dangerous practice, one that Judy Allison, for one, really hated. She had spoken to NASCAR officials in the past about it, but was told that it had been the practice for years and wasn't going to be changed.

Jocko Maggiacomo, a sometime Winston Cup driver who had first raced in 1977, was racing toward the back of the pack, and to keep up, he kept his foot on the gas despite the caution flag. He never saw Bobby's gold Buick sitting stock-still directly in front of him until it was too late. When the car loomed large, there was nothing he could do. Maggiacomo's Chevrolet, going 160 miles an hour, struck the driver's side of Bobby's car head-on. It was a miracle Bobby Allison wasn't killed. Everyone who witnessed the collision thought he might be.

"I had made a pit stop," said Benny Parsons. "Something had happened, and when I rode by I couldn't believe the damage to his car. It was just sitting there horseshoed, and it was really, really bad."

After Jocko was brought into the infield trauma center, Judy confronted him.

"Why didn't you slow down?" she wanted to know.

"The rule is you race to the flag," he replied.

Maggiacomo, forty-one, rarely was mentioned in subsequent stories. He suffered in silence after sustaining a broken ankle, fractured ribs, and a twenty-six-stitch gash to his chin. He also suffered severe emotional trauma and never raced on the Winston Cup circuit again.

As soon as Bobby crashed, Robert Yates called Davey on the walkie-talkie to tell him there had been an accident, that his father was involved, and that it was "very bad." He wanted to prepare Davey for what he was about to see.

As Davey Allison came around turn two, he saw a mangled race car, his father slumped over the wheel. It took work crews forty-five minutes to pry Bobby's limp body out of his wreck while the race continued under a yellow caution flag.

Davey could see that his father was not moving and that it looked very bad, and he was determined to find out his father's condition. Allison stopped four times to try to find out what was happening. Track workers, trying to keep the area clear, kept waving him away. Finally, on his fourth stop, Davey called one of the workers over. He was then told that his father was breathing and that he was unconscious.

Davey Allison was out of his mind with grief.

"Several times in the pits they started to say something to me and stopped, and I'd lose it," said Davey. "I was going crazy in the car, thinking that what they were going to tell me was he didn't make it, that he'd died."

Davey Allison continued the race and finished fifth, but his effort to find out more about his father was futile. Robert Yates, Davey's team owner, thought that he would have to get a relief driver for Davey, but Davey insisted on racing to the finish.

Judy was in the pits when she first heard a crew member say something about there being a caution. The next thing she heard was "There's a big wreck in the turn, and it's Bobby."

Jimmy Fennig said, "Judy, we have to go." Officials wouldn't let them approach Bobby's car, so they waited in the track infirmary. The doctors and nurses were keeping her apprised of what was going on.

"Some people think Bobby was knocked out, but he wasn't," said Judy. "He was aware, and he could talk to the medical people, but when they got him into the infirmary, the nurse had to put a trach in him and a collar on him because the helicopter they were going to transport him in didn't have enough room for her to do that in transit. So she had to knock him out a little bit, give him a sedative, in order to do that. Then when other people came in and started bunching around Bobby, they assumed he had been knocked out and was out of it in the car."

Judy didn't know it, but Bobby had actually stopped breathing, only to be resuscitated by the Pocono track's emergency crew. He was taken by helicopter to the Lehigh Valley Hospital Center in Allentown with a concussion, a bruised heart, a broken left ankle, broken left ribs, a broken left femur, blunt abdominal trauma, and internal bleeding.

Hours after the accident Allison remained unconscious, in critical but stable condition.

Humpy Wheeler, the head of the Charlotte Motor Speedway, was listening to the race on the radio.

"You can tell by listening to the radio when there's really been a bad one," he said. "'Cause they won't talk about it. The race was stopped, and they were working to get Bobby out of the car, and I knew something really, really bad had gone down.

"I got Joe Matioli, the president of the Pocono Speedway, on the phone, and I said, 'Joe, how bad is it?'

"He said, 'It's bad.'

"I called up Dr. Jerry Petty, who is beginning to become the lead doctor in NASCAR. He's a neurosurgeon who shuns publicity, but if you ask any driver who they'd go to, it's Dr. Petty. I called him. He knew Bobby well. I said, 'It looks bad.'

And from tire testing there, I figured they would take him to a pretty small hospital. I knew it was a head injury, and they had one neurosurgeon in the whole hospital.

"We got the president of Piper, a friend of Bobby's, to fly down to pick up Dr. Petty and his partner, Scott McLanahan.

"Bobby would have died had the quick-thinking nurse in the helicopter not intubated him. He got to the hospital, and it was touch-and-go, and these two doctors from Charlotte performed surgery on him, and inserted a shunt, and that helped save him.

"Surviving a full T-bone crash in the door at a high-speed track— It's what killed Tiny Lund and a number of other drivers. The fact Bobby survived it is pretty incredible."

Nevertheless, Judy was upset because Dr. Harry Stevens, who was a leading neurosurgeon, wanted to install a plastic shunt, so he could perform MRI exams. Dr. Petty and Dr. McLanahan insisted on the traditional steel shunt. Judy backed Dr. Stevens.

Bobby's brother Eddie, for one, was mightily impressed by Dr. Petty's knowledge and skill. Eddie was seated at the dining room table eating Father's Day dinner in Hueytown and listening to the race on the radio when the crash occurred.

"We didn't know how bad it was," he said. "Someone called the house, and then Davey called and said, 'Sam will come and get you.' Sam was Davey's pilot. Davey had a Cheyenne, a six-seater, and Donnie and I left about four in the morning.

"We got there, and the first time I saw Bobby, he wasn't one-tenth as dead as Donnie had looked after his wreck at Charlotte in 1981. Still, Bobby looked really bad.

"We walked into the room, and Dr. Petty took his fist, and he hit Bobby in the sternum so hard that everybody in the room jumped. And Bobby's eyes opened.

" 'That's the only way you can open their eyes,' Dr. Petty said. 'If you want to see what their eyes say, you have to open them.' He said you can tell a lot more if they open their eyes themselves rather than if you have to pry them open.

"Dr. Petty said that Bobby was alive because the doctor and the paramedic on the helicopter were the best. She did everything right in those eleven minutes from the racetrack to the hospital. She got his airway open, got the collar on him, did all of that."

Later that day Bobby suffered another emergency. All the platelets had gone out of his blood, and Dr. Harry Stevens, one of the top neurologists in the country, couldn't figure out why.

"He had broken his leg pretty badly," said Eddie. "I happened to be with him, and the doctor took Bobby and rolled him over, and he said, 'There they are.' From the top of his shoulder to the bottom of his ass, the middle of his backbone was solid black.

"What had happened, the seatbelt stretched and banged him back in the seat and bruised all that right side of his body.

"The same thing later happened to Dale Earnhardt, only Dale's head went back so far, he broke his neck. When Dale's head went forward and snapped back, it cracked the bones that his head sat on.

"Bobby's fourth vertebra was bruised so badly it swelled shut, so the water in his brain didn't run down to his abdomen, and that's what the pressure was.

"When he hurt himself in the crash at Elko in '74, doctors had put a plastic socket under his right eye, and in that wreck he banged his ear, and so the fluid tried to push his eye out of that socket and his ear out of the side of his head. As I said, he was supposed to be dead."

Judy arrived at the Allentown hospital about eleven minutes after Bobby. She was taken in the helicopter owned by the Matiolis, the owners of the Pocono racetrack. Meeting her there were Bobby's cousins, Dave and Millie Demerest. Dave drove from the track infirmary to the hospital in record time.

Judy stood in the hallway, waiting for the neurosurgeon, when "I saw a man about six foot six, shoulders about three feet wide, his hair and clothes all messy, and he was wearing Bermuda shorts and sandals. He told me he was Dr. Stevens, the neurosurgeon. I was so concerned about Bobby that none of that registered until later. In a big, deep, gruff voice, he said, 'We have a situation where I have to have your permission to do an outside shunt immediately.'"

Judy kept her composure. "Let me tell you," she said, "Bobby doesn't want to be a vegetable."

"We'll give you back your husband," he said.

Judy was very upset, because she was facing a decision she had always dreaded making: whether to let the doctors do something to keep her husband alive. He had always been very clear about not wanting to survive on life support.

Dr. Stevens told her he had to perform an operation right away or Bobby would die. He needed to drain fluid from his head and relieve pressure in his skull. The chance of its being successful was slim, he said, and the other possibility was that Bobby would remain in a vegetative state. The doctor promised Davey that his dad would not be a vegetable or on life support.

Davey convinced his mother to have the operation. "We've got to take the chance," he told her. They then prayed for a miracle.

After Judy signed the papers, she went to pieces. She got out her rosary, and then she called Bobby's mother on the phone and told her to get out hers. She asked the Demerests if they would go with her to the chapel downstairs.

Judy and Dave and Millie Demerest knelt in front of a crucifix. Judy was crying. And then, she says, "All of a sudden a feeling came over me. It was like, *Judy, you have to straighten up. This is a big job, and you have to do it.* It was something in my head saying this to me. So I regained my composure, and from that moment on, there was a feeling in that hospital. Other people said they could feel it, too, though they didn't know what they were feeling.

"Somebody told me it was the feeling of love. It was, but to me it was the presence of Jesus. It was just too overwhelming a feeling. Some people mistook it for my love of Bobby, which was there, but what they were *really* feeling was the presence of Jesus."

Bobby got lucky in that Dr. Stevens was supposed to be on vacation but hadn't left yet, hence the Bermuda shorts and the sandals. He was at the hospital doing a last-minute check on his patients before he left. So he stayed to head the medical team that implanted a metal shunt in Bobby's skull to drain fluids from the brain.

Said Eddie Allison, "Dr. Stevens told us when he drilled a hole in his head, the blood hit the wall twenty feet away. He said the cranial pressure of the skull when they drilled that hole was 260. You should be dead at 260. And he wasn't dead.

"The doctor was heavyset, a big blowhard with an ego as big as the hospital," said Eddie, "but he knew exactly what he had to do, and he did it, and he saved Bobby's life. He was the man for the job. He did it perfectly.

"After the surgery, he told us, 'We guessed right.'"

After the emergency neurosurgery, said Davey, "The doctor called me over into a corner. He said, 'Son, tonight you're going to have to make yourself be the man of this family. Because if your daddy lives through the night, he'll probably never be able to do anything again.'

"It took the breath out of me," said Davey. "It took the legs out from under me. I fell straight down to the floor."

Doctors also inserted pins in Bobby's shattered left thigh. The rods later would cause him excruciating pain as they ground against the pelvis. After the operations Bobby was in stable but very critical condition.

Davey Allison said at the time, "Dad has control of his body. He moves his fingers, and that seems to be normal. He took a pretty good shot and he's busted up pretty bad. It's going to be a long haul."

Bobby was unconscious for four days. Said Benny Parsons, "I went to Allentown to see him. Bobby didn't even know I was there."

As Bobby lay motionless, Davey realized, "He might never remember me again or remember us being in racing." More frightening was the thought of his having to race without him.

"When he was around," said Davey, "it was like I had a security system. All of a sudden, I had to be able to do it on my own. I was determined to keep racing because that was my life." Davey had to grow up in a hurry.

Eddie told Judy, "If you need a shoulder to cry on, we'll cry together, and we'll get through this.'"

Bobby was conscious but in the twilight zone. He even spoke to people, calling them by name. Told of this later, he had no memory of doing so.

"Even when I was totally conscious and talking to people, I have no lasting memory of it," Bobby said. "I was told people would ask me a question and I would squeeze their hand one for no and two for yes, but I don't remember doing that."

One memory he would never regain was his one, two finish with Davey at Daytona in February. He would read accounts of the race, but when he thought back to recall it, nothing came to mind. In addition to having little memory, he also suffered from double vision.

When Bobby finally regained consciousness, he realized he was not in his own bed.

He thought, *Why am I here and how did I get here?*

He had another thought, *This is just a terrible dream and I'm going to wake up.*

For a couple of days Judy had been trying to get Bobby to squeeze her hand. Finally, he was able to do it. Judy's spirits soared.

The first week Judy spent at the hospital, she lived day and night in the waiting room. Her sister Carolyn kept her company, as did son Davey, who had kept a round-the-clock vigil at his father's bedside. For four days he, too, slept in the waiting room of the hospital. Then he went off to race again.

Before he left, Davey impressed Judy with his devotion to his dad.

"He had a lot of growing-up experience through all of this," said Judy. " 'Cause when it came to anybody being sick, even himself, he was real wimpy."

One time when Davey came to see his dad, he saw that his urine bag had gotten tangled, and Davey, not even realizing what he was doing, picked it up and untangled it.

"I can tell you that afterward, he was beside himself," said Judy. "I said, 'Davey, let me tell you something. When you love somebody, you will do *anything*.' And he proved it again when he had his first child, Krista. Another lady was delivering at the same time, and she was having complications and needed the same doctor, even though Liz was having complications, too. The cord was around Krista's neck and had to be cut, and so Davey had to cut the umbilical cord. She wasn't even cleaned up, and I said, 'Davey, how could you possibly do that?'

"He said, 'Mom, you don't see or hear or feel my knees. They are knocking like crazy.' "

During Bobby's first three weeks in intensive care, they put in three extra phones, two extra computer systems, and equipment to handle all the phone calls coming in. Baskets of flowers came in. Before the first week was up, Judy had to tell the florist to put on a hold until some of the others withered out. Two waiting rooms were filled with flowers. She had to give many of them away. Judy ordered the nurses to take them down to their other patients. And she donated a lot of them to the nursing homes around Allentown.

Dale Earnhardt came to visit. Earnhardt considered Bobby to be almost a second father.

"I think so much of Bobby," he said. "He raced with my dad for years back. He helped me a lot when I first went to Daytona. He's just an all-around good person. He takes time with everyone, not just certain people."

Earnhardt was devastated when he saw Bobby lying there helplessly.

"It was a pretty tough deal to go see him in the hospital," said Earnhardt. "Bobby was lying there like there would never be another day he would walk or talk. But it was amazing the strength that came from Judy. The strength was in that room, and you could feel it."

Said Earnhardt about the risks involved, "It was a freak deal. I feel that Bobby and the majority of people in racing are at home with what could happen. I know I'm at peace with the danger and risks I take."

Davey, showing his toughness, surprised no one when he said he would race at Brooklyn, Michigan.

"I'm sure he would want me to go on with what I'm doing. I will be able to concentrate, especially after the progress he's made today."

By Saturday, said Davey, "He can communicate with his fingers and appears to recognize family and friends. He opens his eyes, he looks around."

But Davey was overly optimistic about his dad, projecting better health than was the reality. Bobby lapsed in and out of consciousness.

Before the Michigan race, Dale Earnhardt asked each driver to wear a Bobby Allison hat during driver introductions for the Miller High Life 400. Davey Allison broke the qualifying record averaging 172.146 miles an hour, breaking Tim Richmond's old record.

On Sunday doctors gave Judy permission to turn on the TV set in Bobby's room so he could watch and listen to Davey race at Michigan.

"They think it will be good for him to hear familiar sounds," said Davey, "and that's definitely a familiar sound. It's what he loves. It's what he's always loved." But it was doubtful Bobby was aware enough to watch Davey's day end when the engine blew on lap 71. Davey was running third at the time.

On June 29, Bobby had four hours of surgery to put a steel rod in his fractured left leg. Doctors repaired his left femur, which had been "splintered, twisted, and was offset."

Later Bobby would ask Dr. Stevens why he waited two weeks to put the rods in his legs.

"Because it didn't seem to make any sense burying a good leg," said Dr. Stevens. "I didn't think you were going to make it."

On June 30, the ever-positive Davey Allison told reporters that despite Bobby's injuries, there was no way his dad would not return to racing.

"There is no question that he would get back in the car if he thinks he can be competitive," said Davey. "The doctors have told us it's all up to Bobby Allison—however far he recuperates from this accident to whatever his decision is going to be afterward."

Davey was being *very* optimistic.

It is fair to say that without Judy's devotion and attention to detail, Bobby's recovery would not have gone nearly as well as it did. After the first week, Bobby was moved to the intensive care unit. Judy watched over him like a mother hen.

When the doctors told Judy she should do everything she could to make Bobby feel at home in familiar surroundings, she snapped into action. She got permission from the hospital to get Bobby a padded lounge chair like the one he had in his bedroom at home. Nathan Sims, a close friend of the Allisons, bought it for him.

The doctors told her, "Give him things familiar to feel and smell and get some of these senses back." So Judy had Clifford bring Bobby his key chain. His granddaughter had made a tag with the word "Grandpa" on it, and Judy wanted Bobby to hold it. Judy also had Clifford bring him a ratchet, and another time she had him bring a gasket from a carburetor so he could feel and smell it.

Judy also did what she could to make sure Bobby didn't become a vegetable, like driver Butch Lynley.

"I was real adamant with Dr. Stevens that I didn't want him to inject any chemicals into Bobby's brain," she said. "Because of Butch Lynley. Butch had wrecked in Bradenton, Florida, and he had a head injury and was in a coma, and they wouldn't get certain responses, and after a period of time they shot him with different chemicals which were supposed to trigger the brain. And nothing happened, and he was in a coma for seven or eight years. After the first year, the bill was $4 million.

"But Dr. Stevens was real good, and the nurses were real good to tell me things and help me, and I in turn could tell them the things that might be relevant for them to know about Bobby. We worked together really well."

Among her other duties, Judy acted as Bobby's guard and protector. She kept a vigil from sunup to sunset. After spending the first week in the waiting room, she stayed for two weeks in Dr. Stevens's home. After that, she rented a room in a nearby apartment that friends fixed up over a NAPA auto parts store.

Early in his hospital visit Judy insisted that no one be allowed to come in to photograph Bobby lying in his bed. When Bobby's brother Donnie crashed back in 1981, pictures of him looking pasty and strange were published, and as a result people in racing were afraid to give him another ride. Judy wasn't about to let that happen to Bobby.

"After a head injury, you have this starey glare kind of face—they have a name for it—and when you have that, you don't look like yourself and you're not responding to people and people get the wrong impression. Bobby's brother Donnie had that accident, and they had to do a radical trach on him, and he lost some oxygen to the brain. Well, he got tagged for the rest of his life as not being normal, and he never had a career after that. Because of that stigma, no one thought he'd ever be normal again.

"And I didn't want that happening to Bobby. I also felt that knowing Bobby and how quickly he recuperated in the past and knowing his character, and how tough his mother is, I felt if anyone was going to make it back into racing after having such a bad head injury, it would be him. It wouldn't be easy, but it would be him."

Judy also took on the job of keeping prying reporters away.

"I had some pranksters, different guys in the media who tried to come up to see Bobby," she said. "They would pull things, saying they were a doctor. I stopped them all. One time I got a phone call from a Dr. Wheeler. Guess who that was? Humpy. He tried to call on the phone and couldn't get through, so he told them he was Dr. Wheeler. Him I spoke to."

When Bobby was moved from the ICU to the constant care facility, he was able to have visitors, who came in a steady stream. Judy stood guard, making sure Bobby was calm. When he became agitated, she quickly shooed them out.

"His agitation came from pain," she said. "His eyes were open, but he wasn't with it. He had the tracheotomy, so he couldn't communicate. They could give him a little painkiller, but when you're in that kind of intense pain, you're still going to feel it. And you're not with it enough to know what to do or say.

"Once we moved over to constant care, where he could have more visitors, then I had to monitor the people, because I had to make sure he didn't get too agitated. Sometimes just having people in the room made him worse.

"If people called me before they came, I could tell them, 'You're taking a chance. You have to understand if he's agitated, you can't see him. You have to be prepared for that.' The bad thing was when people didn't call before they came."

Most of all, Judy provided the positivity needed to boost everyone's morale. When doctors predicted complications and other possible dire outcomes, Judy would counter, "Not him." More often than not she was right.

"If you had cut Bobby through the middle, he would have been white on one side and black on the other," she said. "His contusion was all the way down the left side, and his left arm wouldn't move. It was limp. He had a feeding tube in him and a catheter to go to the bathroom, and a device in his stomach, and they were giving him [blood] platelets because of that contusion, and they were worried where that contusion was going to go, because in most cases head injury victims have other failures like kidney failure, bladder failure, infections, pneumonia, just one thing after another. And it can go back to the brain and cause a seizure or it can go to your heart.

"Within seven days, those possibilities were gone. None of that stuff happened to him. He was very, very fortunate.

"During the first two weeks of intensive care, Dr. Stevens, the head doctor in Allentown, would come in, and he'd say, 'Your husband is going to do this, and he's going to do this, and we have to keep doing so and so.' Problems. Complications.

"And I would say, 'Not him.' And he would look at me kind of funny, like who was I to tell the great doctor?

"And then he would come in a couple days later and say, 'Well, he did really good. He did this okay, and he did that okay, but he's still going to have this problem.'

"And I would say, 'Not him.'

"He did this for the second and third week, and then we moved over into constant care, and he came in and started telling me, 'This is what he's going to do,' and I said, 'Nope. He ain't.'

"And finally he said, 'You know, you're right. He hasn't been doing what I've been predicting.' He finally gave in."

Gradually Bobby would recover his mental faculties. But it would take ten years.

Everyone agreed that Bobby's enormous will had kept him alive. He went from being close to death, to being in a coma, to consciousness, to walking.

On Thursday, July 7, three weeks after the near-fatal crash at Pocono, Bobby was able to sit in a wheelchair and leave his hospital room. He had a tube down his throat to help him take deep breaths and stop fluid buildup in his lungs. He could move his hands, perform certain limited exercises, and respond to commands.

Said Eddie Gossage, the PR representative for Miller Beer, "He's very strong. They're amazed at his strength."

Gossage wouldn't have been so optimistic had he seen Bobby in his sixth and final week at the Allentown Hospital. He was suffering from diarrhea and projectile vomiting, which caused him to lose forty pounds from his once robust frame.

"He couldn't eat," said Judy. "It seemed all he could keep down was apricot nectar. Anything else he couldn't handle. And we had one incident where a nurse tried to force-feed him, and it was my understanding that wasn't good—it could set him back—so I reported her, and she was taken off the case. It wasn't that easy to get her off. I had to convince the doctor that she didn't need to be on the case."

Before Bobby left Allentown, there were more than a few nurses glad to see Judy go.

During his six weeks in the Allentown hospital, Bobby had had many visitors. Most seriously doubted that Bobby would ever be mentally capable again.

CHAPTER 36

Bobby and Judy:
The Long Road Back

"You have to understand, he still hadn't woke up. His eyes were open, but his brain hadn't woke up yet."

—**Judy Allison**

After six weeks in the Allentown hospital, Bobby was allowed to return to Alabama. A med jet flew him to the Lakeshore Rehabilitation Hospital in Birmingham. When he got there, doctors put him on a 3,000-calorie-a-day regimen. They gave him five glasses of Ensure with ice cream mixed in. Judy watched as he made a face when he was given chocolate and then vanilla ice cream. When they tried strawberry, he didn't complain.

"You have to understand," said Judy, "he still hadn't woken up. His eyes were open, but his brain hadn't woken up yet."

During the first week Bobby was at Lakeshore, Judy stayed in his room. The second week she was allowed to stay in a room across the hall.

"Once again, they were real good about working with me and letting me work with him," she said. No visitors were allowed. It was Bobby, Judy, and the medical staff only.

When Bobby first came to Lakeshore, he had to be in a wheelchair because he had bad vision, dizziness, and equilibrium problems. His wheelchair had a high back that could be tilted backward. He had to keep it at an angle, because, the doctors discovered, Bobby had walleyed double vision.

"The whole time he was in Pennsylvania we didn't know what was going on with his vision," said Judy. "They made him special glasses, and gave him an eye patch, and then he got better."

Judy did all she could to make Bobby feel comfortable. Because clothes and even his sheet caused him pain, most of the time Bobby lay on his bed naked. When he got agitated, it seemed the only thing she could do to settle him down was to rub the soles of his feet.

"I don't know why that seemed to help, but it did," she said.

The doctors at the clinic wanted Bobby to immerse himself in the swimming pool. First Bobby seemed to indicate he didn't want to wear swim trunks. After she brought him shorts, he made another face. Judy finally figured out that what Bobby was trying to say was that he didn't want to go in the pool at all.

When Bobby "sort of" woke up—conscious but not all the way to awake— "awake enough to 'sort of' know where he was," said Judy, Bobby decided he was in prison. He mumbled to Judy, "I want you to get my red and white thing and bring it around back so I can get in it, and I can get out of here."

The "red and white thing" was his truck.

"He was wanting to escape," said Judy. "I knew he felt he was in a prison, so I tried to bring awareness around to him, which is what they tell you to do." Judy rolled him in a wheelchair down the hall, asking him, 'Do you see the wall? Do you see that baseboard? What color is it? What does it look like?" She did anything she could to bring Bobby back to reality, though at times she balked at a treatment if she felt it upset Bobby.

When the doctors told Judy they wanted Bobby to watch *Sesame Street* on TV, Judy noticed that he became unsettled.

"You could see it was below his dignity," said Judy. "That was showing on his face."

As an alternative, Judy went out and bought him taped performances of his favorite singers, Marty Robbins, Johnny Cash, Jim Reeves, and Patsy Cline. Bobby was having a tough time sleeping, and Judy would put them on at around eight at night and let them run until he finally fell asleep.

As part of the occupational therapy, Bobby was asked to take large pegs and place them in a colorful pegboard. The blue pegs were supposed to go in the blue holes, the yellow pegs in the yellow holes, et cetera. Once again, Bobby made it clear to Judy that this was an activity he didn't want to do.

"You could read his face once again that this was below his dignity," she said. "And Bobby was color-blind, so it was going to be difficult for him anyway."

Since it was mostly an eye-hand coordination exercise, Judy decided she would find an activity that Bobby would find more appealing. She ordered Clifford to bring over some pistons along with a carburetor. Clifford brought them to Bobby, set the parts on a table, and Judy instructed Bobby to handle them.

"He didn't have any expression of a smile while he was doing that," said Judy, "but he didn't have that look of distaste. He probably didn't want to do it, but it was better than doing the other."

He also began doing crossword puzzles, something he had never done before, but an activity he continues to do to this day.

"That's very good for everything," said Judy.

———

"In truth," said Judy, "Bobby went all the way back to being a baby. He had to be re-taught everything: going to the bathroom, brushing his teeth, taking a bath, getting dressed. He had to be taught everything all over again. Who do you think did that [with him]?"

Judy did. She also helped him relearn how to write.

"When he first started writing, it was so tiny and scribbled it didn't look like anything," she said. "But little by little it started getting a little bigger and a little bit longer, and within three or four weeks, he was writing normal."

On the day Bobby first regained his ability to talk, he made it clear he thought he was still living in the year 1979.

"Nineteen-seventy-nine?" said Judy. "It isn't 1979. It's 1988. You won the championship in 1983."

"No, I haven't won the championship yet," said Bobby.

"Yeah, you have," she said.

To prove it to him, she went home and got the program that recorded his having won the driving championship in 1983. In the cover shot, there was Bobby, standing in front of the Waldorf-Astoria in New York. Once she showed him the picture, he accepted his winning as fact.

Nevertheless, his short-term memory loss was severe. A driver or friend would come in the room, and he would always put his hand out as a greeting. Judy would whisper in his ear, "So and so is coming to see you." While they were there, he would call them by name, speak to them, but by the time the meeting was over, he couldn't remember who he had just seen.

"If they came back in and I didn't tell him again, he wouldn't know," said Judy.

"I was in Lakeshore a couple weeks," said Bobby, "and one day I woke up and said, 'Where am I? What's gone wrong?'

"From that day on I started putting things back together," he said. "I had incredible memory loss. I didn't know what year it was, didn't know what state I was in. I knew Judy and knew my parents and I knew the kids. But close friends would come to my hospital room, and in my early recovery—they say this is fairly common with head injuries—I had an incredible loss of self-confidence that made me so timid. I feared everything.

" 'What's that person doing here? What's he want? What's he doing?' And it might be someone who sat beside me at the airplane hangar or went to lunch with me. It was horrible."

Bobby's recovery was painfully slow. It wasn't until the middle of August that Bobby felt he "had a grasp on things."

As Bobby lay in the hospital bed, his first memory was the driver's meeting before the Pocono race. Dick Beaty called the roll, he remembered, asking everyone,

"Before we start the meeting, are there any questions?" Bobby recalled that he said, "Hey, Dick, I have a question."

"What's that?" asked Beaty.

And he remembered asking the question, "What should a guy do if some asshole spins him out?" He also recalled that Michael Waltrip said he was just the brother.

"And that's all I remember," said Bobby. "I don't remember any more. I don't remember what Darrell said. I don't remember what Dick Beaty said. I don't have any other memory."

According to Judy, for the first four weeks of his six-week stay at Lakeshore, Bobby wasn't very cooperative, but the last two weeks he showed tremendous improvement. He had done so well that his therapist decided it was time for Bobby to leave the hospital for a few hours and take a trip to a local mall. Judy objected to his choice of location.

"Bobby is not a mall person," she said. "He has never been a mall person." And so Judy went to the head of the rehab clinic and asked if she could take him to church for his first outing instead. The therapist resented her meddling but said okay. Judy took Bobby to church.

What hurt Eddie Allison more than anything was that most of Bobby's friends didn't call Bobby during this trying period, and as a result Bobby spent a lot of this recuperation period alone. True, Bobby was having a great deal of difficulty communicating, but brother Eddie felt that even though he couldn't talk very well and had little memory, he would have been buoyed in spirit had they called.

"I can't tell you how many people he has given money to and never asked for it back," said Eddie. "That's why he's poor.

"And what tore my butt up the worst when he was laying up here at the house after he got hurt, and nobody could even call him. And if I spoke to someone, he'd say, 'What am I going to say to him?' I'd say, 'Don't say anything. Just call him up and say, 'Hi,' and let him talk. He'll get into the conversation he wants to have. Get him well. The only way he's going to get well is to talk to people he knows.

" 'What am I going to say?' Like I said, let him do the talking. He'll talk. That's one thing he could do, even though he was brain-dead. He still could talk. And people bringing back memories of the past helped him remember. But that really tore me up."

He continued, "Pat Dye, the head coach of the Auburn University football team, and Bobby did a Vance Auto Parts commercial, and Pat Dye came to an Alabama football practice one day, and I introduced myself to him, and he just went on and on about Bobby. It makes you feel so good to know that your brother is that good a person. Because Bobby and I are the same. We come from the same place. He doesn't need to credit himself, and neither do I. I thank God he gave me a brother like Bobby Allison."

Davey Allison, meanwhile, had a job to do. After blowing engines at Michigan and Daytona, he returned to Pocono on July 24, 1988, and finished third to Bill Elliott and Ken Schrader.

On August 21 at Brooklyn, Michigan, Davey won the Champion Spark Plug 400, breezing to the lead and finishing with little competition. It was his first win of the year. He set a track record of 156.86 miles an hour.

Davey dedicated the win to his father.

"I almost broke down in tears in Victory Lane," said Davey. "That's as close as I've ever come to it.

"It has just been a real tough year for us," said Davey. "We've had injuries, equipment problems, you name it. It's been real tough on me."

Before he left Lakeshore Hospital, doctors suggested Bobby revisit the crash site at Pocono. He flew back to Pennsylvania, was taken to the track, and stood on the spot. He could remember nothing. His only shred of memory was the drivers' meeting before the race.

While he was in the Lakeshore Hospital, Robert Markus of the *Chicago Tribune* interviewed Bobby. Allison told him he was still racked with pain. He talked about how he once broke both feet and shattered a cheekbone in a short-track race at Elko, Minnesota, and how he was back in the race car eight days later.

Not this time. This pain "is about as bad as anything I've ever been through, even a short-term injury," Bobby said. "It hurts constantly. Right now, talking to you on the telephone, it hurts really, really bad, and there's nothing I can do about it."

Bobby didn't know it—no one knew it—Bobby's driving career was over. He would never race again.

Said Bob Tomlinson back in 1991, "It's too bad Bobby got hurt, because he'd be driving right now, and he'd be just as competitive as anyone. I really believe that man could have driven a car until he was sixty or seventy years old, because he was another smart one. He was a charger, but he learned over the years the main thing is to stay on the lead lap, wait for a caution to come out, catch a break, and as a result you'll be right back up front, and you'll win the race."

Humpy Wheeler, for one, was worried less about whether Bobby would drive again than whether he would ever return to normalcy.

"He went back to Birmingham and did his rehab," said Wheeler. "Still there was a lot of wonderment, because the problem with a severe brain injury, you can do the tests, and most of the tests won't show anything. It's how the person comes back, and it just didn't look good."

Hidden from everyone, including her children, was Judy's pain. Everyone was aware how hard it was for Bobby. No one was aware of her ordeal: Bobby's request for a divorce followed by his almost fatal accident and months of around-the-clock care. The whole time Judy was working like a trooper to nurse Bobby back to health, she wondered what would happen to them after he got well.

"You had to laugh at things most people didn't think I should be laughing at," she said, "but you had to. If you let it get you down, where would we be now?"

"I gather," I said, "with all that sitting in the back of your head, you're saying to yourself, *Where is this going?*"

"Yeah. Yeah," she said. "Crazy deal." And then she chuckled, despite there being precious little funny or amusing about the whole, long, painful ordeal.

CHAPTER 37

Bobby and Judy: A Miracle

"Now when the sun goes down, I get tired."

—Bobby Allison

On Tuesday, October 5, 1988, four and a half long months after his crash at Pocono, Bobby Allison went home. He was released from the Lakeshore clinic, and the next day he surprised everyone when he paid a visit to the Charlotte Motor Speedway where the Winston Cup drivers were testing for the Oakwood Homes 500 race.

Bobby told reporters he still suffered from short-term memory lapses and double vision. Dr. Greg Miller said he didn't see any reason why Bobby couldn't race again, despite the tube in his head to drain excess fluid and sustain normal pressure.

Bobby was going to the hospital three days a week for therapy.

"I think he lifted everyone's spirits," said Davey. "I know he sure lifted mine."

Allison, who owned a condo overlooking the first turn at the Charlotte track, remained for the race.

When he returned home to stay, Bobby was deeply depressed. "I wasn't enthusiastic about anything," he said. "I wanted to go to the hangar and sit by my airplane."

But the first couple of times Judy tried to drive him out there, they'd get halfway, and Bobby would ask her to take him back home.

"It was too hurtful that he knew he couldn't fly," said Judy.

Incapacitated, Bobby no longer could work on refitting his Aerostar. His one employee working on the plane, Chuck Stallings, was out of a job after Bobby's accident, and so Bobby got his friend Stuart Millar to hire Stallings, who moved to Vero Beach.

The hangar, bereft of activity and silent, was closed. The plane, with no one to fly it, sat idle, its turbine engines pickled to prevent rust.

Bobby sat at home alone, depressed and in pain. The person who suffered equally in her own way was his wife Judy, who found herself just as alone, while also having to take on much of the responsibility formerly borne by her incapacitated husband.

"Judy was trying so hard to get me recovered and to deal with all the things which now all of a sudden were going upside down," said Bobby.

"Before I got hurt, I know I was very demanding. I did my stuff my way, period. It had caused our relationship to be not as good as it should have been. And after the accident, we were arguing. Here I was in recovery, and I was thinking I ought to have a brand-new airplane and have a new race car. I couldn't fly. I didn't even have Chuck Stallings to sit beside me. As for the race car, Dick Trickle was driving the car, subbing for me."

On January 14, 1989, Bobby returned to the Charlotte Motor Speedway as part of a media tour. He spoke haltingly, pausing between words. He said he still had a hazy memory, but said he was determined to go back and race.

"The one thing I've done all my life is drive race cars," he said. "I certainly miss it a lot, and I long to return." He added, "I guess I could live without racing if I had to, but my wish is to return. I want to get back in there and go."

When one reporter asked him, "How are you feeling?" Bobby replied honestly, "I'll tell ya, I've felt better."

Bobby said the memory lapses continued to haunt him. The doctors said his memory could return any time, but not to expect it to return overnight. He said he could remember very little about the 1988 season.

"Winning the Daytona 500 sounds more like a fiction story to me," he said. "It seems like the account of someone else's experience." He did, however, remember winning the fishing tournament the same week on Lake Lloyd in the track's infield. And he remembered some details of his trip to Australia in 1987.

He said he has seen photos of the gold number 12 Miller High Life car he drove to victory that day, but did not recognize it.

"The last car I can recall driving was red and white, and it was number 22," he says. That was in 1987.

Bobby could accept the fact that he had won at Daytona the last year and would be the defending champion. When doctors decided he should not attend the race because of the crowds, his first reaction was to be upset over having to miss the annual bass fishing tournament.

"The fish are going to get off easy this weekend," he said.

When the Daytona track opened to mark the beginning of Speed Weeks, Bobby made an appearance. What was most notable about his getting there as far as Judy was concerned was the fact that Bobby drove his car to Daytona Beach all the way from Alabama. For several weeks Judy, a strong proponent of tough love, had been pushing him to drive, and he had resisted. When Judy told him the only way they would go to Daytona would be if he drove there himself, Bobby put away his fears and got behind the wheel of the car, driving first to and from church on Sundays, and then to Daytona.

When Bobby limped onto the Daytona track that day, it seemed like a miracle.

"I . . . am . . . very . . . glad," Bobby said with heartbreaking difficulty, "that . . . both . . . Davey . . . and   Clifford . . . are . . . out   there . . . racing . . . because . . . there is . . . a lot . . . more good . . . out there . . . than . . . bad."

If any good had come from Bobby's accident, it came in an announcement from NASCAR that it was raising its drivers' insurance coverage from $50,000 to $500,000.

Said Bobby's spokesman, Eddie Gossage, the $50,000 "was probably used up the first twenty-four hours."

Bobby Allison had begun to campaign for drivers to take out catastrophic insurance on themselves after younger brother Donnie suffered a severe head injury in a crash in 1981.

"It's been very difficult to get the point across," said Donnie. "You don't buy insurance until you think you need it."

Bobby went to the races to be seen because his doctors felt it was good therapy, and Judy made him go. In truth, Bobby continued to be reserved and extremely timid. He didn't want to see people, didn't want to talk to anyone.

Few understood just how hard living was for him.

"Here I was with the whole world upside down, and not on a level page with you."

Bobby was also feeling unneeded—son Davey was becoming a huge success without him—and feeling frustrated that his mind was so scrambled that he was unable to help younger son Clifford, who had settled down in a second marriage, and who at age twenty-five was finally starting a career in racing. As much as Bobby wanted to be part of that, he just wasn't ready. It was all he could do to just deal with the constant pain.

In mid-February 1989 Bobby returned to the Lehigh Valley Hospital in Allentown to have the rods removed from his fractured left leg.

He was complaining of dizziness and nausea. Dr. Stevens removed the metal shunt from his head and replaced it with a plastic one, allowing him to perform MRI exams.

Taking the rods out of his leg made him feel a lot better.

"I just wish my head had improved as quickly as my leg," he said.

When the 1989 Speed Weeks rolled around, Bobby, who was the defending Daytona 500 champion, wasn't in attendance. As announced, he didn't even enter his beloved fishing tournament on Lake Lloyd in the track infield. Bobby had not missed a Daytona 500 since 1964. He watched the race at home in Hueytown.

During the week Clifford crashed in the ARCA race and spent a night in the Halifax Medical Center in Daytona Beach for observation. Davey rolled his car over in the Daytona 500 but wasn't hurt.

Said Bobby after the race, "For me, it was a tough deal not to be there racing, but at least I know it's there, sort of a carrot dangling in front of me. But I'll be trying to get the carrot. That's what's giving me the desire to work hard to improve from my injuries."

Three months later, Bobby wasn't feeling a whole lot better than before.

"My progress is too slow to suit me," Bobby said in May 1989, "but that's just the way it is, and I want to recuperate fully before getting back into a race car."

Bobby was asked if he wanted to own a race team. He was torn, because if he ran a race team, that meant someone else would be driving.

"I guess I'm just not totally convinced about running a car for someone else," he said. "What I can say, though, is that I couldn't turn my back on the sport."

During an interview with *Toronto Star* writer Graham Jones, Bobby talked about how much pleasure he was getting from Davey's success. He also praised Judy for being such a trooper.

"I've always loved her," he said, "but since this happened, I not only love her but also feel I can't go on without her. She's just done so much. She's taken the responsibility to make decisions and looks out for me every step of the way. She steps right in to take the pressure off me. She's a great gal."

Bobby said he was homebound most of his days, "which is a lot different from the way it used to be when I'd stay on the road six days a week and often do a couple of all-night sessions a week to get the car ready for the next race. Now when the sun goes down, I get tired."

After Davey won the Pepsi 400 at Daytona on July 2, 1989, he talked lovingly about his dad.

"I wouldn't be here if it wasn't for him," Davey said. "There's no way I can ever repay him, except to go out and try to win some more races."

"You know," he said, "I once read this great article about an outdoorsman who took his young son out fishing and hunting and passed on all his knowledge to him. Then one day, when the son and the father were older, they went back out into the woods and he saw through new eyes all that he had taught his son.

"That's how I feel about my dad. I feel like I'm his new eyes now. If it hadn't been for him and all that he had done for me and all he had showed me, then I wouldn't be where I am today."

Bobby had business associates and friends who thought it would help Bobby's state of mind and also benefit NASCAR if Bobby was involved in running a race team. Don Hackworth, who had been the general manager of Buick during the 1980s, introduced Bobby to Bob Bilby, who had bought Junior Johnson's race team when Junior switched from Chevrolet to Ford. Bilby had teamed with John LaFere to form a new race team. Two other partners, Nathan Sims and Frank Plessinger, were added to the management of the team.

On August 25, 1989, at Bristol prior to qualifying for the Busch 500, Bobby announced he would be the co-owner of a race team in 1990 and that he hoped to race again. He did not name a driver or a sponsor. The new team, he said, "will drive a Buick and will keep number 12."

When the Stavola Brothers decided to cut back to one team from two, Bobby Allison Motorsports was able to hire his old crew.

Being part of the race team was supposed to give Bobby some purpose in life. But Bobby's pain was too great for him to function, and the team would be run by his brother-in-law, Tom Kincaid, out of Charlotte, while Bobby stayed back in Hueytown recovering.

"I wasn't connected to it," says Bobby.

"While Bobby was recuperating, the two people who made the decisions for the race team were my brother-in-law Tom Kincaid, the PR guy in the business, and Jimmy Fennig, the crew chief," said Eddie Allison.

"Bobby had driven a car for Fennig in Wisconsin and Michigan on Saturday nights. There were ill feelings in the organization because Bobby had brought Jimmy in, and so Bobby Allison Motorsports was screwed up from day one."

Tom Kincaid, a lawyer by trade, was married to Cindy Allison, Bobby, Donnie, and Eddie's younger sister.

"The thing could have been great if Kincaid would have waited for Bobby to be well enough to stand on his own two feet," said Eddie. "Kincaid argued we couldn't wait. 'His name will go away,' he said. How was that going to happen? Bobby is more popular now than when he was driving."

Bobby's first choice to drive was Jeff Purvis, but Tom Kincaid didn't think he was good enough, so Bobby gave in and allowed them to pick another driver.

"They never did get a driver who was as good as Purvis," said Eddie.

Eddie told Kincaid to get Terry Labonte, the 1984 racing champion. Labonte had quit a race team and was on his own. When Kincaid didn't move fast enough, Labonte signed with Rick Hendricks. Kincaid and Fennig chose Mike Alexander to be their driver.

"They were grasping at straws, because Bobby didn't have any input into the race team," said Eddie. "Mike Alexander drove for his daddy's race team. His daddy owned a Ford dealership in Franklin, Tennessee. He was a good friend, and his kid was a pretty good race car driver.

"Mike got in a wreck in Pensacola, and it messed up his head. He had a brain injury. The kid had some potential, but he was not what the race team needed under the circumstances, and when he got hurt, it destroyed him."

Bobby's head injury prevented him from making decisions on his own. Worse, if he did try to say something, he would be treated as though he was a simpleton and ignored.

"He needed a loving, supporting atmosphere, and he wasn't getting it," said Eddie. And the egos of the people around him could not be reined in. Like I say, the ego in the sport is so big."

Bobby needed an activity he could enjoy without facing criticism or rejection. For reasons even Bobby doesn't understand, the one thing in his life he was most connected to was his beloved airplane. Once he could drive again, he enjoyed driving to his hangar in Bessemer to sit with his Aerostar.

"You have to understand," said Bobby, "I was so confused, so screwed up, that there was no peace anywhere except in that hangar. At that hangar I could close the door, and nobody came in there with me. I could sit in my chair next to my beloved little turbine Aerostar.

"I was kinda connected to the airplane," said Bobby. "It was way ahead of everything else in my eyes and in my thoughts. I don't know why. That airplane was the personal accomplishment that meant so much to me."

Then about a year after his companion and friend Chuck Stallings had left to go to Vero Beach to work for Piper Aircraft, Piper let him go and he returned to Hueytown.

"Which was perfect for me," said Bobby, "because I needed him back."

Bobby's greatest desire, greater even than racing again, was going back up into the air. With Chuck Stallings back in town, Bobby was able to climb into his plane and fly again.

"It was my recuperation and recreation all in a package," said Bobby.

The credit for his learning to fly again belonged to Judy.

"I had to convince Chuck that Bobby could be retaught," she said. "Chuck really didn't want to do it. I said, 'Chuck, if I go with you, will you do it?' He said yeah. So I went the first three or four lessons to get his confidence up."

Beginning in the summer of 1989, Bobby and Chuck would fly to the races to watch the Stavola car race.

"I did a lot of that," said Bobby. "I was asked to come to places to sign autographs, and this was income for me, earning like I had done before I was hurt, so Chuck and I would jump in the plane and go zooming off and then return to Alabama."

In November 1989, Bobby met the Bobby Allison race team at Atlanta to test. He sat behind the wheel, pondering what it would be like to go back out on the track. Thirty cars were out there speeding past.

It just isn't the time, Bobby had to admit to himself. Bobby told a reporter, "Owning a car is not as good as driving, but it's way better than lying in a hospital bed."

When the Daytona 500 rolled around again in 1990, it had been two years since Bobby's terrible accident. He told reporters that it looked like his racing days were over, that he just didn't have his balance back like he should.

"The hip and legs still hurt," he said. "I don't understand why it has got to hurt."

After the 1990 season Mike Alexander was let go, and Tom Kincaid decided that the driver to replace him should be Hut Stricklin, who had been fired by Rod

Osterlund at the end of '89. One of the plusses for hiring Hut was that he was married to Donnie's daughter Pam.

"Hut's daddy owned a junkyard," said Eddie. "He got started running here in Alabama, and he was a pretty good race driver. Hut had ability. Hut raced against Davey, and I heard people say how Hut would get after it, so I figured Hut would make it as a racer. And then Hut and Davey got to be friends, and Davey introduced him to Pam, and they ended up getting married. So there were a lot of connections, and when the time came, everyone pushed for Hut to drive Bobby's car."

Bobby had no role in picking Hut.

"I was there," said Bobby. "I was asked to sit over to the side and keep my mouth shut, which was difficult, but in truth I wasn't capable of helping much. The accident had scrambled me. The biggest emotion I had, if somebody did something I didn't like, I would cry. If I couldn't do something about something, I would sit down and cry. I really did see some things on the race car. I could have been a really big help, but I couldn't communicate with the people I needed to communicate with, and I didn't have the confidence to be assertive."

Hut could see immediately that Bobby was in no condition to run a race team.

"Basically at that time Bobby was just a figurehead," said Stricklin. "He really didn't have a whole lot to do with the day-to-day stuff. He had good people to run it. They did an excellent job. I don't think things would have been much different if he had been able to run it. That's how good I felt his people were.

"Jimmy Fennig was our crew chief. He came from Wisconsin. He had worked with Bobby when Bobby came north to drive the ASA cars. He also worked on the ASA cars that Mark Martin drove. So Bobby and Mark were like teammates.

"I can't say anything bad about the relationship I had with Jimmy. We got along good. We were compatible."

On October 23, 1991, Bobby Allison Motorsports had a red-letter day when Hut finished second to Davey at Michigan. It harkened back to the Alabama Gang days when Bobby and Donnie would finish one, two, or vice versa, or to the race where Bobby defeated Neil Bonnett. This was a victory for the second-generation Alabama Gang and also for Hut Stricklin, who led the race for twenty laps.

The man who made it all possible, as it turned out, was Bobby Allison. The race team had been fighting all weekend over a balance problem with the car. Either it was loose into the turn and tight out, or it was tight in and loose out. No one was able to fix the problem.

"We could never get a happy medium," said Hut.

On Saturday, after qualifying, Bobby came into the garage.

"People were aware he was still very slow with his thinking, but he was still Bobby Allison, someone to pay attention to," said Hut.

Bobby walked up to Jimmy Fennig, and said, "I've been thinking about this all night. Here's what I want you to do to this car."

"We were in Michigan, and they were not going to make the show," said Bobby.

"I told Jimmy Fennig, 'You must make this one change to the car. If we're not going to make the show, at least blame it on me. Make this one change. I'm insisting you do it right now, and I'm insisting that you don't tell Hut.

"By then I could see that Hut couldn't relate to what the crew was doing or saying or to the adjustments they were making. If the car was right, he certainly could drive the car good. What happened, Jimmy made the adjustment to the car, and the car went from not making the show to qualifying way up front, fourth."

Hut said to Bobby, "You have to tell me what you did."

"I can't tell you," Bobby replied.

"Whether Bobby was right or wrong, good, bad or indifferent, when he spoke, we tried it," said Hut. "He wanted to change the caster setting on the left front end. We made that change and went out and we were fast right off. It made a whole different car out of it.

"Fennig always said, "I don't care *why* it works, but if it works, we'll stay with it." And that's what we did."

On Sunday, the day of the race, the Raybestos car driven by Hut Stricklin was the fastest car on the Michigan track.

"It was pretty cool," said Hut. "It was the first time I had a dominant car, though that car was a good race car about every week.

"We struggled on our short-track cars, the cars for North Wilkesboro and Martinsville. We couldn't get out of our own way there, and on the half-mile tracks we were terrible. But on the tracks a mile or longer, we were big-time good."

The race began. Davey Allison had the outside pole. He took the lead, and Hut went with him. The two moved out front and ran together, with Davey leading and Hut second.

Then Hut began complaining about the handling of the car.

"So Jimmy made the adjustment Hut was asking for, and that slowed the car down," said Bobby. He said, 'I have to have more of that. You didn't do it enough.' So Jimmy adjusted it a second time, and Hut went from running second, fifty feet behind Davey, to third.

"I told Jimmy, 'You must put the car back like we had it, but you can't tell Hut.' So Jimmy put the car back like it was, and Davey won and Hut finished second. Hut said, 'Boy, that was so good. You have to tell me what you did.'

"So I told him. And the next race he went out on pit road for the first lap of practice, and he came back and said, 'You gotta get that shit off the car. I can't drive it like that.' So it was never done again.

"Unfortunately, we didn't communicate, which was my big, big deficit after I had been hurt, Before the injury, if somebody would argue with me, I responded, forcefully, vocally. After the crash, I could buy a fifty-cent item and hand you a dollar bill and if you told me I didn't have enough money, I'd say, Okay. I don't. And I'd walk away with my tail between my legs."

At Michigan, though, Bobby had had a hand in the best performance in his race team's history. Toward the end of the race, Hut was right behind Davey, when Bobby ordered Hut to pass his son. It was reported in the papers that Hut said, "I can't, Bobby. I might lose my ride home."

To which Bobby replied, "Don't worry about that. We'll get you home."

I asked Hut if he actually said that to Bobby.

"Sure did," he said.

The race was close and exciting right down to the end. Even with Bobby's adjustment, the Raybestos car didn't have enough to catch Davey's Texaco-Haviland machine.

"Our car was so much faster than his through the corners, but his car was so much faster down the straightaways," said Hut. "That's what made it such a good race that day. Whoever got out front was the one who made it hard for the other to get around."

Hut and Davey came into the pits, and when Hut's crew was slower servicing the car, Davey beat Hut out of the pits.

"We never had good pit stops," said Hut. "That was one of our weaknesses. I don't remember why, but Davey and them beat us out, and I couldn't overcome him.

"The race was exciting and memorable without a doubt, and Davey and I joked back and forth about the race in the garage afterward.

"But the thing I remember more than anything was the plane ride home. It was no one but me and Davey. Not even a pilot. Davey had a two-engine Aerostar like Bobby had. We flew back together, and it was just our own personal bragging time.

"It was 'Hey, two guys from Alabama went up north and kicked everyone's butt.' Of course, we didn't want anyone to know we were saying that.

"Davey was very proud of me. Whenever I did well, Davey was always the first one there to congratulate me. We were like brothers. We had a really great relationship."

CHAPTER 38

Neil: Amnesia

"I don't know why Neil had so many serious crashes."

—**Liz Allison**

Neil Bonnett was racing through his fourteenth season when, at Charlotte, on October, 11, 1987, he blew a tire and was injured seriously for the first time. His hip was crushed.

"One time, driving for the Wood Brothers at Dover, he broke his breastbone, but he never had anything as major as this," said Susan Bonnett. "I was at Charlotte with Jesse and Carolyn Cunningham, good friends who live in Lynchburg, Virginia. They had a motor home, and they traveled to all the races. We were up on their motor home watching the race, and I saw Neil hit the wall, and the car veered on around where it was out of our view."

There were no radios to the pits. Susan was listening to the radio broadcast, and when the announcer said the rescue crew couldn't get him out of the car, but that he was conscious, Susan knew he was alive.

"I just didn't know how serious it was, because they weren't saying much on the radio, and they would not let me go through the gate—another one of their rules."

Susan went to the hospital at the racetrack and waited until they brought him in. Bonnett looked green.

"He wasn't saying much, but I could see he was in terrific pain," she said. "I knew he had a broken leg, because that's what he was holding. They immediately said they were taking him to the Carrabas County Hospital. They would not let me go in the ambulance, so the Cunninghams and I got in my rental car and followed behind."

When she arrived at the hospital, she was told that Neil had been put in intensive care. The doctor told her they were going to have to operate, but because he had undigested food in his stomach they would have to wait several hours.

"The doctor showed me the X-rays and said he wasn't sure about his hip, but they were probably going to put a plate and some pins in there because he had a lot of bone that was floating," said Susan. "It was pretty scary. Neil was in horrible pain. That was not easy to watch."

The day before the operation, Neil had but one worry: How long would it be before he would be able to race again? He knew his race team would have to get another driver. That bothered him more than the pain.

"He crushed his femur, so he had a plate with a lag bolt and ten screws," said Susan. "When they operated he lost quite a bit of blood, and they gave him several pints. He was concerned about that because of AIDS. He had never had to take blood before. He was concerned he'd get some kind of disease."

Bonnett lay unconscious for three days, and when he finally awoke, he was in terrible pain. He was hooked up to a morphine drip. Every so often he would press a button and receive a dose of morphine. He was told he had to be able to do it himself, but he said to Susan, "If I fall asleep, you mash it."

Several days after the surgery Bonnett suffered a hematoma in the upper part of his leg. He was in great pain, and when Susan tried to get in touch with his surgeon, Dr. Wassel, she was told he was in surgery. Even with the morphine, Neil was in such pain he was literally pulling his hair out by the handfuls. He told Susan, "If they can't bring me anything, I'm going to send you out on the street to buy drugs. Either you do that, or you're going to have to roll me over to the window and throw me out."

Susan told him, "That won't help because there's a floor right underneath the window. All you will do is fall and break your other leg."

Bonnett stayed in the hospital for ten days, and he was still in pain when he and Susan left there and returned to Alabama.

"He lost so much weight and so much blood that he just didn't look right for a long time," said Susan. "He was very pale."

Bonnett missed the remainder of the 1987 season and returned for the Daytona 500 in 1988.

"He had to work out a lot in order to be able to come back," said Susan. "He had a lot of therapy. We had home health care that came out. Neil had a gym already set up downstairs, so they showed him what to do, and they came out three or four days a week and worked with him, and he would work till it would be painful for me to watch."

When Bonnett returned to racing, he did so with a bang, finishing fourth in the Daytona 500 in the race won by Bobby Allison with son Davey Allison second and Phil Parsons, Benny's baby brother, third.

"We were real concerned about his endurance," said Susan. "He felt confident of the car's capacity, but we were not sure about his physical condition. But he did well. He felt good after he got out. We were just ecstatic. We thought that was great."

The next race was held at Richmond, the last race ever held at the Fairgrounds. Bonnett trailed by two full laps but made it up and won the race. He then flew to Australia and won a race on the other side of the world. And when he came back and raced at Rockingham, he won again, coming from thirtieth place to win in a Pontiac. The Rockingham win was Bonnett's nineteenth Winston Cup win, and it gave him the lead in the standings for the championship.

"He beat Dale Earnhardt," said Susan. "He did. Neil was running Hoosier tires, and a lot of drivers were real upset about guys driving Hoosiers. But Neil had known the Hoosiers man for years when he was in Sportsman racing, and he always thought they were good tires. They were having problems with Goodyears, so they allowed him to use Hoosiers for two or three races. It ticked a lot of people off. I remember Neil saying something to Dale Earnhardt about it. Dale was all up in the air about those Hoosier tires. They just yan-yanned back and forth."

What began as a most promising season turned scary when Bonnett began suffering heart-attack-like symptoms.

"He would get deathly sick and his chest would hurt," said Susan. "We thought they were heart attacks, because it would act like a heart attack. He'd get out of breath and his blood pressure would run up."

One night at Wilkesboro he had an attack. Susan called Dr. Jerry Punch, NASCAR's doctor, because, she said, "you have to keep those things private." Dr. Punch came and checked him. All his vital signs were okay, but his chest was hurting. Dr. Punch gave him some nitroglycerin tablets, which eased the pain. He said, 'You might have gallstones.'

Bonnett told him, "I've been tested, and they didn't find any." He ran the race the next day.

On Monday, Neil went to the doctor's office, and they ran tests, and this time they found them. He would have to have surgery. Wanting to go to a hospital where he could get laparoscopic surgery, he kept putting off the operation, but the pain got worse and worse.

"I would have to pack lunches and travel with him to the races with the things he could eat," said Susan. "He was a meat and potatoes man, so he could not eat all the things proscribed to him on the diet. After you eat lean roast beef, jello, and jelly beans every day, you finally get tired of it. So he couldn't wait any longer, and in July he had to have surgery, which put him out for a bunch of races."

If 1988 wasn't good to Bonnett, it was devastating to his friend and benefactor Bobby Allison, who had crashed at Pocono and almost died.

"I wasn't at Pocono, so I didn't know how serious it was," said Susan. "I don't think Neil knew how serious until he got ready to head for home. I remember when he called me, he said it was very serious. He talked about Bobby having a head injury, saying it was touch and go, and it was so hard to believe. It was a long, long recovery for Bobby."

Neil and Susan went to the rehabilitation center several times to visit him after Bobby returned home.

"Bobby was having a real hard time talking," said Susan. "It was hard for him to communicate. I felt like it taxed him so."

In 1989 Neil returned to racing. In what would turn out to be his last year with RahMoc, Bonnett's season did not include a single victory or even a top five. The car experienced a lot of motor trouble.

In 1990 he returned to the Wood Brothers amid high expectations. "He was excited about it," said Susan. "They had taken on Citgo as a sponsor, and he got close to the top guy representing Citgo. They played golf together, and they had a good relationship, and he felt the Wood Brothers were doing all they needed to do to become a top team. He wasn't running as well as he had hoped, but he was with people he felt confidence in."

And then on April 1, 1990, at Darlington, Ernie Irvan, who was hopelessly out of contention, was battling to get his lap back after a caution, and he spun and set off a wreck involving thirteen cars. Bonnett's Ford was caught up in the wreckage. When they took him from the car, he didn't seem badly injured. But when he arrived at the hospital, he didn't know where he was or why he was there.

Davey and wife Liz Allison were among the first to see Neil in the hospital.

"We went to the hospital right after the race was over and spent some time up there," said Liz. "Luckily for us, we were able to see Neil right away so we weren't quite as shook up over his amnesia as we would have been if we had not seen him firsthand and known the situation. Even at this point, it hadn't hit me or Davey, but we were starting to get a little rattled with some of the stuff going on. When you start seeing people you love and care about getting truly injured to where in his daddy's case it ended his career, you look at racing in a different way. But we still, as hardheaded as both of us were, we still had not gotten it through our heads yet.

"I don't know why Neil had so many serious crashes. Since the time I met Davey, Neil was out of the car more than he was in it. I don't know what it was. Sometimes it's just bad luck. It could be the equipment. It could be the eye of the tiger, when you lose that drive. I'm sure it was a combination of all of the above."

"Neil crashed a lot because he had a big foot," said Eddie Allison. "And nobody can understand why. It happens to a lot of drivers. As good a race car driver that Bobby Allison was, he had some ferocious wrecks. Richard Petty had some ferocious wrecks. It's part of the game, but some guys seem to get away with it."

All through 1990 Neil Bonnett suffered from amnesia.

"It was come and go," said Susan. "It wasn't that he couldn't remember anything and anybody. He was rattled enough to know that at that time he wasn't capable of getting back in the car."

Neil's amnesia was so bad he didn't know his wife and children. He didn't know his home and yard. He was a stranger among his loved ones.

"When I first got there, Neil would look right through me," said Susan. "It was like he didn't know me. So I knew something was wrong. He looked glassy-eyed. For a while he called me 'that woman.'

"They brought him things to smell—cinnamon, garlic—and he couldn't smell them. They brought him things to eat, and he didn't know what they were.

"After they did some tests, the doctors said, 'We're very sorry to tell you, but he's had a stroke.' I thought, *These people don't know what they are talking about.* I said, 'Is there anyone else you can call in?' I called our doctor at home and told him what they were saying, and he said, 'They may be seeing injuries he's had in the past.' Finally, they decided he didn't have a stroke, but the doctor said, 'He has had a head injury, and it's pretty severe, and even though he's okay—doesn't have swelling—he can't remember anything.'"

The doctor added, "It could last a long time. It could last forever. Or it could last a short time. We have no way of knowing."

Neil was suffering from the same sort of agitation as Bobby Allison, who also had serious short-term memory loss.

"We had to protect him from people who came to the hospital to see him," said Susan. "The doctor said, 'The worst thing a person can do is say, "Do you remember me?" Because he can't remember, and he'll get upset, and it will cause other problems.'"

When Neil was released from the hospital, Dale Earnhardt's pilot flew Neil and Susan home. Their doctor was waiting with an ambulance when they got to Birmingham. Neil's parents and his children were waiting for them. Neil was up and walking, but he didn't recognize them or the children, and he didn't have a clue where they were going. He and Bobby had flown in and out of that part of the airport for years, but Neil was scared to death because he didn't have a clue where he was. When Neil walked past his doctor and didn't know him, the doctor said to Susan, "Oh, my God, this is heartbreaking. I've never experienced this."

When Susan visited a neurosurgeon in Birmingham, the doctor asked her, "Does Neil normally have a temper?"

"Yes, he has a terrible temper," she said.

He said, "Look for it to get three times as bad, because he will get frustrated. Whatever you do, don't force him into anything, and keep a close watch on him."

Susan did that.

"When we got home, Neil didn't know where anything was," said Susan. "He would go out the door and start walking, and we'd have to go get him because he didn't know where he was going. It was very bad. The doctor said, 'Some things may trigger memories, but don't force him into anything.'"

Their son was working on a car in the garage, and she'd take Neil out there and let him watch, because she thought this might help him remember. He'd stand around, and when someone would drive up, he'd come running into the house and hide, because he didn't want to have to try to figure out who it was.

Said Susan, "One day someone came up to him and said, 'Don't you know us?' He had a drill in his hand because our son David was trying to show him how to use it, and he came in the house, and he was so frustrated he drilled a hole in the kitchen countertop. The hole is still there. He went into a terrible rage, and when he would do that, he would cry, and it would take him two or three days to come out of it. It was horrible to watch. He would be so mad, and then he wouldn't know why he was mad, and he didn't understand what was happening to him. It was a tough time."

Susan took him to the doctor, and he was tested. The doctor asked her, "Have you noticed anything?"

She said, "I know he would never sit at the table if any of us ate fried eggs. He would make us leave, because he couldn't stand to look at them. And he would never let anyone eat blue cheese because it made him sick to smell it. But now he is eating it."

Said Susan, "So we knew he didn't remember that he didn't eat it, couldn't stand it.

"This went on for several weeks. Then one day he was sitting in the living room when a hunting magazine came in the mail. Usually I didn't let him see those things, but the mail was lying there, and the magazine was there, and he started looking at it, and he started to put some things together. Little things started coming back. He said, 'I know I've been here.' He recognized some of the places where he and Dale had gone to hunt. That was how it started, and then almost every day he started remembering things. He remembered the hunting first. But for a long time he did not remember that he drove a race car."

"Tell me about the day he first remembered you," I said.

"He said he always knew he knew me and that I was someone important," she said. "He said everyone was in there, but he couldn't put them together. He knew he knew some faces, but he didn't know who they were. After he read that hunting magazine, it wasn't a week or two later when he called me by name. He was blessed. There were people who we talked to who had had this for years. I was told, 'His short-term memory will probably be terrible.' We saw that with Bobby. Before his accident Bobby could meet you one time, and he could meet you ten years later and remember who you were. After his accident, we watched that dissipate. After Neil's accident, he never had a lot of short-term memory, though there were things he never could remember."

I said to Susan Bonnett, "Bobby never could remember the Daytona 500 when he came in first and Davey came in second."

"Right," she said. "When Neil's memory started to come back, Bobby came over to see him, and Bobby could hardly talk and Neil could hardly remember, and I was sitting in the living room in between the two of them, and I was trying to speak for Bobby and think for Neil. Bobby would say, 'Hey, do you . . . ,' and he'd look at me and I'd say, 'Remember,' and I'd finish talking for Bobby, and Neil would say, 'Susan, do I remember that?' And I would say, 'You remember when so and so and so and so . . .' He'd say, 'Oh yeah.' In retrospect it was really hilarious, but I was worn out. It wasn't funny at the time, but after Bobby left, I just had to lie on the floor and laugh."

"Did Neil suffer from depression?" I asked.

"Yes, absolutely," she said. "Very deep depression."

"What were you able to do for that?"

"Nothing," she said. "Not a thing."

"I gather he eventually remembered that he was a race car driver, but he knew he wasn't going to be able to do it," I said.

"The doctor kept telling him that it would all depend on how he recovered," she said. "He said, 'Another lick on the head would not be good.' He told Neil, 'When you damage the brain, you don't even have to hit your head. With the speeds you go, and with stopping so quickly, your body stops, but the fluid in your brain does not stop. The movement can cause damage. You have scars from the time you're born, all the little nicks and knocks you had as a child growing up that damage your brain. Those cells never regenerate. It would be a big risk for you to drive again.'

"To begin with it wasn't hard for him not to race, because even though he had begun to remember things, he just didn't remember that he was good at racing. That took a while. The doctor told me, 'When it comes back, if it comes back, it will come back with a passion.' And of course, it did."

But before it did, Neil Bonnett recovered sufficiently to become a fine broadcaster of the Winston Cup stock car races on the Nashville Network and CBS. He was so charming and insightful that quickly he became recognized as one of the best ever to analyze the sport on TV. He even hosted his own weekly show, called *Winners*.

"Neil had done some commentating of Sportsman races," said Susan, "so they knew he was capable of doing that. He had known Ken Squire for years, and whenever Ken did his radio show at Daytona, he would invite Neil to be a guest because he said that Neil was quick-witted and was so good on TV. Ken was in business with Fred Reinstein, and they were the ones who approached Neil, and they did quite a few things, including the *Winners* show, in which he would go out and interview different drivers. Fred Reinstein and the whole crew would come here every so often to film the openings and closings of the show downstairs in the house. Before Neil died, they were planning a fishing program, because Neil loved hunting and fishing. They were going to do some deep-sea fishing, and it was going to be an extremely busy year for Neil."

CHAPTER 39

Davey:
Robert Yates Hires Larry Mac

"Davey asked, 'You got some doughnuts in them pits?'"

—Larry McReynolds

Davey's 1991 season started with a run-in at the Daytona 500 with Dale Earnhardt. With two laps to go, Earnhardt pulled in behind him, took air off his spoiler, and sent him spinning. It was an effective ploy to bury the competition used regularly by Earnhardt to great effect. His opponent ended up stranded in the infield, and he was able to say, "I never hit him."

Davey finished fifteenth.

Without naming Earnhardt, Davey let him have it.

He said, "I passed him clean on the outfield, but then I got hit. I ain't happy. I had a shot to win the race. Racing is a business where you have to use your head. I was using mine. Someone else wasn't.

"What burns me up is he is so dad-blame lucky. He always comes out smelling like a rose. He still finished fifth, and we're here with a torn-up race car."

After the race Allison, whose outspoken criticism of his opponents was viewed as whining by other drivers and fans of those drivers, announced he would no longer be intimidated by the black-suited racer from Kannapolis.

In the next three races the 28 Havoline car was so far out of contention that Davey's state of mind was irrelevant. In the fourth race, at Atlanta, Allison finished fortieth.

Team chemistry was bad. Davey, who was bullheaded, certainly was part of the problem. He argued with his crew chief—stern, gruff Jake Elder—and chided and berated his crew members over the fact the car wasn't running better. Davey's father,

Bobby, tried to lecture Davey on the importance of getting along with his crew, but the youngster refused to listen.

At the Coca-Cola 600 at Charlotte, Allison was leading. The caution flag came out, and when his competitors went in for tires, Jake Elder told him, "Stay out there. You don't need tires." But Allison didn't trust Elder and his crew, and he insisted he needed fresh tires, and he wrongly came in and lost the race.

Afterward Bobby Allison was so angry with his son he could barely speak to him. Davey asked Ralph Moody, who was in the pit, "What do you think?"

Moody told him, "You're stupid as hell is what I think. Listen to your pit crew."

Robert Yates decided he had to make a personnel change to improve the chemistry of the race team. In April 1991 he fired Elder, and hired Larry McReynolds, a hard-working, tough-but-gentle soul with a soothing effect on all around him.

Yates first had asked McReynolds to leave his job with Kenny Bernstein and come to his race team in 1989. McReynolds had been with Bernstein since 1983 and he felt loyalty to him.

"I don't believe in job-hopping," McReynolds said.

Then, right before the 1990 season, Yates asked him again. Even though McReynolds was from Birmingham, and he and Davey were friends, McReynolds had been looking forward to running with Brett Bodine in the Bernstein car in '90, and again he turned the offer down.

Yates persisted. In late February 1991 at the Rockingham race, he tried a third time. He told McReynolds, "Jake Elder is cussing, raising Cain, can't get along with anybody. I want you to replace him."

McReynolds told him, "I haven't shut the door on it, but right now I'm here where I'm at."

Then came the Atlanta race. The Bernstein car didn't work right, and worse, Brett Bodine spent the whole race complaining about the motor.

Said McReynolds, "On the ride home my wife, Linda, and I didn't say five words to each other. I said to her, 'I can't believe I let that twenty-eight-car deal slip through my fingers again. I ought to be over there working right now."

She said, "All you have to do is call Robert."

McReynolds said, "No, Jake is there. I'm not going to change jobs in the middle of the season. If you remember, I did that once when I left Blue Max, and I was left with a wife-to-be and no job."

McReynolds and his wife got home about ten. Larry was unloading his van. They had barely walked in the door when the phone rang. Larry said, "Linda, if that's for me, tell them I'm out feeding the dog, or asleep or something."

Linda came to the door and said, "Telephone."

Larry said, "Linda, I told you . . ."

She said, "You just might want to take this phone call."

It was Robert Yates. He said, "Larry, I am going to make a change, one way or the other. I'm going to offer you this deal one more time."

McReynolds said he'd be at Yates's office at seven the next morning. They shook hands, and McReynolds left the Bernstein team and reported to work as Davey Allison's crew chief.

The season was four races old. A week after McReynolds joined the Yates team, they went to Darlington and tested for two days. His car had horsepower he never had before. That night Larry called his wife and told her he had made "the best move of my life."

For McReynolds, another plus was getting to work with Davey Allison. Said McReynolds, "Davey's very aggressive, and that means a lot. He runs every lap like it's the last one."

"Davey and Larry all kind of grew up together at the Birmingham racetrack," said Liz Allison. "Davey had known him for years. I don't want to take anything away from Larry, because he was great at what he did, but everything was kind of coming together anyway. The engine program was getting there. Robert Yates had hired some great people, and then he brought Larry in, and everything kind of clicked, and in racing that's what it takes. It's the whole package. It all has to click for it to work."

In May 1991 Davey won the World 600 at Charlotte.

"It's a tough race to win," said McReynolds. "It's tough to be there at the end, much less win it.

"With about thirty laps to go, you get that empty feeling, *Something will happen any minute. The engine will blow, the gear will tear up, we'll blow a tire.* You get that way, because at the World 600, you have to run a hundred miles more than any other race, so you get that feeling."

Davey had a nine- or ten-second lead. Thought McReynolds, *Nothing can stop us, unless . . .*

Davey and McReynolds were not saying much on the radio. Every five or ten laps McReynolds kept his driver posted as to the whereabouts of the second-place car. Davey came on the radio, and he said, "Larry, you aren't going to believe what's happening." McReynolds's heart went up into his throat. McReynolds said to himself, *Well, here it is.*

"What happened?" he asked, prepared for the worst. He was expecting, "We lost a cylinder," or "The motor is tightening up," or "Something just fell off or went through the windshield."

But Allison said, "There's an Earnhardt fan hanging through the backstretch, and every time I go past him, he flips me off."

McReynolds was relieved, and miffed. He said to Davey, "Man, what are you doing that to me for?" Said McReynolds, "Here he was, talking just like he was on a Sunday drive."

At Dover the next week, the 28 Texaco/Havoline car handled and ran poorly.

Under McReynolds, the car only had three bad races in 1991, and Dover was one of them. Every fifty laps the car was getting lapped.

About four hundred laps into the race, Davey came on the radio. He said, "Larry." McReynolds acknowledged him. Davey asked, "You got some doughnuts in them pits?" Krispy Kreme, makers of some of the best doughnuts in the world, was an associate sponsor.

McReynolds said, "Yeah, why?"

Davey said, "Man, we ain't got a chance of doing much good today. I'm just trying to ride the thing out, but at the next caution, have Robert hand me a couple. I'm about to starve to death."

McReynolds was duly impressed that Davey Allison could be the same person, whether he was winning or running poorly.

Said McReynolds, "When you have a driver like that, it keeps the crew members pumped up, and they don't get discouraged. When you have a driver out there screaming and yelling and telling you how bad the car is, the crewmen finally say, 'Why am I working seventy hours next week for this cat? He's going to walk away after the race and not know we exist until the next Thursday.' With Davey, we had fellowship and unity."

Even with McReynolds at the helm, Davey still had outbursts of temper, a character trait inherited from dad Bobby. At Darlington, Davey was accused of giving Darrell Waltrip the finger.

The next week the two went at it during the race at Bristol. On turn three of the 367th lap, Waltrip brushed Davey's car. The next time around, Davey hit Waltrip's rear bumper so hard he lifted his rear end off the ground. Waltrip then spun out. After a caution, Allison was forced by NASCAR to restart the race at the end of the pack for rough driving.

During a rain delay shortly thereafter, Davey started yelling and screaming at Darrell, saying he had had every right to bang him because of an earlier incident during which Waltrip had tapped the back of his car.

After the race, which Waltrip won, Davey and Waltrip exchanged angry words.

Waltrip was furious. Said Waltrip, "He must have a problem with me, and I don't know what it is. He gave me the finger last week down at Darlington. We're going to have a little father-son talk."

Said Allison, "He came over to me mouthing off about spinning him out in the fourth turn. I didn't spin him out intentionally, but I guess it's all right if he runs all over the side of my car. I've got Western Auto colors all over the side of my car. I guess when you're Darrell Waltrip and do that to people, it's okay."

Answered Waltrip later, "That little kid, just because he's an Allison he thinks he can do anything he wants. He can't get away with this stuff."

Darrell was right and Davey wrong, and the race fans knew it.

There was more controversy surrounding Davey following the Sears Point Raceway at Sonoma, California, in June. Ricky Rudd trailed Davey nose-to-tail as they battled on the final lap. There's a hairpin turn just before the start-finish line that requires a driver to brake hard. With Allison in the lead and Rudd right behind him, the two cars came up on veteran driver Dave Marcis. Marcis moved to the outside to let them pass.

Davey went into the turn, hard. Ricky Rudd came up behind him and barely tapped him. When Davey spun out, Rudd went into the lead.

Rudd crossed the finish line first, but as he passed the line, he received not the checkered flag, but the black flag. After reviewing the films, NASCAR did something it had never done before in the history of the sport: It stripped the apparent victor of his spoils, taking away his trophy. Rudd was awarded second place.

Dave Marcis, who had the best seat in the house, testified that Davey had gone into that final turn so hard he would have spun out even if Rudd hadn't hit him. Davey's Dad, Bobby, who saw the whole thing, says there is no question that Rudd was at fault.

"Rudd took a short cut in the tight part of the track where he could get ahold of Davey and spin him out," he said. "Rudd was definitely at fault. He ran into Davey on purpose. Davey should have won the race. NASCAR rightly gave the race to Davey, the first time NASCAR had ever done that."

When NASCAR ruled that Rudd had deliberately spun Allison out and awarded Davey the race, the Chevrolet fans charged conspiracy: that NASCAR had ruled the way it did as a result of pressure from Ford, which had been threatening to pull out of racing.

Adding insult to injury, after the race Davey Allison blamed Rudd for his spinout.

"NASCAR did the right thing; they deserved to be disqualified," Davey said.

"Whiner," said race fans, who harked back to the first Bristol race when Davey complained about Darrell Waltrip's rough driving when he had acted just as badly.

So when NASCAR set a precedent by placing Rudd second in the Sears Point race and giving the victory to Allison, everyone was upset, because they felt Allison didn't deserve to win. Rudd was doubly hurt, because he was attempting to catch Dale Earnhardt for the driving championship, and he needed every point he could get.

Davey felt certain that he had deserved the win. But what made him mad was that he had driven an outstanding race on a road course, but because of the brouhaha, no one had noticed.

"Davey felt that Rudd had always been the Superman of the road races and that Davey had really learned how to drive those tracks," said Liz Allison, "so he was disgusted that he had driven such a great race and that his performance was overshadowed by the controversial finish. Though Davey said a win is a win, he was sorry it ended the way it did because nobody had noticed what he had done in the race."

The date June 24, 1991, was one of the highlights for the Allison clan. On that day Davey Allison won the Miller Genuine Draft 400 over Hut Stricklin, who had led earlier in the race. It was Stricklin's best effort since he started racing Winston Cup in 1987.

Davey and Hut had been friends ever since they were kids. "We came up through the short tracks together," Hut said. "But the next time, I want the one, two finish to be the other way around."

After the race Judy Allison was asked who she was rooting for.

"Of course, I was pulling for Hut at the end. That's what pays my bills, not Davey."

Davey was driving a Ford Thunderbird the team nicknamed "James Bond." It had won four of the six races it had entered. Its serial number was actually 007. The first three wins were at Charlotte, including the Winston.

"We're looking forward to the day when we can get the Raybestos Buick in front of that darned old Ford Davey's driving," said Bobby. "Davey has been a lot of pleasure to me along the way. I've talked to Hut about that. I told him on account of that, I just want to beat Davey by a little bit—but I do want to beat him."

It was Davey's third win in five races, not including the Winston, which he also won.

"[Michigan] was great," said Liz. "Bobby's team had been struggling financially, trying to get things going sponsorship-wise. They had struggled. With Hut being a member of the family, it was just a really neat experience for everybody. Just to see Hut run good was just great, and for him to finish second to Davey, that was a great moment, something every one of us was proud of. I know Hut would have loved to have won that race, but now he'd probably say he's glad it ended just the way it did. It was pretty neat."

At Talladega in late July, in an attempt to catch Dale Earnhardt, Davey desperately sought to enroll a drafting partner from among his fellow Ford drivers. None would come forward and cooperate, and Earnhardt won the race. Afterward a furious, out-of-control Davey Allison punched a wall and broke his hand.

McReynolds, in his mild manner, told Allison that if he wanted to win, he had to do it Larry's way. Concentrate on driving, the new crew chief told him. Tired of feeling frustrated, Allison consented, and in 1991 a more in-control Davey Allison became a star.

Winning five races in 1991 under McReynolds's leadership made Davey's bursts of childishness incidental. The other drivers made fun of Allison's tendency to complain when things went wrong, but at the same time they were having to eat his dust.

Feelings were running raw between the Allison camp and the Rudd team as they prepared for the second-to-last race of the year at Phoenix. All season long Rudd had either led or was the second in the points standings for the driving championship, but at Phoenix, Ricky had a bad run and Davey won the race, thereby overtaking Rudd for second place in the standings.

In the final race at Atlanta, Davey's car died when the battery gave out, and he lost four laps in the pits while his crew changed batteries. Rudd finished on the lead lap, with Davey two laps back, earning Rudd some vindication and enabling him to wrest back second place from his Texaco tormentor.

"Davey finished third in the points, and that was a great year for him," said Liz Allison. "There was no frustration at the end of that year, not like it was at the end of '92. It may have been a little disappointing not to have finished second, but we were thrilled with third."

After the race, Davey said, "In one way I really wish 1991 would never end. In another way I wish 1992 would start tomorrow.

"The only way this year could be better is that if my dad were still racing and we were fighting back and forth every week for the win."

NASCAR held its annual awards ceremony at the Waldorf-Astoria in New York City in December. It was televised nationally, and during the program Ricky Rudd, in a surprise, presented Davey Allison with what he called a "crying towel." It was an antagonistic gesture made with a smile. A quick thinker, the surprised and angered Davey Allison took the handkerchief and wiped Rudd's face with it. People in the audience in the ballroom and on national television watched with amusement and fascination. It was a page more from professional wrestling than from stock car racing.

Despite Davey's clever rejoinder, observers silently applauded the normally placid Rudd for expressing his true feelings. It became Ricky Rudd's symbolic revenge. In what appears to be the closest thing to a feud in the racing world at the time, everyone wondered how the bad feelings between Davey Allison and Ricky Rudd would manifest themselves in 1992.

CHAPTER 40

Clifford: "Crazy Wild"

"Clifford didn't get the break that Davey got. And that's fine. Some people do, and some people don't."

—Hut Stricklin

It's not easy to follow in the footsteps of a famous father. It's even harder when your older brother has become a star as well. That's what Clifford Allison was up against.

Uncle Eddie Allison remembers Davey as being level-headed and Clifford as always being "crazy wild."

According to Eddie, when Davey was eight or nine and Clifford five or six, they drove one of those plastic Hot Wheels bikes with the big wheel in front.

Bobby's street started in the parking lot of a big Baptist Church, which is why it was named Church Street. It went for a block and a half and made an ess, and after another half a block it ended at a T. On the left you went up to Bobby's house. On the right the trail went to Kitty's house. The shop was straight ahead.

The driveway of Bobby's house ran down a pretty steep slope, and Clifford would take that three-wheeler up the hill as high as he could go, and he would race down the slope as fast as he could possibly run.

At the bottom he would spin it out and slide the bike sideways. Later when he graduated to Go Karts, he raced down that slope the same way.

"You couldn't keep the tires on the Go Kart for his sliding it sideways going down the hill," said Eddie.

"Davey had to work at it, where it came natural to Clifford. Clifford just had to learn how to hook the gas pedal to his brain."

"I don't think Clifford had the desire that Davey did," said Red Farmer. "I don't know whether it was because he was younger, and he had other things on his mind, or what."

Another reason it took Clifford longer than Davey to get to the top was that Clifford didn't have the focus on racing that Davey did, much the same way that Donnie didn't have the intense focus that Bobby had.

"Where Davey was focused, Clifford was all over the place," said Bobby. "Clifford's a little different in personality. He's interested in racing and other things, too. He'd be doing one thing, and then he'd go to motorbikes. Davey pretty much talked about racing from the time he woke up until he went to bed at night. He liked to hunt and fish, but mostly he liked racing. Clifford didn't mind working for what he wanted, but he was not as sure about what he wanted to do."

There was another reason for Clifford's lack of focus on racing.

"Clifford was very attractive to the female gender, and they to him," said Bobby. "When Clifford was sixteen he tried to get married to the girl who ended up being his first wife.

"Judy was really upset with him, and upset with me. Tammy was the daughter of a local minister. And a different religion. She wasn't Catholic, but Presbyterian."

They tried to run away and get married three times.

Said Bobby, "We'd get them back home and tell them, 'You're too young. You're not allowed to do this. Give me the keys to your car."

After the third attempt, Judy was so furious she threw out Clifford and his belonging—including his clothes and the papers he had written in the second grade that she had saved.

Judy's anger cooled, and while still teens, Clifford and Tammy married in a ceremony held at the Allison home. Conducting the service was the Rev. Charles Hall, Tammy's father, and Father Dale Gruba, a priest from Wisconsin who was one of Bobby's close friends.

Now married, Clifford's life still had little direction. Bobby and Judy worried about his future.

"Clifford didn't know for sure what he wanted to do," said Red Farmer. "A lot of times you ask any teenager, 'What do you want to do for a living?' They tell you a dozen things. They aren't sure about any of them. I think that's the way Clifford was. He didn't know whether he wanted to be a driver or a mechanic like his Uncle Eddie."

Bobby was dismayed by Clifford's lack of purpose, and at one of the races was talking with J. D. Stacy, a car owner and also the owner of a large coal mine.

"My son Clifford is giving me more gray hairs," Bobby told Stacy.

"Bobby, send him up and let him come up to Kentucky, and I'll give him a job in the coal mines. I'll give him a job taking care of my equipment doing maintenance of my coal-mining equipment and my trucks."

"Boy, this was perfect for Clifford," said Bobby.

Clifford and Tammy drove to Kentucky to work for J. D. Stacy.

Tammy became pregnant, and she returned to Hueytown to have the baby while Clifford commuted back and forth for about a month.

"I have a really good job," Clifford told Bobby. "It's the night shift, but I take care of the equipment, and they really like me, and I like it. I'm making good money."

After the baby was born, Tammy returned to Kentucky with Clifford, and it wasn't long before the two began to have personal problems. Tammy moved back to Alabama with the baby. For a while Clifford remained in Kentucky, but he was lonely without his family, and so reluctantly he quit his job and returned home.

When he returned to Hueytown, Clifford reconciled with his parents, which made Bobby feel good. Clifford and Tammy moved into a double-wide trailer in a trailer park not far from Bobby and Judy's house, and he set up a car repair shop in the basement of his trailer.

After Clifford returned, things turned sour and they were divorced. Clifford returned—with the baby—to his parents' home on Church Street.

Free from his emotional attachments, Clifford worked harder on the race cars being built in Bobby's shop, and he worked in earnest on his short-track car that he raced at the Birmingham and Montgomery racetracks.

Bobby had hired Clifford to be crew chief of his Grand National car, but after Bobby's crash at Pocono in June 1988, the race team was disbanded. Clifford got a job at an auto repair shop, and during evenings and weekends beginning in 1989 he worked on his own race car in Bobby's shop.

"Dad, I want to go racing," Clifford told Bobby.

"Clifford began to get more serious about being an adult and doing something with his career," said Bobby.

When Clifford began building his race car during the evenings, he would go into the house and get Bobby to come and help him, even though Bobby was still too banged up physically and emotionally to teach him about building cars.

"I couldn't give him a hand," said Bobby, "but it was so good for me. 'Dad, would you put in a spark plug like this?' He was constantly having conversations with me, which was doing me so much good. 'Come on, Dad, come to the racetrack with me.' 'Come on, Dad, tell me what you would do with the car right here?' I would say something like, 'Tighten the lug nuts.' Which everyone would know, but Clifford made me say it. But it was good for me."

"He had a really good feel for the car," said Bobby of Clifford's talent.

"Bobby was living through Clifford," said Judy. "Working with Clifford was his therapy."

"Bobby was able to get in the picture at the end," said Eddie Allison. "He was trying to see if maybe he could repair his Winston Cup race team with Clifford as the driver. It would have been hard because Clifford was still inexperienced, didn't have many hours in the car, but look at the kids today. They jump in the thing and run two hundred miles an hour."

When Clifford met and married Elisa, a divorcee with two kids of her own, he added a stability to his life that he had never enjoyed before.

"Hey, you talk about the marriage made in heaven," said Eddie. "Those two people were one, and it was really neat. I was so proud of the boy, because he had fought such a battle, and here he finally got a woman who really loved him the way you're supposed to love somebody to marry him, and it worked out."

By 1991 Red Farmer could see the change in Clifford.

"He had changed his whole perspective on racing," said Farmer. "He was really starting to blossom into a good driver. I think he made up his mind that was what he wanted to do. It took him that long to determine that.

"When he made up his mind that 'I want to be a driver like Davey and Daddy,' that's when Clifford started turning everything around. The last year he was here he was really making big strides. He was coming on as a driver."

In 1991 Clifford was driving in ARCA and some Busch races. The first couple of years, he hadn't had a lot of success. More often than not, he crashed or finished back of the pack.

"Clifford had a big foot," said Eddie. "That gets you in trouble. He had to learn how to overcome that, and he was starting to get the hang of it."

Most of Clifford's efforts didn't amount to much. On March 3, 1991, for instance, he finished twenty-eighth at Rockingham in a Busch series race. On March 14, at Atlanta, he was involved in a twelve-car pileup in the fourth lap.

Then there were encouraging performances: On November 8, 1991, practicing before the ARCA 200 at the Atlanta Motor Speedway, Clifford hit some debris, cut a tire, and crashed, damaging the car. After the crew patched it up, he finished a more-than-respectable fifth.

By 1992 Clifford was showing the promise everyone predicted for him. On April 10, 1992, he sat on the outside pole for the Slick 50 ARCA 500K race at the Texas World Speedway. He had the pole won until Loy Allen Jr. outran him in a car Allen had bought from Davey two years earlier.

Two days later, Clifford was leading the race, when Eddie Bierschwale passed him on turn one of the final lap to win the race by 0.32 of a second.

Clifford had led 145 of the 156 laps before oil and debris brought out a caution flag. After the green flag came out, Clifford and Bierschwale battled side by side and traded leads several times. The race showed Clifford was learning discipline.

"Going into turn one of the last lap," he said, "the car got really sideways, and I had to lift. That's when Eddie took the lead."

Hut Stricklin, who was close to Clifford, felt that Clifford had a disadvantage in that his equipment was less than top quality.

"I never felt like he ever had a chance," said Hut. "He never got in a good, good car. The equipment was whoever Bobby could talk into giving him a break."

Hut was aware that when Davey broke into the racing game in 1987, Bobby was still driving and his name had huge clout. When Clifford broke in in 1992, Bobby was out of racing, and his name didn't mean quite as much.

"Being Bobby's son may have gotten Davey the ride with Robert Yates in the beginning," said Stricklin, "but it was still up to Davey to perform, and let's face it, when Clifford came along, Bobby Allison's name didn't mean quite as much as it did early on. That was a lot of it. Clifford didn't get the break that Davey got. And that's fine. Some people do, and some people don't."

Reporters all the time asked Bobby whether Clifford was going to drive for Bobby Allison Racing. In April 1992 Bobby told reporters, "I'd love to have Clifford in my car, but he's not had enough experience to put him in the Winston Cup driver's position.

"I'm a firm believer that you've got to go to school and pass each grade before you can go on to the next grade."

Two months later, at Sears Point, Bobby talked about his dream.

"Davey's doing too well right now to disturb him, and Clifford still needs more experience, but if I can put together a team with my two boys, it will be the happiest time of my life."

On July 18, 1992, Clifford proved that his second-place finish at Texas wasn't a fluke. In an ARCA race at Pocono, Clifford passed Jeff McClure, but Bob Keselowski passed him to take the lead at the end for another fine second-place finish. Victory and the step up to Winston Cup racing now seemed within his grasp.

CHAPTER 41

Davey: The Lost Championship: Part I

"When things were really good, he just beamed. So it was really cool to be around him and experience that."

—Liz Allison

Davey and Larry McReynolds couldn't wait for the winter to be over and the 1992 racing season to begin. Their race team was intact—no one important had defected to another team—and their only fear was losing momentum. Their expectations were that, barring some kind of disaster, the title in 1992 would be theirs for the winning.

When the Texaco/Haviland team arrived in Daytona to run the 500, it came with as much confidence as any race team could have had.

Said Larry McReynolds, "Davey was at the peak of his career, and Robert Yates was the car owner and engine builder. If you got the rest of it just halfway right, how could you go wrong?"

Said Liz Allison, "Going into the Daytona 500 of '92, we *knew* he was going to win that race. We just knew it. The writing was clear on the wall for us. They had run so good at the end of '91, and everyone felt they were going to take that momentum right into '92, which they did. I mean, Speed Weeks was pretty neat, because we could feel the power. We knew it was there, knew it was going to happen. The reporters were all around Davey. He had all that attention. And Davey, too, he was a pretty remarkable person. He always had this confidence about him, and I really admired that in him. Because nothing got him down. He might get mad and bummed for a second, but he basically was very upbeat, a very motivated person, and people loved that energy, so people were around him anyway. But when things were really good, he just beamed. So it was really cool to be around him and experience that."

During the eleven days of Speed Weeks at Daytona, the 28 car showed its strength. McReynolds was one crew chief who believed deeply in a team trying its hardest to win the pole. McReynolds felt that if they could win the pole, it would signal to everyone else their strength.

"It sets a precedent for the rest of the week and for the next two or three months really," he said. McReynolds had been on teams that had struggled in the contest for the pole, and that struggle had continued throughout the week and then through the season.

McReynolds wanted to build momentum. When Davey qualified sixth, no one was happy. Then came the Busch Clash (now the Bud Shootout), a race of pole sitters from the previous year. Most teams, not wishing to risk tearing up their good Daytona 500 car, ran one car in the Busch Clash and the better one in the 500.

McReynolds wanted a race under his belt where he could learn something about his race car, so he made the decision, "rolled the dice," as he described it. He would qualify their Daytona 500 car on Saturday and race it in the Busch Clash on Sunday.

Davey finished third.

"We learned a lot," said McReynolds.

The team practiced Monday, Tuesday, and Wednesday for the 125-mile qualifying races. The two pole winners set the front row of the 500 in stone, and the twin 125 qualifying races on Thursday set positions 3 through 43. If a driver wins one of the 125s, he not only starts up front for the 500, but he also wins a pretty good payday for the race team.

Davey went out to practice the Wednesday before the 125-mile qualifiers. He was out on the track running in a big pack in the final minutes of the last practice, when a car got loose, hit his car, and the car was torn up.

Even though practice was officially over that day, Larry McReynolds went to NASCAR and asked if he could run his backup car a few laps. He was given five minutes.

They had tested this backup car, and it had run well, but during the five laps of practice, a valve cover leaked. That wasn't a big deal, since McReynolds intended to switch engines anyway to run the 125-miler. But because they were using a backup car, they had to start the Daytona 500 at the rear of the field.

McReynolds was particularly impressed with Davey's optimism and confidence despite the setbacks.

"Davey was the most determined individual I ever worked with in my life," said McReynolds. "You couldn't get Davey Allison down if you tried. It was almost as though the more pressure you put on him—the bigger the pressure cooker situation you put him in—the better he performed.

"Davey had a lot of confidence in himself and in the people around him. After the five practice laps, he said, 'We'll get them tomorrow. We'll be just fine.'"

Davey finished third in the 125-miler. Which put the car in sixth on the grid for the Daytona 500.

McReynolds and his team worked hard on the car all Friday and Saturday to make it run better. On Sunday, in a backup car, Davey saw a dream come true when he won the Daytona 500.

The favorites in the race were Junior Johnson's two cars driven by Sterling Marlin and Bill Elliott. Ernie Irvan in the Kodak 4 car also was strong. Those three cars dominated the first half of the race.

Gatorade paid a bonus of $10,000 to the car that led at the halfway point, and those cars battled for that bonus money, which in 1992 was significant. Off turn two, a couple of them got together, and both Johnson cars and the Kodak car were wiped out while Allison slipped through unscathed.

With his strongest competition gone, McReynolds played it cool the last 250 miles. His only competition came from Morgan Shepherd in the Wood Brothers car. Shepherd chased Davey hard the last part of the race but couldn't catch him.

Several days before the 500, McReynolds couldn't find one of his two-way radios. It had disappeared, and he had forgotten about it. With fifteen laps to go, suddenly Davey was getting instructions from a fan sitting in the grandstands.

He was saying, "You better go. He's coming. You better get on it." McReynolds was furious. Davey found it amusing.

Said McReynolds, "Same ole Davey. No big deal. Davey Allison being the cool, calm, collected guy that he is, never let controversy bother him."

After Davey climbed out of his car, Davey told the press, "This is a sweet race right now. I just can't believe it. I'm just shaking all over. We finally won the Daytona 500.

"In about thirty minutes I will probably collapse from disbelief. I spent about ninety percent of each lap looking in the mirror trying to figure out when Morgan was going to go."

Davey's win at Daytona earned the Robert Yates team a purse of $244,050. Allison became the second son to join his father on the roll of Daytona 500 winners—along with Lee and Richard Petty. Davey paid tribute to the King, who had announced he was retiring at the end of the '92 season and who was driving in his final Daytona 500.

"Richard Petty won two hundred races," Davey said solemnly, "I don't think I'll get that far, since I've only got fourteen so far. But sitting here, at the age of thirty, I'm happy that I've done just one of the things he did."

Afterward, Davey led his father Bobby to the press box to celebrate the victory. Only four years earlier Bobby had won this race, with Davey second, though sadly for both, Bobby's subsequent brain injury had erased it from his memory. Bobby told reporters that seeing Davey win the Daytona 500 had been "a goal of mine as long as I can remember."

Said Davey, "I watched my dad win this race a couple of times, and I followed him across the finish line a few years ago. That day is such a special day I don't think anything could replace it." Davey looked lovingly at his dad. "But this is the best race I've ever won."

Said Bobby, "I feel like I'm sitting here next to the best youngster there is out there, and he's the son of Bobby and Judy Allison."

The press ate it up.

"I'm prejudiced," said Liz Allison, "but I like to think Davey was good with the press. He took time that so many drivers didn't take, and some of that was overlooked. He could sit and sign autographs and talk to the press for forty-five minutes, and you could get up and leave one person, and they'd bash you. But yes, for the most part the press enjoyed him because of the energy around him."

Winning the Daytona 500 started the season rolling for the team of Robert Yates, Larry McReynolds, and Davey. But for every high, it seemed, there would be a corresponding low.

On April 1, Davey's grandfather, Pop Allison, passed away. Said Davey, "My dad has always been my hero, but my grandfather has always been my best friend. He drove the school bus [in Hueytown] from St. Teresa's parish to St. Aloysius when I was a little kid, and I used to sit up on the box beside the driver's seat and ride with him. I went wherever he went, and later he went wherever I went. We were very close."

Said Liz Allison, "He was leading in the points when he lost his grandfather, whom he loved, just before the Bristol race in early April. This was the absolute year from hell in our lives. His grandfather, Bobby's dad, was kind of the ringleader of the Alabama gang. Everybody called him Pop Allison, and though Davey suffered, he drove at Bristol. I admired the fact he was able to go and run that race and put every emotion out of that car and still drive unbelievably. But there were times I wanted to choke him because of it, too."

Before he could bury his grandfather, as Liz said, he had to race at Bristol. He had an accident, breaking his lower right ribs and separating cartilage. He also bruised a lung, though they didn't discover that until after the Martinsville race, when he cut a tire and hit the wall, aggravating all his injuries.

Said Liz Allison, "He crashed during the [Bristol] race and hurt his shoulder badly, but he went to North Wilkesboro and won it. I wasn't able to go to that race. I had something going with Krista back home and couldn't go. It was a very emotional race. He dedicated that race to his grandfather.

"He was in a lot of pain. It took me a while to realize how much pain he was in because he never complained. He had all these little stimulators strapped on him like you get at the chiropractor and the battery pack to try to keep his muscles relaxed. I thought, *If that was me, I'd be in a hospital bed.* He was out driving a race car."

Davey, indominable, also made McReynolds a believer when he came back from his Bristol injuries and won at North Wilkesboro. Then he recovered from his Martinsville injuries and won the Talladega race on May 3.

The next week, at Charlotte, in the first-ever night race, Allison figured out how to both win *and crash.*

The race was called the Winston. It was the All-Star race, initiated in 1985. Then in 1992 Humpy Wheeler, the president of the Charlotte Motor Speedway, decided to change the format to make it more exciting.

First the racers would compete for twenty-five laps. The order of finish would then be reversed for another twenty-five laps. And then there would be a ten-lap shootout. The contact rules, moreover, would be relaxed.

Said Wheeler, "It's a race where the owner of the car tells the driver, 'Bring me back the trophy or the steering wheel.'"

Davey was driving "James Bond Double Oh Seven." The car was competitive every time it ran. It had won several races in '91.

Driving car 007, in 1992 Davey won the Daytona 500 and the Winston 500 at Talladega, which meant he had won the first two legs of the Winston Million. All he had to do was win either the World 600 at Charlotte or the Southern 500 at Darlington, and he would win the million dollar prize.

Most car owners would have saved 007 for the World 600 and the try for a million dollars. Not Robert Yates.

Said Larry McReynolds, "What was unique about Robert Yates was that the very next race—whatever it was—was the most important race you were going to run. It didn't matter whether it was the 125-miler, the Bud Shootout, the Daytona 500, or the Coca-Cola World 600."

And so McReynolds prepared car 007 for the Winston, even though it was just an All-Star race that didn't even count in the points standings.

Early in the Winston, McReynolds rated the car as "okay," not great, but with every pit stop he and his crew improved it.

When the flagman waved the white flag, signifying there was only one lap to go, Dale Earnhardt led, Kyle Petty was running second, and Davey was a distant third.

Said McReynolds, "As he took the white flag, I commented to Davey, 'One more lap, Buddy. We're going to be okay. We've learned a lot tonight. We've learned things we need to do differently for next week. Let's just get this next lap in.' I figured we'd be happy taking third."

Davey didn't answer McReynolds, which was his usual modus operandi late in the race. He was focused on what was going on around him.

Roman Pemberton, Robin and Ryan's brother, was standing on top of the toolbox, and he watched Davey go down the backstretch. McReynolds couldn't see him, and about the time the cars were due to go into turn three, McReynolds could see Roman turn around and clench his fist. McReynolds didn't know what was happening, but he figured it was something good. In the stands, meanwhile, the fans "looked like they were about to rip the grandstands down."

What Pemberton couldn't see was Earnhardt taking the lead coming off turn two, with Kyle Petty second, and Davey third. They were running one after the other. Earnhardt went into turn three hard, going up the track a bit but not enough for Kyle to get by, so Kyle dove down and hit Earnhardt's quarter panel, and Earnhradt crashed. Kyle slowed enough that Davey was able to pass both of them.

When McReynolds looked down at turn four, Davey was leading. McReynolds wondered, *How the hell did he do that?*

Kyle Petty was half a car length behind Davey when they crossed the finish line. Kyle had gotten a good run on Davey, but fell just short. After they crossed the line, Kyle gave Davey's car a little nudge. Davey won the race by inches, but his car turned, and he hit the wall hard on the driver's side.

"I still to this day question whether Kyle gave Davey a little nudge that didn't need to be nudged," said McReynolds.

Eddie Allison didn't fudge. He *knew* Petty had made a mistake.

"At the end of the Winston, Kyle just made a tremendous blunder," said Eddie. "He didn't take his foot off the gas pedal after he crossed the final line. If he'd have lifted, Davey would have been okay. He just drove right through Davey's side, not dreaming it would end up like it did, but when you're going 180 miles an hour, you can't control what's going to happen. It bummed Davey up pretty good.

"Kyle and Davey were good buddies. They grew up together with my son Mike, buddied around. I had Mike in the summertime, and we would go to the Marco Polo Motel in Daytona Beach, and they would play the water game Marco Polo. And so it wasn't intentional, it was just dumb. And in the process Kyle hurt Davey pretty badly."

The race over, the two cars slammed together. When Davey lost control of his car, it turned around as it flew down the straightaway. It hit the retaining wall down at the end of the dogleg going off into turn one and came to a halt near where the pace car was parked.

Humpy Wheeler was in the control tower when the crash occurred.

"We've got signals between the head rescue guy, the EMT at the scene, and us to find out how bad a crash is," he said. "Four you don't ever want. He said it was a three, which meant the driver was unconscious and unresponsive. Which I couldn't believe. I knew the hit was really hard. So I took off for the trauma center while they were cutting Davey out of the car.

"All of the Allison clan was there, and it was bedlam, because they had just gone through this with Bobby.

"Up to that point Bobby was walking with a cane. He was slurring his words, not in very good shape. But when Bobby walked into the trauma center, he yelled, 'Shut up. Everything is going to be okay.'

"And everybody—here was the leader of the clan addressing them—calmed down.

"That was the night Bobby came back as a human being."

McReynolds and the Texaco crew sprinted to the car, and when they got there, they could see Davey slumped over in the crumpled car. Workers would have to cut him out of the car.

Said Brian vanDercook, Texaco's PR man, "That one could have killed him. Davey just sat there unconscious with his chin on his chest while the fans went wild. It was very scary."

Larry McReynolds thought, *Man, he's out*. But shortly after that, Davey started coming to, and they got him out of the James Bond 007, which would never race again. Said McReynolds, "The poor James Bond 007 was absolutely destroyed. It went to the graveyard. It was killed."

As they were getting Davey out of the car, the racer in McReynolds came out: He kept looking at the scoreboard. The board had Kyle's 42 on top and Davey's 28 underneath, but he was sure Davey had won the race. About the time they got Davey out of the car and put him in the ambulance, he looked at the scoreboard one more time, and they flipped the numbers. He thought, *Yeah, at least we won the race.*

Davey was put in the ambulance, and Bobby Allison and McReynolds got in with him. Davey awoke, but he was still pretty foggy. From the start of the trip to the infield center, Davey must have asked McReynolds a half a dozen times, "What happened?" McReynolds said, "You wrecked pretty hard, but you won the race." And Davey would say, "You're shitting me." And then Davey would ask McReynolds again, "What happened?" "You wrecked hard, but you won the race." "Man, you're shitting me." They kept this cycle of conversation going all the way to the infield care center.

Because he was knocked out for so long, Davey was airlifted to the nearest hospital by helicopter. He was banged up pretty bad, still suffering from broken ribs he had sustained at Bristol and at Martinsville a couple of weeks earlier. But despite the mild concussion, Davey was conscious enough to become enthralled with the controls and instruments of the helicopter he was riding in. Before the ride was over, he asked the pilot, "Would you mind letting me fly it?"

"If you can get up off the stretcher, we'll let you take over," said the pilot. Davey stayed strapped to the stretcher.

According to Liz Allison, the crash at the Winston made Davey realize that he had not spent as much time with his wife and family as he should have.

"The Winston changed everything for him and for me forever," said Liz. "We have a first-turn condo at Charlotte, where we were looking down at the race. The children were up there, all the family. With five laps to go, I decided to go down to the infield so I could see Davey when he got out of the race car. At that time he was not running up front. I didn't think he had a shot at winning. But as I got down there, I heard people screaming, 'Davey Allison's won the race.' I thought, *What? What happened?*

"Then came the ordeal. The children saw the wreck from up in the condo. He was knocked unconscious, and he had a really weird experience from what happened to him there. He really felt like he should have been killed in that wreck. He really felt he had been given a second chance, and at that point it was time for him to get his life straightened out, to get it in line the way the Higher Power felt like he needed to have it in line. That experience changed Davey Allison forever.

"Up to that point Davey had felt that the race car came before anything else. He loved his wife and children, but the race car still came first. It's hard to explain this to someone else, but that's what makes them the drivers they are. But after the crash, all that changed. Everything came second to me and the children and our family. From then on Davey felt there was nothing in the world more important than that. Not that he wasn't a wonderful husband and father before, but he had been very driven by what he was doing."

The next week Davey was right back at work preparing for the World 600. Back then the World 600 week was really stretched out. Everyone checked in on Tuesday, practiced Tuesday afternoon, qualified Wednesday, practiced Thursday, Friday, and Saturday, and raced on Sunday.

On Tuesday Davey was still hurting pretty bad. He had just gotten out of the hospital Monday morning. He was driving a brand-new, untested race car.

Said McReynolds, "We had killed a car at Daytona, killed a car at Bristol, killed a car at Martinsville, and now we had killed a car in the Winston. We were running out of cars, fast. In fact, when we showed up on Tuesday we didn't even have a backup car on the top of the truck. They were at the shop working feverishly trying to get another car done."

McReynolds didn't want Davey to practice the first day in order to give Davey an extra day to recuperate. In his place they recruited Neil Bonnett, who had retired after his head injury and who was a color commentator on TNN. Neil was thrilled to get his chance to get back behind the wheel.

Partly because Davey wasn't feeling a hundred percent and partly because his car was new and untested, Davey finished fourth in the World 600. It was a good finish, but the Winston Million was still up for grabs. Davey had one more shot at it in the Southern 500. At this point in the season, Davey and McReynolds still figured they were the favorites to win the driving championship. Bill Elliott, driving for Junior Johnson, was his strongest competition. Independent driver Alan Kulwicki, the eventual winner, wasn't even a consideration.

After Charlotte, Davey went on to Michigan in late June, and then just before the Pocono race on July 19, 1992, he checked himself into the local hospital. He had been suffering from a mysterious virus, and he had no strength. He was treated and released.

His lead over Bill Elliott was more than 100 points. Driving a brand-new car, Davey qualified on the outside pole. Despite his weakened condition, he set a new Pocono track qualifying record.

Davey was running so strong that he led the first fifty laps of the race. Then, just after the halfway point, he pitted under a caution. The air gun broke, and the pit crew had to go to a backup air gun. He had been leading, but because of the malfunction, he left the pits twelfth.

Before they restarted the race, McReynolds said, "Davey, we still have ninety-something laps. We'll be okay. You just need to be patient." He said he agreed. More than two hundred miles remained, a long way. Davey had plenty of time to go back out front.

At the restart Davey had led 115 of the 150 laps run so far. Darrell Waltrip had a strong car that day. McReynolds had watched Darrell go into turn one about two laps after the restart, and as Davey went in on Darrell, he watched as Darrell pinched him. McReynolds was pleased that Davey was smart enough to back off.

They came back around, and on the next lap McReynolds saw the caution flag waving, and he could hear the team's spotter saying, "Davey, are you okay? Davey, are you okay?"

McReynolds said, "Terry, what is going on?"

He said, "Larry, it's pretty bad."

What had happened, as Davey and Waltrip went through the so-called tunnel turn, Davey got under Darrell again. Darrell got a little momentum up and hit him in the left rear quarter panel and turned him. Davey slid across the grass out of control, and as he hit one of the access roads, he became airborne and started to roll. The car flipped over, and over, and over, and over . . . countless times (eleven, actually), horrifying for everyone to watch, landing with a sickening thud, a tangled, smoking heap. The car had disintegrated. The question was whether Davey had survived.

As the car spun over and over in the grass like a top, dirt flew everywhere, hitting him in the helmet and across his face and body.

Davey would have been unhurt had his arm not stuck out of the roof of the car. When the car hit the guard rail, his arm was crushed. He suffered a dislocated and broken right wrist, a broken right forearm, and a broken collarbone.

Said McReynolds, "I remember seeing the look on Robert Yates's face, because he was scanning the other drivers passing by on the caution. Robert heard Mark Martin make the comment, 'There is no way Davey is alive. They need to get a body bag.'"

"I thought that was it," said Robert Yates.

While Liz and Judy watched in horror at home on TV, workers threw a blue tarpaulin over the car to keep the curious onlookers from watching the relief workers struggled to extricate Davey from the wreckage. The blue tarp was usually used in fatalities.

This was the same track where Bobby had almost died in a horrific crash in 1988, a crash that had ended his driving career.

"I don't know why Pocono was so dangerous," said Liz Allison. "It's where Bobby ended his career. Judy, Davey's mom, told me, 'Good Lord, if I never go back to Pocono again, it will be a day too soon.' That wreck, which involved Darrell Waltrip, was a bad one. It was weird. It didn't look like much, but it turned into a lot. Davey fractured his skull. It was horrible, terrible."

The last thing Davey remembered before crawling out of the wreckage of the car was seeing Kyle Petty upside down.

"I was thinking, one of us is not going in the right direction, and I have a feeling it's me," said Allison.

Davey also described having an "out-of-body experience." He would later tell family members he felt he was hovering above the car, watching himself be removed from the wreck, convinced he was dead. That eerie experience, Davey said, changed his life. After that night Davey vowed to get his priorities back in order. He vowed to become a better husband and father.

Yates and McReynolds ran to the infield care center, where they unloaded Davey from the ambulance. When Davey saw McReynolds, he looked at him in such a way that McReynolds was sure Davey would survive.

Said McReynolds, "His arm was hurting him, but he was alive, and he was going to be okay."

While Davey was taken by ambulance to the Allentown hospital, McReynolds and his crew loaded up—"it took us forever"—and then they drove to the hospital to check on him. Judy, his mom, met them in the lobby and said, "He doesn't look very good. His head is very swollen."

Liz wasn't at the track because she was home with strep throat. When she saw Davey crash on TV, she knew she had to get to Pocono. But Davey's twin-engine Cheyenne was already at the track. She chartered a plane and flew to Allentown.

When she arrived at the hospital, Davey was on a stretcher, and his arm was splinted. Liz noticed that his head was huge, about "four times" the size of a normal head. She also noticed his face was still caked with dirt.

"It was jammed in his ears, in his nose, in his mouth, and all of his face," she said. "I thought, *Why hasn't anyone cleaned this man up?* I guess they were so busy with his injuries they didn't have time."

When they wheeled Davey into his hospital room, Liz cleaned him up herself. Davey was laughing while she attempted to clean the dirt from every nook and cranny of his face and neck.

Liz said to herself, *Okay, this is it. You're not going to get into a race car the rest of the year.*

When Liz finally told Davey what she was feeling, he didn't utter a word in reply.

"In my heart I knew there was no way he would stop racing," said Liz.

She said, "The next day the swelling went down, and he told me, 'I'm racing on Sunday.' I told him right then, 'You're insane. You're *in-sane*. You are made out of something the rest of us don't understand.' And he was. Absolutely."

When Larry McReynolds and a couple of the crew members walked into Davey's room, they, too, saw how bloated his face was.

"Davey was a pitiful-looking sight," said McReynolds. The g-forces had changed his face into a mask, but he was alert and sitting up. The first thing he said when his crew walked in that door was, "I'm going to kill that son of a bitch. I'm going to kill him dead when I see him." Meaning Darrell Waltrip.

McReynolds said, "No, you're not going to kill anybody. You just need to get healed up."

If Davey was mad at Darrell Waltrip, his uncle Eddie and his dad Bobby have never forgiven him for what happened to Davey that day. That Waltrip went on to win the race only made the Allison clan more bitter about it.

Said Eddie Allison, "Then came the Pocono race, and that was sick. I watched it on TV, and when I saw Darrell turn his wheel to the right, I said, 'Darrell, you sorry, low-down, no-good rascal.' Not only did Darrell take the boy out of the race, he hurt him really bad.

"Bobby can't stand Waltrip. Waltrip is not a good person. And I like Darrell, and I love Stevie. I didn't have problems with Darrell the way Bobby did, at least not until he crashed Davey at Pocono. 'I'm going to kill you,' is what he said when he turned his steering wheel to the right. He spun Davey out, because he knew Davey had the only car that could beat him in the race.

"Darrell's car wasn't even good enough to finish second, but he knew if Davey finished, he couldn't win. So Darrell took him out of the race. I don't think he intended what ended up happening—Davey turning over eleven times and ending up in the hospital—but you can't say you had no idea what the end result was going to be, if he did it intentionally.

"He could have killed Davey. If the car would have stayed on top of the fence as it rolled those eleven times, instead of rolling in the dirt, Davey would have been dead. Because it pushed the windshield roll bar down, and the fence would have started cutting the metal up, and the minute the rollbar became weak enough, it would have gotten in on his head."

Bobby publicly accused Waltrip of being responsible for the accident, calling it a "cheap shot."

When asked about it again, Bobby told reporters, "My mother was on me for saying the things I said. I said, 'Mom, is it worse to say how I feel about somebody or to tell a lie?'

"What [Waltrip] did to Davey did not change my general opinion of him. It just emphasized it even more. The trailing car has an obligation to not make contact with the car in front of him, no matter who is driving."

Commented Larry McReynolds, "There is no love lost between the Allisons and the Waltrips—you know NASCAR history—never has been. It's a battle that goes back to the seventies between Bobby and Darrell. How unique it is that Darrell and Bobby have both retired tied with wins [84, third all-time] with the bad blood that is there.

"I couldn't help feel how unfitting it was that Darrell ended up winning the race on a fuel mileage deal. Darrell and I are best friends today. We never talked about the Pocono situation. I consider him one of my best friends, even though I disagree with what he did that day at Pocono, but that was [a long time] ago."

Ironically, the only one who refused to blame Waltrip was Davey.

"There are times when you overextend or underprotect yourself," Davey said, "and you have to be willing to accept the circumstances. There are things I could have done to prevent it, and there are probably things Darrell could have done to prevent it. But that's not the nature of the sport."

Doctors had scheduled an operation to fix his broken arm and put pins in it. Before he was wheeled out for the operation, Larry McReynolds said, "Davey, what do you think here?" Allison knew what his crew chief was asking him, though others needed a translator. What McReynolds wanted to know was whether Davey wanted him to get a replacement driver for the next race at Talladega on July 26, just seven days away.

Davey said, "What do you mean, what do I think? I want you-all to get you-all's asses on that airplane and get back to Charlotte and get my Talladega car ready, because I *will* be there, and *we will win Talladega.*"

If anyone thought Davey was out of his mind, no one let on, except his surgeon, who had inserted eight screws in his arm.

As Davey checked out of the hospital, one of the doctors passed along a message from the doctor who had operated on him.

"He said I was insane," said Davey.

Davey said he drove in pain because his father did. He said, "My dad crashed in the mid-1970s in Minnesota, breaking ribs, fracturing his face and smashing both his feet. He stayed in the hospital until Thursday, and was back driving in Nashville on Friday. When it come to driving in agony, he's the toughest SOB there ever was."

Now Bobby and Davey would become the toughest father-and-son SOBs there ever were.

Davey wasn't released from the hospital until Thursday. McReynolds went ahead and hired Bobby Hillin to qualify the car, and he qualified third. Robert Yates's and McReynolds's scenario, which had the blessing of NASCAR, was to start Davey in the race, let him run one lap, and then Hillin would finish the race. That way Davey would still get whatever points Hillin could amass in the race as Davey continued to battle for the racing championship.

Yates and McReynolds objected. "If Davey is forced to get out after only one lap under green, it'll cost us a lap and destroy our day," McReynolds said. The NASCAR officials agreed to "play it by ear" and let Davey run until the first caution.

It's hard to believe that NASCAR had approved Yates's and McReynolds's plan. Davey would be getting behind the wheel of a race car going 190 miles an hour with pins in his broken right arm, the arm he would need to shift the car. It didn't seem possible.

Said McReynolds, "Had it not been Davey, and had Davey not been so close to the points leader—he was second to Bill Elliott by a little bit—I don't think NASCAR would have ever agreed with him starting in that race car."

When Davey arrived at the Talladega racetrack on Saturday to practice, he was determined to start the race without showing he was hurt.

"I would not let anybody ever hear me say ouch," said Davey. "I felt like if I could get in that race car without showing any sign of pain and other people were watching, they might say, 'Hey, there's something here.'"

By midafternoon Saturday his medication was down to Tylenol and aspirin. A bigger problem was that he had zero strength in his right arm. McReynolds and his crew came up with a clever improvisation. One of McReynolds' strengths was his ability to solve problems, and this time he came up with a beauty.

The crew put Velcro on Davey's cast and Velcro on the shift lever, and they Velcroed his hand to the shift lever so he could shift for restarts and leaving the pits.

"Davey pretty much drove the car one-handed," said McReynolds, who was impressed mightily by yet another example of the Allison determination.

Said McReynolds, "Even today, when I think I can't do something, or if I can't overcome some obstacle, if I can't get something done, all I have to do is close my eyes and think about Davey, and then I say to myself, I can do *anything* if I want it bad enough.

"You know, Davey was a Christian, and he had a little saying, 'There is nothing that can't come my way that God and I can't handle together.' Race fans have sent that saying to me on a little card that's sitting right on my desk today. That was Davey Allison's attitude and approach."

Because Bobby Hillin had qualified the car, Davey had to start the Talladega race at the back of the field, which was probably not a bad move, because if Davey was going to have trouble steering the car one-handed, he wouldn't put other drivers in harm's way.

The race began, and by lap 4 Davey was still behind the wheel. McReynolds was thinking, *Shoot, what are we going to do? We got to get him out of that car.* Suddenly, it began to rain, a two-minute rain shower in the middle of July without a cloud in the sky, but it was long enough for the officials to throw the caution so McReynolds could get Davey out of the car and put Bobby Hillin in.

Said Davey's wife Liz, "He drove the first four laps at Talladega the next Sunday. That was a very emotional and difficult day for me, but at the same time it was also pretty amazing. I cried all the way out there. I was a crying idiot on pit road. I couldn't contain my feelings. I wanted to know, *Why are you doing this? What are you trying to prove?* There was no answer. I knew the reason, of course. Davey was in the points lead. He felt he'd worked for this all his life, and, by God, he was going to make this happen. The whole time they were putting him in the car, he was moaning and groaning, hollering out from the pain. They had to Velcro his hand to the stick shift, which I still can't believe NASCAR allowed him to do. He needed to drive until the first caution.

"Well, I just didn't see that there was going to be a caution for a long while. The sun was out, but after one lap, it started raining down in turn one. It was the weirdest thing. I thought to myself, *Your guardian angel is looking out for you. Now you can get out of the car.*"

Hillin went on to finish third that day, and Davey wrested the points lead back from Bill Elliott. To outsiders, the day was a rousing success, but Larry McReynolds was upset that Hillin hadn't won that day. He had panicked at the end, and it had cost him the race.

The race came down to a battle of the same four cars that had battled at Daytona, Junior Johnson's two cars driven by Bill Elliott and Sterling Marlin, the Kodak car driven by Ernie Irvan, and Hillin's 28 Texaco car.

There were three Fords and a Chevy, driven by Irvan, but as McReynolds told Hillin with thirty laps to go, "This is *not* about manufacturers. Your best friend is Ernie Irvan in that 4 car."

McReynolds figured that the 11 and the 22 cars of Junior Johnson would help each other, leaving Hillin and Ernie Irvan to team up.

The four cars were running out of gas. Everyone was scheduled to run one more lap, pit on the green, and get gas and two tires.

McReynolds was in communication with Tony Glover, Ernie Irvan's crew chief. McReynolds figured correctly that the 11 and 22 cars would pit, and McReynolds and Glover agreed that after one more lap, they'd both pit and maybe they'd come out in front of them.

When he saw the 11 and 22 headed for the pits, Bobby Hillin panicked. Instead of staying out and running one more lap, he hit pit road with them, leaving Ernie Irvan to run by himself and angering both Tony Glover and McReynolds.

An unhappy Glover said to McReynolds, "What happened? You threw us in here."

McReynolds said, "I didn't throw you in. The driver threw you in."

It ended up working out just fine for Glover and Ernie Irvan, who ended up winning the race.

After it was over, reporter John Romano of the *St. Petersburg Times* asked the question that was on a lot of people's minds. He said, "NASCAR has seen plenty of drivers return from injuries to resume careers, but Allison's determined comeback may reach new extremes. Just days removed from a horrific crash and with a hospital bracelet still on his wrist, it begs an obvious question: Is he nuts?"

In sports there's often a thin line between being nuts and being brave and determined. Nothing was going to stop Davey Allison from winning the points title in 1992 if he could help it. After Talladega came Watkins Glen, and once again Davey strapped on his Velcro and insisted on starting the race.

"I really wanted to tie him up," said wife Liz, "but at that point I gave up. I felt,

If you're going to do this, I'm going to have to support you, because I married you, the race driver, and here we are. So if you're going to do it, what do I have to do to help you do this?"

Before the Watkins Glen race, Davey sat among a large group of enthralled reporters and told them, "Evidently, there is a mission left for me on this earth. I just hope I can figure out what it is I can do for the man upstairs, because the good Lord has definitely given me a second chance."

Davey started the Watkins Glen race, drove eighteen laps, and handed the car over to Dorsey Schroeder. When Schroeder finished twentieth, Bill Elliott took over first place in the race for the driving title.

But losing the points lead was a minor bump in the road for Davey compared to the tragedy that confronted him at Michigan in August. On Thursday, August 15, three days before the Winston Cup race, the Busch cars were practicing when Davey's younger brother Clifford unaccountably crashed and was killed.

Said Larry McReynolds, "We were getting ready to go to the Charlotte airport and catch our flight to Michigan early in the afternoon on Thursday. We had worked at the shop that morning. Davey was already in Michigan. He had some good friends up there he always stayed with. We got word before we left that Clifford had been killed, and of course Robert Yates and I tried to get in touch with Davey to find out what was going on."

CHAPTER 42

The Death of Clifford Allison

"We're gonna get 'em, dad."

—Clifford Allison

Bobby and Clifford were at Michigan practicing for the Detroit Gasket 200, a Busch race. It was August of 1992, and after a half-dozen years racing ARCA and now Busch races, Clifford had put his childish ways behind him and settled down. He was serious about moving up to Winston Cup racing.

"Clifford was trying to make a name for himself," said Liz Allison, "and he had not been able to get in there and do that yet. He hadn't had the opportunity Davey had, hadn't had the same equipment, what a lot of race car drivers battle. Clifford was a funny little guy. He had a great personality. He and Davey were very different. Davey was real straitlaced, hardly drank anything. Clifford drank and smoked. They were just very different.

"They had the same brother-thing every family has. They fought with each other, but they loved each other.

"I remember Davey telling me that Clifford had more born talent as a race car driver than he felt he had himself, but he just felt that Clifford hadn't gotten to the maturity level yet to put it into action. It frustrated Davey so much, because he knew how capable Clifford was. And for a while Davey really battled with the question, *Should I put him in my Busch car?* That haunted him until the day he died."

For inspiration and guidance, Clifford had the attention and devotion of Bobby Allison, his dad. When Davey was coming up, Bobby had been too busy racing himself to help him. Moreover, Bobby was of a mind that since he had had to come up the hard way, by his own bootstraps and ingenuity, what was good enough for him was good enough for Davey.

Not that Davey didn't have help. He had had the expertise of Uncle Donnie and Red Farmer to rely on. Clifford had Bobby's undivided attention. After Bobby's near-fatal crash at Pocono in 1988, Bobby, too impaired and unsure of himself to run his Winston Cup team, had time to work with Clifford, and his greatest pleasure came from showing his younger son the ropes.

Clifford also had Davey's enthusiastic support. Davey was hot on the advantages of the new radial tires. He told Clifford they were tougher to control and more expensive than bias-ply tires, but faster on the track. Clifford told Davey he didn't have the money to spend on the more expensive tires.

"I'll buy the tires if you're not too chicken to drive on them," Davey teased.

Racers are always looking for more speed, and Clifford was a racer. Clifford took the challenge. Davey bought him a set of the radial tires, which were on the car when he went out to practice at Michigan on August 13, 1992.

Clifford turned in a particularly fast lap, and he came into the garage. His crew made some minor adjustments. As he backed out of the garage to go back out onto the track, he looked at Bobby and grinned.

"We're gonna get 'em, Dad," Clifford said.

He went back out. Bobby remained in the garage area.

Suddenly Bobby could see Clifford's crew chief, Reds Cagle throw down his headset. He told Bobby, "He crashed."

Bobby asked him, "Is he okay?"

Cagle put his headset back on and yelled, "Clifford, are you okay? Clifford, can you hear me? Clifford? Clifford?"

Some witnesses said they thought a tire blew. Others said no, that Clifford had lost control.

The car spun, and when the driver's side of the car slammed flush with the concrete, Clifford Allison died instantly. The experts, looking for a reason for the accident, focused on the radial tires. They noted how radials are less forgiving of a lack of smoothness by a driver and cause the car to turn more abruptly once they break traction. Clifford had had no experience whatsoever on the stiffer tires, and most likely it was this lack of experience that caused the crash, they said.

"Bobby has talked about it a lot, said Eddie Allison. "The radial tires stick the cars so good that when they do come loose, you can't get the car back."

Bobby, unable to run because of his injuries at Pocono, started walking from the garage area to Clifford's car. He watched as the safety vehicles raced down pit road the wrong way, an ominous sign. Out on the track Bobby saw racer Bobby Labonte stop his car, get out and look at Clifford's car. A grim Labonte climbed back in his car and drove away.

Bobby kept walking toward the car, even as NASCAR officials yelled at him to stay back. One official told him point-blank, "Bobby, they don't want you out there."

"That's my son," Bobby said. "I'm going."

"I'll walk with you," the official said.

Twenty feet from the car Bobby could see Clifford through the windshield slumped over the wheel.

"I could see his helmet, his suit, but it was already obvious he wasn't moving," said Bobby. "I walked to the front of the car where I could look in, and then I was really sure he was dead."

When Clifford's wife Elisa tried to reach his car, she was told by some of the other wives not to go. She went anyway. When she got to the wreck, Bobby told her, "Don't look."

Clifford's was the first fatality at the Michigan track and the first crash fatality in the history of Busch Cup racing.

Liz Allison, Davey's wife, learned of Clifford's death on the flight from Huey-town to Michigan.

"I remember sitting there thinking of the pain Davey was going through, and that I loved this man so much and could not take his pain away," she said. "I busied myself trying to help everybody else. I was trying to be Miss Fixit. I felt, *Okay, we've got to go home. We've got to go home.*"

Liz went to the hospital where she met Clifford's wife, Elisa. One by one the members of the Allison clan headed home. She kept waiting for Davey.

"I certainly wouldn't ask," she said. "At that point I wouldn't ask anything. I kept waiting for him to say, 'We're going home.' And he never said it. I thought, *Are they going to have the funeral without us?*"

Davey had a long talk with Bobby and Judy. Bobby told Davey to stay up at Michigan, to "do what Clifford would have wanted him to do." And so Davey stayed and raced.

"I don't know how the boy got through that weekend," said Liz. "I just don't know."

When Davey wasn't driving the car, he sat by the side of the truck crying.

"He truly had a strength that was unbelievable," said Liz.

Despite the pain he continued to bear from his terrible crash at Pocono and despite the psychic pain from Clifford's death, Davey drove the entire Michigan race and finished fifth. Only then did Davey and Liz return to Alabama to bury Clifford.

"If he sat out and didn't race today, would that make things better?" Alan Kulwicki asked. "This can happen to anybody at any time, yet I don't think the odds are very high. Yesterday was very tragic, but I probably know more people who died from a heart attack or cancer than from race cars."

Dale Earnhardt agreed. "He was in that race car by his choice. The sad thing is his family is left behind to mourn him and his kids are left to grow up without him. It's no consolation to them he died doing what he wanted to do."

Robert Yates said, "I've been racing since 1969 and never had anyone even hurt badly before. You get to thinking it can't happen to you. When something like this happens, you can't just say, 'Life goes on.' We don't want to lose our kids. But we want to do it because God gave us the competitiveness and ability to do things safely. That's what we have to focus on."

"That's what racers do," said Eddie Allison. "We can relate this to the world. I was listening to Governor Pataki of New York this morning talking about the Al-Quaeda threatening New York, telling the people to do what they're supposed to do and carry on. If we cower, then the terrorists have done what they wanted to do. We're tougher than that."

After the race Davey told reporters, "I hope everyone understands. I'm going to the truck, and I'm going home." Clifford's funeral was the next day in Bessemer.

The pain of Clifford's death would haunt Davey the rest of his life.

"Davey didn't know how to talk about it," said wife Liz. "He never dealt with Clifford's death. Never. No. He never went to the cemetery after the burial. He barely would talk about it. It was so painful for him that he chose to do everything but, and he went out of his way to do whatever he could to help Elisa and the kids and be a father to them. He gave Elisa a job as a secretary in his race shop. There was just a lot of unresolved stuff for him. Davey took all that upon himself."

At first Davey refused to talk about his brother's death. He told reporters, "Honestly, I don't have a lot of self-confidence right now. I need some time to get myself tuned back up."

In the following weeks Davey tried hard to cope.

"Clifford is gone, and there's nothing I can do to change that," he said. "The thing to do is retain memories and prepare to live every day the best I can—on and off the track."

Davey told reporters, "The bottom line is, I know every time I step in the car there is an element of danger. For me not to get right back in would have been giving up everything I've ever believed in."

Davey was convinced Clifford shared that conviction.

"The difference is when I crashed, I got rejected [by the Lord]; he kicked me out. Clifford didn't need a second chance when it came to [his relationships] with family; there's obviously something left for me to do.

"All our lives, Clifford was the more affectionate and thoughtful person, while I was always focused on my career and what might happen down the road. I let the excitement put something other than my family in a priority position; that's something he didn't do.

"Racing is my life, so it has to be high, but there's a way to deal with it so it's still important, but not first or second.

"If there's one thing I've learned this season—other than I am not indestructable—it's that you never know what's in store for you from one second to the next or how you're going to react."

Clifford's death left Davey with the haunting thought that if he should suddenly die he might leave Liz and his children without financial means, as Clifford did.

"I ain't out there for the money," he said. "I'm out there racing every week because it's what I love to do. But what I want most is to be able to raise my kids and know that, should the day come that I'm in the same position as Clifford, they'll be taken care of when I'm gone."

After Clifford died, Davey was very generous with Elisa and her children. Said Eddie Allison, "Davey was well into the money, and Davey was as good a person as his daddy."

The experts generally believed that Clifford had hit the wall because he hadn't had enough experience driving at high speeds on the radial tires that Davey had goaded him into buying.

At the funeral Davey became hysterical. He kept saying, "I killed Clifford. I killed Clifford." He was so distraught Bobby had to slap him across the face to calm him down.

Later, Davey composed himself. He told his cousin, Joe Allison, "This will make us be the best we can be, because we don't know when our time will come." Joe Allison, a struggling field goal kicker for Memphis State, never forgot that. With Davey as his mentor, he practiced with renewed vigor, and the next year won the Lou Groza award as the country's best field goal kicker.

"If I had sulked and become unproductive, Davey would have been very mad at me," said Joe.

His senior year, Joe Allison wore jersey 28 during warm-ups, number 12 during, the game. He kicked a record 89 PATs in a row, a Memphis State record.

Bobby Allison sat with Clifford's widow Elisa at her home after the funeral. She said to Bobby, "I just feel like taking a sledgehammer and going outside and smashing that race car."

Bobby said, "Don't do it."

He then went and got the local Birmingham newspaper. There were ten traffic fatalities, one boating fatality, one drowning, and a worker killed at a shop.

Bobby told her, "These people were killed just like Clifford. They're not going to come back and their families are grieving just as bad. But stopping racing does nothing. It's just part of what goes on out there."

Elisa also had a conversation with Eddie Allison in which she said she was so distraught she was going to "lock the door to any future relationships."

"Elisa, you can't do that," Eddie told her. "You're too young."

"It's turned out nobody could replace Clifford. She married a high school coach, but it didn't last. A couple years ago," said Eddie, "she married a lawyer, and she's doing fine with him."

———

In 1997 Bobby talked about the fact that he still had great physical pain from his accident at Pocono in 1988. He said, "I have been hurting for eight and a half years. I'm hurting right now, sitting here talking to you."

Then he said, "But when I walked up to that car, as close as from me to you, and saw that boy was dead—knew that boy was dead—there began a pain that I had never known before, never imagined. And it kept hurting. Kept hurting. Kept hurting. And it never went away."

In a whisper, Bobby said, "Clifford still stares at me. He had a wound on his face that never even bled—that's how fast his heart stopped."

"Every time Bobby talked to someone about him, he'd have to cry," said Eddie Allison. "But the thrill of what Davey was doing alleviated a lot of it."

CHAPTER 43

Davey: The Lost Championship: Part II

"I guess it just wasn't meant to be."

—**Davey Allison**

After Clifford was killed, Robert Yates and Larry McReynolds assumed that Davey would go back home rather than drive in the Michigan race. When they were finally able to get in touch with him, they asked, "Do you want us to get Jim Sauter?"

Davey said, "Wait a minute, guys. Yeah, my brother was killed today, and it's killing me inside, and I'm hurting a lot, but I'm up here to do a job, and I'm going to do my job. We're going to win this race on Sunday, and then I'm go home on Monday, and we'll bury my brother."

Said Liz Allison, "Don't forget, this was only a month after the Pocono crash, and he was still hurting from those injuries."

Despite his anguish and physical pain, Davey qualified third and finished fifth in the race.

Said Larry McReynolds, "That shows you the guts and determination and the role model that Davey Allison was."

A huge disappointment for the race team was losing the Winston Million at Darlington. Before the race, Davey, still wearing a flak jacket and bandages, told reporters that winning the million would be a just reward for his crew.

"Those are the guys who work nonstop to build new cars after I destroy them," he half-joked.

Davey had the victory within his grasp. But late in the race he came in to pit for gas and tires, while Darrell Waltrip stayed out in a desperate gamble. Had the race run to its conclusion, Davey would have won easily on his new tires. But with five laps to go, rain moved across the track with Waltrip in the lead. The red flag came out, and two hours later, the race was called. Davey finished a heartbreaking fifth in a race he was sure he was going to win.

After the race, Davey was, as usual, sunnily philosophical. "It just wasn't meant to be," he said. "We'll just leave here with a smile and know that we ran a good race."

Waltrip, for one, knew exactly how Davey was feeling. Back in 1989 he was running for the Million when a tire went down and he lost a sure win at Darlington.

"I know how Davey must feel," he said. "Why couldn't this be 1989?"

Reporters wanted to ask Davey if he thought he would have won had the race gone the distance. When they arrived at his trailer, they discovered that he had left the track.

His wife felt worse about the loss than Davey did.

"He led until the final six laps, and then it rained," Liz said. "At that point, I was feeling the frustration of the whole year. I felt, *Why is this guy having to go through so much?* And then he doesn't get the Million. It wasn't the money as much as it was the fact that he deserved the win, deserved the prestige and honor, and for it to start raining so they couldn't finish the race . . .

"Davey came in for gas, Darrell Waltrip took the lead, they were under caution, it started raining, and they didn't even get to finish the race. They called the race. So that was very frustrating, and I was more frustrated than he was."

Nothing, however, matched the frustration that was to come. The Dover, Delaware, race was seven races from the end of the season, and Davey was leading Alan Kulwicki by over 300 points for the racing championship. Neither Davey nor McReynolds thought Kulwicki had it in him to win. In fact, they felt that if they didn't win, Bill Elliott, driving for Junior Johnson, would. As it turned out, both Davey and Awesome Bill from Dawsonville finished poorly.

Said McReynolds, "We could not find our butt with either hand. Neither team could. It was pathetic. All of a sudden, for whatever reason, we fumbled the ball every single week. In the meanwhile, ole Alan was just coming. He wasn't winning, but he was top five, top ten, top five, top ten."

The month of September was terrible for the Texaco team. The car blew up at Dover and finished forty-first. They ran terribly at Wilkesboro, a race they had won in the spring. They then wrecked at Martinsville, when Rusty Wallace and Davey traded paint and spun each other out of contention.

"We just couldn't do anything right it seemed like," said McReynolds. "The month of September just destroyed us."

Tempers reached a boiling point for Davey and the crew after the Rockingham race on October 25. Davey finished tenth, far behind winner Kyle Petty. In the garage area, Davey ripped into his crew members, including team owner Robert Yates and crew chief Larry McReynolds. Some wondered whether the team was breaking apart under the pressure.

Davey, realizing his outburst was uncalled for, called a meeting of the team. He began by apologizing to Yates and McReynolds.

"It had all gotten to me," said Davey. "I told them, 'Look, our strong point has been from the beginning of the race team forming, our communications, the constant way we talk to each other.' We don't go for long periods of time without saying something. If any of us sports something that may be an asset or may be detrimental, we say it. It very seldom causes a problem.

"This time it did. I was saying, 'It's time to get it out of our system and get beyond that.' We have to remember we don't expect the other guy to be a superman, and we don't have a magic wand. We just have to keep working as hard as we can and keep our chin up and keep an enthusiastic attitude."

The meeting had a calming affect. The team relaxed. Davey grew a beard for good luck.

McReynolds didn't want to have to go all the way to Phoenix to test, so the team went to Richmond and tested for two days, running almost six hundred laps. Mike Laughlin had built a new type of chassis, a three-quarter low snout used mainly for short tracks. McReynolds took his regular car and the low-snout. Two hours into the test, Davey was ecstatic about the car with the new design. He said, "You can put a fork in that other one. This is my race car right here for Phoenix."

On the flight to Phoenix, the cabin of Davey's small plane began to fill with smoke. Davey was able to make an emergency landing. On the ground it was determined that a piece of insulation had fallen against the heating system, causing the smoke. When Davey personally inspected the plane, he noticed that one of the engines had a serious oil leak. He felt lucky he hadn't lost the engine during flight.

After fixing the plane, Davey flew safely to Phoenix.

Davey won the Phoenix race, and regained the points lead over Alan Kulwicki, though by a margin of only 30 points. Going into the final race at Atlanta, six drivers could have won the championship: Davey, Bill Elliott, Alan Kulwicki, and three drivers with an outside chance, Kyle Petty, Mark Martin, and Harry Gant. It was the closest championship battle with that many drivers in the hunt ever.

Robert Yates paid Bob Latford handsomely to set up a chart with all of the possibilities in order to find out where Davey needed to finish at Atlanta in order to win the championship.

Latford showed them if Davey finished fifth, or if they led one lap and Davey finished sixth, they couldn't be beaten.

Atlanta would mark one of the most memorable races in NASCAR history. Richard Petty, the King, would be racing in the last of his 1,184 starts in his legendary career. A young kid with a funny-looking mustache, Jeff Gordon, would be competing in his very first Winston Cup race. Though any of six drivers could win the racing championship, Davey was favored.

When the team arrived in Atlanta, Robert Yates let McReynolds run the show.

Had he been more hands-on, he would have seen that the race team made one serious strategic error and was way too cocky and overconfident.

McReynolds chose to take the same car that had won at Phoenix. In hindsight, said McReynolds, "It was not the right race car to run at Atlanta. It was a flat track, but it was a short-track car, and here we went to Atlanta with it."

Davey qualified seventeenth. On Saturday three practices were scheduled: morning, midday, and late afternoon. The car ran decently in the morning practice, so McReynolds and Davey thought they would send a message to the Elliott and Kulwicki teams by leaving their car covered during the midday practice and going to the Ford hospitality tent to eat lunch.

Said McReynolds, "We should have been practicing. But we were on track to do what we needed to do on Sunday. We were beaten by inexperience," McReynolds lamented. "Davey was inexperienced. I was inexperienced."

If Davey had won the race, he would have gone down as the bravest, most indomitable champion in the history of the sport. He would have overcome seven crashes, including the horrific Pocono smashup, serious injury, and the death of his younger brother. If Hollywood had written the script, Davey would have won. And two-thirds of the way through the Atlanta race, it appeared that he would.

Things were going smoothly when Davey came into the pits. McReynolds ordered a two-tire change. Davey took the lead. All he had to do was finish sixth, and the championship was his.

Bill Elliott and Alan Kulwicki were two cars that were running stronger than his car. Were there three other cars better than his? That was the question.

Said McReynolds, "If we were to win the championship, it was not going to be by a whole lot."

In the end, bad luck did them in. Davey was running sixth with 125 laps to go, two-thirds of the way through the race, when Ernie Irvan, who was running right in front of him in the 4 car, blew a tire, hit the outside wall, and came back across the track in front of Davey—there was nowhere for Davey to go. They collided and the car was a mess.

McReynolds yelled to Davey on the radio, "Get it going, The leaders are coming." But the car couldn't go. The steering was bent.

McReynolds refused to let the season end. He knew his crew wasn't going to be too excited about fixing a race car that was going to finish far out of the running, but he said, "Look, guys, we're going to fix this race car, and we're going to finish this '92 season on the racetrack." Everyone went to work.

With Davey out of contention, the points race was then between Alan Kulwicki and Bill Elliott. Kulwicki, one of the few independent drivers, had turned down a million dollars to drive for Junior Johnson. He didn't need anyone else, he said. He could do it by himself. Everyone thought he was nuts.

Kulwicki was an engineering graduate of the University of Wisconsin, the first of many science-minded brainiacs who soon would invade the garages of NASCAR. He had redesigned the rearview mirror and constructed a noise baffle.

Kulwicki was an untiring worker who harangued and ripped his crew members for any imperfection. They rarely stayed with him for long. He drank champagne instead of beer. He didn't own an airplane or a motor home. No one thought he could win it.

Said Kulwicki, "I'm just a guy from the Midwest who works hard."

Kulwicki, who possessed the precision of the engineer he was, made sure he led the most laps in the race, giving him a five-point bonus. As long as he finished second, he knew, Elliott couldn't catch him for the points title. Kulwicki stopped chasing Elliott and tried to stay out of trouble the rest of the way. He was a lot luckier than Davey had been.

Toward the end of the race both cars came in for a splash of gas. Kulwicki only had fourth gear, and his crew had to push him back out. Elliott won the race, but when Kulwicki finished second, he won the points championship. Davey was third.

Meanwhile, as Elliott and Kulwicki raced for the championship, Davey's Texaco car motored slowly around the bottom of the track. Adding to the drama, the damaged 43 STP car of Richard Petty, in his final race, had caught fire and had to be towed back to the garage area. Papers wrote about Petty's "flaming exit." But Petty was determined to finish his final race on the track. In the end Richard Petty, too, ran very slowly around the apron as the winners sped by.

McReynolds could have just as easily parked the car in the garage, since they were as many as sixty laps behind when they finished fixing it, but McReynolds had wanted to make a statement about the courage and determination of the Robert Yates race team. At the end of the day, there was great disappointment, but a great deal of accomplishment—and hope.

"Yeah," McReynolds said, "we finished third in the points, we won five races, we sat on two poles, we won the Winston, we won the Daytona 500, but we didn't accomplish what we really thought we could do, which was win the 1992 Winston Cup championship."

Added McReynolds, "It was an awfully good day, but I will still go to my grave believing that the Pocono crash was the loss of our championship right there. It broke our momentum, even though we came back and still won one more race and actually took back the points lead."

Eddie Allison, for one, blamed Davey and Ernie Irvan equally for what happened at Atlanta.

"I sat here and watched it on TV and said the same dang thing I once said to Donnie at Daytona: 'What is the point of messing around with cars that don't have any chance of winning the race?' he said.

"Ernie knew that tire was flat the lap before, and he still drove that stupid car in the corner until he crashed it, and it ended up running right into Davey. It was a sad, sad deal.

"It was almost impossible for Davey to lose that title. But when he didn't win it, he didn't worry about it. It didn't bother him, because he figured he was going to win the next one.

"Davey knew what he had to race with and what he was going to do and how good he could race. He wasn't worried about winning the championship. But the Lord had other ideas."

The angriest spectator of them all was Liz Allison. She desperately wanted Davey to get the recognition she felt her husband deserved. She, too, blamed Ernie Irvan for depriving him of it.

"Lord only knows what happened that day," she said. "That was the most upsetting thing for me of Davey's whole racing career. I absolutely drove every lap with him. I felt, *Lord, let this race be over.* And then came the accident with Ernie Irvin. Ernie wasn't really well liked at that point anyway. He and Davey had had a few spats, a few things going on, so of all people to wreck him, Ernie Irvin, it was just beyond me. I thought, Jiminy Crickets, everything that this man has been through this year, all the ups and downs, and to come in from Phoenix leading in the points and to lose the damn race now, it just doesn't seem fair.

"I was very angry. I was *so* angry. I just cried, and I felt so sorry for Davey. I wanted to hit Ernie. I wanted to choke Alan [Kulwicki]. And when I got to the infield center, Davey was just as calm and peaceful as he could be, and I felt stupid for feeling the way I felt.

"I kept saying, 'I'm so sorry,' crying on and on, while Davey was trying to see if Ernie was okay. Davey was very disappointed, don't get me wrong. He just— At that point it just wasn't meant to be. He had truly done everything in his power, the best of his ability to make it happen, and it just didn't happen."

Davey Allison showed a lot of class refusing to blame Irvan for his losing the racing title.

After the race, he told reporters, "I watched my father finish second four times before he finally won the championship when he was forty-six. I'm thirty-two-years-old. That gives me at least fourteen more years to win a championship."

Said Davey, "I guess when I look back on 1992 five years from now, I'll look back at the good things. Of course, my grandfather and my brother passed away, but the good things are going to stand out."

When he was asked months later why he didn't criticize Ernie, he said, "If it had been intentional on Ernie's part, or caused by someone trying something they weren't capable of and spun me out, I wouldn't have been a happy person.

"It's been my experience you never make a bad situation better by thinking or saying something negative."

Eddie Allison, who had been out of racing fulltime since 1975, was also affected when Davey didn't win the racing championship in 1992.

He said, "Davey and I talked and talked and talked and talked about my building motors for his Busch car on Saturdays. He said that if he won the championship, he would have the money to pay me. Of course, Alan Kulwicki won. If Davey had won, I'd have been working for him, and in six months I'd have been out of a job."

CHAPTER 44

Davey: Life on the Edge

"Hang up the phone. And get on the other line."

—**Donnie Johnson**

The off-season between 1992 and 1993 was a very special time for Davey and Liz Allison. In January 1993, they renewed their wedding vows in a ceremony with their two children in attendance.

They were busy building a new 8,000-square-foot home in Hueytown, a Taj Mahal of homes. The builder wanted the place to house a Davey Allison Museum. Liz talked him out of it. But the house *was* a palace.

Davey had worked on earning a helicopter license during a stay in Charlotte in 1992. He rented a copter and practiced landing it in the parking lot of the turn-one condos at the track.

Said his wife, Liz, "Davey loved to fly, and then all of a sudden, he wanted to buy one. I was totally against it from the beginning. In '92 he bought a small helicopter. Lord, I don't know why."

Liz only flew with him in his helicopter once. She didn't like flying, and she *certainly* didn't like flying in a helicopter.

"I just felt it was one more big, expensive toy that was not needed," she said.

When Davey arrived in mid-January to start testing for the Daytona 500 he was in an expansive mood. While he was talking to reporters in the garage about what happened in 1992, he rolled up his sleeve and showed two foot-long surgical scars on his forearm, the aftermath of his crash at Pocono.

He said he was at 85 percent of his strength. "That's great considering the damage and the rehabilitation I've gone through. It feels great," he said.

Davey also talked of the hardships of 1992. He said, "I figure if the good Lord thinks I'm capable of handling what comes along, I'll try and do my best.

"We could have just chucked it, rolled over, and quit. But it's like climbing a ladder. Every step you make gets you closer to your goal, and you can't give up along the way."

Allison said it was best to look at the positives: "It was the first time someone won back-to-back Winstons. We were the first to win two events at Phoenix. It was our first time leading the standings and the second year in a row to tie for the most wins.

"And we found that every time there was adversity, we didn't lose but gained in strength."

Davey then talked about his goals.

"I want that Winston Cup championship," he said. "That's something that's etched in the hardest material there could possibly be inside me, like it's written across my heart."

He talked about a conversation he had had with a Catholic priest who was also a friend. "I asked him, 'Is it wrong to want to win all the time?'"

"He said, 'No, it's not. Why do you ask?'

"I said, 'There's just this part of me that won't go away. I'm never satisfied with losing, and I want to win all the time.'"

But Davey and the Texaco team began the 1993 season with two poor performances, a twenty-eighth-place finish in the Daytona 500, and a fourteenth at Rockingham. It made for some tense times in the garage.

Said Davey, "You just can't believe what was going through my mind and the pressure that these guys have had on them after the first two races."

The pressure eased at Richmond, when Davey led 152 of the last 157 laps and beat Rusty Wallace to the finish. It was his nineteenth Winston Cup win.

Then it was back to mediocrity: In the next two races he finished thirteenth at Atlanta and eleventh at Darlington.

Then on April 1, prior to the Bristol race, the racing world was shocked and saddened when Alan Kulwicki, his pilot, and three executives of the Hooters Restaurants chain, died in a plane crash not far from the Bristol racetrack. Kulwicki had been in Knoxville, Tennessee, on a promotional visit. He was signing autographs at a Hooters there.

The twin-engine turboprop, registered to Hooters Restaurants, was five miles from the runway and approaching from northeast of the Tri-Cities Airport when the control tower lost contact with it around 9:30 at night. It went down just off a main highway between Bristol and Blountville. As it made its approach, it suddenly spiraled downward, nose first, and crashed into a hillside. The plane was engulfed in flames. Though five people were aboard, only four bodies were found.

Said Davey, a Catholic like Kulwicki, "One of the things that most impressed me about him was that he was single and he was thirty-eight years old, but he was at Mass every week, just like me and my family. I don't think there's any question that he had his priorities in order."

Liz Allison, who learned of the crash before Davey did, was the one who called up Davey to tell him what had happened to Alan.

"Alan was a great guy," said Liz. "I always really liked Alan. Alan, like Davey, was Catholic, and neither of them would miss Mass for anything. Davey would get me up at five-thirty in the morning before the race, and I'd be complaining all the way, but, by golly, we were going. And Alan would always be there right with us. He was very driven, too. He was rather amazing.

"I was going to Bristol the next day. I called Davey and woke him up, and he was very shaken. He wouldn't even watch the TV to see any of the news. Davey told me, 'Now I know why I didn't win that championship. Alan won't have any other chances, and I'll have lots more.'

"What I wish Davey had said was, 'Alan crashed in his plane. Maybe we shouldn't be flying.'"

Less than twelve hours after Kulwicki's death, Davey and the racers began qualifying for the Bristol race. Rusty Wallace won the pole for the Food City 500. In the race Davey finished fifth to Wallace, who was on a roll.

When Wallace won at North Wilkesboro and Davey finished fourth, Wallace took over the points lead.

At Martinsville, Wallace won again, but Davey stayed close and finished second. At Talladega, on May 2, Davey finished seventh. In that race Rusty Wallace had a terrible crash as his car spun across the finish line. He suffered a broken wrist, a concussion, and facial cuts.

At Sonoma, Davey finished a mediocre fifteenth.

On May 20, Davey, Kyle Petty, and Ty Norris, the R. J. Reynolds assistant manager of the NASCAR Winston Cup series, were flying into Indianapolis when Davey, at the controls of the plane, noticed another plane coming right at them.

Norris had no idea he was seconds from a head-on collision and instant, violent death until he heard Davey discuss what had happened with Ernie Irvan the next day in the garage.

Said Norris, "He was telling him that we were going 180 knots in one direction, and this other plane was going 160 in another, and in another ten seconds we would have hit head-on. I didn't know it was that close until then."

After blowing an engine and finishing thirtieth at Charlotte, Davey finished third at Dover and sixth at Pocono. Davey was still second in the points standings, 225 points behind Dale Earnhardt.

At Pocono, Davey had a reunion with the emergency helicopter rescue team that had airlifted him to the hospital after he had flipped twelve times the year before. He spent about an hour with them, talking about flying helicopters and how they reacted in different situations.

"He really had the bug," said Wayne Estes, a Ford racing executive who often flew with Davey.

While in Charlotte, Davey decided that his little helicopter wasn't fast enough. He traded it in for a turbo copter.

Trading up wasn't unusual for Davey. Two months after he bought his first airplane, he traded it in for a faster plane. In those days he had driven 220 miles an hour at Talladega, and his plane would not go that fast.

"I don't want my airplane going slower'n my race car," Davey said. "That sucker wouldn't go 220 with a tailwind."

Davey's wife Liz did not want Davey flying his newfangled toy. Neither did his family, even if he was only using it to fly from the shop to the airport. But Liz knew there was no point badgering him about it.

Said Liz, "He was taking lessons in it and got upgraded to fly it. Davey was a hardheaded person. And so, I knew I was going to lose, so I might as well be quiet about it."

Larry McReynolds, Davey's crew chief, was another person who objected to Davey's flying the helicopter.

Said McReynolds, "Nobody I knew wanted Davey flying that thing. Davey would ask me to fly with him, and I would say, 'Davey, I will fly around the world with you in an airplane.' He was as good an airplane pilot as there was—I had flown through the middle of a lightning storm with him. But I said, 'Davey, I'm not saying you can't fly a helicopter. I know you have all the papers saying you are certified to fly it, but you have not got nearly enough seat time in that helicopter that I'm going to put my butt in a helicopter with you.'

"He flew around Charlotte a lot in the helicopter in which he took his courses and certification. He'd fly to the shop. He'd say to me, 'Come on. Let me take you to lunch in the helicopter.'

"I'd say, 'I'm not getting in a helicopter with you. I'm just not.'

"I don't know a lot about flying, but you do a lot of things in a helicopter you don't do in a plane and vice versa. I know he had a license. But with Davey Allison, if you told him you needed your book written by August, he'd have it ready by July. He put every ounce of energy and effort he had in a short time to get certified to fly a helicopter.

"He was always focused on what he was doing. There was no way Davey Allison would eat his lunch and talk to you. He would say, 'Let me eat my lunch, and *then* I will talk to you.' First focus on lunch and then focus on talking to you. That was the way he was.

"As long as everything was good and fine in the [helicopter], he was okay. But if something went wrong. . . ."

Jake Elder, a longtime crew chief and another member of the Texaco crew, thought Davey was foolish to fly his helicopter.

"Said Elder, "He did a lot of what I call foolish things. He got that ole helicopter. I said, 'What the hell do you want that thing for?' Davey said, 'I like to fly. It's a lot of fun.' What can you say to a driver making money and winning races? What can you say? You can't tell him no, tell him he's doing crazy things. 'Cause Davey was a good race car driver. He was a likable person, friendly. I don't know what happened to Davey, but if he was here today, he'd be winning a lot of races. The people would take notice, wouldn't they?"

The one person who approved of Davey's new toy was Bobby.

"People warned him about the danger of flying helicopters, but not his daddy," said Eddie Allison. "Bobby was building a heliport on his property so Davey could land it in Hueytown so he wouldn't have to go to Bessemer."

On June 20, 1993, Davey traveled to Michigan to test tires. It gave him a few moments to confront his feelings about Clifford's death there the year before. Davey drove by the spot of Clifford's accident, and he said to himself, *There it is. There it goes. I won't have to look at the wall this weekend and wonder what emotions it might dredge up; I believe I've put them to rest.*

Davey told another reporter, "I can't say that I haven't been thinking about what took place up there last year because I have, and I think about my brother every day. Life still has to go on, and I know he would want us to remember the good times."

Davey finished thirty-fifth at Michigan, thirteenth at Daytona—more mediocrity. The pressures on the team were mounting.

"We did not run very good the first part of 1993," said Larry McReynolds. "We were struggling severely. We struggled at tracks we had dominated and run well. Yeah, we were sitting okay in the points, but we were struggling.

"Davey and I were even battling a little bit out of frustration, even though Davey and I were best friends. If I've ever had a best friend who I've worked with as a driver, it would be Davey Allison. His family and my family did things together. We are both devout Catholics. We had our sons baptized together. We are Alabamans, though we really didn't get to know each other until we moved to North Carolina and Davey started driving Winston Cup. We were not battling away from the racetrack, and our friendship was still strong, but we were starting to question each other a little bit. When you have the success we had, and then all of a sudden it goes away, you start questioning everything and everybody. 'What are you doing?' "

The next race was at Loudon, New Hampshire. It was the inaugural race for the track, the first Winston Cup venue in New England. The race had been sold out since January.

Rusty Wallace won after a terrific pit stop to take on four new tires. Said Larry McReynolds, "We were leading with thirty laps to go—we had that same low-snout car that had won at Phoenix—and a caution came out. The thing about our car, it was not very good on the short runs. It needed long runs to go, and I knew when the caution came out that we were dead in the water, and Rusty Wallace ended up winning that race, Mark Martin was second, and we finished third. But it was like we were finally starting to get this thing figured out. Here we go!"

Since Clifford's death, Davey had become very attentive to Bobby. He would say, "Come on, Dad, go with me in my plane." Or "Come with me for a bite to eat."

After the Loudon race Bobby rode home with Davey in his Cheyenne airplane. Bobby sat in the copilot seat. They talked about Davey's outlook, his ambitions. Davey was in a very positive, upbeat mood.

Said McReynolds, "What made me know Davey was feeling good about it was we all flew back in the plane with Davey. He dropped us off in Charlotte and then went on to Alabama. And his dad was on the plane with him. It was Robert [Yates], Raymond Fox, Eli Gold, the announcer, Sam Manzes, his pilot, and Bobby.

"When we got on that plane, Davey said, 'I'm going to let Dad fly up there. I'm going to sit in the back with you guys and drink a beer and enjoy our ride home.'

"You could see the confidence in him after the day we had at Loudon."

Said car owner Robert Yates, "We left there like we'd won the race. We were making a lot of plans for the future."

Larry McReynolds and the Texaco crew went to the shop on Monday to get ready for the Pocono race. It was a normal day, or so they thought.

Said McReynolds, "Every time we buckle these guys into a race car, whether for practice or qualifying or especially for the race, we don't know if it might be our last conversation with them.

"When you look back at the 2002 Daytona 500, you remember the shot of Dale Earnhardt and Dale Jr. embracing each other, and I keep seeing that picture of Teresa giving Dale that extra little kiss after she gave him a kiss after he got into the car. And you just wondered whether she had a feeling it would be the last time she was going to give him a kiss. But little did I know as we got off that airplane in Charlotte that day that it was going to be my last conversation and last time to ever see Davey.

"Because on Monday in the shop, the phone rang, and it was Bill France Jr., and I heard them page Robert Yates to the phone, and I remember Robert turning white as a ghost.

"He said, 'It's not good. Bill France Jr. just called and wanted to know if I knew about the situation with Davey.'

"With Davey you never knew what the situation was. I wondered whether Davey had called up NASCAR and cussed them out about something or what?

"Robert said that Davey had flown to Talladega and crashed the helicopter, and it was not good. It wasn't good at all."

That morning Bobby Allison had had a physical therapy session and then went to his office down the hill from his house in Hueytown. He was talking on the phone when the other line rang. Donnie Johnson, Bobby's business manager and brother-in-law, answered it. He looked at Bobby and said, "Hang up the phone." Bobby looked at him quizzically. Johnson repeated himself. "Hang up the phone. And get on the other line."

Neil Bonnett was on the phone. He was calling from the Talladega racetrack. There had been an accident with Davey's helicopter. He was being taken to the hospital in Birmingham.

Judy was in Davey and Clifford's room when Bobby came in the house and told her about the accident. Bobby and Judy arrived at the hospital before Davey did. The life of their remaining son was hanging by a thread.

CHAPTER 45

The Death of Davey Allison

"As the shock wears off, the fear sets in, and it just grips your heart."

—Liz Allison

O n the morning of July 12, 1993, Davey and Red Farmer, sixty-one, Davey's mentor and the crew chief of his Grand National car, ate breakfast at Bill's Farmhouse Restaurant in downtown Hueytown. Red, whose whole life revolved around racing, had traveled to Hueytown to race against Bobby and Donnie thirty years earlier and had become family.

"I work at Davey's shop until five o'clock and go home and work on my dirt car from six to ten every night of the week," said Farmer. "I don't really get tired of it. If I did, I'd quit."

That Bill's Farmhouse Restaurant was open was in large part due to Davey's caring nature. In May of 1992, Bill Wesson Sr. the founder of the restaurant, was mysteriously murdered there. The next day the doors were locked. His son, Bill Jr., was too distraught to reopen it.

When Davey returned to Hueytown after racing, he sought out Bill Wesson Jr., finding a sad, solitary figure sitting numbly on the banks of the Black Warrior River, trying to escape from the cruelty and horror of the real world. Davey talked to the distraught Wesson about his own near-death experience when he crashed at Pocono and about the death of Clifford, and he encouraged Wesson to return to the land of the living.

"He said he could have quit racing and I could have just shut the door," said Wesson, "but that we both had to keep living and doing what we loved."

Ten months later Wesson reopened Bill's Farmhouse Restaurant, much to Davey's delight. After eating breakfast there that day with Red Farmer, Davey and

Red hung around Davey's shop until lunchtime, when they went to the Iceburg Cafe in Hueytown. Though Davey usually ordered fried chicken, on this day he ate catfish fillets and french fries.

When the catfish seemed long in coming, Davey and Red pestered waitress Cathy Cole to hurry up.

In the cafe Davey ran into Horace Gray, a friend and an Allison Racing employee. He asked Gray if he wanted to fly with him and Red to Talladega in his new helicopter to watch David Bonnett test his Busch car. Gray declined, saying he had something he had to do.

Shortly after lunch, Davey and Farmer drove to the helicopter pad at Bobby and Judy's house. They strapped themselves into Davey's Hughes 369HS turbojet chopper. The fifty-mile trip east to the Talladega track would take fifteen minutes. The stated reason for going was to see David Bonnett test, but he also was going because it was a good excuse to get in his new toy and fly around. Davey was to be gone for such a short time he didn't even tell Liz he was going. Sue Bonnett saw the helicopter flying overheard as she drove home from food shopping.

As the helicopter reached Lincoln, Red could see the huge Talladega track looming below. Davey decided to land in a paved area near the track's care unit. As Davey brought the craft in for a landing, nurse Ursula Smith waved to Red Farmer, who waved back at her.

The helicopter was hovering just inches off the ground, when suddenly, without warning, it shot straight up and began shuddering from side to side. Smith said she thought Davey was showing off. She didn't think there was trouble.

When the blue and white helicopter jerked up to about thirty feet, its body began to turn counterclockwise under the rotor blades. Witnesses recall hearing a whining sound. The helicopter then rolled on its side and plunged straight down to the macadam.

Farmer described what he recalled: "I could see the sun. I could see the ground, I could see the sky, I could see the dirt and the asphalt, and everything was spinning and the helicopter was just going crazy, and Davey was fighting the controls.

"I braced myself. I put my left hand against the console and my right hand against the window. I guess natural instinct from driving race cars tells you to always brace yourself when you figure something's going to happen. Davey was still fighting the controls and couldn't brace himself. When it went down on the left side, he probably hit his head against the side of the helicopter. Then it flipped over and spun a couple of times and landed on its side."

When the aircraft struck the ground, it crashed hard on the pilot's side. The bubble of the cockpit was shattered by the rotor blade, which had broken off on impact. A couple of witnesses said they thought the back rotor of the helicopter had hit the chain-link fence nearby, but that had not been the case.

According to Eddie Allison, "What happened was, the [main] rotor blade hit the ground, and it broke off, and it rebounded through the cab of the helicopter and cut off the back of Davey's head."

Davey was especially vulnerable because the twenty-year-old helicopter didn't have shoulder harnesses, and Davey wasn't wearing a helmet. None was required. Only a lap belt held him in his seat.

Farmer, in the passenger seat, was lucky not to be hit by the errant rotor blade. But he did not escape unscathed. The force of the impact caused him to suffer broken ribs, a ruptured lung, a broken collarbone, and a broken nose.

As the helicopter lay in a crumpled heap, the motor continued to run wide open. Farmer knew Davey had filled the chopper full of fuel and that the tank was still nearly full, and he was concerned the helicopter was going to blow.

Farmer yelled, "Davey, we gotta get out of here before it catches on fire."

Farmer was desperate to extricate Davey from the wreckage, but he was too badly injured to help. Even if he could have freed Davey, he probably wouldn't have. He had seen wrecks where friends had turned over in race cars.

"If they were hanging upside down," Farmer said, "you don't pull the belts, because if you do, they crash down, and sometimes that hurts them worse than hanging there. And with one arm I couldn't undo the seat belt and hold Davey up at the same time."

Davey did not answer Farmer's plea to get out.

Even though Farmer couldn't help Davey, he was aware help soon would be on the way. He kicked at the broken windshield, shattering it more, and he began to wriggle out.

Neil Bonnett was inside the garage area working on his son's car when he heard the crash.

"What's that?" he asked.

"A helicopter just crashed," he was told.

When Bonnett ran outside, he saw Red Farmer trying to climb out of the helicopter, its motor still running full out. Bonnett helped drag Farmer twenty feet from the craft, out of harm's way.

"Neil, go get Davey, because he's unconscious," Farmer said. "He's got to get out before it catches on fire." While Bonnett ran toward the helicopter, rescue workers from the Talladega track care unit took Farmer to the infield hospital to wait for a rescue helicopter to take him to the Carraway Methodist Medical Center in Birmingham. Farmer would never see Davey again.

Bonnett ran back to Davey even though he was aware the motor was still running and he feared an explosion. As blood poured out of Davey's head, Bonnett tried to undo his seat belt, but because Davey was doubled over, he couldn't do it by himself. Davey was trapped on the upper side of the cockpit by his own weight against his belt.

Bonnett boosted nurse Ursula Smith into the cockpit, and she cut the harness straps, freeing Davey. According to Eddie Allison, "The German nurse told me she had to put his brains back in his skull with her hands. He was about dead, and they just kept him alive because he was an organ donor."

Rescue workers put Davey on a stretcher, and he was taken by a second helicopter to Carraway.

Neil Bonnett, meanwhile, took it upon himself to call Bobby Allison with the tragic news. Bonnett, guilt-ridden, apologized over and over to Bobby for not being able to do more. And then he drove home and sat beside his pool, vainly trying to make sense of it all. Bonnett had owned the pool for perhaps ten years and hadn't spent two hours sitting by it all that time. Now he didn't want to be anywhere else.

Neil, more than anyone, was feeling responsible for Davey's death.

"I think, if I hadn't told him to come [to Talladega to watch David drive], Davey would still be here," he said.

"I almost could not cope with it," said Bonnett. "It really knocked me for a loop because I couldn't do anything. I couldn't help him and I felt so helpless."

At the time of the crash, a helicopter pilot needed to spend fifty-five hours in the air to get a license. According to Davey's instructor, Glen Wenzel, of Mount Airy, North Carolina, Davey had only flown between sixty and sixty-five hours when he went down. As a result, some experts were saying that the copter crashed because of Davey's inexperience.

Eddie Allison, for one, doesn't buy that.

"Davey was a super airplane pilot," Eddie said. "I'm sure he knew what he needed to know to fly that helicopter before he sat in it."

I said to him, "He took a very short period of time to learn to fly that thing."

"When you have that kind of talent," he replied, "why should it take you longer?"

A few days after the crash, as the helicopter was being held upright by a backhoe, Rolf Sasser, a National Transportation Safety Board inspector, declared that there was "no indication Davey had hit the fence and no sign of mechanical failure."

Why the copter did what it did was a mystery, he said.

Eddie Allison, for one, believes otherwise.

"Davey died because something broke," he said. "I know it."

Eddie was working on a crane in Birmingham when he heard the news of the crash.

"I jumped in my truck and hauled ass to the hospital," he said. "I beat the helicopters to the hospital, and I watched them roll both Davey and Red in." Even though Davey was on life support and was breathing, Eddie was told, "Davey's dead." Said Eddie, "You could tell Red would be fine, but Davey looked like a piece of board on a gurney—as flat as a pancake."

Bobby Allison stood in a corridor of the hospital talking to two Catholic priests. Allison looked dazed and unresponsive. Six floors up, Davey was lying in a hospital bed, clinging to life.

"He is in serious, serious condition," said Bobby.

"I'm hoping to hear better news," said racer Mark Martin. "Everybody's praying for him tonight. Miracles do happen, medical or otherwise. He may wake up and be fine tomorrow. That's what we're praying for."

"It's really bad," said Benny Parsons. "It looks like it's going to take a miracle."

Judy Allison had worried every time Bobby, Davey, or Clifford got into a race car. She never once worried about Davey piloting his helicopter. When she saw him, Judy was appalled at what Davey looked like lying there unconscious.

Years later she said, "One of the things that haunts me is that Davey did not like scary movies or spiders. Those were his two big things. He particularly didn't like movies that had mummies in them. And that's kind of what he looked like at the hospital.

"His head was bandaged and swollen and flat on the top. He had blood running out of his nose and his mouth. It really looked bad. And I knew that he himself would not want to look like this."

Sitting beside him, Judy tried to get Davey to communicate with the family, just as Davey had tried to get Bobby to communicate after Bobby's crash at Pocono four years earlier.

"I said to him at one point, 'Davey, you know that we love you, and you know that your dad had this type of injury. You know that when your dad was in the hospital, we didn't know what he was capable of hearing or doing, so we would ask him to do whatever he could, like blink an eye, move a finger, wiggle a toe, anything. If you can do that, would you do it for us?'"

Judy swears that Davey winked an eye, moved a finger, and wiggled his toes. The nurse told Judy she thought Davey had heard her. Judy wanted badly to think he had.

Eddie, who was standing beside her, told Judy, "I think that was Davey's way of saying good-bye."

Eddie went upstairs to see the badly injured Red Farmer. Said Red's daughter Bonnie, "He can't even raise his head. The only thing he can eat is jello, and he vomits that up."

Eddie could see how terribly distraught Farmer was over what had happened to Davey.

Years earlier Eddie and Red had been at Daytona when Don McTavish was involved in a horrendous crash. The front of McTavish's car had been cut off, the engine lying on the ground, as McTavish sat dead in the stopped car, his legs dangling, facing the oncoming traffic. Sam Sommers, seeing the wreckage too late, ran into the debris and cut off Don McTavish's legs.

After the race Eddie and Red sat with the dazed, guilt-ridden Sommers for two hours "to bring him back to the world," as Eddie described it. "He was so shook up."

Eddie said to Farmer, "Do you remember what we had to tell Sam? This is the same deal, man. You weren't supposed to die. You didn't die. Davey did because he was supposed to die."

Later Farmer told reporters he would never get over the pain of Davey's death.

"He's just like my son," he said. "I've known him since the day he was born."

Robert Yates and Larry McReynolds flew immediately to Birmingham, and they spent the evening at the hospital with the family, sure that Davey was going to die.

McReynolds also went to see Red Farmer, who told him, "Larry, we were not five feet off the ground. We were fixing to land. It was so close to the ground I was about ready to open the door to get out. All of a sudden the helicopter started oscillating, and it just got up further and further, and the next thing you know it was up and down on its side. I just don't know what happened.' He said, 'Davey is hurt, and he's hurt bad, and there's no way he'll make it.'"

Larry was asked whether he wanted to go in to see Davey, but after talking to Red, he declined the offer.

"If I thought it would help Davey in any way I would have," said McReynolds, "but I wanted to remember Davey Allison sitting in the back of his airplane, drinking that beer and having a good time with us, cutting up, aggravating me. I didn't want to see him hooked to tubes and wires and breathing machines just keeping him alive for whatever reason. And I'm so thankful I did that."

Davey Allison never regained consciousness. Just after dawn, at seven o'clock on the morning of July 12, 1993, Davey was pronounced dead. He was thirty-two years old. A Georgia heart patient who had been waiting fifty-one days for a new heart received Davey's. It saved his life.

"I was in Davey and Clifford's room when Bobby came into the house and told me about Davey," said Judy. "I was just out of it, but it was worse when we went to the hospital and they said, 'He's gone.' Then I did go crazy. I went *very* crazy. It's just one of those things."

"In the middle of the night, early Tuesday morning, they pronounced him dead, and we flew back to Charlotte," said McReynolds. "Then we went back to Hueytown Wednesday evening with our race team. Our race team was small. Back then we probably weren't more than twenty-five strong, but it was such a close-knit group of guys. Everybody got along, and we always supported each other. Through our struggles in '92 and into '93, you never saw anyone pointing a finger or saying, 'I told you so.' A lot like when a family loses a family member, we all brought our families over to Robert Yates's house. We gathered together, and Robert and I looked at those guys, and we said, 'What do you all want to do? Where do we want to go from here?'

"It was pretty unanimous that we didn't want to go to Pocono. We were going to bury Davey on Thursday, and we just did not feel we could go to Pocono and do a good job with a substitute driver. Because we still had a lot of tears in our eyes. Did we want to send a driver at two hundred miles an hour on a straightaway when we really weren't with the game? No, it wouldn't be fair to anyone.

"Davey would have been real pissed off knowing we didn't go to Pocono, but he wasn't the one having to deal with it. We were. So, like a big family, Robert didn't make that decision. I didn't make that decision. We made it together.

"We went back to Alabama and buried Davey, and we shut the shop down until Monday morning when everyone could get themselves together.

"My wife and I have two children. I said to her, 'I just want to get away for a few days.' We went to the mountains, and nobody knew where we were. I didn't want to have to deal with anything for a few days. I wanted to be with my wife and two kids.

"I don't think you ever get it out of your system. Here it is, years later, and there isn't a day that goes by that I don't remember Davey. I think about him a lot. One reason was that he was such a role model to me, from his attitude toward God, his determination, his constant confidence in the people around him.

"You can't find a bad characteristic about Davey Allison."

Eddie Allison was one of the few who didn't take Davey to task for risking his life flying a jet helicopter.

"Davey was doing exactly what he wanted to do when he got killed," said Eddie. "Davey loved that helicopter.

"I'm with Red; I said it first. I said, 'If Davey malfunctioned and crashed, if he was standing right here right now, he would tell you it was his fault. See, that's why he was such a good race car driver. He would not lie to himself about his weakness. So he could fix it. That's the trouble with the drivers today. They are all hot dogs, so they can't fix what's wrong.

"We don't believe in predestination, but we do believe that God has a plan, and Davey Allison died because he saved everybody on earth he could save while he was alive. The way he brought more people to the Lord was to die, and if you had been to the funeral you'd have seen it. And that's how we get through that."

Liz Allison suddenly was a widow too soon. On the day Davey died, Liz didn't even know he was going to fly. Davey left her a widow with two young children, Krista Marie, three, and Robert, not quite two.

Liz had watched how both Bobby and Davey had handled tragedy, and she, too, decided to soldier on. Said Liz in 1997, "I don't really know what happened. I really don't. I'm probably better off that way.

"People ask me how I handled a tragedy like that. By the grace of God. I mean, that is the truth. When you have children, you take your strength from them. You know you have to get up every day and make things work. I just truly believe that the Lord will not put you in a situation that you can't handle, and that you simply do what you have to do. What people see on the outside is not what is on the inside. So it's a long process, and when little ones are involved, it's even more detailed and confusing.

"I, of course, was not the only one devastated. Unfortunately for Davey's parents, his death tore them apart. Davey will be dead four years, and they have been separated for a year. They are waiting on a court date for their divorce. I'm sure they wouldn't mind me saying this, but as in any marriage, Bobby and Judy had problems off and on. They had separated in the past, worked through the problems and got back together again, and this time I thought they would work through this and be fine. They have been through an awful lot. The two of them have been through more than any two people should have to go through. In situations like this, they either pull together or tear apart. For both of them, I know anger has been a real part of grief. They both have been eaten up with it, and it just tore them apart. And I hate it for them. Hate it.

"I'm still very close to Judy and to both of Davey's sisters. I don't see Bobby quite as much. That's kind of a man thing. But I'm close to them, and I only want the best for them, and I do hate that they have had to go through more heartache.

"When Davey died, immediately afterward I questioned my faith in God. I remember telling someone, 'I prayed with all my heart, prayed on my hands and knees, prayed with everything I had, and Davey still died. And having little ones involved, holy cow, it's very hard to understand. It's hard enough to understand, but when you have little people involved, little hearts, it's even more difficult.

"I felt *very* angry with Davey. And I probably still do. It'll be four years this summer. I feel very angry because of the helicopter. 'Why in the heck did you have to have that helicopter, Davey? Why did you have to have these expensive toys?' "

It had not always been easy for Liz. During the early years of their marriage, Davey was not a dedicated husband and father. Like Bobby, racing was his first love, and everything else came second.

But then Davey's first wife wanted to remarry, and to do that she had to get an annulment from the Church. Once she did that, Davey was free to marry Liz in the Church. And after that ceremony was held, Davey decided to do everything he could to make his marriage to Liz work. During the last two years of his life, Davey was doing all he could for Liz and his children. Liz, for one, clearly saw the change in Davey.

"It's hard to understand those things, but I can say, as weird as it sounds," said Liz, "I am thankful that Davey and I had the two years we had before his death, when Davey became a different man and dedicated his life to his family. Not that the years when we got engaged and married and first started our family weren't wonderful. But those last two years were really special, and because of what I brought away from that, I'm okay where I am now, and it has a lot to do with the way I raise our children.

"I want people to know that Davey was truly an exceptional person. He was a special person. No doubt people will remember his driving talent. That will be remembered forever, but I also want people to know the incredible man he had become in the last years of his life. It's what everybody should strive to be.

"That's how I want people to remember him: as a God-driven person with family number one in his heart and doing something he loved. Davey was a very blessed man."

The next day banners flew in Hueytown with the message: "He's not gone. He's just gone one lap ahead."

CHAPTER 46

Alabama Mourns

"It hurts. Oooh, it hurts. All the joy, all the success, now all the heartache."

—Bobby Allison

On the day of Davey's passing all of Alabama mourned: The loss of a loved one. Promise unfulfilled. The end of a dream.

At the Iceburg Cafe in Hueytown, where Bobby and Davey had eaten lunch three or four times a week, tears flowed.

One customer came in, hugged Davey's picture on the wall, broke down and cried. Another man walked in, saw Davey's picture on the wall, started crying and walked out. He sat in his car and cried for about thirty minutes.

Kenneth Dunlap, the son of Iceburg owner Gay Ann McCrary, said he saw Davey almost daily.

"He was a friend of mine," said Dunlap. "He came in here and would go to the back room just like anybody else. He was always laughing. He wasn't any different than when he was in high school. He still hung out with the same people and did the same things.

"When he got big it didn't change him a bit. It made him a better person."

As soon as he learned of Davey's death, Father Dale Grubba left his home in Princeton, Wisconsin, and traveled to the Allison compound at the end of Church street the morning of July 14.

Father Grubba and Bobby Allison had been longtime friends, and Grubba knew that now, more than ever, he was needed.

Grubba drove to the gates of Bobby's home and saw police turn away grieving fans at the gates. When Grubba drove up, the policeman saw Grubba's collar and let him pass.

Grubba drove up to the house and sat in the car for a few minutes. He thought back to the funeral of President John Kennedy. He had been a seminary student in 1963 and had taken part in that service. He thought back to Rose Kennedy. Father Grubba would say later, "Those of us who lived through that era said the same thing: "How many more of these does the lady have to endure. She, too, was the epitome of tough Irish Catholicism. That deep, deep faith."

As he sat in his car, Kitty Allison, Bobby's eighty-six-year-old mother, walked up to him.

"How much more can Bobby and Judy take, Father?" she asked. "God give them strength."

"They've got people like you, though, who are examples of strength," he replied.

"I just hope I can be enough for them, that's all," she said. "You have to go on and accept it. You can't ask why. Someday we might know. You've got to say, like Davey said, 'When my time comes, I'm gonna go,' and he was philosophical about it right along."

She sighed. "Have you seen them, Father?"

"Just going in now, Mom. How are they doing?"

"It's terrible hard, Father. But everybody has been so wonderful. From all over. All over."

Bobby was standing in his race shop that he and Donnie had built in 1964. Father Grubba walked down the hill to the shop with writer Ed Hinton, who had known the Allisons for twenty years. The shop was crowded with men.

Bobby embraced the priest and told him, "I know I'm a walking miracle. Honestly, I asked for a miracle again when we were in the hospital [with Davey]. I didn't get a miracle. But it doesn't mean I won't ask for another miracle again sometime."

Bobby then looked at Hinton. Their relationship had had its ups and downs. Once Bobby had threatened to punch him in the mouth. The two embraced and both wept.

"It hurts. Oooh, it hurts," Bobby said. "All the joy, all the success, now all the heartache."

"Mine was a racing accident," Bobby said. "Clifford's was a racing accident. But now this. I guess what I'm trying to say, nowhere is safe."

Hours later Bobby stood in the front yard of his home. He attempted a smile and told Hinton, "My religion teaches me that I have to forgive everyone of everything. But no one can convince me that I have to forgive Darrell Waltrip."

As much as the presence of Father Grubba and Ed Hinton buoyed Bobby's spirits, that's how much it infuriated Judy. She had specifically requested no press at the service or at the house, and so when Grubba, who was a newspaper columnist as well as a priest, showed up with Hinton, Judy blew her stack.

"I tried to be there for everybody—for Bobby and our kids and in-laws," she said. "And I wasn't dealing with my own feelings. On the day we buried Davey, we said, 'No press.' And Ed Hinton and Father Grubba showed up at my house, and they had Bobby pinned outside and were interviewing him, and we had just laid Davey in the ground, and I thought that was so uncalled for that I don't have anything for them anymore like I would have. Not even for a priest. Him of all people. He should have known. 'Cause he was the one who got Ed Hinton in there. It just really disturbed me for so many years and upset me so bad. It's only been a couple of years that I can even talk to those guys. I thought it was very uncalled for. They had him pinned there for more than an hour. I mean, it was so uncalled for. I not only was mad at them, I was also mad at Bobby for allowing it. I expressed my anger to all three of them, and I went storming into the house. I was slamming doors. My sisters didn't know what was wrong with me."

That evening Bobby called and invited Neil Bonnett to come over to his house. "I know you have a lot of business deals coming up," Bobby said. "Don't cancel any of them."

"I was totally amazed," said Bonnett. "There he was, in more pain than any of us can imagine, and he took time to worry about me and give me peace of mind.

"He told me he knew I was suffering too, but that the only way to get over it was to go on and live my life."

Inside St. Aloysius Catholic Church a standing-room crowd of over 750 gathered to mourn and pray. Among the mourners was Mario Andretti, himself a racer and proud father of racers.

"Why?" asked Andretti. It was the question on everyone's minds and lips. "It is beyond my comprehension. If ever there was goodness in anyone, it is in that family. The whole family. They are the example of goodness."

At the start of the service, four jet fighters flew over in formation. During the service Judy and Liz Allison spread a white cloth marked with three crosses over Davey's coffin. They wept. Bobby wept. All of Alabama wept.

"Now he's with his brother," said Michael Waltrip. "We have to look at it that way."

It took every piece of fire and police apparatus from Hueytown and Bessemer to block off the two-mile route from the church to the Highland Memorial Gardens in Bessemer. Cars stretched for miles behind the white hearse. The route was lined with thousands of people, many crying. Some held the sign, "Davey's gone one lap ahead." As the funeral procession left the church, one sticker in the rear window of a beat-up Ford read, "If only I had one wish, number 28."

The funeral was attended by an estimated five thousand fans under a relentless summer sun. Davey was buried in his black, red, and gold Texaco driver's suit and hat in a grave only a few feet from where Clifford was laid to rest. Floral arrangements blanketed the grave for weeks. During the ceremony, country and western singer Joe Diffie, accompanied by his guitarist Lee Bogan, played a version of Davey's favorite song, "Ships that Don't Come in." Liz had called Diffie's office seeking the sheet music to the song. Diffie, who had met Davey and Liz "a couple of times," was in California when he got the message. He called her and said he would be honored to sing it at Davey's funeral.

He brought Bogan, and they played dual guitars at the grave while Diffie sang.

The mourning for Davey continued unabated for nearly two weeks. The Bessemer newspaper had an editorial advising parents how to help their children cope with Davey's death. Letters, cards, notes, poems, and telegrams poured in to the Allison family.

"It was as big as Bear Bryant's funeral," said Hut Stricklin. "It was huge. Davey had come into contact with an unbelievable number of people in such a short time. He was the Elvis of Alabama."

Said Eddie Allison, "Today you can go to that cemetery and sit on that marble bench a little bit away from his grave, and somebody will come by and look at that grave."

After the funeral Donnie Allison stood in Bobby's front yard and stared at his mother's house across the street. He was asked if Davey's death finally was too much for the family to bear.

"I don't know if there is too much," said Donnie. "That lady right over there and our dad raised us to believe from the time we were little bitty kids that you put it in the good Lord's hands, and you don't question his decision."

The death of Davey Allison left a huge void in the racing world. Not only was he perhaps the most popular driver on the circuit, he was also the driver anti-Earnhardt fans were counting on to defeat the Intimidator on the racetrack. Davey, like Kyle Petty, was an important link to NASCAR's past. And now he was gone.

The gaping hole in NASCAR's fabric became evident at the Pocono race on July 18. Two drivers, Jimmy Spencer and Hut Stricklin, were there to carry on for the Allison family, but with little enthusiasm. Spencer, who drove for the Bobby Allison Race team, said before the race, "My heart's not in this race like it should be. Bobby's not going to be here.

"This isn't a perfect world. You've got to do what's right. What's right is coming here to the racetrack . . . It's easier said than done."

"I never had a brother," Stricklin said. "Davey was like a brother to me . . . It's very hard to keep focused. As long as I've been running Winston Cup there's always been a number 28 and a Davey Allison out there. Sunday there's not going to be."

In fact, there was no Allison in a Winston Cup race for the first time since November 2, 1975.

The spot where Davey's Texaco transporter would have been was roped off and empty, except for flowers and wreaths that began to pile up there. Allison's pit and his garage areas were unoccupied and bare.

Before the Pocono race, taps was played and tears were shed.

Said Dale Earnhardt, "Davey was a heck of a friend. It's tough to describe the emotions. I want Davey back. We were always competitive and raced hard . . . I want him back."

Earnhardt won the Pocono race, and immediately after crossing the finish line, was handed a flag with the number 28 on it. He waved it as he circled the track on his victory lap. Jimmy Spencer finished twenty-fourth. Hut Stricklin was twenty-eighth.

The next race on the schedule was Talladega, Davey's hometown track. Before the race Liz Allison stood a football field away from her husband's race car, another football field away from the spot where he was killed.

As the assembled multitude stood in silence, Liz stepped forward to the microphone and squeezed both hands of the Rev. Hal Marchman.

"The last two weeks have been really difficult for Robbie, Krista, and myself, and the whole Allison family," she said. "There have been times when we felt that we couldn't go on. But the love and the support that all of the fans have shown to us have been just overwhelming. There's no way we can ever thank each and every one of you for that love.

"Davey is looking down on us today with a big smile on his face for all the love you've shown. These are the things that will help Robbie and Krista know how very special their daddy was to so many people. There's something I would like to share with all of you today that has brought some peace to me, and I hope it will to you."

Over the loudspeaker a recording of "The Fan," a song by the group Alabama, blared out. As the black Texaco Thunderbird with Donnie Allison behind the wheel drove through the track infield and onto the track, the song, written especially to commemorate Davey, was played.

Track officials explained that the members of Alabama had intended to sing the song in person, but were too distraught, hence the recording.

The teary-eyed fans listened to the soothing lyrics:

"Please don't sing sad songs for me,
 Forget your grief and fears.
 For I am in a perfect place.
 Away from pain and tears."

There is no question that Liz Allison had loved her husband very much. She would later say, "I felt like my life was shredded in a million pieces and thrown in front of a fan and blown out across the room."

But life became more difficult for Liz Allison when Davey's friends and fans became aware that she was getting her solace in the arms of another man, in this case country and western singer Joe Diffie, the ex-foundry worker who performed regularly on the Grand Ole Opry in Nashville. Diffie had vaulted onto the charts with his first single entitled, "Bigger Than the Beatles." His other hits include "Prop Me Up Beside the Jukebox" and "John Deere Green," but it was his "Ships That Don't Come In" that Davey Allison loved most and which brought the singer to his funeral.

By mid-October of 1993, newspapers were reporting a Diffie–Liz Allison romance. That Diffie was being sued by his wife Debra for divorce was also fodder for the tabloids.

A lot of Davey's friends and fans were livid. Said one of the customers at the Arts 'N' Hair & Nails beauty parlor in Hueytown, "Three months, heck. He isn't even cold yet. I mourned Judd longer than that. Judd, my dog."

But some were understanding. Said Bill Wesson, "Maybe we expected her to sit around and mourn longer than she did. But Davey was a strong believer that no matter what, life must go on."

Diffie and Liz were stalked by the paparazzi and blitzed by the entertainment media. Film crews camped out on Diffie's and Liz's doorstep trying to interview them. Snoops went through their trash cans. With all the publicity about his affair with Liz Allison, Diffie became a megastar, and his album *Honky Tonk Attitude* climbed to the top of the charts.

Before long, Diffie couldn't go anywhere around the country and western circuit without being mobbed.

In January of 1994 Liz and Diffie went on a cruise together. That summer his wife Debra sued Diffie for divorce. Even though Diffie didn't contest, in July of 1994 the Franklin, Tennessee, family court chancellor turned Diffie's life into even more of a soap opera, as articles abounded throughout the land about Diffie's "cheating heart." When the chancellor ordered him to make a list of all the women he had had relations with during his marriage, there was a great clamor to see who was on it. He acknowledged his relationship with Liz, but the rest of the list was kept secret when the chancellor ordered it sealed. Debra won a "very generous" settlement. Diffie also had to pay all court costs.

By October of 1994 there were published reports that Liz's romance with the singing star had cooled. By November of 1995 it was over, as he announced he was concentrating on making his next album, *Life's So Funny*.

"It's almost like that never happened," she said.

In 2000 Liz married Ryan Hackett, a therapist who works at Vanderbilt University Hospital. They live in Brentwood, Tennessee. Liz has written several books, including one on racing wives, and in 2003 she was hired by TNN to be a color commentator at the Nextel Cup races.

There was one unfortunate ramification of the Diffie-Liz romance. At the time Liz and Diffie were dating, Judy and Bobby had widely divergent views on what she was doing.

"As long as she isn't doing anything illegal and is taking care of my grandchildren, that's all I care about," said Judy.

Bobby for his part was adamant and furious that what she was doing with Diffie wasn't right.

"I was furious that Liz was living with Joe Diffie right after Davey's death," said Bobby. "To my mind, he certainly was making the most of the opportunity. It was obvious he was living at the house. I still don't know the right way to even talk about it. It was something I didn't like, and a lot of people didn't like. If I had had better mental health, I'm sure I could have dealt with it, but in my condition, it was way better to run."

According to friends, the issue was one that helped drive a wedge between them.

CHAPTER 47

Hut: Scarred

"It seemed like the people from Alabama were doomed. And I was next."

—**Hut Stricklin**

Throught the 1992 season Hut Stricklin complained he wanted a race team that would bust its butt to help him win, and he felt he wasn't getting that. He would go into the garage area on a Saturday night when he felt his crew should have been working on the car. Instead, he would see them at the nearest bar or club.

"I was getting paid on time, and I was getting treated more than fair," said Stricklin. "The only thing—and Jimmy [Fennig] has changed, and I have changed—Father Time has taken his toll; he settled down, and I'm sure I did, too, our biggest disagreement was that the team loved to party. More than anything, it tore our team apart.

"Every weekend was a big party. What I complained about was that we would always be the first ones out of the garage on a Saturday evening.

"I'd say, 'That's fine if we're winning races, but when we're falling out of races because stuff is breaking or is getting overlooked,' that's where I had problems.

"I said, 'We need to put more focus on the car and let's get our priorities straight.' When I started complaining, that's when things started to turn sideways.

"I went to Bobby and I said, "We have a possibility of a championship-caliber team here. But we've got to slow down on the partying. We've got to get our focus on racing."

"Bobby didn't say a whole lot as far as wanting to do anything about it. I don't know if he was capable of doing anything about it at the time.

"To make a long story short, I didn't feel things were going to change, to get any better for me, and if I was going to take a chance and better myself, I needed to move on."

Late on the 1992 season Junior Johnson called Stricklin to drive the prestigious McDonald's car the next year. When Bobby overhead his driver bragging about it, he fired him on the spot. "Okay, go now," he said.

"Hut reminds me a lot of Bill Elliott or Darrell Waltrip," said Johnson, who won driving championships with both. "He's really a calm driver. He has a gentle feel for a car. I think he'll be just as good as Darrell or Bill or David Pearson." Unfortunately, it didn't work out that way.

At any other time in Johnson's long and celebrated career, it would have been a coup for Stricklin, who had been wooed by the Petty organization and a couple of other race teams as well. But this was 1993, and at the age of sixty-one, Junior had two serious problems that would curtail his racing activity. He and Flossie Johnson had been married for forty years, but their love had cooled, and Junior fell in love with a younger woman. When Flossie sued him for divorce, it was ugly. Junior, moreover, would have triple bypass heart surgery in March 1993. His days as a car owner, as successful as he had been, were coming to an end.

"I thought it was my best opportunity," said Stricklin. "Of course, I didn't know Junior had all the personal stuff going on. The timing was off."

When he arrived, the thirty-one-year-old Stricklin found that Junior's shop was a whole lot more laid back even than Bobby's.

"I might pull into the shop and find none of the guys there. They were out in the back working in the garden," said Stricklin. "But I saw a lot of things that gave Junior an advantage over other people. They weren't afraid to cheat. That was to their advantage, but as things changed, you couldn't bend the rules as much as you used to. I think that was one of the reasons Junior got out of racing. They took out a lot of the ingenuity."

Stricklin was joining a two-car race team. Johnson's other driver, Bill Elliott, was a taciturn, humorless, private man who, curiously, ended up being voted NASCAR's most popular driver year after year.

"It took me the better part of a whole year to get to know Bill," said Stricklin. "I thought, This guy is something. He doesn't talk. Finally, he started loosening up, and the more I was around him, the more I liked him. He didn't really communicate a whole lot with the outside world. At that time so many people were pulling and tugging on him, it was hard for him to decide who to talk to."

Stricklin wasn't part of the Johnson race team a week before Junior fired Elliott's crew chief, Tim Brewer, and replaced him with Stricklin's crew chief, Mike Beam. Stricklin and Beam communicated well. When Junior moved Beam to Elliott's team, he replaced him with an old-timer, Mike Hill.

Stricklin began the 1993 season in grand style, finishing fourth in the Daytona 500. Three car lengths was all that kept Stricklin from winning what would have been his first, and certainly his most memorable, Winston Cup race. After the race, a sub-dued Stricklin confided in Pam that he was sure the season was going to turn out to be a disaster. No one but he knew it, but he had constantly fought with Mike Hill, for whom he had no respect.

"After the race Pam and I went back to the motel," said Stricklin. "We were rid-ing up the elevator, and I looked at her and said, 'We're in trouble.'

" 'What?' she said. 'You just finished fourth in the Daytona 500.'

"I said, 'I know we're in trouble. I don't think we're going to click with these people.'

"And boy, that came true. Things progressively got worse and worse and worse through the whole year. I didn't get along with the crew, and Mike Hill, the crew chief, was the worst one. First of all, in my opinion he was not crew-chief capable. He got handed the job, and where Junior was at the time, either he couldn't get someone else to come up there because of the location . . . I know money wasn't the problem. Junior would have spent the money.

"We fought. If I wanted it tighter, Mike wanted it looser. If he wanted it looser, I wanted it tighter. If I wanted black, he wanted white. It was a big ego thing for him. He wanted to be the one to make the calls. And I didn't care who made the calls. I just wanted the car to run as fast as it could run."

Red Farmer, for one, could feel Stricklin's pain.

"Doing well has a lot to do with chemistry," said Red Farmer. "Hut almost never got with a crew chief who made him feel comfortable in a car. Or maybe he needed something no crew chief could give him. A lot of times people just don't hit the right combination together. It's one reason they don't put two bulls in the same pas-ture. Bobby Allison and Junior Johnson should have been terrific together, but Ju-nior had his way about things, and Bobby had his way about things, and they never could bend to get it together. They were always pulling the wagon in two directions. Hut faced a lot of that. There are so many reasons behind it, you don't ever know what the reasons are."

Stricklin, fighting with Hill all the way, was convinced he was snakebit. And then on July 13, 1993, his emotional state worsened when Davey Allison crashed his helicopter at Talladega and died. Had circumstances been different, Hut, too, would have been in the helicopter that day.

"I flew to Loudon, New Hampshire, with Davey, and after the race I was going to fly home with him to Alabama," said Hut. "But I ate dinner in Loudon, and four of my teammates and I got food poisoning, and I couldn't leave until Monday morn-ing, so I told Davey to go on home without me.

"If I had gone with him, I know what would have happened. Neil Bonnett's son, David, was testing the very next day at Talladega, and I know Davey would have said, 'Hey, go with me tomorrow, fly with me in my helicopter, and we'll go see him race.' And I would have gone. Instead, I wasn't there. I was glad the way it turned out."

Davey's death was just one in a string of several incidents in 1993 to scar Stricklin.

"A lot of things affected me that year," he said. "Not only Davey's death. Mike Crawford, my best friend growing up in Calera, got killed two or three months later in a car wreck, and then Stanley Smith, who I was friends with, got injured real bad at Talladega in the very next race.

"It seemed like the people from Alabama were doomed. And I was next. Oh yeah. You couldn't help but feel it. You tried to put it on the back burner, but still it was there, especially when people kept bringing it up. I was the last of the Alabama Gang."

CHAPTER 48

Bobby and Judy: No Peace

"It was so incredibly wonderful for people to feel that way about Davey, but it kept us torn up all the time. It didn't allow any healing."

—Judy Allison

After Davey died, Bobby and Judy were inundated with well-wishers and fans seeking to pay their respects. They were well-meaning, but every visitor brought fresh pain to their lives. Bobby's brother Eddie suggested the two get in their motor home and disappear for a few weeks, drive around the country and try to find some joy in life. Judy embraced the idea. She even brought a jug of wine with her as she went out the door. Bobby, who loved the attention from the fans nearly as much as Judy hated it, reluctantly went along. They headed for the Land Between the Lakes in northwest Tennessee and Kentucky.

"During the trip I was in a daze," said Bobby. "She was suffering with the facts of what happened. I was just suffering. I really believe if the whole thing had been left up to me, we would have stayed home in Hueytown and people would have come. But my brother Eddie said, 'Get in that thing and get out of here.'"

"Bobby was in his own mode, and he was a little distant," said Judy. "We didn't communicate as well as maybe we should have during that period. Mostly, he wanted to go somewhere, stay one night, and move on, not staying in any one place. A couple of times we stopped where he could go fish, but he didn't want to help me fish, so it was kind of one-sided. But we did have a bit of a break. One time we got off the beaten path, and we drove the back roads, really skinny roads, up and down and twisted, and we had to figure our way out. We were in Tennessee, even Kentucky, and we ended up coming out at I-77 in North Carolina."

While they were on the road, they kept in touch with relatives via their cell phone, a recent phenomenon. Like a lot of new cell phone customers, they weren't aware of the steep roaming charges, and after two weeks on the road, they came home to find a bill for six hundred dollars.

Bobby finally got tired of being a nomad.

"I wanted to go home," he said.

When Bobby and Judy returned to Hueytown, they found that little had changed. After they returned, Bobby stayed in his home, secluded and alone.

"Where could he go?" said Eddie. "He was devastated. We were in his bedroom sitting on the floor talking after we buried Davey, and Bobby wanted to go out to the airport and fill the plane full of fuel and head southwest and turn it on autopilot, and just go to sleep and let the plane run out of fuel and land in the ocean. But he stopped himself. He was still strong enough in his faith, even though that's what he wanted to do."

"It was really tough, because I was in recovery, mentally as well as physically," said Bobby. "I still had a reasonable amount of memory loss, even though I had regained quite a bit of memory, especially stuff away from racing. Some of my different projects did come back to me, including the memory that I had been flying an airplane, which meant an awful lot to me."

Thanks to Judy's prodding, Bobby was able to learn to fly again, and after Chuck Stallings returned from Vero Beach, Bobby once again had someone to help him work on his airplane. He decided that he wanted to take the turbine engines from his first Aerostar and put them in his newer Aerostar Superstar. He hired Stallings to do that, but this time, he found a different, less tolerant Chuck Stallings.

"Chuck wanted to do what Chuck wanted to do," said Bobby. "He found out real early in my recovery that if he wanted to do something I didn't want to do, all he had to do was yell at me. And if he yelled at me, I'd sit down and cry, and I'd tell him, 'Do what you want to do.'"

It pains Bobby to talk about it, because Chuck Stallings for quite a while was his closest companion, and it wasn't very long before they became estranged.

"My relationship with Chuck was so good," said Bobby, "and I lost him. As I think of the guy now, I liked him so much, but then all of a sudden, we couldn't agree on things, and he was doing what he wanted to do."

When Bobby asked Stallings to install the turbine engines in the second Aerostar, Bobby says Stallings told him, "All right, I'm doing what you want done. Get out of here and shut up."

Said Bobby, "He destroyed the first airplane taking it apart. He took the engines off, unbolted them, and took what he needed as far as what had to be bolted onto the second Aerostar, but he cut wires and actuator cables just because they were in his way, instead of unbolting the thing and moving them aside so the parts could be reused. And his remark to me was, 'This plane has to be grounded, so I don't have to save anything.'

"I allowed that, because at the time I had no ability to reason or resist. So here was airplane number one sitting outside the hangar destroyed. It was so sickening. I never should have allowed him to take that airplane apart."

According to Bobby, Chuck Stallings began to resent him.

"I paid him well," he said. "I had given him a bonus when we flew the first airplane, but he wasn't getting the big dollars, and he wasn't getting the credit by Piper and the aviation magazines for the things that we were getting done."

Despite the disharmony, Bobby continued to tolerate Stallings's behavior while his Aerostar Superstar was being refitted, but their relationship ended after he, Judy, and Stallings flew to the funeral of Benny Parsons' wife in late spring 1991.

They got in the Aerostar, and Bobby flew the plane to North Wilkesboro, Benny's hometown, for the funeral. The plane was fitted with all the modern gear, including top radio equipment and equipment for instrument flying. Bobby even had a radar unit that had graphics on it for the radio.

"You could put a radio station in its location on the screen," said Bobby, "but then you could make a phantom station by entering the right coordinates. To make an approach to the North Wilkesboro airport, you had to enter a phantom station.

"North Wilkesboro is Hickory VOR 32 degrees, 16 miles."

In preparation for landing, Chuck Stallings entered the coordinates, only instead of entering them correctly, he inadvertently switched the two numbers, putting in "VOR 16 degrees, 32 miles."

It was overcast, and the plane was in the clouds. When they arrived within radio distance of the airport, Stallings called and got permission from Greensboro to make an approach to land. They would have to fly below radar coverage. The airport was nestled between tall mountains.

Bobby knew the area. He had flown into the North Wilkesboro airport dozens of times to race. Stallings had also been there before.

Bobby did not want to drop below the minimum, the lowest attitude you can legally go under in instrument conditions. If you don't see the ground at those minimums, you are supposed to pull up and go around again.

They dropped down to where they were supposed to see the ground or call for a missed approach, and they didn't see the ground, so they called in a missed approach. They climbed back up, and they were back in touch with Greensboro approach control, but they were not yet on Greensboro radar.

"We had a missed approach," Bobby said. "We have to go back and try again."

"Okay, you're cleared for another RNav approach to North Wilkesboro airport," replied the voice in the tower. RNav was the phantom station.

They went back around again. The phantom airport was set up on the screen. They were inbound again, back down to minimums, still in the clouds, and suddenly Chuck Stallings shouted, "Goddamn, pull up. I just killed us all. I just killed us all. Goddamn."

The top of the clouds was very low, and Bobby pulled the plane higher and higher until he could see sunshine.

"Chuck, we ain't dead," Bobby said. "Shut up."

Stallings, petrified, turned toward his window and didn't answer.

"He wouldn't answer me," said Bobby. "He wouldn't do anything, and I was flying the airplane, and we'd made this second missed approach, and we're so late we were going to miss the funeral."

Bobby told the air traffic controller, "We missed again. We want to call it off and return to base." Base was Bessemer, Alabama.

"Climb to 10,000," the controller told him.

"I was on top of these clouds," said Bobby, "but now I see I don't have enough fuel."

Bobby said to the controller, "We have to land." He didn't say "for fuel," because a pilot is never supposed to put himself in a position where he doesn't have the fuel to get where he's going. "You tell them you have to go to the bathroom or something," Bobby explained.

The controller said, "Asheville is below minimums. Charlotte is behind you 150 miles, and it is right at minimums. Spartanburg is below minimums. Where do you want to go?"

"Look and see if Knoxville is okay," Bobby said.

"Knoxville is okay" was the reply.

"We want to make a rest stop at Knoxville," said Bobby.

"Okay, you are cleared to Knoxville."

As they flew west, they could see patches of ground below, holes in the clouds. Bobby saw the Severeville airport, not far from Kingsport.

Bobby said something to Stallings, but Stallings would not respond. He continued to stare out his window.

"I see Severeville," Bobby said to the controller. "Cancel IFR and land at Severeville."

"Okay. Cleared to the frequency."

Bobby called Severeville and told the tower he was landing, and requested fuel while he was on the ground. He landed and taxied to the fixed base operation.

Judy went to the bathroom, and so did Bobby, who instructed the young man with the fuel truck that his plane took jet fuel, unique for an Aerostar.

"My turbine engines took jet fuel," said Bobby. "I had to be careful every time I flew my Aerostar."

When Bobby exited the bathroom, Chuck was going in. After he returned to the plane, he went back to where he was sitting in the copilot's seat and again turned toward the window in silence.

Bobby flew the plane back to Bessemer. Stallings never said a word the entire trip. After Bobby landed the plane and taxied it to his spot in the hangar, Judy got out first. Chuck exited next. As he came out of the door of the plane, Judy pushed her finger into his nose, pushed it sideways, and said, "I will never fly anywhere with this guy again."

Their Buick Park Avenue was waiting for them in the hanger. She went in the car and slammed the door.

"Which told me this was a done deal," said Bobby. "I turned to Chuck and said, 'You're finished. You get your stuff and get out of this hangar. I will see you later.'"

Bobby drove Judy home and then drove back to the hangar. Chuck was loading his tools into his pickup truck.

"What went wrong?" Bobby asked him.

"I put the numbers in the RNav in backwards," Stallings replied. "I put 16 degrees and 32 miles instead of 32 degrees and 16 miles. We must have flown down somebody's driveway there in the mountains."

"We should have been dead," said Bobby. "We should have flown into the side of a mountain." Almost ten years later a plane carrying Rick Hendrick's son and nine members of his family and race team did exactly that not far from that spot.

"He felt so bad he never really talked to me much after that," said Bobby. "No apology, no nothing. His answer was, 'I put the numbers in backward.' That's why he said, 'I killed us. I killed us.'

"So now I have this really neat airplane, and I have a little Grumman Cheetah. But I have nobody to work on my plane. I decided if I needed to do any more work on the plane, I would do it myself."

It would be one of the last trips Bobby and Judy would take together for a long while. A wall was going up between the two of them. More than anything, Bobby wanted to be alone with his misery, and he had finally developed enough confidence to be able to fly off by himself. Sometimes he would get shaken when things about a flight weren't going perfectly, but nothing so bad he couldn't eventually get out of it. It wasn't too long before Bobby would get in his plane and fly off. He might go anywhere. He might visit Jim Reaves, a friend from Atlanta who was with the FAA. Or he could go to his condo at the Charlotte Motor Speedway.

"I would sit in my chair and watch TV and be mad at the world," said Bobby. "I spent a lot of time where I actually accomplished zero. For meals, I'd go to one of the markets and get some kind of prepared food and take it back and eat it."

Back home, Judy had to entertain the guests, who continued streaming to the house in search of Davey's spirit, pay the bills, keep up the spirits of her surviving daughters. By 1996, Judy couldn't take it any longer.

"She wanted to be away from the house on Church Street," said Bobby. "The fans never quit coming. Every day fans came. On some weekends it was almost a parade. People would get out of the car and come ring the bell and cry and carry on. It was so incredibly wonderful for people to feel that way about Davey, but it kept us torn up all the time. It didn't allow any healing. There was no getting away from the problem and letting things heal. So Judy moved to an apartment on the east side of Birmingham."

There was another reason for the rift between Judy and Bobby. Clifford's widow had two daughters who Clifford had adopted and one they had together. Clifford's wife and Judy hadn't gotten along, and after Clifford died, Judy claimed she kept getting rebuffed when she wanted to see her three grandchildren, especially Clifford's daughter. So Judy took Clifford's widow to court. Bobby, who disliked any and all confrontation, didn't agree with what Judy was doing.

"During this time I had difficulty with Bobby not understanding certain things that were going on," said Judy. "One of them was the trouble I was having with Clifford's wife. I wanted visitation rights to see our grandchildren, and she wouldn't agree to that. I thought it would be a great healing process for us and for her daughter. I wasn't excluding her other daughters, but she was in a frame of mind at the time that she didn't understand what was going on, and you couldn't reach her. So we had difficulties.

"I had difficulties with Bobby, because he had suffered a trauma, and then Clifford was an added trauma for him, and Davey was even worse, and so his thinking went backward rather than forward. And so it ended up Bobby and I were in conflict about a lot of stuff, mostly over the grandchild and what was going on. I wanted grandparent visitation. Bobby thought I wanted custody. And I couldn't reach him. So it caused such a thing in him that then it was like we didn't agree about anything.

"So I moved out, thinking that maybe we could get it back together. And that didn't work. I stayed in the apartment in Birmingham two years, hoping things would get back together, but they didn't. And I did get grandparents' visitation, and I did it like I should, and I did have all the kids together at times."

CHAPTER 49

The Death of Neil Bonnett

"As long as we have life, we'll have death."

—Bobby Allison

Those who knew Neil Bonnett best understood that he was miserable when he wasn't back behind the wheel of a race car after his crash at Darlington and his recovery from amnesia in 1990. For three years Bonnett sat on the sidelines while he worked as a TV commentator for CBS, TBS, and TNN.

One of the commentators alongside him, Ned Jarrett, said that Bonnett "was a natural for it. Neil was destined to become one of the best analysts ever to come down the pike."

Buddy Baker also worked with Bonnett in the announcer's booth. Baker could see firsthand how badly Bonnett wanted to drive again.

"I feel like I knew Neil quite well, because he and I broadcast together for three years," said Baker. "After his crash at Darlington, he sat out those three years. People say he never should have gone back to racing, but I can tell you why he did it. All the time he was broadcasting, he was testing for Dale Earnhardt, and he was running lap times that were as good as anybody.

"He told me, 'This is what I'd really like to do.' TV was just a sideline for him. When he got healthy enough, he said, 'I'm going back out there. I haven't done the things I want to do yet.' We talked about it, and I said, 'Neil, you are so good on TV.' He said, 'Buddy, driving is what I want to do.' I said, 'Well then, go for it.'

"I've often said, it's not how many years you are here, it's how well you've lived the ones you're on."

And Bonnett was unhappy.

Bobby Allison, Davey Allison, Dale Earnhardt, and car owner Richard Childress all had seen this, and each in his own way did what he could to nudge a hesitant, depressed Bonnett back into racing.

In May of 1992 Davey let Neil substitute for him driving the car in practice at Charlotte. In February of the next year Dale Earnhardt let Neil test his car before Dale won the Goody's 300 at Daytona. Neil also drove Earnhardt's backup car in a Winston West event in Texas, and in Winston Cup events at Talladega and again at Atlanta.

Bonnett credited Earnhardt for the improvement of his mental health after his amnesia.

"People joke about Earnhardt and myself," said Bonnett. "But I don't care how much therapy you do, what he did was incredible. He stuck by me more than anybody when I was down. My best rehabilitation was when Dale asked me to climb into his race car."

Said Susan Bonnett, "Dale Earnhardt encouraged him a lot, and he would tell me, 'There is nothing wrong with Neil except he has lost his confidence.' Which had happened even before the accident. Things hadn't been going well, and Neil was questioning himself. Davey Allison, too, had encouraged Neil, had him warm up his car in a couple of places, and Richard Childress also kept encouraging him."

When Richard Childress and Dale Earnhardt gave Neil Bonnett the opportunity to race again, Bonnett's doctor in Birmingham was dead-set against his driving. Earnhardt decided what his buddy needed was a second opinion.

"The doctor here told us it wouldn't be a good idea for Neil to get hit in the head again," said Susan Bonnett. "Neil was wanting to race again but didn't feel he had the confidence to do it. Dale said, 'There is nothing wrong with him except his confidence level.' So he took him to a well-known doctor in Charlotte and had him checked out, and NASCAR had him checked out, and they felt he was in good shape physically."

A lot of people didn't want Bonnett to race again, but Richard Childress chided them.

"No one knows what's inside a man and how much this chance means to him. No one should tell another person what to do."

Bonnett first announced his return to racing at a press conference at Talladega the morning of July 13, 1993. Later that afternoon, Davey Allison crashed his jet helicopter at the track and died. Bonnett's stated return was obscured in the avalanche of news about Davey.

Bonnett returned to racing after a three-year absence at Talladega on July 25, 1993. When he went out onto the track, he began to cry, so happy was he to be back behind the wheel of a race car. But a third of the way through the race, Bonnett's Richard Charles Racing Chevrolet turned sideways, became airborne, flew over the hood of Ted Musgrave's car and crushed a chain-link fence. Bonnett miraculously wasn't hurt. The race was red-flagged for an hour and ten minutes while repair crews fixed the fence. The last time that had happened at Talladega was back in 1987, when Bobby Allison did it.

Said Bonnett, "That wreck wasn't near as bad as it looked."

The next day Eddie Allison had to visit a friend who lived on Sylvan Springs Road, about five miles from the Bonnett residence, and on the way back he decided to have a talk with Neil.

"I pulled into Victory Lane, the street to his house, and we got to talking," said Eddie. "I said, 'Neil, for gosh sakes, you don't need to drive the race car any more. There is no point. You have your TV show. I'm telling you, you don't need to do it anymore.'

"His personality really came across great on the television. He had it, but he wanted to drive.

"Neil said, 'I gotta drive. I gotta.'

"I said, 'No, you don't.' But he *had* to drive."

The fact was, the other drivers were worried about him. He had suffered injuries bad enough to send him to the hospital seven years in a row. They didn't want him driving.

"Fact is, none of us wanted him to race," said Morgan Shepherd. "Even at Talladega, and that was an accident he could get up and walk away from. We told him he should stay away."

Neil then entered the final race of the season, but only managed a single lap before the engine quit. But Bonnett was undeterred. When it was announced that NASCAR would race at the Indianapolis Speedway in August 1994, Bonnett was determined to be one of the drivers in that inaugural race.

The offer Bonnett received to drive again came from James Finch, who was being sponsored by Country Time lemonade drink. Neil was to run at Indianapolis, Charlotte, and Talladega. Daytona was not on the schedule. Then the Country Time executives decided they wanted to run at Daytona after all.

Said Bonnett, "It took only two seconds to talk me into it." Bonnett was predicting that his would be one of the greatest comebacks of all time.

On February 11, 1994, forty-seven-year-old Neil Bonnett went out onto the Daytona track for the first day of practice before qualifying trials, which were to be held the following day. About ten laps into the session, Rick Mast dropped a driveshaft and left oil on the track in turns one and two. Practice was halted. Crews went and cleaned it up, and minutes later practice resumed.

Bonnett drove another ten laps. Shortly after noon, while speeding around the track in his pink and yellow Country Time Chevrolet with the number 52 on its side, he drove into the fourth turn, and then without warning, veered down toward the safety apron. To correct for the skid, he turned his wheels all the way to the right. When the nose of his car hit the apron of the track, the wheels hooked, and the car shot nearly head-on into the unyielding concrete wall.

Driver Jerry Hill was right behind Bonnett when he crashed.

"All I saw was him spinning toward the apron, and then he went head-on into the wall. It just seemed like he lost control for some reason."

Kyle Petty said he thought a strong gust of wind might have pushed Bonnett's car toward the outside wall, making him lose control. Hill thought Bonnett might have hit a slick spot on the track. But NASCAR officials said the track had been checked for oil before practice was allowed to resume.

Said Chip Williams, the PR director of NASCAR, "The best we could tell it was driver error." The statement upset race fans and the Bonnett family terribly. "People knew it wasn't that," said son David. NASCAR later retracted its statement.

The *Orlando Sentinel* did an investigation and found the probable cause of the accident was a three-dollar screwlike piece called a shock absorber mounting stud that held the right shock absorber to the car. According to experts, when the stud fails, the car goes straight into the wall.

A rescue crew ran to cut Bonnett out of the car. When a blue tarp was thrown over the car, everyone knew it was bad.

"You just feel sick inside," said Darrell Waltrip.

Bonnett was taken by ambulance to Halifax Medical Center, where he was pronounced dead at 1:17 P.M. He had massive head injuries.

Said Butch Nelson, president of Bonnett's Honda dealership and his friend of twenty-five-years, "I guess if Neil could have written his exit out of this life, this is the way he'd choose. But it's sure not the way I wanted it to happen."

Said racer Dale Jarrett, "I'm sure a lot of people wonder why Neil Bonnett ever got back into a race car again after what he had gone through in 1990 and then the things he had seen happen to his very close friends, the Allison family."

Said Dale Jarrett's dad, Ned, "If there's any consolation, he died doing exactly what he loved doing. He wanted to drive a race car again. He knew the risks involved."

Dale Earnhardt echoed those sentiments. He said, "Racing was everything to him. He wasn't happy when he couldn't race. It really meant something to him for somebody to say, 'Hi,' or 'How ya doing?' or to talk to him instead of ignoring him because he wasn't a race car driver. He had a lot of people ignore him that he thought were friends, and that hurt.

"You try to say, 'Why did this happen? Why did he come back? He wanted to drive a race car. He never wanted to stop. For everything to happen like it did, it seems . . .'"

Earnhardt turned melancholy. He added, "That first couple of laps on the racetrack, and he's gone after getting his own car, his own deal. Is that fair?"

After Bonnett's wreck, Bobby Allison was driven to the hospital, where he and several longtime friends kept a quiet vigil. Bonnett was more of a brother than a friend to Bobby, who spent much of the day trying to comfort Bonnett's relatives and friends.

"He was one of the best friends I've ever had," he said. "Neil was a person who cared for me individually in a really special way. It was his basic makeup anyway to care for people. But I had the good fortune of having a special relationship with him.

"How do you judge if it makes sense or not? What do we know? What are we supposed to be entitled to?"

Raad Cawthon, reporter for the *Atlanta Constitution,* asked Bobby whether the death of his two sons, the crippling of his own body, the injury to his brother, and now the death of his close friend, whether the accumulation of all this tragedy made things harder to accept.

"Oh yeah," said Bobby. "But when the line of whether too much is being asked of me tries to come into my mind, I make myself say, 'I don't have to like it, but I have to accept it.'"

Bobby said he told a close friend that he wondered whether he should quit. "But quit what? That's the part you don't get to choose. I don't know that I'm looking for solace in anything. I either have to accept what happens or stop the world and get off."

Said Allison, "As long as we have life, we'll have death."

The day of Neil Bonnett's fatal crash, his wife, Susan, and a friend had left her Hueytown home at seven in the morning.

"We were driving from here to Daytona," she said. "I had never had a cell phone in the car before. My daughter had given me hers. She said, 'You don't need to be traveling without a cell phone.' I said, 'Don't call me on it, because it will scare me to death.'

"As I was nearing Tallahassee, Florida, the phone rang. It scared me and my friend who was with me. My daughter called, and I told her, 'Don't call us anymore unless it's an emergency.' She just laughed. She said, 'I wanted to make sure you knew how to answer it and work it.'

"And when the next call came, that really did scare us.

"James Finch called me first. He told me that Neil had been in a bad wreck in practice and wanted to know where I was. He said, 'We're going to see if we can meet you and pick you up.'"

Track officials wanted to fly Susan to Daytona, but it was quicker for her to continue driving than to detour to a local airport where she could be picked up.

"Of course, they didn't tell me that Neil was gone," said Susan. "They told me it was bad, and I should get there as fast as possible.

"It was just a horrible time, stuck in the car. I wouldn't let my friend turn on the radio. I didn't want to hear anything. Then my son called, and he said, 'We'll meet you there.' He was home in Alabama.

"I said, 'How are you going to get there?'

"He said, 'James said he was sending a plane to pick us up, and we'll be there to meet you.' He sent the plane to pick up my children and Neil's parents. They knew before they left home that Neil didn't make it. But they had not told me.

"When I called the hospital back, they would direct me to a girl named Stephie, who worked for World Sports. I kept asking her, 'Is he alive?' She kept saying, 'Last we heard, he was.' She never did tell me.

"When I got about an hour from Daytona, Max Helton, the pastor with Chapel at the Track called me. He said, 'We know you're almost here. We debated whether to tell you, but we don't want you to hear it on the radio,' and before he could say another word, I handed the phone to my friend because I knew what he was fixing to tell me.

"We were stuck in traffic, not even moving, when they met us with a police escort and took me straight on to the hospital. My family was already there. It had been a long ten-hour trip. It seemed like forever."

I said to this remarkable woman, "What was amazing to me was the patience you showed when Neil was first becoming a race driver. If you had been some other wife, my guess is you could have derailed that from the start."

"I don't know," she said. "I've always been told that two things I am are faithful and patient. If Neil were here, he probably would not agree with the second one, but, yeah, I think I'm pretty patient, and I think when you love somebody totally you have to honor what they love to do.

"I might not be so patient today as I was then, because I realized I could have changed some things, but I can't go back and do that, and I won't live in the past.

"Who of us doesn't wish there are things we could change? Thank God, everything that has happened in my life has brought me to today. I'm happy. I'm healthy, and I give abundant thanks to God. I don't know if I would have gotten here any other way."

"He had made a comeback," said Humpy Wheeler, "and a lot of people didn't think too much of that. He drove hard, so he crashed hard. Unfortunately, the wreck that claimed his life was something I'm sure he told many, many rookies not to do, and that's try to save the race car. He lost the car and he tried to save it. It bit, and it came right back out and hit the wall at that horrific one o'clock angle."

"He was so far behind in his steering he just got the car where he couldn't steer it, and he ended up dead," said Eddie Allison. "It's really sad, but again, I'm a firm believer in how few people die doing what they love to do.

"And basically, the danger factor is small. You can get killed walking across the street. You don't get killed in a race car wrecking, because race cars are built to wreck. If you get killed, it's because something abnormal happens."

It was Sunday, the morning of the 1994 Daytona 500, and Dale Earnhardt was philosophical.

"We lost a lot of guys in the old days, many more than now," he said, "but racing is a tough sport. It's tough to follow it and see some of the tragedy that can happen. And it doesn't happen often. Our safety record is pretty good.

"You know, if the Lord's willing, and we win this race, I can truly dedicate it to Neil, because Neil has had such a hand in preparing my race car.

"You know, he's pretty much with me all the time, in mind and thought, and I think he'll be even closer today.

"I'm going to take him along with me in my heart."

After the race, won by Sterling Marlin, someone asked Earnhardt why he was smiling.

"Because it's Daytona," he said, "and I'm alive."

On Monday, February 13, 1994, there was a memorial funeral service for Neil Bonnett at Garywood Assembly of God in Hueytown. His coffin lay under a black and white floral display designed to look like a checkered flag.

During the service, Lynn Northcutt, a cousin, sang "Oh, What a Beautiful Morning." According to Northcutt, Neil woke up every morning singing that song.

"He was just fun to be with," said Northcutt. "He was a humble man. He never wanted the fame that was his."

During the service NASCAR chaplain Max Helton talked about how Davey Allison had gone to see Neil at Talladega on the day his helicopter crashed.

"This past Friday, Neil went to see Davey," said Helton.

Those who couldn't get into the church for the service lined Forest Street near Forest Memorial Gardens, where he was buried.

Susan Bonnett issued a statement to stop rumors that she had been bitterly against Neil's racing again.

"I'm not bitter," she said. "Neil always knew that whatever he decided to do, that I'd go along. The day after he decided to start racing again, he came home with a big smile on his face and asked me that I thought. I just smiled with him."

CHAPTER 50

Hut: A Career Fizzles

"Kids at school were saying, 'Your daddy can't drive.'"

—Hut Stricklin

In 1993 Hut Stricklin switched from Junior Johnson's McDonald's race team to Travis Carter's Camel's Smokin' Joe team.

Carter was the titular owner of the team, but according to Stricklin, Johnson was the real owner.

"I had a two-year contract with Junior when I went there," said Stricklin. "It was one year with McDonald's, and one year with Smokin' Joe's. That was one thing about Junior. He honored his deal with me fully, totally, unlike some of the others I drove for. Junior was a man of his word. To this day I will go eat with him sometimes.

"The shop was run in Wilkesboro, but we weren't in the same shop as the Budweiser and McDonald's cars. We were a little further down the road.

"Junior had very little input. He didn't come by very often. He hired Travis, and Travis ran it.

"We struggled real bad. We had a lot of hand-me-down cars. It really didn't pan out either."

Two years later Junior Johnson would himself get out of racing. On November 14, 1995, without fanfare, Johnson sold one of the winningest race teams in the history of NASCAR to Brett Bodine, ending his thirty-year run as car owner.

One reason Johnson got out of racing was that he found it no longer fair. Racing against him were ruthless teams with seemingly unlimited funds.

"Money is the root of all the problems we have in our sport," he said, "and it's basically the problem of any sport. As the money gets bigger and the supply gets more plentiful, the people get more vicious. A lot of us out here have to work within a certain figure, because our sponsorship is what we work off of. There's several out there—and you know who they are—that have finances other than racing and can afford to do a lot more than we can.

"You can't buy everything you want. You've got to be smart enough to figure out how to do it without the finances everybody else has, and I've always been able to do that."

As a symptom of the ruthlessness that he decried, experienced crew chiefs and other valued employees had left Johnson after being seduced by significantly higher-paying job offers. The final blow came in May 1995 when crew chief Mike Beam and three other crew members left him to go work for Bill Elliott, who had started his own race team.

"Stealing away other team's employees is not something I am willing to do," said Johnson "I don't see where you get any gratification taking people away from other teams just because you've got a little money and can do it. Some of the stuff that's gone on this year is disgusting."

The sixty-four-year-old father of two infants was out of racing after almost fifty years.

Johnson told a reporter, "There's two things I ain't gonna have ever again—an old woman or an old car."

In 1995 Hut Stricklin was out of a ride after he and Junior's Smokin' Joe's team parted company. With no offers on the horizon, he announced he would attempt to put together his own Busch Grand National team.

Then he got a call from Kenny Bernstein, owner of King Racing. Steve Kinser, the sprint car champion, was trying to make the switch to Winston Cup cars and wasn't having a lot of success. Bernstein asked if Hut would help and advise him.

"I was running out of money, and I needed to do something," said Hut.

Bernstein was a very interesting car owner, a man who wore a lot of different hats. He was the King of the Top Fuel dragsters and Funny cars. A racer since 1973, he won the NHRA Winston Funny Car championship four times, and six times he was named to the American Auto Racing Writers and Broadcasters Association Auto Racing All-America team. When he became the first NHRA racer to surpass 300 miles an hour on March 20, 1992, he was crowned "King of Speed." Two years later he reached 310 miles an hour. In 1996 he became the only driver to win both the Top Fuel and Funny Car championships.

He didn't fare nearly as well in Winston Cup racing. Bernstein founded the King Racing team in 1986. After Joe Ruttman and Morgan Shepherd each drove a season, Ricky Rudd won a race each in 1988 and 1989 and Brett Bodine won another in 1990. Bodine also managed three seconds in the four years he raced, but then Bodine departed at the end of 1994, leaving a ride to be filled. That's when Bernstein thought he'd hire Steve Kinser. After all, Kinser might have been the greatest sprint car driver who ever lived. If he could make the jump to Winston Cup, Bernstein might have the winning race team he had never had before.

"I went and started helping them with their testing, trying to help Steve," said Stricklin, "but he just couldn't seem to adapt to the heavier cars. There's an edge, and you have to run up to that edge—that's as far as you can take it—but he'd go over the edge, and he'd wreck a lot."

Stricklin had taken the job because he needed the paycheck, but he was a straightforward, honest-days-work-for-an-honest-man's-dollar kind of guy, and Bernstein came to appreciate him as a driver as well as a person. When Bernstein finally became convinced that Kinser would not be able to make the switch to Winston Cup, on April 11, 1995, he announced that Hut Stricklin would replace Kinser in that car.

Stricklin was thrilled. Bernstein was a racer, which meant that he took his sponsorship money and put it in the car, rather than put it in his pocket. Finally, Stricklin felt, he had a car and a race team that could win races. In his first race driving for King Racing, he finished seventh in the Coca-Cola 600 at Charlotte.

"We had an incredible team there," said Stricklin. "Everybody jelled. It looked like we were on the brink of something. It was one of the better rides I had, without a doubt.

"Richard Broome was the crew chief. I loved that guy. We got along great. Anything I wanted to do, he did it. We had a communication between us. Neither one of us took anything personally. It was just for the betterment of the car, to make the car run the fastest."

Hut continued to impress, finishing fourth at Dover, a tough track.

"We should have won. We were leading it with about twenty laps to go, and we had to stop for fuel."

He came in a solid fifth at Pocono.

"We went four or five weeks, ran great, and then Bernstein came up and said, 'That's it. I'm going to sell the team and get out of Winston Cup racing.'

" 'You're going to do what?' I said. 'You can't do that.' "

" 'I've had enough,' he said. 'I want to focus on my drag racing and try to win a championship.' "

"I always try to put myself in someone's shoes," said Stricklin. "He had been doing it for quite a few years and hadn't seen much success at all, especially for what he put into it, because he put the money in it. He gave you what you needed to do it, and it never materialized."

Hut tried everything in the world to try to change Bernstein's mind, but it was made up.

"That was pretty incredible," said Stricklin. "It was one of the best situations I'd ever been in, and to have that happen . . . He tried to sell it, tried everything, but the bad part was once Bernstein announced what he was going to do, all the employees just started scattering. One guy left, then another, then two more, then one, and before long, there wasn't anything left; nothing but the car."

And Hut Stricklin.

On October 21, 1995, driving a car with no future, Hut astonished everyone when he won the pole at Rockingham.

"That was pretty incredible," he said, "because that wasn't supposed to happen. Here we were going out of business, but I still wanted to show people we had a good thing and if someone wanted to step up and put it together, buy the thing . . . but it never materialized."

In 1995 Stricklin had his best year financially, winning $486,000 in purses.

"I don't remember how much I got, but I didn't starve," he said. More important, he established himself as a driver who was on the cusp of winning.

His success with King Racing in 1995 afforded him an extended life in racing. After Bernstein folded his team, Stricklin signed a three-year contract to drive for the Stavola Brothers, a team that had begun in 1984 with Bobby Hillin. The young Hillin had won a race for them in 1986, and then Bobby Allison had won three races for them, one each in 1986, 1987, and 1988, but after that they had hit a dry spell. It was 1996, and the Stavola Brothers hadn't won a race since. Stricklin replaced Jeff Burton in the car. In the two and a half seasons he was there, Stricklin didn't win either.

"The first year we had some ups and downs," said Hut. "We almost won Darlington [he came in second], but we just couldn't put together the consistency the Stavolas and I wanted.

"Then in the second year, we brought in Richard Broome to try to, as Bill Stavola put it, 'bring some gray hair to the team,' meaning experience. But it was a whole totally different deal than what I had with the King Racing team, and in '97 we didn't hit on much. We started trying to build our own engines. We tried different things. We couldn't seem to get any part of it together. We couldn't seem to get the engine stuff or the bodies right on the cars. After the season everyone quit or was fired."

In 1998 the Stavolas hired a new crew chief, Bill Engle. Once again it was two bulls in a pasture.

"He and I just butted heads right from the start," said Stricklin, who says Engle was another crew chief who wanted to call all the shots, leaving him out of the decision-making process.

"We didn't pan out," he said. "I was there basically half a season, and then we split up."

The Stavolas would run five more races with Buckshot Jones and two more races with Morgan Shepherd before folding their race team after fifteen years.

In 1999 Stricklin began the season running a second car for Brad Akins in the Busch series and driving a Winston Cup car for Scott Barbour, who owned a Florida company called Turbine Solutions, which sold used or remanufactured aircraft engines.

Stricklin became the answer to a quirky trivia question driving on the Busch circuit. He won the pole at Homestead in the final race of 1999, and he won the pole at the first race at Daytona in the year 2000.

"I kid everyone," said Stricklin. "I was the last guy to sit on the pole in the nineties, and I was the first to win a pole in the 2000s."

He had little to speak about in Winston Cup driving for Scott Barbour, who ended up not having the resources to compete.

"The aircraft business took a turn for the worse," said Stricklin, "and he ended up basically going out of the racing business."

Stricklin drove nine races for Barbour, earning one top-ten finish, before signing with Junie Donlavey. Barbour finished out the season with Ricky Craven and Loy Allen Jr. before he closed up shop.

Stricklin drove for Junie Donlavey in one race in 1999, seven races in 2000, and twenty-one races in 2001. Donlavey had been in racing since 1952, when Joe Weatherly drove for him in one race. Some of his drivers were Sonny Hutchins, Bill Dennis, Jody Ridley, Dick Brooks, Ken Schrader, Bobby Hillin, Mike Wallace, and Dick Trickle, capable drivers but not household names. Some years Junie ran part-time. The few seasons he had the money, he ran most of the races. Of the 863 races he entered through 2002, Junie's race team had won one race, the Mason-Dixon 500 at Dover on May 17, 1981, but the win was a disputed one: Bobby Allison actually finished the race a lap ahead of his driver, Jody Ridley, but a scoring error gave the victory to Ridley.

In the time he drove for Junie, Stricklin could only manage one top-ten finish, but it was an experience he cherished despite the lack of success. When he finished fourteenth at Indianapolis in 2001, he was thrilled just to be able to race at the hallowed Brickyard.

"You can't imagine how important that was to me," said Stricklin. "Here was a team that didn't have any money, and our pit stops were terrible. But it was a good group of guys, everybody had fun, I loved them all, we all had a lot of fun together. Nobody was really what they called a trained professional, but it was a fun time."

It was also a lot of hard work for Stricklin, because he was doing double duty as driver and his own crew chief.

"I'd spend two days setting up the car," he said, "and then I'd go to the racetrack. It was a pretty tough deal."

But mostly, according to Stricklin, it was fun.

"I enjoyed working with Junie," said Stricklin. "He would continually tell stories about how they used to do things. Of course, things now change weekly. But I had a blast driving for him.

"When something worked, he would never say anything. When it didn't work, he wouldn't let you forget it. If you pulled too low a gear in the engine, he'd come in the shop, and he'd look at you and say, 'You dumb SOB.' He didn't mean it personally. That's how he was."

After 2001, Hut's sponsor, Hills Brothers, decided it wanted to spend more money, but it wanted Hut to run for a more competitive team. Hut had to leave Donlavey if he wanted to keep Hills Brothers as a sponsor.

Hills Brothers interviewed three teams, all of which were fine with Stricklin, and chose the Bill Davis race team for Hut to drive in 2002. Felipe Lopez, Hut's old friend, was the crew chief.

Though Hut earned $1,255,000 in purses in twenty-two starts, he wasn't able to accomplish even one top ten.

"We didn't have any problems," said Hut. "No fighting or arguing. But we couldn't ever seem to get it right. We'd unload the car, and we'd be so far off when we got there, we'd spend all weekend trying to catch up, and by the time the race was done, we'd be as fast as anybody there, but we'd be ten laps down."

Before the 2002 season was over, Hut was out of a ride. He had driven in 329 races and hadn't won a race, and after fifteen years of trying, at the age of forty-one he had become the poster child for futility in Winston Cup racing. Hut began to hear the whispers that he was washed up. So did his children. Hut became frustrated, unhappy at not having success doing what he was doing. He talked with several race teams, and when he didn't get any bites, he decided to retire.

"I had reached a point in my career, I wasn't happy with what I was doing," said Hut. "It was hard on my family. Kids at school were saying, 'Your daddy can't drive.' I reached the point where I just got burned out doing what I was doing."

His dad had been in the automobile salvage business, a business he knew well. Stricklin decided to open his own automobile salvage business in Cleveland, North Carolina, between Statesville and Salisbury. (You can find Hut's business on the web at www.hutstricklinusedparts.com.) "Right now I'm spending everything I ever made in my life on it," he says.

The Stricklins live in Mount Ulla, North Carolina, near in-laws Pat and Donnie. Donnie's boys have a shop just three miles down the road where they build Legacy cars.

For a while, Hut's son, Taylor Lane, was racing Go Karts, but once Stricklin opened his auto salvage business, Taylor quit racing to join him, and that doesn't bother Hut one bit.

"He's just strictly been sticking here and helping me," said Stricklin. "He really likes what he's doing. We've turned this into a family operation."

CHAPTER 51

The End of Bobby Allison Motorsports

"The agony of losing my sons and then Neil . . . my concentration could be better."

—**Bobby Allison**

In the seven years between 1990 and 1996, in 207 starts, the Bobby Allison Motorsports team never won a single Winston Cup race. The team's best effort came at Michigan in 1991 when Hut Stricklin finished second to Davey. Jimmy Spencer had a second in 1993, and so did Derrike Cope in 1995.

Bobby Allison Motorsports, according to Eddie Allison, was missing one key ingredient—Bobby Allison.

"Bobby wasn't well enough to have any input to the car, so it never could work," Eddie said. "He still wasn't well enough mentally to really make decisions. He was so tired. I talked to him and talked to him.

"I told him he should walk into his shop and say, 'You're going to do what I want, or you guys are all leaving.' Because he never lost what made the race car go. He still had that. But nobody would believe him, because he had had a brain injury. They wouldn't let him have any input, and they kept trying to tell me, 'He won't do anything.' Well, he wouldn't, because when they started, they stopped him. And with him in the mental condition he was in, he couldn't fight them. He needed a loving, supporting atmosphere, and he wasn't getting it. And the egos of the people around him could not be reined in. Like I say, the ego in that sport is so big.

"While Bobby was recuperating, the two people who made the decisions for the race team were my brother-in-law, Tom Kincaid, the PR guy in the business, and Jimmy Fennig, the crew chief.

"Bobby had driven a car for Fennig in Wisconsin and Michigan on Saturday nights. There were ill feelings in the organization because Bobby had brought Jimmy in, and so Bobby Allison Motorsports was screwed up from day one.

"Kincaid, who married my baby sister Cindy, is a lawyer. I told him when he started it, 'Get Terry Labonte. Get someone who can do it.' Terry had quit and was going to start his own race team, and it fell through, and he ended up driving for Rick Hendrick in 1990."

The driver Kincaid hired was Mike Alexander. Eddie wasn't impressed.

"They were grasping at straws, Bobby didn't have any input into the race team," said Eddie. "Mike Alexander drove for his daddy's race team. His daddy owned a Ford dealership in Franklin, Tennessee. He was a good friend, and his kid was a pretty good race car driver.

"Mike got in a wreck at Pensacola, and it messed up his head. He had a brain injury. The kid had some potential, but he was not what the race team needed under the circumstances, and when he got hurt, it destroyed him."

After Mike Alexander left the team in May 1990, Hut Stricklin became the team's driver.

"It just didn't jell. Hut had a real bad problem that cost him a chance to be a longtime driver in Winston Cup: He couldn't turn a steering wheel. He wanted the car to do the work. Which is true of ninety percent of the drivers. They all holler they can't drive the cars.

"When Hut was driving for Bobby, Bobby would tell him, 'Turn the steering wheel.'

"Hut would say, 'But I'll spin out.' They all say that. If the car spins out when you turn the steering wheel, you better fix it. After you go into the corner, you have to turn.

"Today the cars are put in the wind tunnel and they figure out how to go faster straight ahead, and *then* they try to figure out how to turn it. So we turn the car with the fenders, and when the fenders get bent in the race, the car doesn't turn anymore. And the fenders *will* get bent.

"I don't want to say it's nerve—everyone talks about having big, brass balls, but I still say it's the *want* to do it, because you have to learn how to drive a car. It doesn't just come to you. Being an Allison isn't enough. You have to work at it. One racer may have a better feel between his foot, hand, and his steering wheel, but drivers are *not* naturally born. You gotta learn how to do it, no matter who you are. And that's just will and determination.

"I've watched and watched and watched. *No one* is naturally born.

"Anyway, Hut ended up in the car, and the only race he ran well in to any extent was at Michigan when he came in second to Davey, and see, that day, Bobby fixed the car in the garage. He said, 'Don't tell Hut what we did.' And the car turned when it got to the end of the straightaway, and so he could drive it.

"But the thing went completely downhill, because Bobby had no confidence in himself to do anything. His mind wasn't clear enough to take charge. It was really screwed up from day one. What sponsor was going to walk away from Bobby Allison? But every sponsor did. Somebody drove the sponsors off, right? Raybestos never would have left unless somebody messed with them.

"In '93 Hut was fired. They hired Jimmy Spencer, and Spencer was good. And Bobby could control Spencer. Jimmy had enough respect for Bobby to listen to what Bobby said."

In 1993 Allison's Meineke Muffler team did well, with five top-five finishes and $686,026 in prize money, but Meineke dropped Bobby Allison Racing at the end of the season. Then after Hut went to drive for Junior Johnson, at the end of the year Junior let him go, and he hired Spencer away from Bobby.

"Losing Jimmy Spencer hurt me a lot," said Bobby. "He couldn't buy a ride when I gave him a car. I thought he would stick with us, but what can you do? You go on. You have to go on."

Said Eddie, "It pissed Bobby off, but that's all it did. Time was running out. Meineke was still sponsoring the car, and then Meineke backed away. It was a crazy deal."

What was crazy was that because Bobby was sure Meineke would be his sponsor for 1994, he turned away other potential suitors. When Meineke pulled out, the other sponsors had already found cars to represent, putting Bobby's race team on life support.

Bobby told reporters it cost at least $65,000 a week to keep the team on the track. No one with deep pockets was paying the bills. Sponsors were offering mostly one-race, small-money deals.

Said driver Chuck Bown, who replaced Spencer, "My biggest challenge isn't driving, it's trying to remember which sponsor signed up fifteen minutes before the race. I bet I'm the only guy out there with cue cards."

Despite the lack of money, Bown managed a pole at Bristol in April, and a seventh-place finish at Martinsville in 1994. After that there were mostly back-of-the-pack runs.

The team's outlook worsened when in June 1994 Bown crashed at Pocono and suffered a head injury.

The team replaced Bown with Tim Steele, a twenty-six-year old ARCA ace from Coopersville, Michigan.

When the team arrived for the inaugural NASCAR Indianapolis 500 in August 1994, Steele's wife, Brenda, had just given birth to a baby girl, and when the crew arrived just after the opening of the track on Thursday, everyone was smiling.

Steele then went out in the first practice session, which began at 9:30 A.M. The throttle stuck on Steele's car, and he became the first NASCAR driver ever to put a car into the wall at Indianapolis.

As crew chief Jimmy Fennig and the crew were tearing the tape off a new paint job on the backup car and working on the engine, Bobby was asked how much time he spent under the hood.

"Not enough," he said. "The agony of losing my sons and then Neil . . . My concentration could be better."

Bobby was asked how he was doing emotionally. He looked across the garage area but didn't speak.

"Good days and bad?" asked the reporter, Patrick Reusse.

"Lately, there have been bad days and then worse days. For a time, the racing helped to ease the pain over Clifford and Davey and Neil, but it's always there now." He said it was worse for Judy because she also remembered Pocono and the two months when they didn't know whether he'd be a vegetable or not, and he didn't.

Reusse asked Bobby whether it was all his money paying the bills for the race team.

"Mine, or what I've borrowed from the bank, or what has been put in by my friends," said Bobby. Then Bobby showed that he had not completed lost his sense of humor. He asked Reusse, "Speaking of friends, how about you? You look like a guy who might be interested in investing $500."

Reusse didn't report what he replied.

Eddie Allison went to the Brickyard for the first race, and he talked to Tim Steele in an attempt to find out why the race team wasn't more successful.

"Again, the same crap: the mechanic was way smarter than the driver," said Eddie. "Fennig was the mechanic. And you cannot race a car like that. I don't care what goes on. You can't be smarter than your driver, or you end up with a crashed pile of scrap iron. And that's what happened.

"They went out and ran two or three laps. The speed sheet said when he turned the corner he was going 191 miles an hour, and that was faster than anybody. But he didn't have any brakes. You have to get the brakes hot to get them to work, and when you are running 191 miles an hour, they better work. And they didn't. The car didn't slow down. It went straight into the wall, *bam*. Can you imagine hitting the wall at 191 miles an hour? It tore up.

"No one would listen to Steele. They told him to drive the car like they had it. They ended up racing a car that Steele owned because they had crashed all theirs. And it was a fiasco."

Bobby had loved Indianapolis when he drove IndyCars there in 1973 and 1975, and in 1994 NASCAR was racing there for the first time. Bobby badly wanted to get in the race car and experience the thrill of Indianapolis. According to Eddie, Bobby just could not summon the courage to do it.

"At Indianapolis I have never seen my brother so distraught in my life," said Eddie. "He and I were in his room back at the hotel. He was distraught that he didn't get in the car and drive it himself. He just wanted to run the car around the racetrack. That's all, just to drive the car around the track. See, he had no intention of racing, but he never got in the car. I asked him why. He didn't give me an answer.

"It broke my heart that he didn't drive a Winston Cup car in Indianapolis. I saw complete depression. He laid there on the bed more distraught than when his son got killed. Because he knew he could drive the car. He had no confidence. If I had known how badly he wanted to drive the car, I would have made him drive it. I didn't know until we got back to the hotel.

"When I said, 'What's wrong?' He said, 'I didn't drive the car.' But by then it was too late. Practice was over."

In 1994 Tim Steele entered five Winston Cup races and had four DNFs. His best finish was twenty-seventh.

The last racer to drive for Bobby Allison Motorsports was Derrike Cope, who had won the Daytona 500 in 1991 when Dale Earnhardt blew a tire within sight of the start-finish line. Cope's win at Daytona prolonged his racing career by ten years. Every owner who hired him envisioned him doing it again. But it never happened.

"Derrike Cope can drive a race car, but he isn't a race car driver," said Eddie. "There's a bunch of them out there who can drive a race car. You can count on one hand the race car drivers."

Bobby's race team signed as a sponsor Straight Arrow Mane 'n Tail, which started as a line of grooming products for horses then switched to grooming products for humans. It wasn't a lot of money, but it kept the team in business.

Cope had more success than any of the previous racers. In the first five races of the 1994 season, he finished eighth, sixth, and fifth. Cope sat fourth in the Winston Cup points standings. But Bobby's Ford was inferior to the Monte Carlo in 1995, and Cope's standings dropped precipitously.

The race team signed Gumout, a carburetor cleaner, as a small-time sponsor and kept afloat. But it was a balancing act that the team couldn't sustain forever.

The beginning of the end of his race team came when Derrike Cope crashed his car at Rockingham, destroying one of the few good cars the team had left.

Just before the crash Bobby felt the car should have been brought to the pits, but he didn't have the self-confidence to give the order.

"If I had said something, taken charge, ordered Derrike in, he wouldn't have been out there where the wreck started. But that old thing keeps biting at me. Lack of confidence."

Said Eddie Allison, "When Cope crashed at Rockingham, Bobby Allison Motorsports was out of money. The race team, not him. Bobby had run out of money years ago before that."

When Bobby Allison Motorsports closed up shop after the 1996 season, Bobby felt a great relief at not having to do it anymore.

"He didn't need it in his life," said Eddie. "His life was not unfulfilled if he wasn't doing it."

"The race team was started because a lot of people were trying to help me," Bobby said. "I did it because people expected me to do it. But we went through a series of driver changes and sponsor changes, and it got to the point, I guess, where it was so frustrating."

When he no longer could get another sponsor, the effort was over.

"I am glad," he said.

Brother Donnie was unhappy that Bobby was disenchanted with racing. "I am trying to change that," he said. "You can't go through every day getting only the bad parts of life. There has to be some good parts, or even the strongest person will be disillusioned.

"He has been so negative about racing. I told him, if his airplanes had blown up every day like his race cars, he'd be negative about them, too. But I can't push him."

The end of Bobby Allison Motorsports "might just be the best thing that has happened to me since 1988," said Bobby. He hated being a figurehead car owner, dependent on the financial backing of partners. He couldn't attract adequate sponsorship. His name no longer carried enough clout. He couldn't even bring himself to give orders in the pits.

"Getting out of racing was the right thing to do," Bobby said. "Now at least I'm aiming toward where I want to go. I just don't know where that is yet."

CHAPTER 52

Bobby and Judy: Financial Ruin and Divorce

"Who else would have the steering wheel in his hand?"

—Judy Allison

Bobby's medical bills had been staggering, as much as $500,000 in all, but Bobby and Judy weren't worried because he was insured under NASCAR's blanket coverage and under two additional personal policies that were supposed to pay his bills in full.

It didn't work out that way, as they learned the harsh reality of the insurance game: Insurance companies are only too glad to take your premium money, but when it comes to paying on those policies, it's a whole other story.

According to Judy, the NASCAR policy, it turned out, paid $50,000 of Bobby's $200,000 Allentown hospital expenses. A policy from Blue Cross Blue Shield was supposed to pay the rest of the bills, and a policy he bought from a close friend was supposed to pay him $2,000 a week supplementary insurance for as long as he was laid up in the hospital. In the end Bobby was paid exactly $100,000 after having to sue, and most of that went to legal fees.

After Bobby came home to Alabama, the billing department of Lehigh Valley Hospital in Allentown called his home.

"You have to refund Blue Cross's payment, and normally we would start a lawsuit right now, but because of who he is, we're going to give him a month to pay his bill," Judy was informed.

"The bill for his first week at Allentown came to $93,000," said Judy. Judy sent in her claim, and Blue Cross sent a check to the hospital. Then Blue Cross called the hospital to say there had been a mistake, and the hospital needed to send back the check."

Bobby was in no condition to battle over anything, so Judy had his lawyer call Blue Cross to ask why the insurance company wasn't paying his bills like it was supposed to.

The answer came back: "If Bobby Allison is acting as a CEO he is exempt from coverage. He had the steering wheel in his hands when the crash occurred, so that made him the CEO."

Say what? Who did they think was going to be behind the wheel at the time they accepted his premiums?

"I was floored," said Bobby. "But I had all this other money, and I said, 'I'll pay the bill.' I paid the Allentown bill out of my own checking account in Hueytown." Bobby got a break on a fee because he had given permission for the hospital to film his shunt operation as a teaching tool.

The bill at Lakeshore Hospital in Birmingham was approximately $1,000 a day. Bobby was there for sixty days. Again, Blue Cross Blue Shield refused to pay.

His catastrophic injury coverage was purchased from an agent he knew. Bobby thought the supplemental insurance policy was such a great benefit that he took the agent to meet Bill France Jr. to make it available to all the drivers. France's response: "If I endorse your guy, I will have to endorse everybody else who comes along selling insurance."

"I wasn't France's most favorite person anyway," said Bobby, "so I couldn't go and say, 'Bill, I'm your buddy, Bobby. I think this is a really neat idea. Will you look at it twice?'

"Anyway, he was turned down by Bill France."

As it turned out, Bobby had to wage war to collect on his policy. When Bobby asked the agent when his bills would be paid, the reply was, "It's coming pretty soon, but we have to do a little more paperwork. Be patient. You're fine."

Bobby, severely brain damaged, had no ability to look into the matter further. But the agent had sold a similar insurance package to Neil Bonnett, and Bonnett also had trouble getting paid. After Bonnett regained his memory, he was in better mental and physical shape to investigate than Bobby. When Bonnett called the agent and was told, "It's coming," Bonnett became enraged. He went to the state of Alabama insurance commissioner, who began an investigation. Lloyds of London finally made good on Neil's policy.

Bobby filed suit against the insurer and the agent's company, who denied any wrongdoing.

Bobby got a lawyer, who told him, "We're going to get a million dollars from Lloyds of London."

They went to court, and a jury was empanelled.

Said Bobby, "The young lawyer for Lloyds of London said, 'I would like to inform the court and jury this is an out-of-country transaction, and the United States has no jurisdiction.' The judge turned to me and said, 'He's right. You're out. You don't get a dime.'"

Ultimately Bobby settled his claims. According to Bobby, Lloyds of London offered him $100,000, and he took it. After his lawyer took his piece, Bobby didn't have a lot left, money he used to pay another lawyer $60,000 up front to sue Blue Cross Blue Shield. Bobby had to sell racing equipment and one of his antique cars to pay the fee to pursue a case he lost.

Part of the problem, says Bobby, was that everyone thought he was rich to begin with.

"These people all know I won $7.7 million in purses, and they thought I still had most of it left," said Bobby.

Bobby remembers that the jury pool was made up of working men and women—not one member of the middle class on the entire panel.

Bobby recalls the winning riposte by the young lawyer representing Blue Cross Blue Shield.

"Why is this guy pushing for this $1 million?" he asked.

Bobby's lawyer, angry, replied, "I'm going to shove that down your throat." And when he said that, the entire jury gasped. With that, the foreman of the jury said loud enough for Bobby to hear, "What's he want more money for? He already has more money than all the people in the world?"

Bobby, in no shape to respond, just hung his head.

"The judge should have called it a mistrial," said Bobby. "My lawyer turned to me and said, 'You just lost the case.' So we left the room knowing we were defeated."

"The Blue Cross case cost us the most," said Judy. "They took $500,000 of our money. They said he was the CEO of the company and they didn't have to pay because he had the steering wheel in his hand. And our attorneys were not able to come up with the right answers. When they sold us the insurance and when we paid the premium, they knew he would have the steering wheel in his hand. He's a race car driver. Who else would have the steering wheel in his hand?"

Of all the illusory insurance, Judy reserves most of her contempt for NASCAR.

"You know what kind of insurance NASCAR had on Bobby?" she asked. "Fifty thousand dollars worth. There are seven Frances right now, and each one is a billionaire. Why aren't the drivers protected when they get hurt? Why isn't there a pension fund for the older drivers? NASCAR could make a big deal out of giving the older drivers who didn't make the millions they do now a decent pension. The PR value would be huge. What can you do?"

And so by 1996 it wasn't surprising that an unemployed Bobby Allison, who once owned a fleet of airplanes and antique cars, found himself in dire financial trouble.

He tried to market his name as best he could, but he found out what every professional athlete knows: Once you retire, your value goes *way* down. Fortunately for Bobby, he was a legend in Alabama, and he was able to use his fame to ease his debt.

The rehab center in Birmingham let him work off much a $60,000 debt by making public appearances and speeches.

He also signed a contract with the Alabama Department of Transportation to do TV spots, personal appearances, and lectures on safe driving in exchange for $75,000 a year.

Bobby had been recruited by Governor Fob James, a Republican. Allison met, and liked, U.S. senator Jeff Sessions, also a Republican, and he went on some bus tours with him.

Then came the criticism. The newspapers blasted the Republicans and Allison, saying that Bobby was "ripping off the state of Alabama." For someone with Bobby Allison's deep sense of morality, nothing could have hurt him more.

On October 23, 1996, on another bus tour, Bobby gathered two Birmingham TV crews and announced he would continue to do his public service work, but at no charge.

"I can take care of my personal bills," he told reporters. "I have been in a financial pinch ninety percent of my adult life. I'm pretty fortunate that people like [ninety-year-old] Mrs. Shepard, who lives up there at the beginning of Church Avenue in Hueytown, will feed me if I show up hungry."

Bobby displayed his old feistiness, and it surprised him.

"It was evidence that a little of the real me has survived all this," said Allison. Meaning he could be vindictive and hateful. Allison told Ed Hinton that he continued to resent all of Richard Petty's wins and that he continued to hate Darrell Waltrip with a passion.

The official NASCAR record win list reads Richard Petty 200, David Pearson 105, Darrell Waltrip and Bobby Allison, 84.

"Eighty-five," says Allison. "I've really got eighty-five." He hadn't challenged it back in 1971 when, after he won on the quarter-mile track at Winston-Salem in his Grand American car, NASCAR didn't give him—or anyone else—the win.

He beat Richard Petty and everyone else that night in his little Mustang. But NASCAR officials ruled that his lighter weight was an advantage, and it gave the win to—nobody.

Bobby believed (wrongly) that NASCAR gave the win to Petty, and he wanted it back. But if NASCAR did that, said Bobby, Petty wouldn't have his magical 200, so he is sure they won't.

"Now who in the world would take one of the King's 200 wins away from him?" asks Allison. "Who in the world would do something that vile?"

As for Waltrip, says Allison, "For career wins, I am tied with a man who will probably break the tie. (He never did.) But if Darrell would only give back all the wins he got illegally, then he would be tied with Joe Frasson for career wins. (Frasson didn't win any.)

Bobby was asked how they were illegal.

"Big fuel tanks, wrong-size engines, wrong tires, you name it. He just got away with murder, race after race."

For his part, Waltrip accused Allison of doing as much or more illegal than he.

"One of Bobby's downfalls was that he was paranoid," said Waltrip. "No matter how well he was doing, he thought everybody was against him. Particularly NASCAR—the officials."

Bobby's thinking was that no one could beat him in a legal race, and so if he lost, he figured the other guy had to be cheating. It became an obsession with him.

Waltrip says Allison's resentment for him surely was centered on his three championship seasons when he drove for Junior Johnson.

"I was driving for the one man Bobby hates more than he hates me: Junior Johnson."

Over the years Bobby has had long talks with Stevie Waltrip, Darrell's wife, who is very religious, and as a result his enmity for her husband has faded some.

"I may—I probably will—end up down there shoveling coal with the little red guy," said Bobby. "But I'm gonna tell you something: I still have forgiven Darrell Waltrip only three-fourths."

As the years after Clifford's and Davey's deaths dragged on, the relationship between Bobby and Judy Allison disintegrated. By 1996, she saw there was no chance of a reconciliation and demanded a divorce. Bobby, too weary to fight back, agreed and hired a lawyer.

As part of the divorce arrangements, Bobby and Judy agreed to split their assets. Bobby signed a contract giving Judy permission to auction off the Church Street house and its contents in order to pay the outstanding bills.

Before he agreed to the auction, he first tried raising the $200,000 or so, which represented half of what everything was worth. Friends such as Bruton Smith and Bill France Jr. sent Bobby significant sums of money, but it came too late to halt the auction. The money was used to pay other expenses, mostly medical bills. Bobby had always been raised to pay his bills in full when they arrived, so when the medical bills rolled in, he didn't pay 10 percent down and save the rest to live.

"I was raised that way," he said, "plus I was so incredibly out of touch with the world out there," said Bobby. "I looked okay, but that was all."

Judy, in splitting their assets, was just being practical, doing what she felt she had to do.

"It took three months' preparation," said Judy. "A lot of times the remark was, 'Bobby came home one day, and Judy had everything out in the front yard for sale.' It didn't happen that way. I kept everything that was important. I gave a lot of stuff away to his family and some of my family and friends. Bobby okayed the things we sold. He was there for the sale day. Some people have since given him back things, and that was nice."

Bobby's brother Eddie, for one, held it against her.

"After Davey was killed," said Eddie Allison, "Judy left. She auctioned off all the stuff in the house. It was ugly."

Before the auction, Bobby waxed nostalgic about the house in which he and Judy raised their children.

"We moved in [to that house] on Christmas Eve, 1969," said Bobby. "Worst day of the year to move. But I thought it would be neat for those kids to wake up in that new house and find that Santa Claus had been there."

"The memories of the children in the house are wonderful," said Judy. "But when you throw in financial problems, and you throw in all these people coming by fairly regularly, and—where was Bobby? Bobby was either in the shop or flying. He didn't have to contend with all this as much as I did. So things just kind of went in a different direction, and the next thing I know, this is where we're at."

"Some . . . incidents . . . in my life kept the agony, kept the agony, kept the agony on her," said Bobby. "So she packed her suitcase, and she left.

"I felt the agony, too. But I handled it differently. I've always had this . . . this . . . ability to . . . go on."

He said, "Racing didn't take Davey. Judy was really bitter about the helicopter. She said racing bought it for him. I said Davey would have mowed grass to buy that helicopter. I think one of the things that happened to Judy and me was that we were not able to give each other the support we should have in this incredible tragedy."

Even before they separated, Bobby said, "We would go in separate directions a lot. She would go stay with her sisters. A friend of mine had a house in Pensacola, and I would get in my plane and go stay with him, and we'd get on his boat. Somehow I could hide."

Judy, who had moved into an apartment in nearby Hoover, said she wasn't bitter about racing.

"And I didn't really leave," she added enigmatically. She refused to discuss the reasons for the separation except to say, "I do not feel it was the deaths of the boys."

In April 1996 three hundred of Bobby's fans and other curiosity seekers flocked to sit on his lawn to bid for his possessions and memories in an attempt to help defray the costs of Bobby's medical bills, which had wiped out their savings.

Auctioneers began by selling off the furniture that filled their ranch-style home in Hueytown. The five-bay garage served as the warehouse for the sale. Everything but the five-bedroom, four-bath house and its 1.5 acres on a lot sloping to a small lake was sold to the highest bidder.

Said Eddie Allison with contempt, "It was sick. *Sick.* They were auctioning off stuff out of the icebox. It was just ridiculous."

I asked him if he attended.

"Hell no," he said. "I went and got my mother and took her out. Ma lived across the street. They had a big auction in the street.

"Why did Bobby stand for it?" I asked.

"He had no strength," Eddie said. "It was so sad."

———

After the auction, Bobby went across the street to live with his ninety-year-old mother in her modular home. Bobby was fifty-nine.

Bobby saw the irony. He would say to neighbors, "This is Bobby Allison. Is my mommy over there?"

The race shop, down the hill from the big house, stood empty.

Wrote Ed Hinton, "He is broke and almost broken, but he does not brood. He goes on."

"I have learned to launder my underwear," says Bobby. "I have learned to cook spaghetti. And I will make it."

Ed Hinton asked him, "Just how much can one man bear?"

"I am afraid to ask that question," he said.

When the house didn't sell at auction, Bobby and Judy made a deal. Bobby could have the choice of keeping either it or the condo at the end of the first turn at the Charlotte Speedway. Bobby chose to keep the house, in part because his race shop was there. He resentfully gave the condo to Judy, who had to pay the mortgage and maintenance fee. As soon as she got the deed, she put it up for sale. But there were no buyers.

A friend in real estate told her she might have better luck selling it if she moved in first. Since she felt it "ridiculous" to pay the mortgage on the condo *and* the rent for her apartment in Alabama, she decided to move to North Carolina.

When Judy moved into the speedway condo, she discovered an unpleasantness that somehow had escaped Bobby whenever he went there. The Richard Petty Driving Experience ran a school at the track seven days a week from eight in the morning until ten at night. The high-pitched whine of car engines made for a noisy living experience. Even in the bedroom Judy could barely hear the TV, unless she turned it way up. There was no garage, moreover, and on rainy or snowy days, Judy had to battle the weather.

Once she moved in, she discovered another grim reality. It had a $100,000 lien, and if she sold it, she would have to pay the lien plus a steep capital gains tax in that she hadn't lived in it for the required two years.

She took it off the market. To avoid the capital gains tax, she was told she could trade it for a residence of equal value. A buyer called her after she took it off the market, and she traded for a house in Mooresville, a suburb of Charlotte.

"It was like the Lord led me to it," Judy said, adding, "I know Bobby has his own feelings about it. He really was still mixed up back then."

CHAPTER 53

Bobby and Judy: Reunited

"I just felt, Something good has happened . . . I thought, I really like this gal."

—Bobby Allison

The home of Kitty Allison, Bobby's mother, was filled with religious artifacts, mostly statues of the Virgin Mother, who stared down from the front room wall. Kitty had a papal blessing dedicated to her on her nineteenth birthday.

"There is some reason," she says, "all of this has happened. We don't know what it is. But there's *some* reason. Someday we hope to find out."

Then she said to reporter Ed Hinton, "Do you realize what a miracle it is?"

"I beg your pardon," Hinton said.

"Just seeing Bobby," she said. "Don't you realize what a miracle it is? They never dreamed he would recover to be the man he is. Not one of the doctors dreamed." She paused and said, "But this latest thing, with his marriage, he's going to have to work out for himself."

She was praying for a reconciliation.

Miracle of miracles, she got one, but it took more tragedy and suffering to bring it about.

The story of their reconciliation began with the wedding of Liz Allison to Ryan Hackett on May 12, 2000, in Nashville. Judy drove from her home in Mooresville. Bobby drove alone from Spartanburg, where he was honoring David Pearson, who was having a road named after him. While in Spartanburg, Bobby got word that Adam Petty, Kyle's son and Richard's grandson, had been killed in a racing accident.

Bobby really didn't want to go to Liz's wedding. He was still angry that she had taken up with Joe Diffie too soon after Davey was laid to rest. Liz had moved to Nashville to live with Diffie, but after they lived together, she discovered they weren't the match made in heaven they thought they were, and each moved on. Liz remained in Nashville, where she fell in love with Hackett, a specialty occupational therapist.

Bobby hadn't spoken to Judy in a long time. If he wanted to tell her something, he would call one of his daughters and say, "Call your mother and tell her." If Judy wanted to say something to Bobby, she'd do the same thing. Bobby's anger at Judy was so great that on his telephone the speed dial name for her was "Whatshername."

"I was having a tough time with the whole deal, for sure," said Bobby.

Bobby's mother and his daughter Bonnie hounded him to go. They arranged for Bobby to meet with them and sit together in the church.

The day before the wedding Bonnie called Judy and asked her if she knew that Bobby was coming, too. She didn't.

The church sat more than a thousand people. Bobby parked his car and walked in. He could see that Judy was sitting near the front with the bride's family, which was fine with him.

"I didn't want to look at her, didn't want to talk to her, didn't want to be there for the wedding," said Bobby. "But my mom said I had to be, so I was there, dressed in my suit."

Bobby sat in about the thirtieth row, a little farther than halfway to the front. He sat on the aisle next to his mom and his niece Michelle, his sister Mary Agnes's daughter.

The wedding ceremony began. Liz came down the aisle, dressed in her long, beautiful gown, and she stopped where Bobby and his mom were sitting, and she said, "Grandma, thanks for being here," and she kissed Bobby's mom. Which floored Bobby, who contends that Liz was never affectionate to his mom in all the years she had been married to Davey.

And then Liz kissed Bobby on the cheek and thanked him for coming, continuing down the aisle to the ceremony.

"It really did floor me," said Bobby. "It disarmed me. I thought, *Wow!*"

The wedding was elaborate. There were ten bridesmaids and seven or eight ushers. Both of Liz's children, Krista and Robbie, had a part. Liz and her husband-to-be exchanged vows and said some charming words of love to each other, and were pronounced "husband and wife."

On the way back up the aisle, walking arm and arm with her new husband, Liz once again stopped where Bobby was sitting, and again she kissed him and said, "I really appreciate your being here." Now Bobby was *really* disarmed.

The bride and her entourage left the church, and after Bobby got up and walked to the door, Judy cornered him.

"Bobby was standing in the back, and as I went by, I grabbed his hand and I said, 'How are you doing?' He wouldn't look at me. I said, 'Well, you look nice.'"

The way Bobby tells it, she then said, "We should put our differences away and go help the Pettys." Adam's funeral in Level Cross, North Carolina, was scheduled for the following day.

"You're right," Bobby said. Says Bobby today, "I feel we have basically been together ever since."

"I will see you at the reception," said Bobby.

"Yes," said Judy.

Bobby and Judy separately walked over to the building where the reception for the eight hundred guests was being held. Bobby was sitting at a table with his mother and Eddie's son Jacob. He got up and invited Judy to join them.

"His mother was sitting at a little table," said Judy, "and people were getting in line for food, so I went ahead and got in line and got my mother-in-law something to eat." The way Judy tells it, it was at this point that Judy said to Bobby, "You heard about Adam Petty? Why don't we put our differences aside and go to the funeral for him and help the Pettys?"

The way Judy remembered it, Bobby was hesitant, but his mother said to him, "That's a good idea, Bobby."

"But I have my car here," Bobby said.

"You can bring it to North Carolina and leave it or maybe somebody here can drive it back," Judy offered. Bobby arranged for Jacob to drive it back to Hueytown. Bobby then drove in Judy's car back to Judy's home in Mooresville.

"We started the trip by me telling her, 'I am really mad at you,' said Bobby. 'I am doing this because it's a really good idea, but you really aggravate me, and I want you to know you have aggravated me.' I spewed off at her for the first lots of miles on the trip.

"Finally I stopped to take a breath, and she said, 'You know, I'm kind of mad at you, too.' I said, 'Oh?' And then she told me a few things she wanted to get off her chest." At the time of Clifford's and Davey's deaths, Bobby could not talk about anything. He knew only he needed to run and hide. Judy needed him, and he wasn't there. In the car Bobby responded in a way that rekindled in Judy a spark from the past.

"During the ride back to Mooresville, we discussed all kinds of things," said Judy. "He said he would like me to do a discount in the alimony. I said, 'Maybe I can do that.' And it shocked him!" She laughed at the memory. "He said something about getting another motor home and traveling around, which I kind of believed but kind of didn't."

"From the time she said we should put our differences aside and go try to help the Pettys," said Bobby, I felt relief I had not felt for years. I just felt, *Something good has happened*, and I don't know how to explain it, or who to thank for it, other than the Lord, but this is one of the best things that's ever happened to me along the way. And I felt that way probably two-thirds of the way from Nashville to North Carolina. I thought, *I really like this gal*."

"He came to the house," said Judy. "He had planned to stay with our youngest daughter, Carrie, who lives about seven miles from us here in Mooresville. But he stayed the first night, and the next day we went to the Pettys."

Pattie Petty stood outside her home in the brown fields of North Carolina. Her eyes were red from three days of weeping. On this day she was going to bury her nineteen-year-old son, Adam, who had been killed when his race car rammed the concrete wall at the New Hampshire International Speedway in Loudon.

It was a private ceremony. No press, no cameras. Only close friends were invited. A handful of the drivers like Dale Jarrett, Bobby Labonte, and Ward and Jeff Burton came to pay their respects.

Suddenly she noticed an unexpected couple.

"Y'all have been there," she whispered to Bobby and Judy Allison. Pattie gave Judy a hug. While Pattie's hands were on Judy's shoulders, Bobby grabbed them in a gesture that involved the three of them. They stood that way for more than a minute.

Standing nearby was Richard Petty, the King.

"He got killed in a race car," Richard said. "And he was in a race car because of me." Petty was wearing sunglasses, as he usually did. "Then last night, I saw [on TV] where two men drowned at the High Rock lake. Then I saw where two men had gotten killed trying to land a private plane at a local airport. And I said, 'Okay.'"

Petty sighed. He was adopting the rationale all racers inevitably employ: When your time is up, your time is up.

"This was one of them deals," said Petty.

The Pettys were grateful for the support of the thousand or so friends and relatives who came to the funeral, but no one could give them the emotional support that Bobby and Judy could bring.

Said Richard, who knew the Allisons had undergone a bitter divorce. "When we saw them, I told Lynda [his wife], 'That's great. They can get along for long enough to come and feel the grief we feel.'"

"This is very tough for us," Bobby said to Richard. "Judy and I talked, and decided that if there was any way to help, we had to try."

Judy said they had needed time to get over the deaths of their sons.

"It's ironic that a tragedy presented the opportunity for us to, first of all, speak, and then to put our feelings aside to help someone else," said Bobby. "We needed the four years to heal. Early on, we didn't support each other in the healing process. I went in one direction, and she went in another."

Bobby and Judy returned to Judy's house after leaving the Pettys. Bobby stayed with Judy for another twelve days.

"During that time," said Judy, "we got all the hurt out."

Bobby and Judy began going to affairs together. In May 2000, they went to a charity ball given by Bruton Smith.

"We went together, and everyone was shocked," said Judy. "We just started traveling together, and he had to make some appearances, some of which I would drive to."

"When it got to be late June, early July, naturally we were sleeping together," said Judy, "so I told him that wasn't a good thing for the grandchildren, so when we would go to Hueytown, we slept in separate beds, and by this time we had feelings for each other, and we said, 'Maybe we should think about getting married.' Which a lot of the family and some friends were *not* in favor of, and his mother in particular was *not* in favor. I think she knew how bad he still was, being a bad boy instead of a good boy."

I asked Judy what she meant by that.

"We're not going there!" she said with a laugh. "But anyway, we got remarried on July 3, 2000. It was just me and him. We went to the Bessemer courthouse and were married by the judge, because the Catholic Church said we really were still married, so if we wanted to do something, that's what we'd have to do. Then we could renew our vows at some point.

"The Catholic Church never recognized the divorce. It had not been annulled. A lot of people were after me to annul it, and I kept saying, 'No, I'm not going to. I feel like I'm still married, and whether he does or not, this is it.'"

"Our marriage seemed natural to me," said Bobby. "It was a simple ceremony. 'Do you take this woman to be your wife?' 'Yup.' 'Do you take this guy to be your husband?' 'Yup.' 'Okay, you're married. Bye.' It might have been a little bit better than that, but not by much. And that was good enough."

Bobby and Judy decided to make their remarriage into a public celebration. They invited a select group, including Dale Earnhardt, to attend a ceremony to renew their wedding vows on Tuesday, February 20, 2001, at St. Aloysius Church in Bessemer. It would have marked forty years of marriage.

Then on February 18, 2001, on the last lap of the Daytona 500, Dale Earnhardt died of head injuries in a crash.

Bobby and Judy were watching the race on TV. When Judy saw Dale hit the wall, she said to Bobby, "Oh my God. This is bad. This is *really* bad."

"No, he didn't hit the wall that hard," Bobby said. But then Judy heard Darrell Waltrip say, "Oh no, oh no," and then she saw Ken Schrader's face, and she said, "That's it. I'm telling you. This is bad."

Bobby and Judy left the house and took Bobby's mother out to dinner at the Red Lobster. There they received a phone call from Nate Sims, their close friend who was also close to the Earnhardts. Sims had sponsored Davey when he was starting out, and he had built the Garage Mahal for Earnhardt. Sims was calling to say that Dale Earnhardt had died of his injuries.

And so rather than renew their vows, they attended yet another funeral, this one for Dale Earnhardt, the Intimidator, a man many believed would never die.

"The thing I get so bent out of shape over," said Eddie Allison, "in 1980 a Hueytown boy, George White, built a head-restraint harness, and to this day NASCAR will not let him in the loop. If we'd had that thing on people, Dale Earnhardt would still be here. I have no idea why they wouldn't let him use it. See, you don't restrain the helmet. You restrain the head.

"The minute Earnhardt's car touched the wall, he was dead. The car stopped. You can't stop after running 180 miles an hour and not kill the driver.

"I talked to Kenny Schrader at Talladega. He didn't believe it. I said, 'Kenny, the car stopped in the wall.'

"Sterling Marlin bumped Dale and got him sideways. Dale had the car taken care of. He had both feet on the gas and had the car in hand to slide down the wall and run third or fourth. But then Kenny Schrader hit him and turned the car straight into the fence. And he had both feet on the gas. Both feet. Because he could drive it that way. He had to get the back wheels spinning to be able to get the front wheels to turn the car so it didn't spin out.

"And so when Kenny hit him, it turned the car straight into the wall, and even though he was going down the racetrack, the car hit the wall straight ahead and stopped. And Dale's head came off his neck.

"That didn't happen to Bobby at Pocono in '88. Bobby didn't go far enough to break his neck."

The Allisons canceled their ceremony and instead went to Earnhardt's funeral.

All that matters to Eddie is that his brother Bobby is happy.

"Bobby and I are today so close it's unreal," said Eddie. "I love him so strong, and I never dreamed that he was going to fix himself back up with his wife. So far, it's looking like a terrific thing. It works, and that's fine. After they got married, Bobby never even told me they got married.

"Before he got married, Bobby and I were planning to do a lot of things, things we didn't get to do, and that's fine. I have plenty to do. I love Alabama football. My son is a senior there.

"He is happy. And that's all that counts, because he's had so much sadness, and he needs to be happy.

"He's such a good person. He needs to be happy before he gets to heaven. Because God intended us to be happy on this earth. He needs some happiness.

"We were sitting up in his office one day, and I grabbed him on the top of his leg and said, 'How are you, bud?'

" 'Good,' he said.

" 'Man,' I said, 'that's all that counts.' "

"So we never did have our renewal ceremony," said Judy. "Our daughters kept saying, 'Why don't you wait until your fiftieth? Which is in 2010. This is our forty-fifth, so we have five more years to go. It's okay. We're doing great."

"People ask me how I survived," said Bobby. "You have to hold onto the dear Lord. You just have to. I don't know how people who don't have religion do it. If they don't believe in God or Jesus, I don't know how they get through things. You look around: I met a woman in California who lost four daughters in a car crash. Two years ago the Dale Jarrett team had three girls who were killed in an accident coming to the races. Look at the Hendrick plane crash. It's just terrible. I don't know how people do it.

"I'm really pleased that I never lost my enthusiasm. I saw plenty of people who did, people with incredible talent who didn't have that last little bit of push.

"My life has been a series of ups and downs, hills and valleys, top of the mountain, bottom of the valley. My whole career, even my early career, was like that. I had really, really good times, and I had disasters, where other people might have quit racing, but every time I hit a valley, I figured there had to be another hill out there and I'd climb that hill. I've been blessed in so many ways. And I'm grateful."

NOTES

Chapter 2: Pop and Kitty
Interviews with Bobby and Eddie Allison.

Chapter 3: Bobby: Exiled to Wisconsin
Interviews with Bobby and Eddie Allison.

Chapter 4: Bobby: Bobby Sunderman
Interviews with Bobby Allison and Red Farmer.

Chapter 5: Bobby: Judy
Interview with Bobby Allison.

Chapter 6: Donnie and Eddie: Built from the Chassis Up
Interviews with Bobby Allison, Eddie Allison, Ralph Moody, and Red Farmer.

Chapter 7: Pat: Alabamy Bound
Interview with Pat Allison.

Chapter 8: Red Farmer: Short-Track Racer
Interview with Red Farmer.

Chapter 9: Bobby: Nose to the Grindstone
Interviews with Eddie Allison and Bobby Allison.

Chapter 10: Donnie and Eddie: Busting Their Humps
Interviews with Eddie Allison, Pat Allison, and Bobby Allison.

Chapter 11: Bobby: Eddie Makes a Sacrifice
Interviews with Eddie Allison, Bobby Allison, Bob Latford, Humpy Wheeler.
p. 65 "It was a thrill": Peter Golenbock, *The Last Lap*, p. 174.
p. 65 "I blew by all the hot dogs": Greg Fielden, *Forty Years*, vol. 4, p. 91.

Chapter 12: Bobby: Bud, Cotton, Harry, and Ol' Ralph
Interviews with Eddie Allison, Bobby Allison, and Fred Lorenzen.
p. 79 "You just work on the car, and we'll go from there": Jake Elder, *The Last Lap*, pp. 202–203.

Chapter 13: Bobby: An Independent Again
Interviews with Bobby and Eddie Allison.
p. 84 "We were settling an old score": Ben White, *The Bobby Allison Story: Circle of Triumph* p. 63.

Chapter 14: Bobby and Eddie: Mario
Interviews with Bobby and Eddie Allison, Paul Goldsmith
p. 92 "I find it financially unfeasible to independently support a car on the Grand National circuit": Greg Fielden, *Forty Years*, vol. 3, p. 346.

Chapter 15: Bobby: Outsmarted by the Pettys
Interviews with Bobby Allison, Eddie Allison, and Humpy Wheeler.

Chapter 16: Donnie: Banjo
Interviews with Humpy Wheeler, Eddie Allison, and Bobby Allison.

Chapter 17: Bobby: Allison Versus the Pettys
Interviews with Bobby and Eddie Allison, Wanda Lund, and Waddell Wilson.
p. 105 "Some people go crying around when they're not in front,": Greg Fielden, *Forty Years*, vol. 3, p. 345.
p. 105 "It's strange how your luck can turn around": Ibid., p. 346.
p. 106 "There's an awful lot of red paint on the side of my car": Ibid., p. 358.
p. 107 "We both had the desire to win": Ibid.

Chapter 18: Bobby: Junior
Interviews with Bobby Allison, Eddie Allison, and Junior Johnson.
p. 114 "Sponsorship is the thing": Greg Fielden, *Forty Years*, vol. 4, p. 8.
p. 115 "Well, hell, why don't you just sponsor the whole show then?": Paul Hemphill, *Wheels: A Season on NASCAR's Winston Cup Circuit* (New York: Simon and Schuster, 1997).
p. 120 "NASCAR has jacked the rules around so much to help that Chevy": Greg Fielden, *Forty Years*, vol. 4, p. 20.
p. 123 "There's not going to be any trouble until he hurts me": Ibid., p. 12.
p. 123 "If I had films of this, I could sue him for assault with intent to kill, or something close to that": Ibid.

Chapter 19: Bobby: IROC and Indy, 1973
Interviews with Bobby Allison, Eddie Allison, and Humpy Wheeler.
p. 127 "I went right home and sold my Porsche as fast as I could": Shav Glick, *Los Angeles Times*, Sports, part 3, p. 14.

Chapter 20: Bobby: The Roger Penske Years
Interviews with Bobby Allison, Eddie Allison, and Humpy Wheeler.
p. 142 "They were good engines, unless you wanted to drive fast": Patrick Reusse, *Minneapolis Star-Tribune*, Aug. 5, 1994, Sports, p. C1.

Chapter 21: Donnie: Outsmarted by the Gardners
Interviews with Bobby Allison, Pat Allison, and Eddie Allison.
p. 148 "I was feeling more sorry for myself": Greg Fielden, *Forty Years*, vol. 4, p. 89.

Chapter 22: Neil Bonnett: Susan
Interview with Susan Bonnett.
p. 151 "When your best friend fell you didn't wonder if he made it . . .": John Ed Bradley, *Washington Post*, April 27, 1984, Sports, p. D1.
p. 154 "What's your trophy look like": Ibid.

Chapter 23: Bobby: Bud Moore Saves Him
Interviews with Bobby Allison, Buddy Baker, and Bud Moore.

Chapter 24: Donnie: Hoss
Interviews with Bobby Allison, Humpy Wheeler, and Pat Allison.
p. 162 "I'm going home": Greg Fielden, *Forty Years*, vol. 4, p. 247.

Chapter 25: Bobby and Donnie: The Fight at Daytona
Interviews with Bobby and Eddie Allison, Bud Moore, Buddy Baker, and Bob Tomlinson.
p. 168 "I can't believe he'd do something like that knowing the points race I'm in": Greg Fielden, *Forty Years*, vol. 4, p. 280.

Chapter 26: Bobby: Butting Heads
Interviews with Bobby Allison and Waddell Wilson.
p. 171 "right now I don't even have the seagulls out there with me": Greg Fielden, *Forty Years*, vol. 4, p. 319.
p. 172 "This is a whole new ball game": Ibid., p. 320.
p. 173 "I sure wasn't going to call anybody and tell them": Ibid.

Chapter 27: Donnie: T-Boned and in a Coma
Interviews with Jimmy Makar, Pat Allison, and Humpy Wheeler, Bobby Allison, and Tommy Johnson.

Chapter 28: Bobby: A Championship—At Last

Interview with Bobby Allison.

p. 188 "I'm going to win some races": *New York Times*, Feb. 14, 1982.

Chapter 29: Bobby: It Gets Ugly

Interviews with Bobby Allison and Robin Pemberton.

Chapter 30: Davey: The Prodigal Son

Interviews with Wanda Lund, Red Farmer, Eddie Allison, Bobby Allison, John Bailey, and Robin Pemberton.

p. 208 "It was the sound a V-8 makes when the driver hits the throttle": Angus Phillips, *Los Angeles Times*, Sept. 27, 1992, Sports, part C, p. 11.

p. 208 "Sometimes they were pictures of my dad's cars . . .": Robert Markus, *Chicago Tribue*, Feb. 5, 1989, Sports, p. 1.

p. 210 "He was like *Ned's First Reader* the first few laps": Bill Robinson, *Atlanta Constitution*, July 16, 1994, Sports, sec. G, p. 2.

p. 210 "And for whatever reason he didn't get it": "How Much Can One Man Bear?" Ed Hinton, *Sports Illustrated*, Feb. 10, 1997, p. 54.

p. 212 "he wanted me to know what was going on in that car": Ron Green, *Chicago Tribune*, May 25, 1987, Sports, p. 2.

p. 213 "you can either be a choirboy or a race car driver": Ibid.

p. 214 "He may be a rookie in some people's eyes, but not in mine": Associated Press, Feb. 9, 1987.

p. 214 "Don't turn your back on the Alabama Gang": Ibid.

p. 214 "I didn't make it back around": Shav Glick, *Los Angeles Times*, Feb. 11, 1988, Sports, part 3, p. 1.

p. 214 "it lifted my heart back to where it belonged": Shav Glick, *Los Angeles Times*, May 4, 1987, part 3, p. 1.

p. 214 "I probably had the mike open and I was screaming": Bill Luther, *Chicago Tribune*, May 2, 1988, Sports, p. 3.

p. 215 "I was never so proud in my life": Ibid.

Chapter 31: Hut: Rookie of the Year

Interviews with Red Farmer and Hut Stricklin.

Chapter 32: Neil: In Waltrip's Shadow

Interviews with Sue Bonnett, Humpy Wheeler, Buddy Baker, Bill Ingle, and Junior Johnson.

Chapter 33: Bobby: The Oldest Winner Ever

Interviews with Bobby Allison and Ed Carroll.

Chapter 34: Bobby and Davey: Father, Son Finish 1, 2

Interviews with Bobby Allison and Eddie Allison.

p. 241 "That's what was happening all day": Michelle Kaufman, *St. Petersburg Times*, Feb. 14, 1988.

p. 243 "the only difference, in my dreams *he* finished second": Ibid.

Chapter 35: Bobby: At Death's Door
Interviews with Judy Allison, Eddie Allison, Benny Parsons, Humpy Wheeler.

p. 250 "I gotta keep my eye on him today" "How Much Can One Man Bear?" Ed Hinton, *Sports Illustrated*, February 10, 1997.

p. 252 Bobby Allison actually stopped breathing: Bruce Lowitt, *St. Petersburg Times*, Feb. 16, 1989, Sports, p. 6C.

p. 255 "I fell straight down on the floor": "How Much Can One Man Bear?" Ed Hinton, *Sports Illustrated*, p. 54.

p. 255 "He might never remember me again": Jerry Potter, *USA Today*, May 3, 1990, Sports, p. 2C.

p. 257 "I know I'm at peace with the danger and risks I take": Robert Markis, *Chicago Tribune*, Feb. 5, 1989, Sports, p. 1.

p. 257 "It's what he's always loved": *New York Times*, sec. 8, p. 8.

p. 257 "The doctors have told us it's all up to Bobby Allison": Bill Luther, *Chicago Tribune*, June 30, 1988, Sports, p. 12.

Chapter 36: Bobby and Judy: The Long Road Back
Interviews with Judy Allison, Bobby Allison, Eddie Allison, and Humpy Wheeler.

p. 265 "It's too bad Bobby got hurt": Peter Golenbock, *American Zoom*, pp. 166–67.

Chapter 37: Bobby and Judy: A Miracle
Interviews with Bobby Allison, Judy Allison, Eddie Allison, and Hut Stricklin.

p. 269 "I'm . . . a . . . very . . . glad": Ed Hinton, *Sports Illustrated*, Feb. 10, 1997, p. 54.

p. 270 "I'll be trying to get the carrot": *Los Angeles Times*, Shav Glick, Feb. 29, 1989, Sports, p. 8.

p. 270 "Now when the sun goes down, I get tired": Graham Jones, *Toronto Star*, May 27, 1989, Wheels, p. 9.

p. 270 "I wouldn't be where I am today": Michael Vega, *Boston Globe*, July 3, 1989, Sports, p. 41.

p. 272 "Owning a car is not as good as driving": Steve Hummersports, *Atlanta Journal*, Feb. 17, 1991, Sports, sec. E, p. 14.

Chapter 38: Neil: Amnesia
Interviews with Susan Bonnett, Eddie Allison, and Liz Allison.

Chapter 39: Davey: Robert Yates Hires Larry Mac
Interviews with Larry McReynolds and Liz Allison.

p. 285 "It's the whole package. It has to click for it to work": Peter Golenbock, *The Last Lap*, p. 373.

p. 287 "nobody had noticed what he had done in the race": Ibid., pp. 373–74.

p. 288 "Of course, I was pulling for Hut at the end": Robert Markus, *Chicago Tribune,* June 24, 1991, Sports, p. 1.

p. 288 "Davey has been a lot of pleasure to me along the way": Ibid., Sports, p. 1.

p. 288 "It was pretty neat": Peter Golenbock, *The Last Lap,* p. 374.

p. 289 "We were thrilled with third": Ibid.

Chapter 40: Clifford: "Crazy Wild"

Interviews with Eddie Allison, Red Farmer, Bobby Allison, Judy Allison, Hut Stricklin.

p. 291 "Clifford was all over the place": Jonathan Ingram, *Atlanta Constitution,* August 16, 1992, Sports, sec. E, p. 10.

p. 292 "Bobby was living through Clifford"; "How Much Can One Man Bear?": Ed Hinton, *Sports Illustrated,* Feb. 10, 1997, p. 51.

p. 294 "I'm a firm believer": *Chicago Tribune,* AP, August 14, 1992, Sports, p. 3.

Chapter 41: Davey: The Lost Championship: Part I

Interviews with Larry McReynolds, Liz Allison, and Humpy Wheeler.

p. 297 "I spent about ninety percent of each lap": *Chicago Sun-Times,* Feb. 17, 1992, Sports, p. 91.

p. 301 "If you can get up off the stretcher": Shav Glick, *Los Angeles Times,* July 13, 1993, Sports, part C, p. 1.

p. 304 "One of us is not going in the right direction": John Romano, *St. Petersburg Times,* July 26, 1992, p. 1C.

p. 305 "The trailing car has an obligation not to make contact": Ibid.

p. 306 "That's not the nature of the sport": Ibid.

p. 306 "He said I was insane": Robert Markus, *Chicago Tribune,* Feb. 12, 1993, Sports, p. 1.

p. 306 "He's the toughest SOB there ever was": Beth Tuschak, *USA Today,* Sept. 3, 1992, Sports, p. 2C.

p. 308 "is he nuts?": John Romano, *St. Petersburg Times,* July 26, 1992, p. 1C.

p. 309 "the good Lord has definitely given me a second chance": Michael Vega, *Boston Globe,* August 16, 1992, Sports, p. 43.

Chapter 42: The Death of Clifford Allison

Interviews with Eddie Allison, Liz Allison.

p. 311 "Clifford? Clifford?"; "How Much Can One Man Bear": Ed Hinton, *Sports Illustrated,* February 10, 1997, p. 51.

p. 312 "Then I was really sure he was dead": Angus Phillips, *Washington Post,* Sept 15, 1992, Sports, p. E1.

p. 312 "If he sat out, would that make things any better?": Robert Markus, *Chicago Tribune,* August 15, 1992, Sports, p. 1.

p. 314 "If I had sulked . . . Davey would have been very mad at me": Jorge Milian, *Fort Lauderdale Sun-Sentinel,* Nov. 26, 1993, Sports, p. 6C.

p. 315 "Clifford stares at me": Ed Hinton, *Sports Illustrated,* Feb. 10, 1997.

Chapter 43: Davey: The Lost Championship: Part II

Interviews with Larry McReynolds, Liz Allison, and Eddie Allison.

p. 318 "We just have to keep working as hard as we can": Cary Estes, *St. Louis Post-Dispatch,* Nov. 15, 1992, Sports, p. 14F.

p. 321 "you never make a bad situation better by thinking of saying something negative": Beth Tuschak, *USA Today,* Feb. 12, 1993, Bonus, p. 3E.

p. 321 "That gives me at least fourteen more years to win a championship": John Sonderegger, *St. Louis Post-Dispatch,* July 25, 1993, Sports, p. 1F.

Chapter 44: Davey: Life on the Edge

Interviews with Liz Allison, Larry McReynolds, Jake Elder, and Eddie Allison.

p. 323 "I want that Winston Cup championship": Robert Markus, *Chicago Tribune,* Feb. 12, 1992, Sports, p. 1.

p. 323 "I want to win all the time": Ibid.

p. 323 "You just can't believe what was going through my mind": Liz Clarke, *Charlotte Observer,* Mar. 8, 1993, Sports, p. C6.

p. 324 "he had his priorities in order": Rick Minter, *Atlanta Constitution,* April 2, 1992, sec. A, p. 1.

p. 324 "I didn't know it was that close until then": Mike Zizzo, *Orlando Sentinel,* July 13, 1993, sec. A, p. A1.

p. 325 "He really had the bug": Shav Glick, *Los Angeles Times,* July 13, 1993, Sports, part C, p. 1.

p. 325 "That sucker wouldn't go 220 with a tailwind": Bill Robinson, *Atlanta Constitution,* July 16, 1993, Sports, sec. G, p. 2.

p. 326 "I believe I've put them to rest": Beth Tuschak, *USA Today,* June 18, 1993, Sports, p. 2C.

p. 326 "I know he would want us to remember the good times": Felecia Rosser, *St. Petersburg Times,* June 18, 1993, Sports, Fanfare, p. 2C.

Chapter 45: The Death of Davey Allison

Interviews with Liz Allison and Eddie Allison.

p. 329 "I don't really get tired of it": Rick Minter, *Atlanta Constitution,* July 13, 1993, Sports, sec. E, p. 6.

p. 329 "we both had to keep living and doing what we loved": *USA Today,* July 26, 1993, Sports, p. 1C.

p. 330 On this day he ate catfish fillets and french fries: Raad Cawthon, *Atlanta Constitution,* July 14, 1993, Sports, sec. D, p. 1.

p. 331 Only a lap belt held him in his seat: Mike Downey, *Los Angeles Times,* July 26, 1993, Sports, part C, p. 1.

p. 332 "if I hadn't told him to come, he would still be here": Ibid.

p. 332 "I couldn't help him and I feel so helpless": Sandra McKee, *Baltimore Sun,* July 17, 1993, Sports, p. G6.

p. 333 "Miracles do happen. That's what we're praying for": *St. Petersburg Times,* wire services, July 13, 1993, Sports, p. 1C.

p. 333 "I knew that he himself would not want to look like this": *Rocky Mountain News,* July 17, 1994, Sports, p. 28B.

p. 333 "I think that was Davey's way of saying good-bye": Ibid.

p. 334 "He was just like my son": Associated Press, July 14, 1993.

Chapter 46: Alabama Mourns
Interviews with Hut Stricklin, Eddie Allison, and Bobby Allison.

p. 338 He sat in his car and cried for about thirty minutes: *Cleveland Plain Dealer,* wire services, Sports, p. F1.

p. 338 "It made him a better person": Raad Cawthon, *Atlanta Constitution,* July 14, 1993, Sports, sect. D, p. 1.

p. 339 "everybody has been so wonderful": "Requiem for a Racing Man," Ed Hinton, *Sports Illustrated,* July 26, 1993, p. 51.

p. 339 "But no one can convince me that I have to forgive Darrell Waltrip": Ibid.

p. 340 "He told me he knew I was suffering, too": Sandra McKee, *Baltimore Sun,* July 17, 1993, Sports; p. G6.

p. 340 "Why?" asked Andretti: Ed Hinton, *Sports Illustrated,* July 16, 1993, p. 51.

p. 341 "I don't know if there is too much": *Ed Hinton, Sports Illustrated,* July 26, 1993, p. 51.

p. 341 "I never had a brother": Mike Owen, Associated Press, July 17, 1993.

p. 342 "Davey was a heck of a friend": Jim Jenks, *Newsday,* July 19, 1993, Sports, p. 83.

p. 343 "I felt like my life was shredded": ABCnews.com, "NASCAR Wives," Nov. 10, 2003.

p. 343 "I mourned Judd longer than that": Ibid.

p. 343 "Davey was a strong believer that life must go on": Ibid.

p. 343 For the terms of the Diffie divorce, see the Associated Press Story by Joe Edwards, August 25, 1994.

p. 343 "It's almost like that never happened": Richard Huff, *New York Daily News,* Nov. 15, 1995, Sports, p. 71.

Chapter 47: Hut: Scarred
Interviews with Hut Stricklin and Red Farmer.

p. 346 "He has a gentle feel for a car": Darrell Fry, *St. Petersburg Times,* Feb. 13, 1993, Sports, p. 1C.

Chapter 48: Bobby and Judy: No Peace
Interviews with Eddie, Bobby, and Judy Allison.

Chapter 49: The Death of Neil Bonnett
Interviews with Buddy Baker, Susan Bonnett, Humpy Wheeler, and Eddie Allison.

p. 356 "No one should tell another person what to do": Sandra McKee, *Baltimore Sun,* Feb. 14, 1994, p. 2C.

p. 357 "That wreck wasn't nearly as bad as it looked": Shav Glick, *Los Angeles Times,* Feb. 12, 1994, Sports, part C, p. 1.

p. 357 "It took only two seconds to talk me into it": Charean Williams, *Orlando Sentinel,* Feb. 12, 1994, Sports, p. B1.

p. 358 "it's sure not the way I wanted it to happen": Cary Estes, *St. Petersburg Times,* Feb. 12, 1994, p. 5C.

p. 358 "Is that fair?": Raad Cawthon, *Atlanta Constitution and Journal,* Feb. 16, 1994, Sports, sec. G, p. 3.

p. 359 "What are we supposed to be entitled to?": Ibid.

p. 359 "As long as we have life, we'll have death": Darrell Fry, *St. Petersburg Times,* Feb. 13, 1994, Sports, p. 1C.

p. 361 "I'm not bitter": *Houston Chronicle,* Feb. 15, 1994, Sports, p. 3.

Chapter 50: Hut: A Career Fizzles

Interview with Hut Stricklin.

p. 363 "You can't buy everything you want": Tom McCollister, *Atlanta Constitution and Journal,* Dec. 10, 1995, Sports, p. 7E.

p. 363 "There's two things I ain't gonna have ever again": Parker Lee Nash, *Greensboro News and Record,* Life, p. D1.

Chapter 51: The End of Bobby Allison Motorsports

Interview with Eddie Allison.

p. 370 "I bet I'm the only guy out there with cue cards": Beth Tuschak, *USA Today,* Apr. 29, 1994, p. 3C.

p. 372 "That old thing keeps biting me": Ed Hinton, *Sports Illustrated,* Feb. 10, 1997.

p. 373 "Getting out of racing was the right thing to do": Sandra McKee, *Baltimore Sun,* May 29, 1997, p. 1D.

Chapter 52: Bobby and Judy: Financial Ruin and Divorce

Interviews with Bobby, Judy, and Eddie Allison.

p. 378 "I was driving for the one man Bobby hates more than he hates me: Junior Johnson": Ibid.

p. 378 "I still have forgiven Darrell Waltrip only three-fourths": Ibid.

p. 379 "we were not able to give each other the support we should have in this incredible tragedy": Ibid.

p. 380 "I am afraid to ask the question": Ibid.

Chapter 53: Bobby and Judy: Reunited

Interviews with Bobby, Judy, and Eddie Allison.

p. 384 "He got killed in a race car": Ed Hinton, *Orlando Sentinel,* May 16, 2000, Sports, p. C1.

p. 384 "I went in one direction and she went in another": *Miami Herald,* July 8, 2001, p. 2D.